Race-ing Representation

Culture and Education Series

Series Editors: Henry A. Giroux, Pennsylvania State University
                Joe L. Kincheloe, Pennsylvania State University

The rise of new media and significant changes in media industries have brought about a major transformation in how knowledge is produced and assimilated. Today, TV, films, CDs, computer networks, and advertising all figure into the construction of cultural identities and social experiences—often in ways that were hard to imagine just a few years ago.

Surprisingly little academic study has been undertaken of these transformations in media, culture, and education. This new book series explores questions about the relationship among knowledge, power, identity, and politics in connection with issues of justice, equality, freedom, and community.

Race-ing Representation: Voice, History, and Sexuality
    edited by Kostas Myrsiades and Linda Myrsiades, 1998

Forthcoming:

Between the Masks: Resisting the Politics of Essentialism
    by Diane DuBose Brunner

Cutting Class: Social Class and Education
    edited by Joe L. Kincheloe and Shirley R. Steinberg

Race-ing Representation

Voice, History, and Sexuality

Kostas Myrsiades and Linda Myrsiades

ROWMAN & LITTLEFIELD PUBLISHERS, INC.
Lanham • Boulder • New York • Oxford

ROWMAN & LITTLEFIELD PUBLISHERS, INC.

Published in the United States of America
by Rowman & Littlefield Publishers, Inc.
4720 Boston Way, Lanham, Maryland 20706

12 Hid's Copse Road
Cumnor Hill, Oxford OX2 9JJ, England

The following essays were first published in *College Literature*: Carr in 20.2 (June 1993); Heller in 21.2 (June 1994); Dukats in 22.1 (February 1995); Brooks, Blackmer, Crooks, and Lock in 22.3 (October 1995); Basu in 23.3 (October 1996); Ongiri and Pellegrini in 24.1 (February 1997); Chowdhury in 24.2 (June 1997); Baker in 25.1 (February 1998). Henry A. Giroux's chapter appeared in *Channel Surfing: Race Talk and the Destruction of Today's Youth*, by Henry A. Giroux, New York: St. Martin's Press, 1997.

British Library Cataloguing in Publication Information Available

Library of Congress Cataloging-in-Publication Data

Race-ing representation : voice, history, and sexuality / [edited by]
    Kostas Myrsiades and Linda Myrsiades.
        p. cm.
    Includes bibliographical references and index.
    ISBN 0-8476-8856-9 — ISBN 0-8476-8857-7 (pbk.)
    1. American literature—Afro-American authors—History and criticism.
2. Literature and history—United States—History. 3. Sexual orientation
in literature. 4. Afro-Americans in literature. 5. Race in literature.
6. Sex in literature.   I. Myrsiades, Kostas. II. Myrsiades, Linda S.
PS153.N5R28 1998
810.9'896073—dc21   97-37072
                                                CIP

ISBN 0-8476-8856-9 (cloth : alk. paper)
ISBN 0-8476-8857-7 (pbk. : alk. paper)

Printed in the United States of America

Contents

II Voice

III History

IV Sexuality

Introduction

Race-ing Representation: Voice, History, and Sexuality

Linda Myrsiades

Toni Morrison speaks of a world of racial tropes in which it is almost always the case that "the exorcism of critical national issues [is] situated in the miasma of black life and inscribed on the bodies of black people" (Morrison 1992, x). She goes on to retell the tale of Robinson Crusoe, this time from the point of view of Friday, who is given his name and presumably his "life" by the man who rescues him, the assumption being that before his rescue he had no language and, even if he had one, he would have had nothing to say in it. Crusoe, in any case, never wanted to learn Friday's language, which Friday himself proceeds to forget in learning how to think *as* Crusoe: "The problem of internalizing the master's tongue is the problem of the rescued" (xxv).

Morrison wrote this account of Friday as the introduction to an anthology of essays on the Clarence Thomas/Anita Hill case. Morrison's linguistic signifier for Judge Thomas was Friday, the black man who had subjugated himself totally to the white master. Friday participates in and continues the dichotomous trope of master/slave. When translated into the present, 1990s Supreme Court decisions to dismantle affirmative action programs threaten to insert an insidious linguistic twist into this debate by adding an element of ambiguity not merely to the master/slave hierarchy but to the Friday/Caliban dichotomy. By interpreting affirmative action as a rescue operation instead of a means to redress centuries of historical oppression, the Supreme Court reinterpreted affirmative action as a stigma, a means of muting rather than voicing African-American experience. In other words, affirmative action is now accused of creating Fridays, of muffling resistance and disguising the politics of the master language. The back and forth between Friday and Caliban, between taking up and resisting the master language, has added a bizarre twist to Toni Morrison's stand.

The problem of representing race in the context of a master language and culture is addressed in this debate in terms of the ongoing struggle to redefine the self through which to speak, that is, to reconstrue our understanding of history, sexuality, and speech itself in a continuing battle for self-definition. Only then, Morrison implies, will the footprint in the sand that figures so prominently in Crusoe's nightmares counter the foot that Friday picks up and places on his head. Indeed, it is only by engaging this "dialectic of the feet" that we can be instructed by it; and it is only by refiguring that we can truly engage it. The essays collected here fulfill just such a function: they refigure; they engage; they instruct. As a totality, they explode the notion of race as a natural boundary between groups, even if their critiques raise the prospect of exposing what Marvin Jones calls "an incoherent fiction" (Jones 1993, 439). The infinite number of possible constructions, she explains, force us to accept that "race is not so much a category but a practice: people are raced." And the practice by means of which they are raced is language, that is, the "making" of race and its meanings in metaphors and narratives. Such constructions go beyond determinate facts to indeterminate imaginings, beyond discovering to evoking and reconstituting, to an interpenetration of past and present in both literature and history. By this understanding, race studies explodes our narrow conception of what texts we will accept for explication and what boundaries we will ascribe to them. The metaphor adopted has become one of a free range rather than a reservation. As this collection indicates, race studies has gone beyond mere questions of race identity and race difference to rewriting race without obliterating the fact of having been raced, a politics responsive not to translation or even transgression but to transformation. The themes thus opened to study in this collection range widely from explorations of origin through Afrocentric theory to the seductiveness and panic inherent in "passing." They cover readings of "whiteness" and of body politics as cultural texts, the representational burdens of sexing race and race-ing sex, and the "tricky positionality" of the multivalent subject. They examine the economies of lynch law and turn the light of Fredrick Turner's frontier thesis on the urban frontier. In the literature of Toni Morrison, Audre Lorde, Maryse Condé, Nella Larsen, Aimé Césaire, James Weldon Johnson, Eldridge Cleaver, Chester Himes, and Walter Mosley and in the films *Young Soul Rebel*, *Fried Green Tomatoes*, *Boys on the Side*, and *Work*, we find that the resistance to race-ing is both meaningfully engaged as a cultural possibility and rewritten as a linguistic practice.

Race-ing Representation

The essays presented here can be divided into four parts that reflect how race-ing is represented through voice, history, and sexuality. In this age of controversy over ebonics—in which a legal scholar as well respected as Patricia J. Williams raises the twin questions of whether black English is not "the perpetual symbol code for ignorance" (Williams 1996, 9) and whether the American vernacular itself can be called English—the idea of race-ing representation has particular importance for real-world race issues. Certainly the Afrocentrism discussed in Kanishka Chowdhury's "Afrocentric Voices: Constructing Identities, (Dis)Placing Difference" gives pause to any serious student of multiculturalism, diversity, and difference. It raises the specter of a new hegemony based on false nationalism and a new kind of exclusionism tied to benevolent solicitude (the contemporary surrogate, for all intents and purposes, for benign neglect). Afrocentrism suggests itself as the black equivalent of a recent American Indian's ironic call to let the Mafia run reservation gambling halls; they couldn't do any worse in terms of generating self-esteem than government agencies, and they would certainly do better in terms of efficient management. But Chowdhury takes the position that alternative visions, whatever their agenda, need as rigorous a critique as "official" perspectives. In this effort, his essay examines the Afrocentrisms of the Senegalese Cheikh Anta Diop, the African-American Molefi Kete Asante, and the "Nigerian troika" Chinweizu, Onwuchekwa Jemie, and Ihechukwa Madubuike. The debate as Chowdhury poses it is between a stable fixed vision and one of stable instability, but also between a presumably corrupt colonialism and a presumably pristine pre-contact culture. Colonialisms, the author insists, must also be pluralized, just as Patrick Hogan, in another context, refers us to the term "post-colonization" for cultures that experienced being colonized (Hogan 1996, 163), both of them ambiguifying the monolithicity of discourses that treat the colonizer as external and singular. Moreover, the colonized, in this reading, must be localized so that their essentialized "center" can be critiqued and its cultural chauvinism exposed. The "rupture and discontinuities" of historical narratives need to be included to diffuse the notion of "total history" (a linear continuous history) to which Foucault refers (McHoul and Grace 1997 44-45).

An alternative critique of raced representation emerges in Henry A. Giroux's "White Noise: Toward a Pedagogy of Whiteness," which provides the necessary context for fully appreciating Afrocentrism. Giroux looks at "'whiteness' as a signifier of privilege and power" (ch. 2, page 43) and a political ideology sowing racism. Giroux's position is that "whiteness" may operate within "fixed boundaries of identity politics" (ch. 2, page 43) but those boundaries need re-imagining. Moreover, whiteness serves doubleduty, that is, as an anti-racist as well as a racist practice, leading us to reconceptualize for future generations of whites an identity that is not merely to be understood through domination and racism. Nor is one condemned to an essentialized whiteness once one understands that the particularities of culture can act as a resource that resists such an identity and that we can enable ourselves to move beyond guilt and resentment. Giroux thus takes on the task of rethinking "whiteness" "as a discourse of both critique and possibility" (ch. 2, page 44), providing for a racial identity capable of enacting "a broader, radical, democratic project" (ch. 2, page 44). He does so by juxtaposing and intertexting two radically differing films on racial identity (*Dangerous Minds*, 1995, and *Sutures*, 1993) to reveal their pedagogical usefulness in reading whiteness as other than a trope for domination and in addressing the shortcomings of recent scholarship in the field.

Houston Baker's piece "Yes, Virginia, There Is an Answer" is a productive complement to Giroux's essay. Baker addresses the black perspective on whiteness through a narrative construction of Virginia Thomas, Justice Thomas's white wife, in the Anita Hill/Clarence Thomas hearings. He takes the position that both parties to the hearing were engaged in finding a "loophole of retreat" (a phrase he takes from Harriet Jacob's slave narrative, *Incidents in the Life of a Slave Girl*), a hidden place from which they can dispatch messages and which gives them the necessary distance to maneuver. Virginia becomes a weapon in the Judge's arsenal, a means of controlling the black woman's body, of brokering his survival. The "they" who would destroy him is the black woman who herself claims "gross *harassment* by the LAW in blackface" (ch. 2, page 80). The white woman in the equation resists being signified in terms of her "relationship to the LAW, their relationship, say, to sexuality and desire in the economies of lynch law" (ch. 2, page 80). Baker thus questions Virginia's role in this bit of American (lynch) law and her implied rejection of the black woman's discourse. To the driving question that acts as the spine to the Judge's case ("Why are they trying to destroy me?"), Baker elliptically responds, "Dear Virginia . . . you, yourself, are precisely the answer" (ch. 2, page 82). The implied narrative is one of interracial rape fantasies and intraracial sexual abuse in which whiteness is the key to the construction.

The last two essays in this section examine the phenomenon of "passing." The first, Neil Brooks's "On Becoming an Ex-Colored Man: Postmodern Irony and the Extinguishing of Certainties in *The Autobiography of an Ex-Colored Man*," takes up James Weldon Johnson's *The Autobiography of an Ex-Colored Man*, a novel disguised as an autobiography on passing as a white man. This breach of the racial barrier required the production of a double self as a means of finding acceptance in an unaccepting society. On the one hand, Brooks represents the novel as a reverse slave narrative and, on the other, as a Horatio Alger story. A truer picture emerges when the narrator's sense of self is destroyed as a cost of passing. He remains, moreover, detached from the community he has presumably "passed" into. Having sold his birthright, the narrator can only claim success as an impostor, a success that constitutes a psychological vacuum in a world of illusion that could at any moment drop away. The narrator has escaped the slavery attached to his skin color only to fall into the self-imposed slavery of his "conflicted positioning" (ch. 4, page 89), having made his fortune from the very underclass he has fled. He remains nameless throughout the novel, and therefore incomplete, even as he fulfills his own ambitious expectations. The narrator can never be validated, for he cannot choose one racial identity over another, having become both in a society that requires one or the other. He can, therefore, no more choose to be black or white, for he is both and, at the same time, neither. The only control he can have over his life is through his representation of it, and that representation, once he starts passing, is bound to be raced in a way that will deny him the dignity he associates with being white. Society will pin a "badge of inferiority" on him whether it is external (when he is black) or internal (when he is white). He is, nevertheless, always an invisible man, either because he chooses to be one (as a white man) or because society chooses for him (as a black man). Representation is here confounded, for the "false dichotomy" of the narrator's position make his exposure, should he truly "represent" himself, a tragic probability. Raced, he is unrepresentable. Represented, he is deraced both as a white and as a black man.

In her essay "The Veils of the Law: Race and Sexuality in Nella Larsen's *Passing*," Corrine E. Blackmer takes up the issue of passing through the interface of literature, politics, and law as they relate to race and sex masquerading in Nella Larsen's Harlem renaissance novel *Passing*. In the context of the Supreme Court's *Plessy v. Ferguson* decision (1896), Blackmer considers the Jim Crow laws (in which seven-eighths Caucasian, one-eighth African blood is sufficient to be classed as "colored") that led to Homer Plessy's ejection from a whites-only railroad car. In Justice Henry Billings Brown's majority opinion asserting that de jure segregation was constitutional and that de facto segregation was unavoidable, the Court regarded the onus of "a badge of inferiority" as an invention of "'the colored race [which] chooses to put the construction upon it'" (as quoted, ch. 5, page 99). The court having thus laid down the gauntlet, it could hardly be surprising that breaching the color line became a desired object for those denied their Fourteenth Amendment right to equality; indeed, *the Brown v. Board of Education* decision (1954), a half century later, declared separate but equal inherently unequal. Black culture would, after all, have to prove its worth to a largely white audience if it was to validate itself. But to do so under terms that effectively declared it "unequal" and laboring under a "self-imposed" badge of inferiority was to ensure that racial stigmas attached to those of mixed blood would become an ideal vehicle to explore racial representation.

In Larsen's novel, passing is explored through the freedom of identity and sexuality of a woman who not only is involved in an interracial union but also is

tempted to cross sexual lines to explore a same-sex relationship. In Larsen's
construction of passing, the experience becomes a metaphor for a range of
"deceptive appearances and practices" (ch. 5, page 100) from those of chance to
those of the subconscious. The central figure, Clare, embodies a "Janus-like
duplicity" (ch. 5, page 101) so that she can maintain relationships in two racial
and two sexual worlds at the same time. When outward appearances are penetrated, Clare, exposed, meets a violent and tragic end. Her death, taken by
Blackmer as "a poignant symbol of the victory of *de jure* segregation" (ch. 5,
page 102), legitimates both racial and sexual taboos at the same time that it
identifies racial and sexual fantasies in a way anticipated by the white racism
that declared segregation constitutional. Blackmer concludes that such an
analysis is an "inevitable corollary of racial panic . . . in an environment governed by the legal and cultural assumptions of Plessy" (ch. 5, page 103).
Moreover, she holds, the same kind of unequal treatment associated with race
has now been extended through the courts to homosexuality, linking race and
sex in a way that makes Larsen's novel prescient and the values of the Harlem
renaissance forerunners of greater social acceptance for gays. What Larsen also
passes on, however, is a strong sense of the moral dilemma that results in race
betrayal in the novel and both the seductiveness and the panic stimulated by
representations that play on the edge and in the dark. The masquerades taken up
by her central character both liberate and enslave, given "the shackles of the
racial and sexual conventions that imprison her" (ch. 5, page 112). Clare's
moves may have been acts of transgression or survival; they were more certainly stratagems made more necessary by a world dominated by the legal representations of race endorsed by the *Plessy* court.

Voice

In the second section of the collection, devoted to the question of "voice,"
Brenda Carr's "'A Woman Speaks . . . I am Woman and Not White': Politics of
Voice, Tactical Essentialism, and Cultural Intervention in Audre Lorde's Activist Poetics and Practice" presents the multiply positioned (African-American,
feminist, lesbian) Audre Lorde as a poet who strategically invokes her multiple
identities, centering both "voice" and "silence" as she does so. Silence is refer-
enced within the context provided by Susan Sontag's aesthetic of "'a mythic
project of total liberation'" (as quoted, ch. 6, page 120)—that is, an "ahistorical
aesthetic of silence"—and the "silence=death" logo that has become the motto
of AIDS activism. Both silences are strategic; neither is without content.
Speaking or refusing speech, hearing or failing to hear, a voice thus becomes
part of the larger question of representation that is itself irrevocably tied to an

understanding of identity. As Carr acknowledges, speaking and hearing across a divide is, however, not merely a question of Lorde's intervening "in the symbolic order with her alternative signifying practice" (ch. 6, page 121) but also an issue for Carr of her own reception (Carr is both white and heterosexual) as a political fact of life: "Those of us writing across difference from variously privileged subject positions are always already inside the activity of appropriation" (ch. 6, page 122). Carr thus speaks from a position of what she calls "honorable appropriation," a negotiation of horizons engaged in a dialogic relationship that takes on other interested readings. Voice is, then, not merely a question of giving voice to or taking voice by the silenced; it is also a question of what "identity markers" shall count in constituting what can be said and how one can separate such markers given the multivalent subject, what Carr calls Lorde's "tricky positionality" (ch. 6, page 124). It is, as well, a question of the voice in which representation happens and how that, too, affects identity, both as experienced and as understood.

In "The Hybrid Terrain of Literary Imagination: Maryse Condé's Black Witch of Salem, Nathaniel Hawthorne's Hester Prynne, and Aimé Césaire's Heroic Poetic Voice," Mara L. Dukats addresses voice through a Cameroon proverb that essentializes women's silence: "Women have no mouth" (ch. 7, page 141). Such a historicized and contextualized image of voicelessness means that a woman must vocalize against the grain and in a circumstance in which there is no tradition of written texts to aid her. She goes unheard because there is no place to hear her. When Tituba of the Salem witch trials is called on to speak in Maryse Conde's *I Tituba, Black Witch of Salem*, she is "represented" by an official document that "records" her as having spoken. She is written-into-being when needed and historically effaced when done with. Tituba is not, however, merely a woman and a black, but also a slave, confined three times over to a voiceless state. Conde gives her a new "hearing," mixing historical and literary constructions to allow her readers to rethink the Caribbean slave and to allow the slave to reclaim her agency. In her newly written state, it is "Tituba as the effaced and unacknowledged presence that conditions the construction of the canonized texts [the *Scarlet Letter*] that it interrogates" (ch. 7, page 144). Taking a page from Toni Morrison's *Playing in the Dark,* Dukats explores Tituba as a mediating force who both allows Hester Prynne to think about herself (once the American literary imagination ceases "playing in the dark") and finds her own place, transforming, in the process, the way we read originary American fiction.

In Biman Basu's "The Black Voice and the Language of the Text: Toni Morrison's *Sula*," the issue of voice is raised in terms of its ability to mediate conflict, that is, as a narrative strategy. In this sense, "mobilization of voice enacts the conflict between cultures" (ch. 8, page 155). The dominating literary frame implies the dominance of one language culture (the written) with which a second culture (the oral) engages in a "colonial interface" (ch. 8, page 156). The narrative strategy of voice constitutes a mode of intervention that can be said to dissolve the frame, without, of course, entirely escaping it. Basu's claim includes the prospect that the oral "implodes the literary voice" (ch. 8, page 156) and that it is in black women's fiction that the oral most successfully reconfigures the literary experience, largely through its use of voice.

But voice does not operate in a vacuum, particularly in regard to "representing" the oral, for although "representation may mark the epistemological limits of access, . . . yet representation itself seems constantly to be disfigured by unrepresentability" (ch. 8, page 156). The text is thus pockmarked with vestiges of the nonrepresentational. In Morrison's *Sula*, indicatively, the title character herself slips and shifts "as the figure of the semiotic," "as the figure of music," as "the figure of language itself" (ch. 8, page 159), recalling for Basu the intractable Bakhtinian grotesque, which, ultimately, becomes "the grotesque body of the community" (ch. 8, page 163) in the novel. Morrison's *Sula* is, in sum, presented as celebrating the signifier. It strains "toward unrepresentability, to be released from referentiality" (ch. 8, page 170) only to be reined in by the materiality of the embodied word. This black speech inhabits the grotesque body of the community and ruptures the written text to resist being incorporated or appropriated by its sterility. Voice, in this reading, is resistance.

History

The effect of history and memory on raced representation is taken up in the third section of the collection. The opening essay, Robert Crooks's "From the Far Side of the Urban Frontier: The Detective Fiction of Chester Himes and Walter Mosley," invokes the frame image of Frederick Jackson Turner's frontier thesis (1893). He cites "'the frontier' as a signifier . . . now cut adrift" (ch. 9, page 175) and free to be attached to other conceptual spaces. Crooks's candidate for that place where savagery and civilization meet in today's world is the city. Here, the racial divide is particularly sharp, and, he contends, in its crime fiction the urban frontier finds its textual space. Substituting "black criminal chaos" (ch. 9, page 176) for Turner's Indian savagery, Crooks maps his unified frontier, his "'common danger' of absolute otherness" (ch. 9, page 176), out of the differences, contests, and class and economic conflicts of the city. The individual against the collective of frontier narratives becomes the individual white man against the "otherness" of the collective black experience, while the culture clash is identified as what occurs between the civilizing purity of the dominant white culture and the inferiority of oppressed black culture. The urban landscape is described as infiltrated by "pockets of racial intrusion, hence corruption and social disease to be policed and constrained—insofar as the 'others' threaten to cross the line" (ch. 9, page 178). The black urban community, by association, is thus reduced to "the criminal side of the urban frontier" (ch. 9, page 178). This war of extermination was to work not through genocide but through hegemony and strategies of containment. The frontier ideology, Crooks's argument, is thereby reinvigorated by its relocation to an urban setting just as it will be re-sisted and defended there. In Crooks's view, it is African-American detective fiction that has the capacity to enact such resistance, carrying the violence of the West forward, as Richard Slotkin puts it in the title of a chapter, "From the Open Range to the Mean Streets," from his classic work *Gunfighter Nation*. And as it does so, urban detective fiction clarifies both the historicized nature of rep-resentation and the race-ing nature of such representation. The frontier adven-ture has, in sum, produced "a single cultural enemy [read 'black'] on which to build a fantasy of a unified American people [read 'white'] pursuing a linear national [read 'hegemonic'] narrative" (ch. 9, page 195).

Helen Lock's "'Building Up from Fragments': The Oral Memory Process in Some Recent African-American Written Narratives" takes us to the role of memory in history, in its historically contextualizing and historically liberating roles, as well as in its ability to excavate repressed history. Examining three novels (David Bradley's *The Chaneysville Incident*, Paule Marshall's *Prais-esong for the Widow*, and Toni Morrison's *Beloved*), Lock moves back and forth between oral and literate conceptions of memory "to energize the dialectic between them" (ch. 10, page 201) and, through the "creative reconstruction" (ch. 10, page 201) they provide, to retrieve the lost past. But memory proves resistant in representing the past, reluctant to confront what it does not wish to revisit. The literate, considered not as a fixed, singular, or true text, is thus used to stimulate recall. Lock's use of memory captures Morrison's "remembering" as a literate way of reassembling parts of the past that is itself characteristic of the oral process. The false objectivity of the literary is absent here as reconfiguring is kept flexible, collective, and improvisatory. History is transcended in its reenactment for it is the process more than the product that is privileged; it is the act of courage at confronting and, as in Marshall's novel, the transformation of both the past and present by the act of memory that are most highly valued. As Bradley's novel makes clear, by abandoning a strict sense of historicity and embracing an actively entered-into experience of remembering, memory comes alive and becomes useful. Representation is, as a result, condi-tioned by memory processes characteristic of an oral tradition that is local and historical. It does not, and cannot, function to unrepress what defines us repre-sentationally; it cannot resist race-ing by others; and it cannot open up to our use inaccessible memory material, unless it is connected to its own history and con-textualized historically.

Dana Heller's "Reconstructing Kin: Family, History, and Narrative in Toni

Morrison's *Beloved*" extends our understanding of the importance of contextualizing representation in its examination of family history and representation in
Morrison's *Beloved*. Family, in Heller's reading, is itself already a raced representation, the "good" family being the nuclear white family, while the "bad"
family is characterized "in recurrent images of family violence, absent fathers,
and women-centered black families" (ch. 11, page 214). *Beloved*'s task, in
Heller's view, is to reconstruct fractured black family relations and reconnect
family with community. Heller's task, by contrast, is to demonstrate the mutually reinforcing structures of African-American kinship and narrative structures.
In the latter, the central females of the novel are represented as connected by a
"specific link between generations of women" (ch. 11, page 216), constrained to
a home dominated by a female head of the house, and inhabited by a ghostly
female demon draining them of life. History and memory dictate the intertwining
forces that hold these women together, forces that both support and threaten
them. Until memory stitches together the pieces of the past and connects them in
and for the present, the ex-slave Sethe will remain the misperceived "bad"
mother who has brought disaster on her family by a bloody act of child murder.
Reconstruing Sethe's act in the light of her own personal and social collective
history, however, yields a representation that not only clarifies how the institution of slavery destroys the possibility of functional slave families but also
makes understanding possible. It dismantles the binary racial opposition of good
(white) and bad (black) mothers so that the story that is recaptured through the
appearance of the ghost-daughter Beloved becomes a representation that, no
longer resisted, can be de-raced and can now begin to heal.

Sexuality

In the final section, on sexuality, raced readings of body politics and cultural
nationalism are taken up in Amy Ongiri's "We are Family: Miscegenation, Black
Nationalism, Black Masculinity, and the Black Gay Cultural Imagination." This essay
addresses the perceived threats posed by miscegenation and homosexuality as disruptions of both the "resistant Black self" and "the narrative of nation" (ch. 12,
page 235). Ongiri raises the prospect of a sexuality that creates anxiety for "the
possibilities of cohesion and wholeness in the scripting of the narrative of the
Black nation directly onto Black bodies in an imagined Black reality" (ch. 12,
page 236). Through her consideration of the personal politics of Eldridge
Cleaver's autobiographical *Soul on Ice* and Isaac Julien's film *Young Soul Rebel*
and the collective politics of such work as Asante's *Afrocentricity*, she outlines
the differences between queer theory and African-American cultural models to
make the point that strategies of representation called for by the former under-

mine the latter. Genetic annihilation represents, after all, both the goal of white racism and the threat of black homosexuality. What is both black and gay finds itself in an "ambiguous space" (ch. 12, page 237) between race and sexuality. It is caught between the homophobia of black nationalism and the sense of brotherhood and family in the gay community (black and white) that make gay politics an anomaly in mainstream black thought. Ongiri raises the possibility that a resistant black masculinity within that ambiguous space may have been "precluded by the historical circumstances that mark desire in the context of black bodies as 'dangerous'" (ch. 12, page 242). Certainly, the two forms of sexuality (miscegenation and homosexuality) joined in interracial same-sex relationships, at present, pressure black cultural nationalism to renegotiate a resistance that is "fixed" and that refuses "a continuous process of location and relocation" (ch. 12, page 244).

Ann Pellegrini's "Women on Top, Boys on the Side, but Some of Us Are Brave: Blackness, Lesbianism, and the Visible" raises questions about black sexuality from the feminist and lesbian perspectives, finding the representations it encounters no less in need of "relocation." Taking up the gauntlet of black feminism, Pellegrini calls attention to "the unmarked whiteness of Women's Studies" and the way in which it places "some subjects out of bounds" (ch. 13, page 247). White scholars of sexuality, she announces, have failed to examine the significance that race has for the ways in which gender and sexuality are represented. Race, for Pellegrini, is not a mere qualifier that specifies particular lesbians and gays. It is, rather, a means of theorizing differences and, with racialization, a means of raising questions that need to be integrated into the study of sexuality. Its instrumentality lies in determining "the ways that 'race' is sexed and 'sex' raced . . . [in a way] that marks out a different set of relations and demands a different mapping" (ch. 13, page 253). Moreover, it must perform its function, we are warned, without falling into the familiar, and by now deadening, mantra of race, class, and gender.

To make her point, Pellegrini offers two negative referents (*Boys on the Side*, 1995, and *Fried Green Tomatoes*, 1991), films that represent lesbianism in ways that should not serve as models for exploring the intersections of race, sexuality, and gender. In *Boys on the Side*, the use of a racial marker (the "blackness" of the lesbian character among three female friends) bears the "representational burden" (ch. 13, page 256) for a threatening difference. The black lesbian is the woman who goes beyond the pale in marking the difference between female homosociality and female homosexuality. In *Fried Green Tomatoes*, by contrast, the heroism of two lesbians who are "raced white" (ch. 13, page 256) is set against white racism to create a normative model for race relations. The film is less about sexuality than about "good" and "bad" white people. In both films, then, differences related to homosexuality are whisked away into questions of race. Nowhere is the interfacing of the two made a part of desire; nowhere are the interstices studied. Sexuality and race are, however, en-gaged in a third film, *Work* (1996), with which Pellegrini concludes. Here, within a homosexual relationship we find intersections of class and race that complicate cross-racial desire and provide a "flip" on rising and falling fortunes that challenges expectations and rewards class-linked and race-linked aspirations. The differences not only do not stand still, but they also negotiate switchpoints in ways that complicate identity and enrich our understanding of cross-racial same-sex desire.

Race studies such as those exemplified in this collection, as Angela Harris's now-classic piece on race and essentialism makes clear, have developed an understanding of the multiplicity of self that postessentialism has brought us. They have brought us to recognize the relational rather than the inherent in raced constructions and to accept that acts of will must replace passive discovery if whole-ness and community are to be achieved. In this sense, race studies is not limited to issues related only to African-Americans but includes other "raced" groups. It acknowledges the considerable contradictions that arise between and among dif-ferently raced groups and respects the ambiguities such contradictions pose, even as it denies, as Harris does, that nuanced borders are all that separate them. And it is in literature such as that examined here that these constructions, this experience, are most brought to life for us and that resistance to race-ing is both meaningfully engaged as a cultural possibility and rewritten as a linguistic practice.

We close this introduction with an image taken from new world exploration and the linguistic colonialism associated with it. To draw the picture, we need to recall Columbian "discovery" as an old world move that that essentially "kidnapped" the new world politico-linguistically with the claim that those of the new world had no culture or, for that matter, language of their own to speak of. The expectation was that new world inhabitants would quickly repeat what was told them and so learn to "speak." It was critical to the discoverer's project that they be regarded as having no language of their own, for only then could they be easily converted. It was equally useful to regard them as naked, both culturally and linguistically, for the same reason. As Stephen J. Greenblatt ex-plores this image, the new world had to be unformed so that the old world could leave its impression on it and so that the former would take its imprint. Linguis-tic colonialism, then, became the perfect instrument of both empire and, in its service, cultural torture. The new world was the old's linguistic plantation.

We can apply this vision to our conception of raced representation by con-sidering that to speak is really to speak in one's own language. From the colo-nizer's point of view, however, speaking one's own language impedes the mis-sionary progress of conversion. The colonizer is thus engaged in the process of capturing what is "savage" to take it "home" and domesticate it. As long as the "kidnapped" keep their language silent, those in control of language find they have a useful screen on which to project their dark fantasies. This process further reinforces distinctions already being made between the "civilized" and the "primitive" to reinforce a status hierarchy that works to the benefit of those with the unfair language advantage.

This is where Caliban comes in. As a figure, he calls into play the relation between Prospero and his library, the source of power, and Caliban himself, the "primitive" without language until civilization arrives. The conflict could be represented as the primitive withdrawing for fear "her" secrets would be captured while the civilized possesses spells hidden in "his" books. Having learned what can be learned of Prospero's language, Caliban has learned how to curse in it. In Prospero's eyes, Caliban is not a noble savage but a debased creature. In Greenblatt's terms, Caliban has to be of Prospero's world to be considered human. To be human is to be civilized in Prospero's sense. In the end, Caliban is acknowledged, a small victory for the creature who is accepted like a festering wound for which society has taken responsibility.

But to leave Caliban and the colonizing perspective, we need to ask from where a truer correction to race-ing is likely to come. If it does not come from recognition of the universality (read here "tyranny") of a single imposed language, it might come, as Lyotard suggests, from a place that preserves the balance of voices and their unique language games. This balance neither insists on difference (which leads to domination and silence) nor requires similarity (and the collapse of identity). It does not make other languages, and thereby cultures, transparent by denial or dismissal but accepts that they are opaque on their own terms. We are thus in a place where neither Prospero's treatment of Caliban nor Crusoe's of Friday matters. Rather, as Edward W. Said would lead us to understand, it is the insider's way of "treating" that ultimately counts.

But representation from the inside has become as complex and problematic as representation from the outside. Gramsci would advise us that historical blocs are not themselves homogeneous. It is thus the case that not only do we now speak of colonization "within" groups and societies and not just "of" societies, but we also recognize that even genders and races representing themselves lack "an Archimedean point" from which to interlocute (Said 1989, 211). We cannot hang free of the history from which race-ing derived and that continues to nurture it. Efforts to speak will remain an inescapable part of the larger discourse that originates in linguistic colonialism, if only by resistance to it. Nevertheless, by taking on their own voice, however impacted and often "unrepresentative," the silenced liberate the "hidden transcripts" of which James C. Scott speaks and thereby provide a fuller picture that is more diverse not only in terms of the number but also in terms of the variations and the depth of those expressions. What was once debased becomes subversive and then normative in the service of a heightened conversation that enriches society as a whole. Without such a variety of voices and their intercourse, society loses the immediacy and accuracy that will enable it to survive in a context that requires "a plural destiny for mankind" (Said 1989, 224). Representation is, in the end, even more significant as a political than as a literary instrument. How we represent ourselves and who represents us are what make it possible to be different. Only when that possibility becomes a reality can we productively reach into the interstices of race and gender as well as historicize race in a way that localizes the voice that speaks and places it more appropriately in the context of larger issues of linguistic and cultural colonialism. Only then can de-racing take place.

Works Cited

Greenblatt, Stephen J. 1991. *Learning to Curse: Essays in Early Modern Culture*. New York: Routledge.

Harris, Angela P. 1990. "Race and Essentialism in Feminist Legal Theory." *Stanford Law Review* 42: 581.

Hogan, Patrick Colm. 1996. "Colonialism and the Problem of Identity in Irish Literature." *College Literature* 23.3: 163-70.

Jones, D. Marvin. 1993. "Darkness Made Visible: Law, Metaphor, and the Racial Self." *Georgetown Law Journal* 82: 437.

Lyotard, Jean-Francois. 1988. *The Differend: Phrases in Dispute*. Trans. G. Van Den Abbeele. Minneapolis: University of Minnesota Press.

McHoul, Alec, and Wendy Grace. 1997. *A Foucault Primer: Discourse, Power, and the Subject*. New York: New York University Press.

Morrison, Toni. 1992. "Friday on the Potomac." Introduction to *Race-ing Justice, Engendering Power*. Ed. Toni Morrison. New York: Pantheon.

Said, Edward W. 1989. "Representing the Colonized: Anthropology's Interlocutors." *Critical Inquiry* 15: 205-25.

Scott, James C. 1990. *Domination and the Arts of Resistance: Hidden Transcripts*. New Haven: Yale University Press.

Slotkin, Richard. 1993. "From the Open Range to the Mean Streets: Myth and Formula Fiction, 1910-1940." *Gunfighter Nation: The Myth of the Frontier in Twentieth-Century America*. New York: Harper.

Williams, Patricia J. 1996. "The Hidden Meanings of 'Black English'." *The New York Times* 29 December, E:9.

I

RACE-ING REPRESENTATION

1

Afrocentric Voices: Constructing Identities, (Dis)Placing Difference

Kanishka Chowdhury

> Each generation must out of relative obscurity discover its mission, fulfill it, or betray it.
>
> Franz Fanon, *The Wretched of the Earth*

In a recent article, "Nubian Treasures Reflect Black Influence on Egypt," published in *The New York Times*, John Noble Winford comments on the growing influence of archeological studies that celebrate the magnificence of the ancient Nubian civilization.[1] Winford explains the significance of these continuing discoveries in the context of current debates over "the relationship of ancient Egypt to other African civilizations and their role in the rise of Western civilizations" (Winford 1992, 8). According to Winford, such research is promoted by an "Afrocentric school" consisting primarily of African and African-American scholars.

Winford's limited definition of "Afrocentric" assumes that it is a contemporary African-American academic theory whose advocates hold a position loosely based on certain archeological and anthropological studies. One of the key goals of these academics, Winford believes, is to establish Egypt as a black society. However, certain forms of Afrocentrism have existed for well over a hundred years in the writings of W. E. B. Du Bois, Ida Wells, and Marcus Garvey and, later on, in the works of black nationalists such as Maulana

Karenga and Malcolm X. None of these thinkers was particularly concerned with the importance of Egypt or its place in black history, even though Du Bois had argued that ancient Egyptians were Negroes. Their principal interest was to resist the cultural, political, and economic domination of Euro-American ideology and establish some form of black autonomy and independence. Among the most extreme Afrocentric positions was Garvey's famous call for a return to Africa.

The current resurgence of Afrocentrism has, of course, attained a certain controversial edge in relation to discussions about multiculturalism within the university. The advocates of Afrocentrism have moved from the liberal approach to multiculturalism, which generally calls for a recognition of cultural diversity, to a more radical call for infusing the curriculum with an entirely new vision. This radical call for curriculum revision has elicited a similar reaction from white liberal and right-wing educators; their response to Afrocentrism has been generally hostile.[2] Even prominent African-American scholars such as Anthony Appiah, Henry Louis Gates, and Orlando Patterson have questioned the political and philosophical usefulness of Afrocentrism.[3] Paul Gilroy, a British cultural critic, in his influential new work, *The Black Atlantic*, also rejects an "African American version of cultural studies [which he argues] shares a nationalistic focus that is antithetical to the rhizomorphic, fractal structure of the transcultural formation that is the black Atlantic" (Gilroy 1995, 4). Their stance, however, has not prevented several school districts—in cities including Sacramento, Detroit, Atlanta, and Washington, D.C.—from developing an Afrocentric curriculum. The Shule Mandela Academy in East Palo Alto and Suder Elementary School in Chicago are just two examples of schools that base their curriculum on African culture. However, these schools do not necessarily identify themselves as "Afrocentric"; they merely attempt to reverse the hopelessly biased educational system in the United States that has kept black history and black achievements completely in the margins. Indeed, as I intend to demonstrate in this study, "Afrocentricity" is a term that is constantly redefined within alternative cultural moments.

I have selected three important Afrocentric voices in order to present a fairly representative sample of the various Afrocentric ideologies: Cheikh Anta Diop's *Civilization or Barbarism* (1991), Molefi Kete Asante's *Afrocentricity* (1990), and Chinweizu, Onwuchekwa Jemie, and Ihechukwu Madubuike's *Towards the Decolonization of African Literature* (1983). These texts are deliberately selected from different fields of inquiry in order to examine the antagonisms among these fields. Furthermore, Diop, a Senegalese Marxist, Asante, a conservative African American, and the Nigerian troika of literary critics represent a broad range of Afrocentric cultural and political positions. The writers have also been chosen from different historical contexts within the African diaspora to demonstrate their different cultural priorities.

These Afrocentric gestures include attempts to rewrite Western histories and to reestablish Africans' cultural heritage, a heritage that includes the oldest known civilization. However, as I will emphasize in this study, that is only one aspect of the Afrocentric impulse. I will also distinguish contemporary Afrocentrism in relation to earlier "African" movements such as Pan-Africanism and Negritude. My primary intention in this study is to map certain key dangers of constructing alternative histories. I believe that alternative historical narratives, whatever their political and emancipatory agendas, must be interrogated with the same rigor as "official" histories. According to Fanon, the newly liberated peoples of the colonies dwell "in a zone of occult instability" that is one result of the cultural fluctuations that accompany the end of colonization (Fanon 1968, 227). Homi Bhabha has persuasively argued that Fanon's critique of "fixed and stable" narratives of national culture is relevant outside the realm of anticolonial struggle. Bhabha insists on recovering Fanon's notion of "the instability of cultural signification . . . that cannot be a knowledge that is stabilized in its enunciation" (Bhabha 1994, 152). While I reject Bhabha's lack of historical specificity and his disavowal of all acts of knowledge formation, I would agree that cultural enactments are never innocent.[4] Furthermore, I would argue that Afrocentric discourse, like some anticolonial narratives, fundamentally works against such instability, trying instead to create an essential zone of cultural oneness. In the final section of my paper I will propose a rationale for a critical Afrocentrism that will call for a radical reimagining of cultural memory within the context of such instability.

Civilization or Barbarism

To emphasize the vital historical specificity of Diop's intellectual contributions, it is worthwhile to contextualize the scholarly terrain on which he rewrote the narratives of historical memory and cultural identity. Western histories of Africa have, of course, done much to obliterate the past of African people and systematically erase social, cultural, and political traditions that existed for centuries. The European dominance over the African continent can be generally separated into two historical moments. The first phase began in the early seventeenth century with the establishment of trading posts along the western African coast and the subsequent exploitation of African people through the massive slave trade. This enforced displacement of millions of Africans finally ceased in the nineteenth century, when both Britain and the United States banned slavery. At about the same moment, the second phase of exploitation of the Africans began with the actual colonization of the continent. This phase commenced systematically with the Berlin Congress in 1885, but in reality it had begun in 1830 with the colonization of Algeria by French forces.[5] Basil Davidson has referred to this second phase as the "new racism." It is these one hundred and fifty years that saw the rise of a form of European scholarship that systematically denigrated African culture and civilization in order to legitimize a particularly vicious form of colonization. The Europeans claimed to bring Christianity, commerce, and civilization to a land of savages, a land without history, as Hegel once described Africa. Despite fierce resistance, imperial representatives managed to impose Western culture on the Africans with the support of colonial armies, and the battle over the ownership of knowledge was made easier since African history was largely unrecorded in textual form. The African people, therefore, became a people without a text, a people without official histories.[6] And colonialism was able to "turn to the past of the oppressed people, and distort, disfigure, and destroy it" (Fanon 1968, 210).

Diop's project, then, is to recover the past and systematically overturn Western cultural assumptions, an effort historically situated in the years since decolonization. As Robert Young points out: "What has been new in the years since the Second World War during which, for the most part, the decolonization of the European empires has taken place, has been the accompanying attempt to decolonize European thought and the forms of its history as well" (Young 1990, 119). Young accurately locates the historical moment in which postcolonial histories were constructed in response to decades of hegemonic European narratives. Diop's Afrocentrism is a direct descendent of this intellectual movement that followed decolonization, but it also has its roots in the earlier political ferment that came out of Garveyism and the Fifth Pan-African Congress convened in Manchester in 1945. Thus, Diop's works must be located within the tradition of Pan-Africanism and the struggle against intellectual colonialism that was "guilty of a deliberate falsification of human history" (Diop 1991, 1).

The publication of Diop's *The African Origin of Civilization* (1967) is regarded as a key moment in the study of African culture. In this work Diop explores ideas that he had already developed in a previous text, *Nations negres et culture* (1955). While *Nations* contained innovative interpretations of African history as well as strategies for African political independence, *The African Origin of Civilization* begins to question decades of European historiography. Diop tries to establish the following key point: "Ancient Africa was a Negro civilization. The history of Black Africa will remain suspended in air and cannot be written correctly until African historians dare to connect it with the history of Egypt" (Diop 1974, xiv).

Civilization or Barbarism (1991), according to Diop, is a "further contribution to the work that has allowed us [black scholars] to elevate the idea of a Black Egypt to the level of an operational scientific concept" (1). It corrects the "distorted perspective caused by the blinders of colonialism [that] had so profoundly warped intellectuals' views of the African past that we had the greatest difficulty, even among Africans, in gaining acceptance for ideas that are today becoming commonplace" (Diop 1991, 1-2). *Civilization or Barbarism* is in many ways the most significant of Diop's works and the culmination of a lifetime of research and study. It is an in-depth scholarly project of cultural restoration and a work where Diop, in John Clarke's judgment, displays his varied skills, "using the disciplines of linguistics, cultural and physical anthropology, history, chemistry, and physics that his research required [to forge] new theoretical pathways and [reveal] new evidence in the quest to uncover the ancient origins and unifying principles of classical African civilization" (Clarke 1991, xiv).

In undertaking this project Diop was responding to European efforts to dislocate Egypt from the rest of Africa and isolate its cultural traditions from sub-Saharan Africa.[7] The motivations for this cultural erasure were, he argues, obviously to discount any historical possibilities for a unified black people and to legitimize colonization. It may be remembered that the great English philosopher John Stuart Mill advocated liberty for some based on the division of the world into civilized and barbaric people. The civilized race was responsible for ruling these inferior people and thus the new "Egyptological ideology, born at the opportune moment, reinforced the theoretical basis of imperialist ideology" (Diop 1991, 1). One of Diop's primary tasks, then, is to set the European historical record straight. According to Diop, the Egyptologists had committed a crime not only against the African people but also against science. The "true" history of humanity had to be recovered as a scientific project; however, Diop makes it clear that his work is not merely an objective search for the so-called truth; for Africans, "the return to Egypt in all domains is the necessary condition for reconciling African civilizations with history, in order to be able to construct a body of human sciences, in order to renovate African culture" (3).

Diop attempts to do just this in a painstaking analysis spread out over eighteen chapters. *Civilization or Barbarism* is a thoroughly researched work that intervenes in European accounts of the origins of humanity. Diop engages in a full-scale empirical study to disprove previous "scientific" claims made by Europeans. His major points may be summarized as follows: Africa is not only the birthplace of *homo erectus* (upright human) but also of *homo sapiens*; Europeans are descendants of the black Grimaldi type who appeared in Europe thirty thousand years ago; Egypt originated in Black Africa, and the Nubian kingdom gave birth to Egypt;[8] the XVIII Egyptian dynasty colonized Crete and the whole Eastern Mediterranean; Greece and Western civilization have their historical antecedents in Egypt (Black Africa). Diop elaborates on this connection by defining "Egyptian philosophical currents and their obvious connections to those of Greece" and also by providing "a proper method for identifying the Greek vocabulary of Black African Egyptian origin" (Diop 1991, 6).

Given the scope of Diop's assertions, the question now arises whether these findings are relevant to contemporary systems of Afrocentric thought. It is necessary to acknowledge that the majority of Diop's works were written and published after the decolonization years in Africa. To some extent the political struggle for freedom had succeeded, which is to say that flag independence had been achieved. How significant, then, are Diop's works in an apparently independent Africa, and how important are they to the Pan-African movement? These questions can be contextualized in the light of Diop's own interests and faith in African social and economic unity. Diop was part of a generation of African activists who had experienced the heady years that followed the independence of Ghana in March 1958 but then "lived to see Africa turn against itself, motivated in part by its former colonial masters, who were still behind the scenes, controlling the destiny of the continent" (Clarke 1991, xiv).[9] Ultimately, then, Diop was interested in recovering the past only insofar as it informed the practices of future African governments. In a work such as *Precolonial Black Africa* (1987), he embarks on a description of "African national life: the administrative, judicial, economic, and military organizations, that of labor, . . . the migrations and formations of peoples and nationalities, thus their ethnic genesis, and consequently almost linguistic genesis" (Diop 1987b, xii). The final purpose of such a project is to establish the cultural oneness of the African people. This aspect of Afrocentrism can be seen in all of Diop's work, particularly in *Civilization or Barbarism.*

Another, more radical, form of Afrocentric reasoning involves placing Africa at the center of history. In this formulation, Africa becomes not only the birthplace of humanity but also the cradle of Western civilization's philosophical and cultural traditions. Furthermore, the future and the hope for humanity can in many ways be located in African systems of thought. This interest in the future is one of the founding principles of Diop's work. For Diop, "the return to Egypt in all its domains is the necessary condition for the reconciling of African civilizations with history, in order to be able to construct a body of modern human sciences, in order to renovate African culture. Far from being a reveling in the past, a look toward the Egypt of antiquity is the best way to conceive and build our cultural future" (Diop 1991, 3). For example, in a work such as *Black Africa: The Economic and Cultural Basis for a Federated State* (1987), Diop presents a detailed analysis of possible methods to safeguard Africa's mineral resources for the future. His efforts to unite Africa are not merely a form of cultural chauvinism, but a strategy based on a sincere determination to strive for the political, cultural, and economic autonomy of the African continent.

Diop does not hesitate to challenge, for instance, the latest theses on the

Asiatic or African Mode of Production (AMP). In an incisive critical review of the Marxist definitions of the AMP, Diop points out that these states are not distinguished by the absence of revolution, but rather by the suppression of revolution due to the "ultrasophisticated interventionist machinery" that these states employ (Diop 1987a, 188). According to Diop, this interventionism is "one of the heaviest legacies that the AMP state has bequeathed to the modern state, and one which explains the enormous difficulties that the world revolutionary process encounters today in different countries" (188). He also looks at various revolutions in history, especially the ones that failed, comparing the revolutions in the Greek city-states with the revolutions in the AMP states. The study of these revolutions, according to Diop, is particularly relevant "when African society is entering the phase of the true struggle of classes in the modern sense of the term . . . the first strike of the African workers against an African industrialist employer would mark the beginning of the new era in the class struggle" (5-6). The questions he raises in these sections lead him to examine the characteristics of African political and social structures, which then guide the reader toward probable answers for the problems facing present governments in Africa. Thus, Diop's engagement with political economy and his materialist reading of the African past prevent the work from sinking into hopeless abstraction. For instance, he takes special pains to historicize the failure of the Negritude artists between the wars and attributes it to "the fact that the intellectual and psychological climate created by all the writings of this type [works produced by scholars such as Count Arthur Joseph Gobineau] strongly conditioned the first definitions that the Negro-African thinkers of the period . . . had tried to give their culture" (217). In its incisive grounding in socioeconomic analysis, then, Diop's Afrocentrism is substantially different from that of Molefi Kete Asante, whose work I will examine later in this study.

However, it is also necessary to point out some major philosophical contradictions in Diop's theories. His theory of history, for instance, suggests a Hegelian notion of totality and continuum that can only be applied by excluding the ruptures and discontinuities of any historical narrative. Diop begins his project with a chapter on prehistory and the origins of humanity and then traces the rise of Nubia and the subsequent evolution of an authentic Black Egyptian civilization. In the process, he constructs a linear, continuous history of Black Africa that Michel Foucault would define as "total history":

> The project of a total history is one that seeks to reconstitute the overall form of a civilization, the principle—material or spiritual—of a society, the significance common to all phenomena of a period, the law that accounts for their cohesion—what is called metaphorically the "face" of a period. (Foucault 1972, 9)

Foucault goes on to explain that such a project depends on supposing "that between all the events of a well-defined spatio-temporal area, between all the phenomena of which traces have been found, it must be possible to establish a system of homogeneous relations: a network of causality that makes it possible to derive each of them" (9). Total history ignores micronarratives, resistances to histories, and thus silences voices that would disrupt the apparent continuum of history. The success of such a project must finally depend on a violent teleological concept of history in which the recovery of a cultural essence provides the route to an imagined future liberation.

Despite these shortcomings, Diop is engaged in an important intellectual project. He is attempting to recover the African past that was formerly the property of the European ruling class. But in an effort to perform a laudatory emancipatory task, Diop succumbs to cultural idealism. He hopes that "the world wide dissemination of information . . . [will force] the ethical conscience of humanity to stick to 'acceptable' limits" (Diop 1991, 376). His theory of the "Progress of the Ethical Conscience of Humanity"—that "humanity's moral conscience progresses" with the acquisition of knowledge—obviously neglects to take into account the immense changes in the global economy that were already taking place. Dissemination of knowledge was never an innocent activity and is now, as in the past, controlled by the metropolitan centers. The Subaltern Studies collective has shown how radical historians are "blinded by the glare of a perfect and immaculate consciousness." These historians see "nothing, for instance, but solidarity in rebel behaviour, and [fail] to notice its other, namely betrayal" (Guha 1983, 40). In the end, it is even questionable how valuable such acts of recovery really are for the contemporary African. Frantz Fanon in his brilliant exposition on National Culture said it best: "on the plane of factual being the past existence of an Aztec civilization does not change anything very much in the diet of the Mexican peasant of today" (Fanon 1968, 209).

It is finally a stark contradiction that, while resisting a European-Hegelian-Humanist view of history, Diop constructs just such a model in *Civilization or Barbarism*. The error lies in part in retaining a binary— barbarism-civilization—that can never be fully reinscribed or reversed.[10] It is only fitting to recall at this instance Walter Benjamin's words on the very same binary:

> For without exception the cultural treasures [the historian] surveys have an origin which he cannot contemplate without horror. They owe their existence not only to the efforts of the great minds and talents who have created them, but also to the anonymous toils of their contemporaries. There is no document of civilization which is not at the same time a document of barbarism. (Benjamin 1969, 256)

Diop needs to recreate an unproblematized view of the past to make a valuable polemical point, and perhaps the absence of a "legitimate" center dictates the "logic" behind his rhetorical moves. Africa, because of decades of scholarly distortion, has no center that can be deconstructed or refigured, and Diop's project primarily consists of constructing just such a center. However, Diop's intellectual redemption of the center "ignores the anonymous toil" of those millions of African men and women who participated in creating Africa's "cultural treasures."

Afrocentricity

Molefi Kete Asante, chair of the Department of African-American Studies at Temple University, has become one of the primary spokespersons for Afrocentric curriculums in the United States. In a recent issue of *Newsweek*, he provides the rationale for such curriculums: "The task of the Afrocentric curriculum is finding patterns in African-American history and culture that help the teacher place the child in the middle of the intellectual experience" (46). According to Asante, such a process is necessary because of the alienation African-American children feel in the face of Eurocentric educational system that places them "outside the information being discussed" (Asante 1991, 46). Asante strikes an extremely reasonable position in this article, presenting his views to a mainstream audience within the boundaries of nonseparationist rhetoric. However, in his recent work *Afrocentricity* (1990), Asante is far less restrained and launches into a stinging attack on Eurocentrism, while providing an Afrocentric manifesto for African Americans to follow.

Asante's philosophical antecedents can be traced back to several African-American intellectuals who have proven to be influential. Indeed, Asante speaks with approval of Marcus Garvey, Elijah Muhammad, Malcolm X, and Maulana Karenga, though he claims that, despite their brilliance, Booker T. Washington, W. E. B. Du Bois, and Martin Luther King were not Afrocentrists. Of course, Asante's list of prominent intellectuals consists of male African Americans. Sidney Lemelle, quoting Francis White, argues that such hero worship and adoption of masculinist discourse "invents a past which is subject to 'sexist pitfalls' and fosters a 'conservative agenda on gender and sexuality'" (Lemelle 1995, 334).

Yet the male African-American influence is not the predominant one; Asante emerges out of a tradition of Afrocentrism that has its roots beyond the United States in the works of Diop. In fact, in a previous work, *The Afrocentric Idea* (1987), Asante identifies himself as a "Diopian":

I consider myself a "Diopian"; that is, the aim of my work is to advance the

study and enhance the appreciation of the complexity and historicity of
African culture. As such, I am a cultural analyst, committed to the systematic
exposition of communication and cultural behaviors as they are articulated in
the African world. (Asante 1987, vii)

However, his latest work, *Afrocentricity*, provides not so much cultural analysis
as a cultural call to arms. But the revolution is a diffused one, specific in its aim,
yet universal in its reach: "Up from the intellectual and spiritual pit which has
held our mighty people! Let each person take his post in the vanguard of this
collective consciousness of Afrocentrism! Teach it! Practice it! And victory will
surely come as we carry out the Afrocentric mission to humanize the universe"
(Asante 1990, 6). It is quite apparent that the intended audience of this work is
African American. Asante is far less interested in accommodating Euro-
American thought than he was in the *Newsweek* interview; instead,
Afrocentricity is now the key to salvation for African Americans. It is no more
merely the means to broaden a curriculum, but a way to achieve liberation:
"Afrocentricity is the belief in the centrality of Africans in postmodern history.
It is our history, our mythology, our creative motif, and our ethos exemplifying
our collective will" (Asante 1990, 6). Of course, Asante never really explains or
problematizes his reference to "postmodern history." He merely assumes that it
is a contemporary "natural" historical moment.

Asante's primary purpose in this work is to preach liberation through
enunciating a politics of difference. African Americans can only attain this
liberation through the doctrine of Afrocentricity, which reclaims their "true"
identity by informing their thoughts and actions. The African-American
community is defined by Asante as a monolithic whole without any gender or
class differences. According to Asante, any differences are eclipsed by
"history": "Regardless of our various complexions and degrees of consciousness
we are by virtue of commitments, history, and convictions an African people.
Afrocentricity, therefore, is only superficially related to color, it is more
accurately a philosophical outlook determined by history (Asante 1990, 27)."
African Americans, therefore, have a core of being, a collective memory that
they can somehow recover. According to Asante, their liberation can be
achieved by following "Nija." This doctrine "is the collective expression of the
Afrocentric worldview which is grounded in the historical experience of African
people. . . . It places Afrocentricity in the African population of the Diaspora
and the continent" (21-22). Asante goes on to explain that practicing Nija
includes a "libation to the ancestors . . . [and] becomes the main source of
meditative activities and spiritual growth" (22). Furthermore, "Nija establishes a
link to our fundamental primordial truths" (22). By focusing on self-
improvement and the notion of fundamental truths, Asante replicates the cultural
conservatism of the right and the ideology of the infamous Daniel Patrick

Monhiyan report "The Negro Family: The Case for National Action." Asante's suggestion is that African Americans need to return to some inner strength and ignore the institutional impact of racism. Job discrimination, low wages, inadequate housing, and educational opportunities are separate from the attainment of Nija.[11] Asante's acontextual call for self-help is particularly disturbing in an age in which politicians disavow any state responsibilty for the ravages wrought by corporate greed and antiminority legislation.

Asante's somewhat naive belief in the universality of the diasporic experience is particularly borne out in the following sentence: "We have always felt that South Africa had to be free and we have always abhorred the United States' investment in that racist country. In this respect our international politics resembles that of African nations more than that of the United States" (Asante 1990, 67). Surely, Asante is aware that several African countries indirectly supported the South African government by engaging in trade and commerce with the apartheid regime. The African diaspora is not an easily characterized political block whose historical destinies are necessarily aligned. According to Sidney J. Lemelle, "Asante, in groping for some timeless 'essence', sees little or no difference between a poor Zimbabwean peasant woman and a rich male Barbados banker. Likewise, for him there is a spatial and temporal connection between Menelik II struggling against Italian imperialism in the 1890s and US Supreme Court Justice Clarence Thomas struggling against pro-choice forces in the 1990s" (Lemelle 1995, 341). Asante's move away from a historical analysis of the continent is also displayed by his statement on Marxism: "Marxism's Eurocentric foundation makes it antagonistic to our worldview; its confrontational nature does not provide the spiritual satisfaction we have found in our history of harmony" (Asante 1990, 80). Instead of accurately focusing on "Marxism's Eurocentric foundations," Asante engages in an utterly idealized faith in some "history of harmony." Such ahistorical mystifications finally disqualify Asante from being, as he claims, a "Diopian."

It should be quite apparent at this point that Asante is asserting a theory of cultural oneness. He posits as its basis the concept of a totalized identity as well as a complete faith in a created "tradition," a tradition that can only emerge from a "history of harmony." However, by implying that traditions are wholly recoverable, Asante ignores the fact that traditions are never fixed; traditions, after all, are constantly changing within different historical moments, and often these changes are brought about by the ruling class to accommodate its power within shifting variants.[12] Indeed, as Eric Wolf points out, cultures are not "integrated totalities in which each part contributes to the maintainance of an organized, autonomous, and enduring whole. There are only cultural sets of practices and ideas, put into play by determinate human actors under determinate circumstances. In the course of action, these cultural sets are forever assembled, dismantled, and reassembled, conveying in variable accents the divergent paths of groups and classes" (Wolf 1982, 390-91). Traditions, then, can become the property of the ruling classes and may not necessarily function as a means of protecting and recovering an ethnic identity or as a form of emanicipation.

In addition, the whole process of claiming an ethnic identity is at best a tenuous project. According to Homi Bhabha, "the enunciation of cultural difference problematizes the division of past and present, tradition and modernity, at the level of cultural representation and its authoritative address" (Bhabha 1994, 128). Ethnic absolutism dismisses ethnic entropy in an effort to place identity within easily negotiable categories. Asante is content to present the African-American community as a monolithic group with a unique past easily represented. Indeed, any acknowledgment of difference would challenge his "sense of historical identity of culture as a homogenising, unifying force, authenticated by the originary Past, kept alive in the national tradition of the people" (130). Asante's philosophy of Afrocentric oneness is ultimately couched in the dubious claims of origin and descent, which are then totalized and textualized into a recoverable way of life easily reproduced and imitated in the present and the future.

The greatest danger that Asante's theories pose resides not so much in their theoretical impossibilities as in their replication of the very same Western hegemonic systems that he so despises. The authentic identity that Asante is so eager to recover reinforces Western constructs. Kobena Mercer is worth quoting on this point:

> the search for an authentic, essential "self" in adverserial ideologies such as black cultural nationalism . . . often replays the vanguardist notion that there can be only *one* privileged agent of social and historical change. However tactically the "war of manoeuvre" against white/male supremacist ideologies, the consequences of such separatism is self-defeating as it mimics the authoritarian power to which it is initially opposed by simply inverting the binaries of discourses that legitimize domination. (Mercer 1994, 281)

While Mercer seems to ignore the political valence of such acts of separatism, he is accurate in claiming that the terms of the battle are finally dictated by Western ideological constructions and that the colonized legitimizes the colonizer by miming his authority.

However, Asante's return to the source for strengthening an identity that has been assaulted by the Europeans is completely understandable. Indeed, even a revolutionary such as Amilcar Cabral advocated a return to the source. But in his book of the same name, Cabral points out that "a thorough analysis of cultural reality does not permit the claim that there exists continental or racial cultures. This is because, as with history, the development of culture proceeds in uneven fashion, whether at the level of a continent, a 'race', or even a society" (Cabral 1973, 51). For Cabral, a return to the source is not an intellectual, escapist form of self-indulgence, but a way in which the people of Africa could mobilize their forces to defeat the forces of imperialism. Cabral's historical understanding of the African diaspora is quite different from Asante's clarion call for a seamless, dehistoricized "cultural rebirth": "there is no other truth more necessary for the intellectual, political, economic, and cultural advancement of the world than African people immersing themselves in the waters of a cultural rebirth" (Asante 1990, 104).

Finally, Asante's faith in a purely autochthonous culture becomes his greatest downfall. Unlike Diop, his study does not even attempt to engage in any archival research.[13] Instead, he relies on hopeless abstractions, calling on African Americans to achieve "liberty through adequate actions and symbols" and to "express the totality of [their] African experience, knowing both its separateness from and its connectedness to a Pan-African world" (Asante 1990, 36-37). It is hard to imagine how an African-American man or woman caught within a cycle of poverty in America's inner cities is to engage in such a project, particularly when it is directed at "writers, authors, and other intellectuals or artists" (39).[14] As Asante tries to "defeat and . . . overthrow . . . one sovereignty" and establish "the emergence and consolidation of an antithetical sovereignty," he succeeds in the "creation of a different . . . repression" (Radhakrishnan 59). "Liberating" primarily the middle-class male subject, in the end, can only be an inadequate project.

Toward the Decolonization of African Literature

In *Toward the Decolonization of African Literature*, Chinweizu, Onwuchekwa Jemie, and Ihechukwu Madubuike, otherwise known as the Bolekaja critics, emulate Asante's objective in that their work is primarily an act of cultural decolonization. Their text was the first concentrated attempt to articulate an Afrocentric basis for the study of African literary works. The troika very correctly responded to the dominant Eurocentric mode of criticism that African and non-African critics employed in their reading of African texts. The years following the political decolonization of Africa had not produced a subsequent decolonization of the mind. Several African critics still practiced European ways of reading and judged African texts by European standards. The non-African critics, such as Charles Larson, John Povey, and Adrian Roscoe, set the guidelines for such criticism. Their primary objective was to portray African literatures as an emergent literature with no prior tradition and then evaluate them according to the rigid standards of universalism, which translated as the standards of the European high bourgeoisie. Chinua Achebe sums up the role of the colonialist critic aptly:

> The latter-day colonialist critic . . . sees the African writer as a somewhat unfinished European who with patient guidance will grow up one day and write like every other European, but meanwhile must be humble, must learn all he can and, while at it, give due credit to his teachers in the form of direct praise or, even better, since praise sometimes goes bad and becomes embarrassing, manifest self-contempt (4).

Writers such as Chinua Achebe, Ngugi wa Thiong'o, and Wole Soyinka have consistently objected to the Western standards to which African literatures have been submitted, so the troika's intervention in this primarily Eurocentric field, of course, is not the first of its kind. What the troika attempts for the first time, however, is to recreate African literatures within the terms of their indigenous traditions and then propose a "correct" way to read these texts. Such a project strives to destroy the remaining vestiges of Eurocentric models of criticism: "The cultural task at hand is to end all foreign domination of African culture, to systematically destroy all encrustations of colonial and slave mentality, to clear the bushes and stake out new foundations for a liberated African modernity" (Chinweizu et al. 1983, 1). To achieve this systematic destruction, the troika once again seeks salvation in the power of "tradition" and folklore. A "liberated modernity" can only emerge if attention is given to the "pure" literatures with their origins in the African soil. In the realm of "poetry," for instance, the battle for liberation has to be waged against those critics who have encouraged "stiff, pale, anemic, academic poetry, slavishly imitative of 20th-century European modernism, with its weak preciosity, ostentatious erudition, and dunghill piles of esoterica and obscure allusions" as opposed to a poetry with its roots in "the vital nourishment of our African tradition and home soil . . . [a poetry] of vibrancy, gusto, and absolute energy of the African oral poetry . . . firmly and deeply rooted in the African home soil" (Chinweizu et al. 1983, 3-4).[15]

The Chinweizu et al. version of Afrocentrism consists of an idyllic return to the past from which the energy will be generated for a cultural liberation. The troika selects a variety of poems and stories to develop its central premise: if African literature is read correctly—read Afrocentrically—the richness of the literature is easily decipherable. Of course, the route to such Afrocentricity is lighted by the intellectual vanguard: "The task of decolonization . . . requires an active nationalist consciousness. It must be conducted within the guiding parameters set by those intellectuals who have upheld black consciousness through the centuries" (Chinweizu et al. 1983, 5). In claiming to define a form of "nationalist consciousness," Chinweizu et al. do not show any recognition of what Gramsci would call "the people-nation." In fact, as Gramsci pointed out, "the intellectual's error consists in believing that one can know without understanding" (Gramsci 1971, 418). Liberating the African continent is not an intellectual project divorced from the interests of the people. Indeed, Chinweizu's privileging of literature also assumes a certain form of bourgeois indulgence that ignores the historical forces that shape the lives of the people of Africa. Gareth Griffiths has criticized the troika on this very same point: "[The troika displays] an inadequate level of theoretical analysis, an analysis which [takes] no account of the determining forces of social and cultural practice, nor of the need to relate this practice very specifically to the distinct articulations of ruling class ideology" (Griffiths and Moody 1989, 75). Their inability to make these very connections between the cultural and the political causes the focus to shift from the very real issues facing Africa's attempts at decolonization. Judging by the troika's diatribe, one would assume that the primary danger facing African authenticity and independence is the cultural ideals of the high European bourgeoisie. That is certainly not the case. The chief assault instead is from the globalization of American capitalism. It is far more common in countries where illiteracy often runs higher than 80 percent to see the influence of the West in its popular iconic forms. For example, in Harare, Lagos, or Nairobi one may observe a young boy don a Lakers T-shirt or imitate Michael Jackson, without being remotely concerned about the form of Eurocentrism that Chinweizu et al. seem to fear. Even in the above examples, it is important to point out that there is no such thing as a homogenized process of Westernization; "Western" styles are assimilated through local paradigms and structures. Africa's reading of a Western text will seldom coincide with a Western reading of that icon.[16] Thus, the image in the process of transference is never only Western, never fully indigenous.

The troika's rather elitist privileging of literature is also demonstrated by their commitment to selecting works based on "excellence." According to the critics, only those authors who are "distinct and consummate have been considered. Materials with engaging themes, but indifferently or ineptly handled, have been excluded" (Chinweizu et al. 1983, 5). Taking refuge in such categorizations gets the troika back to a cycle of value hierarchies that are ultimately a return to canon formation and intellectual elitism. It is ironic that the very same critics who are responding to Western-biased perceptions of excellence immediately set up their own categories of aesthetic judgment. Furthermore, their notions of "excellence" based on written work in English ignore African oral/popular genres and languages. Perhaps the final contradiction in any form of reverse discourse is that the nature of the argument prevents it from erasing the dominant from its system of analysis. Anthony Appiah accurately sums up the philosophical oversights of the troika:

> [In] the establishment of a "reverse discourse" the terms of resistance are
> already given us, and our conversation is entrapped within the Western
> cultural conjecture we attempt to dispute. The pose of repudiation actually
> presupposes the cultural institutions of the West and the ideological matrix in
> which they, in turn, are imbricated. Railing against the cultural hegemony of
> the West, the nativists are of its party without knowing it. (Appiah 1990, 69)

The troika can never escape this "ideological matrix." Even while it nobly
attempts to "[root] out from African literature colonial attitudes, norms, world
views, values, and techniques," it inevitably condemns itself as it "endeavour[s]
to [replace] them with others that are conducive to African dignity and
autonomy in the world" (145). It is as if it believes there is a simple choice to be
made between Afrocentric and Eurocentric ways of seeing the world.

One of the problems the troika refuses to recognize is that the Afrocentric
interpretation it imposes on a text is finally dependent on exterior factors, most
of which are outside its realm of control.[17] Texts, after all, are not produced
independently of ideological practices. Meaning is negotiated between the
writer, the reader, and the critic within ideological configurations. The
production of the text, therefore, has no idealized moment of creation, and its
consumption is dictated by a combination of cultural, historical, and political
circumstances. Finally, what is this Eurocentric "literary" criticism that must be
decolonized? Can we any longer sustain the field of literary studies independent
of anthropology, sociology, or political economy? Are these seminal works—
Talat Asad's *Anthropology and the Colonial Encounter* (1973), Johannes
Fabian's *Time and the Other* (1983), Edward Said's *Orientalism* (1978), Eric R.
Wolf's *Europe and the People without History* (1982)—Eurocentric and
nonliterary? How do Chinweizu et al. set up autonomous fields of inquiry
without destroying that text that they so dearly want to historicize? And, in the
end, what are "African" literatures?[18] A writer such as Ngugi has even
proclaimed that the literature produced in European languages "is not African
literature at all"; it is "Afro-European" literature, "written by Africans in
European languages in the era of imperialism." According to Ngugi, "African
literature can only be written in the African languages of the peasantry and the
working classes" (Ngugi 1985, 125). The troika, in a manner similar to Asante,
assumes a homogeneity of cultural expression and thus incorrectly formulates a
watertight plan for decolonization.

Toward a Critical Afrocentrism

but the work of man is only just beginning
and it remains to man to conquer all

the violence entrenched in the recesses
of his passion
and no race possesses the monopoly of beauty
of intelligence, of force, and there
is a place for all at the rendezvous
of history

Aimé Césaire, *Return to My Native Land*

Despite some of the more severe criticisms I have leveled against these specific Afrocentric texts, it is important to recognize that the movement in its contemporary form is a strategic response at a given historical moment. Its primary intention has been to "break with Euro-modernist power/knowledge" and "simultaneously [propel] a release from its strictures of authorised expertise and professionalization, recognizing them as agencies of dominant discourse, gate-keeping mechanisms of approved 'knowledges'" (Taylor 1989, 103). The Afrocentrism of these scholars is thus an understandable historical response to years of epistemic imperialist violence. They have attempted to situate sub-Saharan Africa in relation to its intricate history with Islam and the West while in some measure recovering a precolonial past, a tradition whether it be in art, literature, or sociopolitics.

The problems, however, surface when the Afrocentrists talk about the "corruption" of indigenous art forms. They assume the existence of a pure originary culture that has moved from the realm of the authentic to the realm of the impure. Such theories are commonly found in postcolonial narratives of pristine precolonial, precontact societies. But what exactly does it mean to say precontact? To assume that sub-Saharan Africa before the European expansion was somehow pristine is unusually naive. Models of distinct and separate systems did not exist before the European expansion. Nigerian Benin and Hausa Kano, for instance, were influenced by traders and merchants from North Africa, while East African kingdoms were inextricably involved with traders and cultures from the Indies and India.

And in viewing the colonial phase, Afrocentrism still constructs a dyadic political structure that ignores two major factors: power cannot simply be located in a single monolithic colonizer, and the colonized is not an exclusive homogenized mass. Even Diop's vast archival discoveries are ultimately unimportant if they do not become part of impure historical circumstances. And, as Fredric Jameson points out, "History" itself has to be part of the equation:

> the restoration of the meaning of the greatest cultural monuments cannot be separated from a passionate and partisan assessment of everything that is oppressive in them and that knows complicity with privilege and class domination, stained with the guilt not merely of culture in particular but of History itself as one long nightmare. (Jameson 1981, 299)

Cultural monuments and texts are irrevocably bound up with both civilization
and barbarism. The exploitative mechanisms of the past cannot be separated
from present and future attempts to form a discourse of liberation. According to
Kobena Mercer, "[what] is demanded . . . is not a history that aims to 'articulate
the past as it really was,' but a mode of storytelling which, in Walter
Benjamins's phrase, aims to 'seize hold of a memory as it flashes up at a
moment of danger'" (Mercer 1994, 278).

In its contemporary explorations, then, Afrocentrism not only has to
interrogate vigorously the structures of knowledge that have reproduced racist
oppressive practices but also has to oppose and call for a dismantling of all
dominant hierarchies of knowledge, whether they be classist, racist, or sexist. A
critical Afrocentrism must not merely revere the contributions of individuals,
but also must have its intellectual and cultural roots within the community from
which will emerge the actors and knowledges that will directly challenge
hegemonic sytems. As Khaula Murtadha puts it, "The communitarian African
worldview contains within it the social and ethical value of social well-being,
solidarity, interdependence, cooperation, and reciprocal obligations—all of
which can contribute to equitable distribution of resources and benefits to
society" (Murtadha 1995, 357). It is in the spirit of this communitarian
worldview that one must use and evaluate the contributions of Diop, Asante,
and the Bolekaja critics.

At a very preliminary level, the changes must originate within the schools.
Afrocentric schools are necessary as long as racist practices enforce a segrated
school system; however, an Afrocentric or a broadly multicultural curriculum
must be more than a celebration of history; it must be socially empowering,
situated within specific cultural contexts. Afrocentric schools must extend their
struggles against Eurocentric curricula beyond the classroom. As the children
begin to be socialized in their cultural heritage, the communitarian worldview of
Afrocentrism must incorporate an understanding of the political economy that
perpetuates cultural hegemony against African-American culture (Phillips 1995,
391).

A good example of such a curriculum is the "Project La Churasano:
Remembering the Past to Control the Future," which was adopted for a group of
African-American students in St. Petersburg, Florida. "La Churasano" means
culture in the Mandinka language. The program "addressed such issues as
historical origins of African Americans, their migration, the power of their
words in rap, blues, and preaching, and the spatial development of the African
American community" (Philips 1995, 380). More importantly, however, the
students were "presented opportunities to critically assess the social history of
African American life in St. Petersburg from the 1920s to the present" (379).
Their classroom materials included interview tapes with older residents of the

city, newspaper articles on "Negro News," maps, city council files, and other unconventional learning aides. Students also visited specific sites in their own neighborhoods to appreciate what relocation projects had done to their own community. Ultimately, "the documentation of the social history of African Americans in St. Petersburg allowed these students to examine historical patterns of socialization and their implications" (390). In this way, an Afrocentric curriculum can have direct political and cultural impact on students' perception of their world.

A critical Afrocentrism, moreover, must be able to locate these specific local histories to an understanding of the workings of the global cultural economy. Indeed, one of the secondary aims of the Churasano Project was to provide students with an opportunity to study the relations between the various African cultures in the diaspora. Similarly, a strength of the Pan-African movement, for instance, was its ability to make connections between communities across lines of global capital. Writers and activists such as Frantz Fanon, C. L. R. James, Malcolm X, George Padmore, and Walter Rodney always located their analysis of specific political situations within larger contexts. Pan-Africanism in the twenty-first century, according to Horace Campbell, must link the liberation of African peoples to the liberation of other oppressed peoples. Campbell adds that "the battle against racism cannot continue to accept the unscientific category of race" (Campbell 1995, 306). A critical Afrocentrism must problematize such categories. Michael Omi and Howard Winant, for instance, posit a theory of "racial formation" that emphasizes the "social nature of race, the absence of any essential racial characteristics, the historical flexibility of racial meanings and categories, the conflictual character of race at both the 'micro' and 'macro social' levels, and the irreducible political aspect of racial dynamics" (Omi and Winant 1994, 4). Moreover, racial dynamics have to be understood in the context of class relations rather than as distinct from them. C. L. R. James had said much the same thing in his classic evaluation of the Haitian revolution: "The race question is subsidiary to the class question in politics, and to think of imperialism in terms of race is disastrous. But to neglect the racial factor as merely incidental is an error only less grave than to make it fundamental" (James 1989, 283). African Americans must be concerned with the depiction of Haitians and Somalis in the media, but they must also interrogate cultural and political policies that continue to demonize all Third World peoples and marginalize the underclass in the United States.

Finally, a critical Afrocentrism must reimagine the cultural priorities that replace great European males with African ones. Indeed, all the Pan-Africanists that I have named and who have been immortalized are men. More attention should be given to retracing the contributions of Pan-African feminists such as Adelaide Casely Hayford.[19] Asante, Diop, and the Bolekaja troika pay little or no attention to the specific issues surrounding women. Black feminist scholars such as Patricia Hill Collins, bell hooks, and June Jordan have written persuasively against Afrocentrists' conservative agenda on gender and sexuality. Angela Davis sums up the terms of the struggle eloquently: "If we are talking about an entire community rising out of poverty and racism, men will have to learn how to challenge sexism and to fight on behalf of women" (Davis 182).[20] Emancipatory politics have to include an overturning of patriarchy as well as of capitalism and racism. Women of African heritage are amongst the poorest in the world, and they bear a disproportionately large burden of labor responsibilities. They can no longer be merely marginal objects of Afrocentric theorizing; they must be full participants in its production.[21]

In the end, cultural liberation cannot be attained by a fight against racism and cultural imperialism because these struggles, however important, are not separate from a fight for economic independence.[22] The ultimate success of such theories as Afrocentrism has to be measured not merely against the overturning of dominant Eurocentric modes of thinking but also against real economic and political liberation for the millions of the black underclass living in Africa and the diaspora.[23] Cultural liberation cannot circumvent or bypass political economy.

Notes

1. I am grateful to Shaun Hughes, as well as three anonymous readers for *College Literature*, for valuable critical comments on earlier versions of this essay. I am also grateful to Jim Berlin, Tim Brennan, Ross Dawson, Aparajita Sagar, and Andrew Scheiber for helping me think through some of these ideas.

2. The attacks have ranged from Diane Ravitch on the right to the more liberal Arthur Schlesinger, author of *The Disuniting of America* (1991).

3. Greg Thomas provides a useful overview of some of the ideological differences between African-American scholars in his essay, "The Black Studies War: Multiculturalism Versus Afrocentricity."

4. It is particularly important to stress that Afrocentrism in the United States has never been a threat to democracy. I want therefore to distinguish my response to these Afrocentric scholars from those conservative, liberal, and postmodern critics who decry all forms of "essentialism" and "extremism." The politics of Afrocentrism are not congruent to the politics of white supremacy. I categorically reject criticisms that collapse theories into a politically neutral category of generalized "isms." Essentialisms and extremisms cannot be judged outside their relation to structures of domination. As long as white supremacy is the dominant logic, Afrocentrism will always operate as a means of resistance.

5. The year 1830 also saw the British secure a protectorate over the Gold Coast as well as establish Khartoum as part of the Egyptian territories up the Nile. Of course,

there had been several pockets of influence before 1830, some of which were established as early as 1507, when the Portuguese occupied parts of Mozambique and adjacent areas on the east coast. In 1652 the Dutch East India Company began settlements on the Cape of Good Hope; the British finally occupied this region in 1798. The final note, however, on the European settlement of Africa must be in reference to the Napoleonic army's arrival in Egypt (1798), which is generally regarded as the first "modern" European invasion of Africa.

6. Hegel's pronouncements on Africa are well known, and the general Eurocentric dismissal of oral history finds its roots in such declarations: "The periods . . . which peoples have passed before the writing of history, may have been filled with revolutions, migrations, the wildest transformations. Yet, they are without objective history because they lack subjective history, records of history" (Hegel 1953, 76). Eric R. Wolf's *Europe and the People without History* (1982) is a direct response to such dismissals.

7. Martin Bernal, the renowned author of *Black Athena* (1987, 1991), documents the systematic attempts by Western cultural historians and anthropologists to develop a view of Egyptian civilization that denied any African contribution.

8. Bernal disagrees with Diop on this issue. He insists that the Egyptian people were a combination of African, Asian, and Mediterranean peoples and not purely a black race.

9. The failure of Nkrumah's revolution in Ghana, the assassination of Patrice Lumumba in the Congo, and the genocide in Biafra offered an early indication of Western governments' reluctance to let the people of Africa decide their own destinies.

10. Adam Kuper, in *The Invention of Primitive Society* (1988), has expanded on the illusory nature of such concepts as "civilization," "barbarism," and "savagery." He points out that they are all intellectual constructions created ultimately to reproduce dominant ideologies.

11. Robert Reid-Pharr points to the similarly conservative agenda of the Million Man March: "African Americans were once again advised that self-help is the best medicine. The black man was instructed to return home and start providing for kith and kin, to stop making excuses about the scarcity of legitimate well-paying jobs, and to access his inner manhood, that great and mysterious wellspring of masculinity hidden deep within his psyche, waiting to be harnessed to the project of a beautiful black tomorrow" (Reid-Pharr 1996, 37-38).

12. Terence Ranger has commented on the "invention" of traditions in colonial Africa by the British ruling class. According to Ranger, the British "set about to codify and promulgate [African] traditions, thereby transforming flexible customs into hard prescription" (Ranger 1983, 212). "Traditions," in this instance, aided the British in subjugating the native population.

13. For a more comprehensive historical manifesto, see Chancellor Williams's *The Destruction of Black Civilization: Great Issues of a Race from 4000 B.C. to 2000 A.D.* (1987). Williams's ambitious title leads him down more complex and detailed passages, but his focus is primarily on the great Nubian civilization. He also ignores the period 1100-1500 A.D., which Chinweizu identifies as the most significant years in African history. Like Asante, Williams is interested in suggesting Afrocentric routes to cultural and political liberation. In such sections as "A Master Plan" and "The Shape of Things to Come," Williams draws up a detailed plan for battle. The significance of Williams's work is in its timing; the study was originally published in 1969, a year that was

significant for African-American political gains and losses.

14. According to Cornel West, "the distrust and suspicion [of the black intellectual] stem not simply from the usually arrogant and haughty disposition of intellectuals toward ordinary folk, but, more importantly, from the widespread refusal of black intellectuals to remain, in some way, organically linked with Afro-American cultural life" (West 1985, 112).

15. The adjectives used to describe Eurocentric poetry—"pale, anemic"—are female/nonmasculine. Afrocentric verse, on the other hand, is "vibrant" and obviously masculine. The binary, ironically, is part of an Eurocentric rhetoric available since the Renaissance with its concepts of male versus female style. This male/female juxtaposition is also not purely incidental; none of the Afrocentrists have very much to say about the specific problems women face in most African societies. Indeed, Chinweizu et al. make only passing references to African women writers.

16. A good example of such a hybrid icon is the Mami Wata (Mother Water), which originated from the Western myth of the siren. It was originally represented in Western styles but has subsequently been transformed through Zairean urban art and become almost unrecognizable to the Western eyes.

17. It is necessary to add that Chinweizu's latest publication, *Decolonizing the African Mind* (1987), is a far more rigorous analysis of a wide range of issues from economics to politics. The work includes trenchant criticism of such European institutions as the Nobel Prize and the Olympic games. And in an earlier work, *The West and the Rest of Us* (1978), Chinweizu had presented a broad, material analysis of the reasons for European domination: "the fundamental conflict between the West and the rest of us is not over ideology. . . . For over five hundred years now the conflict has been over the control and use of the resources of the non-western peoples" (481).

18. Chinweizu himself expresses some measure of disquiet in a recent anthology, *Voices of Twentieth-Century Africa: Griots and Towncriers* (1988), when faced with the task of defining "African" literature. Indeed, it is a political and intellectual issue that has periodically plagued African writers. The very same question had been the topic of discussion at a historic meeting of African writers at Makerere, Kampala, Uganda, in 1962. At this conference of "African Writers of English Expression" an attempt had clearly been made to limit the boundaries of the discussion.

19. Although Hayford's focus was primarily on the middle-class subject, "her intellectual vision of feminist Pan-Africanism . . . remains an important one. It represents one of those 'reflexive moments of consciousness' which Edward Said has described, that 'enabled the African . . . citizen inching toward independence through decolonization to require a theoretical assertion of the end of Europe's cultural claim to guide and/or instruct the non-European or nonmainland individual'" (Blair 1995, 139).

20. Michael Awkward's recent engagement with black feminism is one example of a male critic's serious attempt to problematize one's own positionality. In a perceptive reading of Hortense Spiller's "Mama's Baby, Papa's Maybe," Awkward claims that "rather than seeing the 'female' as strictly other for the Afro-American male, Spiller's afrocentric revisioning of psychoanalytic theory insists that we consider it an important aspect of the repressed in the black male self." Awkward goes on to argue that "black feminist criticism has not only created a space for an informed Afro-American male participation but it heartily welcomes—in fact, insists upon—the joint participation of

males and females as comrades" (Awkward 1995, 52).

21. Recent global conferences have seen an increased participation by women. Women's groups have contributed significantly to such meetings as the Conference on Environment and Development (Rio de Janeiro, 1992), the World Conference on Human Rights (Vienna, 1993), the International Conference on Population and Development (Cairo, 1994), and, of course, the United Nations Fourth World Conference on Women (Beijing, 1995), where they issued a strong Platform for Action.

22. The 7th Pan-African Congress has endorsed precisely such a struggle: "The 7th Pan-African Congress has been convened to formulate a general programme of action for an overall political and economic strategy for the final liberation of Africa under one union Government with full citizenship rights to Africans in the diaspora. Economic integration must be guided by creating the material basis for objective economic complementarity" (Lemelle and Kelley 1995, 364).

23. Recent figures show a dismal rate of economic growth for the African continent—a mere 2 percent as compared to 6 percent in the rest of the developing world. This rate is partly affected by the increasing foreign debt that African nations inherit every year. In recent years, severe drought conditions, especially in the Sudan, have caused widespread hunger and poverty.

Works Cited

Appiah, Anthony. 1990. "New Literatures, New Theory?" In *Canonization and Teaching of African Literatures*, ed. Raoul Granqvist. Amsterdam: Editions Rodopi B.V.

Asad, Talat. 1973. *Anthropology and the Colonial Encounter*. Atlantic Highlands: Humanities.

Asante, Molefi Kete. 1987. *The Afrocentric Idea*. Philadelphia: Temple University Press.

_____. 1990. *Afrocentricity*. Trenton: Africa World.

_____. 1991. "Putting Africa at the Center." *Newsweek,* 23 September, 46.

Awkward, Michael. 1995. *Negotiating Difference: Race, Gender, and the Politics of Positionality*. Chicago: University of Chicago Press.

Benjamin, Walter. 1969. *Illuminations*. Trans. Harry Zohn. New York: Schocken.

Bernal, Martin. 1987/91. *Black Athena: The Afroasiatic Roots of Classical Civilization.* 2 vols. Brunswick: Rutgers Univesity Press.

Bhabha, Homi. 1989. "The Commitment to Theory." In *Questions of Third Cinema*, ed. Jim Pines and Paul Willemen. London: British Film Institute.

_____. 1994. *The Location of Culture*. New York: Routledge.

Blair, Barbara. 1995. "Pan-Africanism as Process: Adelaide Casely Hayford, Garveyism, and the Cultural Roots of Nationalism." In *Imagining Home: Class, Culture, and Nationalism in the African Diaspora*, ed. Sidney J. Lemelle and Robin D. G. Kelley. New York: Verso.

Cabral, Amilcar. 1973. *A Return to the Source*. New York: Monthly Review.

Campbell, Horace. 1995. "Pan-Africanism and African Liberation." In *Imagining Home: Class, Culture, and Nationalism in the African Diaspora*, ed. Sidney J. Lemelle and Robin D. G. Kelley. New York: Verso.

Césaire, Aimé. 1969. *Return to my Native Land*. Trans. John Berger and Anna Bostock.

Handsworth: Penguin.

Chinweizu. 1978. *The West and the Rest of Us: White Predators, Black Slavers and the African Elite*. New York: NOK.

____. 1987. *Decolonizing the African Mind*. Lagos: Pero.

____, ed. 1988. *Voices of Twentieth-Century Africa: Griots and Towncriers*. London: Faber and Faber.

Chinweizu, Onwuchekwa Jemie, and Ihechukwu Madubuike. 1983. *Toward the Decolonization of African Literature. Vol. 1, African Fiction and Poetry and their Critics*. Washington, D.C.: Howard University Press.

Clarke, John Henrik. 1991. Foreword. *Civilization or Barbarism*, by Cheikh Anta Diop. Trans. Yaa-Lengi Meema Ngemi. New York: Lawrence Hill.

Davis, Angela. 1992. "Nappy Happy." *Transition* 58.

Diop, Cheikh Anta. 1954. *Nations negres et culture*. Paris: Presence Africaine.

____. 1974. *The African Origin of Civilization: Myth or Reality*. Trans. Mercer Cook. Westport: Lawrence Hill.

____. 1987a. *Black Africa: The Economic and Cultural Basis for a Federated State*. Trans. Harold J. Salemson. Trenton: Africa World.

____. 1987b. *Precolonial Black Africa: A Comparative Study of the Political and Social Systems of Europe and Black Africa, from Antiquity to the Formation of Modern States*. Trans. Harold J. Salemson. Westport: Lawrence Hill.

____. 1991. *Civilization or Barbarism: An Authentic Anthropology*. Trans. Yaa-Lengi Meema Ngemi. Westport: Lawrence Hill.

Fanon, Frantz. 1968. *The Wretched of the Earth*. Trans. Constance Farrington. New York: Grove Press.

Foucault, Michel. 1972. *The Archaelogy of Knowledge and the Discourse on Language*. Trans. A.M. Sheridan Smith. New York: Pantheon.

Gilroy, Paul. 1995. *The Black Atlantic: Modernity and Double Consciousness*. Cambridge: Harvard University Press.

Gramsci, Antonio. 1971. *Selections from the Prison Notebooks*. Trans. Quentin Hoare and Geoffrey Nowell Smith. New York: International Publishers.

Griffiths, Gareth and David Moody. 1989. "Of Marx and Missionaries: Soyinka and the Survival of Universalism in Post-Colonial Literary Theory." In *After Europe: Critical Theory and Post-Colonial Writing*, ed. Stephen Slemon and Helen Tiffin. Sydney: Dangaroo Press.

Guha, Ranajit. 1983. "The Prose of Counter-Insurgency." *Subaltern Studies II: Writings on South Asian History and Society*, ed. Ranajit Guha. Delhi: Oxford University Press.

Hegel, Georg W. H. 1953. *Reason in History: A General Introduction to the Philosophy of History*. Trans. Robert S. Hartman. New York: Bobbs Merrill.

James, C. L. R. 1989. *The Black Jacobins: Toussaint L'Ouverture and the San Domingo Revolution*. New York: Vintage.

Jameson, Fredric. 1981. *The Political Unconscious: Narrative as a Socially Symbolic Act*. Ithaca: Cornell University Press.

Kuper, Adam. 1995. *The Invention of Primitive Society*. New York: Routledge.

Lemelle, Sidney J. 1995. "The Politics of Cultural Existence: Pan-Africanism, Historical Materialism and Afrocentricity." In *Imagining Home: Class, Culture, and*

Nationalism in the African Diaspora, ed. Sidney J. Lemelle and Robin D. G. Kelley. New York: Verso.

Lemelle, Sidney J. and Robin D. G. Kelley, eds. 1995. *Imagining Home: Class, Culture and Nationalism in the African Diaspora*. New York: Verso.

Mercer, Kobena. 1994. *Welcome to the Jungle: New Positions in Black Cultural Studies*. New York: Routledge.

Murtadha, Khaula. 1995. "An African-centered Pedagogy in Dialog with Liberatory Multiculturalism." *Multicultural Education, Critical Pedagogy, and the Politics of Difference*, ed. Christine E. Sleeter and Peter McLaren. Albany: SUNY Press.

Ngugi wa Thiong'o. 1985. "The Language of African Literature." *New Left Review* 150: 109-27.

Omi, Michael and Howard Winant. 1994. *Racial Formation in the United States from the 1960s to the 1990s*. New York: Routledge.

Phillips, Evelyn Newman. 1995. "Multicultural Education beyond the Classroom." In *Multicultural Education, Critical Pedagogy, and the Politics of Difference*, ed. Christine E. Sleeter and Peter McLaren. Albany: SUNY Press.

Radhakrishnan, R. 1990. "Ethnic Identity and Post-Structuralist Difference." *The Nature and Context of Minority Discourse*. Ed. Abdul Jan Mohamed and David Lloyd. New York: Oxford University Press.

Ranger, Terence. 1983. "The Invention of Tradition in Colonial Africa." In *The Invention of Tradition*, ed. Eric Hobsbawm and Terence Ranger. Cambridge: Cambridge University Press.

Reid-Pharr, Robert. 1996. "It's Raining Men: Notes on the Million Man March." *Transition* 69: 36-48.

"Resist Recolonisation!: General Declaration by the Delegates and Participants at the 7th Pan-African Congress." In *Imagining Home: Class, Culture, and Nationalism in the African Diaspora*, ed. Sidney J. Lemelle and Robin D. G. Kelley. New York: Verso.

Said, Edward. 1978. *Orientalism*. New York: Vintage.

Taylor, Cylde. 1989. "Black Cinema in the Post-aesthetic Era." In *Questions of Third Cinema*, ed. Jim Pines and Paul Willemen. London: British Film Institute.

Thomas, Greg. 1995. "The Black Studies War: Multiculturalism versus Afrocentricity." *Village Voice,* 17 January, 23-29.

West, Cornell. 1985. "The Dilemma of the Black Intellectual." *Cultural Critique* 1: 109-24.

Williams, Chancellor. 1987. *The Destruction of Black Civilization: Great Issues of a Race from 4000 B.C. to 2000 A.D.* Chicago: Third World.

Winford, John Noble. 1992. "Nubian Treasures Reflect Black Influence on Egypt." *The New York Times*, 11 February, B5.

Wolf, Eric. 1982. *Europe and the People without History*. Berkeley: University of California Press.

Young, Robert. 1990. *White Mythologies: Writing History and the West*. New York: Routledge.

2

White Noise: Toward a Pedagogy of Whiteness

Henry A. Giroux

> The crisis of leadership in the white community is remarkable—and terrifying—because there is, in fact, no white community.
>
> James Baldwin, "On Being . . . and Other Lies"

"Whiteness" is no longer invisible. As a symbol of cultural identity and an object of critical scholarship, it has become both a symbol of resurgent racism and the subject of a rising academic specialization. For conservative ideologues, whiteness has been appropriated as a badge of self-identity and fashioned as a rallying point for disaffected whites who claim they are the victims of reverse racism in a country that is becoming increasingly racially diverse and hybridized. Under attack by multiculturalists, radicals, feminists, gays, lesbians, and other subordinate groups, such whites feel besieged and persecuted.

At the same time, whiteness has become the object of critical analysis in a number of academic fields. This new scholarship, named by some as "whiteness studies," has attracted a great deal of media attention; it is best known for revealing how whiteness in its various ideological and institutional forms over time has worked to perpetuate relations of domination and oppression against nonwhites while simultaneously securing whites with a disproportionate amount of power and privilege.[1]

While the "old" view of whiteness as a signifier of privilege and power is enjoying a resurgence in the United States, it appears mainly as a rear-guard attempt to ward off those forces chipping away at the remaining, though far from weak, vestiges of racism that structure all aspects of public life. The new scholarship on whiteness provides an enormous theoretical and political service in revealing and deconstructing how the ideology of whiteness worked histori-cally and how it operates politically in the service of racism currently in Ameri-can life. And yet, the new scholarship is troubling in its inability to capture the complexity that marks whiteness as a form of identity and cultural practice. The distinction between whiteness as a dominating ideology and white people who are positioned across multiple locations of privilege and subordination is often sacrificed in this work to the assumption that whiteness is simply "the terrifying attempt to build an identity based on what one isn't and on whom one can hold back" (Roediger 1991, 13). Being white in this context appears by default to make one a racist.

Defining "whiteness" largely as a form of domination, such scholarship, while rightly unmasking whiteness as a mark of ideology and racial privilege, fails to provide a nuanced, dialectical, and layered account of whiteness that would allow white youth and others to appropriate selective elements of white identity and culture as oppositional. This theoretical lacuna suggests that work-ers, educators, and students face the task of rethinking the subversive possibility of whiteness. Such a pedagogical and political challenge means, in part, reimag-ining whiteness both beyond the fixed boundaries of identity politics, defined primarily through a discourse of separatism and white supremacy, and no longer as an act of bad faith—whites exhibiting what Eric Lott calls "blackface's un-conscious return."[2]

While it is imperative that a critical analysis of whiteness address its histori-cal legacy and existing complicity with racist exclusion and oppression, it is equally crucial that such work distinguish between whiteness as a racial practice that is antiracist and those aspects of whiteness that are racist.[3] Where whiteness has been dealt with in pedagogical terms, the emphasis is almost exclusively on revealing whiteness as an ideology of privilege mediated largely through the dynamics of racism.[4] While such interventions are crucial in developing an anti-racist pedagogy, they do not go far enough. I am concerned about what it means pedagogically for those of us who engage in an antiracist pedagogy and politics to suggest to students that whiteness can only be understood in terms of the common experience of white domination and racism. What subjectivities or points of identification become available to white students who can only imag-ine white experience as monolithic, self-contained, and deeply racist? What are the pedagogical and political stakes in rearticulating whiteness in antiessentialist terms so that white youth can understand and struggle against the long legacy of white racism while using the particularities of "their own culture as a resource for resistance, reflection, and empowerment?"[5]

At the same time, there are too few attempts to develop a pedagogy of whiteness that enables white students to move beyond positions of guilt or resentment. There is a curious absence in the work on whiteness regarding how students might examine critically the construction of their own identities in order to rethink whiteness as a discourse of both critique and possibility.[6] Cultural critics need to connect whiteness with a language of possibility that provides a space for white students to imagine how whiteness as an ideology and social location can be progressively appropriated as part of a broader politics of social reform. Whiteness needs to be theorized carefully in terms of its potential to provide students with a racial identity that can play a crucial role in refashioning an antiracist politics that informs a broader, radical, democratic project. In what follows, I want to delineate in more detail the dialectic of whiteness as it has been embraced by both conservative whites and in the new scholarship.

The Conservative Politics of Whiteness

In the early 1990s the debate over race took a provocative turn as whiteness became increasingly visible as a symbol of racial identity. Displaced from its commonsense status as an unnamed, universal moral referent, whiteness as a category of racial identity was appropriated by diverse conservative and right-wing groups, as well as critical scholars, as part of a broader articulation of race and difference, though in different ways and for radically opposed purposes. For a disparate number of whites, mobilized, in part, by the moral panic generated by right-wing attacks on immigration, race preferential policies, and the welfare state, "whiteness" became a signifier for middle class resistance to "taxation, to the expansion of state-furnished rights of all sorts, and to integration" (Winant 1992, 166). Threatened by the call for minority rights, the rewriting of American history from the bottom up, and the shifting racial demographics of the nation's cities, whites felt increasingly angry and resentful over what was viewed as an attack on their sense of individual and collective consciousness.[7] As whiteness came under scrutiny by various social groups as an oppressive, invisible center against which all else is measured, many whites began to identify with the "new racism" epitomized by right-wing conservatives such as talk show host Rush Limbaugh.[8] Winning over vast audiences with the roar of the "angry white male" bitter over imagined racial injuries committed against whites, Limbaugh's popularity affirmed that race had become the most significant social force of the 1980s and 1990s. In an era of unprecedented unemployment, poverty, and diminishing opportunities for most black Americans, right-wing whites had convinced themselves of their loss of privilege. For these groups, archconservative actor and mythic white male Michael Douglas becomes less a symbol of "falling down" in a tragic Hollywood morality tale about white supremacy and paranoia and more a moral crusader fighting a holy, if lost, war. Thus, the discourse of race became a vehicle for appeasing white anxiety and reinventing both the subject and meaning of what one might loosely call "social justice." The progressive legacy of identity politics as "a crucial movement to expand citizenship to people of color and other subordinated groups" was either trivialized or dismissed as conservatives appropriated the politics of identity as a defining principle of whiteness (Yudice 1995, 268). John Brenkman highlights this appropriation by claiming that "the constituency whose beliefs and fears have been most significantly molded to their racial identity in the 1980s are white" (Brenkman 1995, 14).

A siege mentality arose for policing cultural boundaries and reasserting national identity. The discourse of whiteness as an ambivalent signifier of resentment and confusion gives expression to a mass of whites who feel victimized and bitter while it masks deep inequalities and exclusionary practices within the current social order. Shifting the politics of race from the discourse of white supremacy, the historical legacy of slavery, and segregation, as well as the ongoing burden of racial injustice endured by African-American and other minorities in the United States, politicians such as Pat Buchanan, David Duke, Jesse Helms, and Pat Robertson mobilized a new populist discourse about family, nation, traditional values, and individualism as part of a broader resistance to multicultural democracy and diverse racial culture. In the rapidly expanding medium of talk radio, conservatives bashed blacks for many of the social and economic problems facing the country.[9] Conservative columnist Mickey Kaus exemplifies this sensibility in his comment: "I may want to live in a society where there is no alienated race and no racism, where I need not feel uncomfortable walking down the street because I'm white."[10] As race became paramount in shaping American politics and everyday life from the 1980s on, racial prejudice in its overt forms was considered a taboo. While the old racism maintained some cachet among the more vulgar, right-wing conservatives (i.e., New York City's radio talk show host Bob Grant), a new racist discourse emerged in the United States. The new racism was coded in the language of "welfare reform, neighborhood schools, toughness on crime and 'illegitimate' births." Cleverly designed to mobilize white fears while relieving whites of any semblance of social responsibility and commitment, the new racism served to rewrite the politics of whiteness as a besieged racial identity. As the racial backlash intensified in the broader culture, whiteness assumed a new form of political agency visible in the rise of right-wing militia groups, skinheads, the anti-PC crusades of indignant white students, and conservative, academic organizations such as the National Association of Scholars and the Southern League.[11] Rather than being invisible, as left critics such as Richard Dyer and bell hooks have claimed, "whiteness" was aggressively embraced in popular culture in order to rearticulate a sense of individual and collective identity for besieged whites.[12] Celebrated in the mass media in the 1990s, the new cartography of race emerges as the result of an attempt to rewrite the racial legacy of the past while recovering a mythic vision of whiteness associated with purity and innocence. Immensely popular films such as *Forrest Gump* (1994) attempted to rewrite public memory by cleansing the American past of racial tensions and endorsing "a preferred understanding of racial relations that work on the behalf of the public mourning of the 'victimized white male'" (Gresson 1996, 13). Widely discussed books such as *The Bell Curve* by Richard Herrnstein and Charles Murray and *The End of Racism* by Dinesh D'Souza revised and reaffirmed the basic principles of the eugenics debate of the 1920s and 1930s and provided a defense of racial hierarchies.

In the popular press, the discourse of racial discrimination and social inequality gave way to lurid stories about black crime, illegal aliens taking jobs, the threat to the deficit posed by government welfare payments to single, teen mothers, and the assertion that black "gangsta" rap artists such as Snoop Doggy Dogg and Ice Cube corrupt the moral values of white suburban youth.[13] While liberal academic journals such as *The New Republic* and *The Atlantic Monthly* shunned the extremist discourses of David Duke, Ralph Reed, and Jerry Falwell, they produced editorials and stories legitimating the popular perception associating black culture with the culture of crime, pathology, and moral degeneracy. *The New Republic* devoted an entire issue to an analysis of *The Bell Curve*, justifying its decision in a shameful editorial statement that declared: "The notion that there might be resilient ethnic differences in intelligence is not, we believe, an inherently racist belief" (*New Republic* 1994, 9). Of course, the refusal to acknowledge that such a position grew historically from a eugenics movement that legitimated diverse racial hatreds as well as some of the most barbarous and atrocious massacres of the twentieth century appeared irrelevant next to the editorial's self-congratulatory assertion of intellectual flexibility. *The Atlantic Monthly* echoed similar racial fears in a barrage of sensationalist cover stories and articles about how crime, disease, the breakdown of public order, gangsta rap, and unwed [black] mothers were about to wreak havoc on "everyone—even white people in Back Bay."[14]

The tawdry representations of black experience that these magazines produced gained increasing currency in the dominant media. Racial coding parading as commonsense populism associated blacks with a series of negative equivalencies that denied racial injustice while affirming the repressed, unspeakable, racist unconscious of dominant white culture. Images of menacing black youth, welfare mothers, and convicts, framed by the evocative rhetoric of fear mongering journalists, helped to bolster the image of a besieged white middle-class suburban family threatened by "an alien culture and peoples who are less civilized than the native ones . . . a people who stand lower in the order of culture because they are somehow lower in the order of nature, defined by race, by color, and sometimes by genetic inheritance" (Hall 1991a, 13).

While the popular press was signaling the emergence of a politics of identity in which white men were defining themselves as the victims of "reverse" racial prejudice, academics were digging in and producing a substantial amount of scholarship, exploring what it might mean to analyze whiteness as a social, cultural, and historical construction. Such work was characterized by diverse attempts to locate whiteness as a racial category and to analyze it as a site of privilege, power, and ideology but also to examine critically how whiteness as a racial identity is experienced, reproduced, and addressed by those diverse white men and women who identify with its commonsense assumptions and values.

In some quarters, the call to study whiteness provoked scorn and indignation. For instance, *Time* magazine held up to ridicule a professor who named a standard American literature survey course she taught "White Male Writers" (Henry 1991). *Newsweek* took a more mainstream position, constructing an image of white men in the United States as undergoing an identity crisis over their changing public image. According to the editors of *Newsweek*, white males were no longer secure in an identity ravaged by "feminists, multiculturalists, P.C. policepersons, affirmative action employers, rap artists, Native Americans, Japanese tycoons, Islamic fundamentalists and Third World dictators" (Gates 1993, 48). Not to be outdone in their equation of feminists, multiculturalists, and Native Americans with Third World dictators, *Newsweek* further lamented the clobbering white men were taking in the media, buttressing its argument with comments from a "rancorous" female employee as well a prominent psychiatrist, who assured readers that "for white men in their 30s and 40s, this is not a joke at all. Their whole future is at stake, in their minds. They're scared" (Gates 1993, 51). While the demise of the power of white men seemed a bit exaggerated to the editors of *Newsweek*, they also made it quite clear that the current white panic was not entirely unfounded, since whites may find themselves in the next century living in a society consisting largely of "diverse racial and ethnic minorities" (Gates 1993, 49). But the imperative to analyze whiteness was not limited to conservatives, right-wingers, and liberals. A new critical scholarship on the subject began to emerge in the 1990s.

The Rise of Whiteness Studies

Building on the work of W. E. B. Dubois, Ralph Ellison, and James Baldwin, scholars from a wide ranging number of disciplines, including history, cultural studies, literary studies, sociology, and speech communication have put the "construction of 'whiteness' on the table to be investigated, analyzed, punctured, and probed."[15] Rejecting the assumption that an analysis of race means focusing primarily on people of color, scholars such as David Roediger, Ruth Frankenberg, Theodore Allen, bell hooks, Noel Ignatiev, Toni Morrison, Howard Winant, Alexander Saxton, and Fred Pfeil address the historical and social construction of whiteness across a wide spectrum of spheres, identities, and institutions and redefine the necessity to make whiteness central to the broader arena of racial politics.[16] While it is impossible to analyze this large body of work in any great detail, I want to comment briefly on some of the theoretical directions it has taken and assess the implications of such work for those of us concerned with issues of representation, racial politics, and pedagogy.

Historians such as David Roediger, Noel Ignatiev, and Theodore Allen, among others, build on the work of previous historians of race by focusing less on the African-American roots of mainstream white culture than on the issue of how white identities were constructed, appropriated, and shaped historically. Challenging both what it means to be white as well as how whiteness was experienced through an often unstable, shifting process of inclusion and exclusion, these historians have rearticulated and broadened the concept of racial identity while simultaneously challenging whiteness as a site of racial, economic, and political privilege. More specifically, such work brings a revisionist history to the highly charged debates about racial and national identity central to contemporary American politics. By focusing on how whiteness as the dominant racial identity shaped at different intervals the history of American labor and configured historical and political relations among ethnic groups such as the Irish, Roediger and others have thrown into sharp relief "the impact that the dominant racial identity in the United States has had not only on the treatment of racial 'others' but also on the ways that whites think of themselves, of power, of pleasure, and of gender" (Roediger 1994, 75).

Central to theoretical work on whiteness is the attempt to confront "the issue of white racial identity [and to raise] the questions of when, why and with what results so-called 'white people' have come to identify themselves as white" (Roediger 1994, 75). No longer the stable, self-evident, or pure essence central to modernity's self-definition, whiteness in the work of such historians as David Roediger and Noel Ignatiev is unmasked in its attempts to arbitrarily categorize, position, and contain the "other" within racially ordered hierarchies. Dislodged from a self-legitimating discourse grounded in a set of fixed transcendental racial categories, whiteness is analyzed as a lived but rarely recognized component of white racial identity and domination.

Roediger, Saxton, Ignatiev, and others have done more than add a historical component to the discourse about whiteness; they have expanded and deepened the relevance of politicizing the debates about the interrelationship between whiteness and race. Roediger, for example, provides three reasons for urging cultural critics who are involved in the social construction of race to focus their political energies on "exposing, demystifying and demeaning the particular ideology of whiteness":

> The first is that, while neither whiteness nor Blackness is a scientific (or natural) racial category, the former is infinitely more false, and precisely because of that falsity, more dangerous, than the latter. The second is that in attacking the notion that whiteness and Blackness are "the same," we specifically undermine what has become, via the notion of "reverse racism," a major prop underpinning the popular refusal among whites to face both racism and themselves. The last is that whiteness is now a particularly brittle and fragile form of social identity and it can be fought. (Roediger 1994, 12)

The notion that whiteness can be demystified and reformulated is a theoretical motif that links historical analyses of the construction of whiteness to the work of prominent theorists in a variety of other fields. For instance, Toni Morrison in her landmark book, *Playing in the Dark*, challenges critics to examine how whiteness as a literary category functions in the shaping and legitimating of a monolithic "American identity." Morrison frames her interrogation of the imaginative construction of whiteness in the following way:

> the readers of virtually all of American fiction have been positioned as white. I am interested to know what that assumption has meant to the literary imagination. When does racial "unconsciousness" or awareness of race enrich interpretive language, and when does it impoverish it? . . . What parts do the invention and development of whiteness play in the construction of what is loosely described as "American"? (Morrison 1993, xii, 9)

In the field of cultural studies, Ruth Frankenberg, Richard Dyer, and bell hooks further probe the role of whiteness as a site of privilege and exclusion. Recognizing that whiteness is produced differently within a variety of public spaces as well as across the diverse categories of class, gender, sexuality, and ethnicity, theorists such as Frankenberg explore how whiteness as a site of racial privilege, location, and standpoint works to shape the lives and identities of a diverse group of white women. Dyer, on the other hand, challenges the representational power of whiteness "to be everything and nothing as the source of its representational power" (Dyer 1998, 45) through an analysis of the racial pedagogies at work in popular culture and provides a theoretical service by analyzing whiteness as a guarantor of beauty and truth within the representational politics of three Hollywood films.

One of the most trenchant criticisms of whiteness comes from bell hooks, who argues that too many white scholars focus on certifiable "Others" in their analysis of race, but are doing very little "to investigate and justify all aspects of white culture from a standpoint of 'difference'" (hooks 1990, 55). According to hooks, "It would be just so interesting for all those white folks who are giving blacks their take on blackness to let them know what's going on with whiteness."[17] Hooks further extends her critique by arguing that while whites are willing to analyze how blacks are perceived by whites rarely are white critics attentive to how blacks view whites. For hooks, whites refuse to see blacks as political agents. Nor do whites, caught up in their own racial fantasies of murder and rape, recognize that in the black imagination whiteness is often associated with terror. But for hooks, more is at stake than whites recognizing that representations of whiteness as pure, good, benevolent, and innocent are challenged by representations of whiteness as capricious, cruel, and unchecked in the black imagination. Hooks also calls whiteness as an ideology into question by exposing its privileged readings of history, art, broader institutional power, and politically myopic forms of cultural criticism. Hooks builds on this criticism by calling for whites to become self-critical about how whiteness terrorizes, to "shift locations to see the world differently" (hooks 1992, 177).

In a decisive theoretical and somewhat paradoxical twist, hooks urges whites not to go too far in focusing on whiteness, particularly if it serves to downplay the effects of racism on blacks. First, she argues that attempts to see racism as victimizing to whites "in the hopes that this will act as an intervention is a misguided strategy" (hooks 1992, 13). Second, disavowing the discourse of white victimization as one that fails to distinguish between racial prejudice, as it is experienced by blacks and whites alike, and institutional racism that victimizes people of color, primarily blacks, hooks agrees with the black theologian James Cone, who argues that the only way in which whites can become antiracist is "to destroy themselves and be born again as beautiful black persons."[18]

Hooks's criticism is echoed in the field of speech communication by Thomas Nakayama and Robert Krizek who also argue that the primary task of whites is to demystify and unveil whiteness as a form of domination. In this case, Nakayama and Krizek go to great lengths to "deterritorialize the territory of 'white,' to expose, examine, and disrupt . . . so that like other positions it may be placed under critical analysis. . . . We seek an understanding of the ways that this rhetorical construction makes itself visible and invisible, eluding analysis yet exerting influence over everyday life" (Nakayama and Krizek 1995, 292).

Heavily indebted to the assumption that whiteness is synonymous with domination, oppression, and privilege, the critical project that largely informs the new scholarship on whiteness rests on a singular assumption. Its primary aim is to unveil the rhetorical, political, cultural, and social mechanisms through which whiteness is both invented and used to mask its power and privilege. The political thrust of such work seeks to abolish whiteness as a racial category and marker of identity. Roediger echoes this sentiment in his comment that "it is not merely that 'whiteness' is oppressive and false; it is that 'whiteness' is *nothing but* oppressive and false" (Roediger 1994, 13). This position is echoed by Noel Ignatiev, who provocatively writes in *Race Traitor* that "the key to solving the social problems of our age is to abolish the white race . . . so long as the white race exists, all movements against racism are doomed to fail [and] treason to 'whiteness' is loyalty to humanity" (Ignatiev and Garvey 1994, 10). Similar arguments conflating whiteness with white racism can be found in the work of Derrick Bell and Andrew Hacker.

In what follows, I want to analyze some of the political and pedagogical problems based on the assumption that whiteness is synonymous with domination and the only alternative that progressive white kids have in constructing a racial identity is to, in fact, renounce their own whiteness. I develop this critique by examining three considerations. First, I focus on some of the issues at stake in understanding the racial backlash that is taking place among many white students in this country. Second, I address how representations of whiteness in two films exemplify the limits and possibilities of analyzing the social construction of whiteness. Third, I explore how these films might be used pedagogically to rearticulate a notion of whiteness that builds on but also moves beyond the view of whiteness as simply a fixed position of domination. In doing so, I attempt to address the possibility of fashioning a tentative and strategic pedagogical approach to whiteness that offers students the possibility for rearticulating whiteness rather than either simply accepting its dominant normative assumptions or rejecting it as a racist form of identity. While white students may well feel traumatized in putting their racial identities on trial, trauma in this case can become a useful pedagogical tool in helping them locate themselves within and against the discourse and practice of racism. White youth need a more critical and productive way of construing a sense of identity, agency, and race across a wide range of contexts and public spheres. Alternatively, linking whiteness to the project of radical democratic change is not a rationale for evading racial injustice, deep inequalities between blacks and whites, or struggling to link individual change with social transformation.

Youth and the Rearticulation of Whiteness

Race increasingly matters as a defining principle of identity and culture as much for white students in the 1990s as for youth of color in the 1970s and 1980s. As a marker of difference, race significantly frames how white youth experience themselves and their relationships in a variety of public spaces marked by the presence of people of color. In contrast to the position popular among white educators, who claim that "we [whites] do not experience ourselves as defined by our skin color" (Scheurich 1993, 6), white youth have become increasingly aware of themselves as white. Two major forces affecting the racial divide have served to make whiteness more visible and fragile as a site of privilege and power, while at the same time offering few opportunities for youth to be both white and oppositional.[19] The first is the rise of identity politics in the United States as it emerged in the 1960s to the present. While contradictory and diverse in its manifestations, identity politics has largely resulted in the formation, consolidation, and visibility of new group racial identities. But such identities have emerged within highly charged public debates on race, gender, and sexual orientation and have made it more difficult for white youth to either ignore whiteness as a racial category or to "safely imagine that they are invisible to black people" (hooks 1992, 168). White students may see themselves as nonracist, but they no longer view themselves as colorless. As Charles Gallagher points out, whiteness has become "a salient category of self-definition emerging in response to the political and cultural challenges of other racialized groups" (Gallagher 1995, 166).

Contrary to its intentions, identity politics did not seek the transformation of society in general, rather it promoted a politics of difference that asserted itself through the separate and often essentialized banners of race, gender, sexuality, ethnicity, and nationality. Within this recoding of the politics of recognition and difference, the experiences, rights, and histories of subordinate groups were affirmed, but such groups were simply unable to articulate a new social vision rooted in the principles of equality or solidarity that organized progressive "interactions between white and black people in addressing such a politics" (Jester 1992, 111).

Unfortunately, for many white youth whose imaginations were also left fallow, unfed by a larger society's vision or quest for social justice, identity politics engendered a defensive posture. White students assumed that the only role they could play in the struggle against racism was either to renounce their whiteness and become black or suffer the charge that any claim to white identity was tantamount to racism. Within this paradigm, racism was configured through a politics of representation that analyzed how whites constructed, stereotyped, and delegitimated racial others, but it had practically nothing to say about how racial politics might address the construction of whiteness as an oppositional racial category. Moreover, while the debate within identity politics made important theoretical gains in rewriting what it meant to be black, it did not question the complexity of whiteness with the same dialectical attentiveness. Of course, whiteness did become an object of critical scrutiny, but it appeared to have no connotation except to "signify the center which pushes out, excludes, appropriates and distorts the margins" (Jester 1992, 115). Liberal ideology provided an agenda for how blacks and whites might work together by substituting tolerance and the appeal to a color-blind society for any viable recognition of the importance of racial identities in the struggle for social and racial justice.

Identity politics, in part, served to undermine the possibilities for white youth to engage critically the liberal appeal to a color-blind society; it also had the unintended consequence of reinforcing the divide between blacks and whites. Furthermore, the absence of an oppositional space between separatism and a power-evasive liberalism provided an opportunity for conservatives and right-wing activists to step into the fray and appropriate whiteness as part of a broader backlash against blacks and people of color. In this case, conservatives and the far right actively engaged in the process of recovering whiteness and redefining themselves as the victims of racial antagonism while simultaneously waging a brutal and racially coded attack against urban youth, immigrants, and the poor. Seemingly unresponsive to the needs of white youth, the white working class, and the white underclass, the discourse of whiteness was easily appropriated as part of a broader reactionary cultural politics that in its most extreme manifestations fueled the rise of white militia groups, the growing skinhead movement among white youth, and a growing anti-political-correctness movement in both higher education and the mass media.

The second force at work in reconstructing whiteness as a racial category among youth is the profound changes that have taken place regarding the visibility of blacks in the media. While it would be foolish to equate the increased visibility of blacks in the media with an increase in power, especially around issues of ownership, diverse representations of black culture throughout the media have made issues of white identity inextricably more fragile, hybridized, and fluid. This is evident in the ways in which popular culture is increasingly being reconfigured through the music, dance, and language of hip hop. Similarly, the emergence of Black Entertainment Television, MTV, and cable television, in general, testify to the ubiquitous presence of people of color in television dramas, sports, and music, while the popular press touts the emergence of the "new" black public intellectuals in academia. All of these changes in the media signal that whites can no longer claim the privilege of not "seeing" blacks and other people of color; white youth now have to confront cultural difference as a force that affects every aspect of their lives. Coupled with the rise of an incendiary racial politics, the racialization of the media culture, and growing economic fears about their future, a significant number of white American youth are increasingly experiencing a crisis of self-esteem. Like their counterparts in Britain, they "do not feel that they have an 'ethnicity,' or if they do, that it's not one they feel too good about" (Jester 1992, 107).

The British cultural critic Diana Jester has further suggested that white youth have few resources for questioning and rearticulating whiteness as an identity that productively narrates their everyday experiences. This seems to be borne out in the ways in which many white college students have reacted to the racial politics of the last decade. One indication of the way in which whiteness is

being negotiated among students is evident in the rising racist assaults on minorities of color on campuses across the United States in the last few years. As a
resurgent racism becomes more respectable in the broader culture, racist acts
and assaults have once again become a staple of college life. At the same time,
large numbers of white students appear to support the ongoing assaults on affirmative action programs that have been waged by the courts and state legisla-
tures. Moreover, white students increasingly express a general sense of angst
over racial politics and an emphatic indifference to politics in general.

Charles Gallagher's ethnographic study of white college students suggests
that many of them view the emergence of multiculturalists, feminists, and other
progressive groups as an attack on whiteness and a form of reverse discrimination. For example, Gallagher writes, "It is commonly assumed among many
white students that any class that addresses issues of race or racism must necessarily be anti-white. More specifically, students believe that the instructors of
these classes will hold individual white students accountable for slavery, lynching, discrimination, and other heinous acts" (Gallagher 1995, 170). Many of the
white students that Gallagher interviewed did not see themselves as privileged
by virtue of skin color; some went so far as to claim that given the rise of racial
preferences, whites no longer had a fair chance when competing with minorities
in the labor market. Gallagher asserts that white students are resentful over being blamed for racism and that "ignoring the ways in which whites 'get raced'
has the making of something politically dangerous . . . [and that] [w]hiteness
must be addressed because the politics of race, from campus clubs to issues of
crime to representation in the statehouse, permeate almost every social exchange" (182, 185). Unfortunately, Gallagher offers little in the way of suggesting how whiteness might be rearticulated in oppositional terms. In fact, he concludes by suggesting that as whiteness becomes more visible it will be further appropriated and mediated through a racist ideology and that any notion of white
solidarity will result in a reactionary politics. Hence, whiteness as a marker of
identity is confined within a notion of domination and racism that leaves white
youth no social imaginary through which they can see themselves as actors in
creating an oppositional space to fight for equality and social justice.

Central to any pedagogical approach to race and the politics of whiteness is
the recognition that race as a set of attitudes, values, lived experiences, and affective
identifications has become a defining feature of American life. However arbitrary and mythic, dangerous and variable, the fact is that racial categories exist
and shape the lives of people differently within existing inequalities of power
and wealth.[20] As a central form of difference, race will neither disappear, be
wished out of existence, nor become somehow irrelevant in the United States
and the larger global context. Howard Winant insightfully argues:

> Race is a condition of individual and collective identity, a permanent, though

tremendously flexible, element of social structure. Race is a means of knowing and organizing the social world; it is subject to continual contestation and reinterpretation, but it is no more likely to disappear than any other forms of human inequality and difference . . . To rethink race is not only to recognize its permanence, but also to understand the essential test that it poses for any diverse society seeking to achieve a modicum of freedom. (Winant 1994, xiii)

Pedagogically, this suggests providing the conditions for students to address not only how their whiteness functions in society as a marker of privilege and power, but also how it can be used as a condition for expanding the ideological and material realities of democratic public life. Moreover, it is imperative that all students understand how race functions systemically as it shapes various forms of representations, social relations, and institutional structures. Rather than proposing the eradication of the concept of race itself, educators and other cultural workers need to fashion pedagogical practices that take a detour through race to address how whiteness might be renegotiated as a productive force within a politics of difference linked to a radical democratic project.

Analyzing whiteness as a central element of racial politics becomes useful in exploring how whiteness as a cultural practice promotes race-based hierarchies, how white racial identity structures the struggle over cultural and political resources, and how rights and responsibilities are defined, confirmed, or contested across diverse racial claims.[21] Whiteness in this context becomes less a matter of creating a new form of identity politics than an attempt to rearticulate whiteness as part of a broader project of cultural, social, and political citizenship.

I want to begin to take up this challenge pedagogically by building on James Snead's pertinent observation that the emergence of mass visual productions in the United States requires new ways of seeing and making visible the racial structuring of white experience.[22] The electronic media—television, movies, music, and news—have become a powerful pedagogical force, veritable teaching machines in shaping the social imaginary of students regarding how they view themselves, others, and the larger society. Central to the formative influence of the media is a representational politics of race in which the portrayal of black people abstracts them from their real histories while reinforcing all too familiar stereotypes ranging from lazy and shiftless to menacing and dangerous. Recent films from a variety of genres, such as *Pulp Fiction* (1995), *Just Cause* (1995), and *Ace Ventura: When Nature Calls* (1996), offer no apologies for employing racist language, depicting black men as rapists, or portraying blacks as savage or subhuman. Antiracist readings of these films often position white students to define and critique racism as the product of dominant racist stereotypes that unfairly depict black identities, experiences, histories, and social relations. As important as these critiques are in any antiracist discourse or peda-

gogy, they are severely limited theoretically because they do not make problematic how whiteness as a racial identity and social construction is taught,
learned, experienced, and identified within certain forms of knowledge, values,
and privileges. Hollywood films rarely position audiences to question the pleasures, identifications, desires, and fears they experience as whites viewing dominant representational politics of race. More specifically, such films rarely make
problematic either the structuring principles that mobilize particular pleasures in
audiences or how pleasure as a response to certain representations functions as
part of a broader public discourse. At worst, such films position whites as racial
tourists, distant observers to the racist images and narratives that fill Hollywood
screens. At best, such films reinforce the liberal assumption that racism is
something that gives rise to black oppression but has little or nothing to do with
promoting power, racial privilege, and a sense of moral agency in the lives of
whites (Frankenberg 1993, 49).

In what follows, I want to explore the pedagogical implications for examining
representations of whiteness in two seemingly disparate films, *Dangerous Minds*
(1995) and *Suture* (1993). Though I will focus primarily on *Dangerous Minds,* it
is through a juxtaposition and intertextual reading of these films that I hope to
provide some pedagogical insights for examining how whiteness as a cultural
practice is learned through the representation of racialized identities, how it
opens up the possibility of intellectual self-reflection, and how students might
critically mediate the complex relations between whiteness and racism not by
having them repudiate their whiteness but by grappling with its racist legacy and
its potential to be rearticulated in oppositional and transformative terms. I also
want to stress that I am not suggesting that *Dangerous Minds* is a bad film and
Suture is a good film given their different approaches to whiteness. Both have
weaknesses that are notable. What I am suggesting is that these films are exemplary in representing dominant readings of whiteness and as cultural texts that
can be used pedagogically for addressing the shortcomings of the recent scholarship on whiteness in particular ways to move beyond the jaundiced view of
whiteness as simply a trope of domination.

At first glance, these films appear to having nothing in common in terms of
audience, genre, intention, or politics. *Dangerous Minds*, a Hollywood blockbuster
starring Michelle Pfeiffer, was produced for a mass, general audience, and
grossed millions for its producers within its first week. The film's popularity, in
part, can be measured by the appearance of a pilot television series called *Dangerous Minds* that premiered in the fall of 1996. In contrast, *Suture* is an independent film that played primarily to highbrow audiences with a penchant for
avant garde cinema. While some may argue that *Dangerous Minds* is too popular and too unoriginal to be taken seriously as a cultural text, it is precisely because of its popularity and widespread appeal that it warrants an extended
analysis. Like many Hollywood films, *Dangerous Minds* is offensive not only in

terms of its racial politics but also in its fundamentally debased depiction of teaching and education. The 1995 summer hit is also symptomatic of how seemingly "innocent" entertainment gains its popularity in taking part in a larger public discourse on race and whiteness largely informed by a right-wing and conservative notion of politics, theory, and pedagogy.

Dangerous Minds and the Production of Whiteness

Dangerous Minds follows a long tradition of Hollywood movies recounting the sorry state of education for dispossessed kids who bear the brunt of poverty, crime, violence, and despair in the inner cities of the United States. Unlike earlier films such as *Blackboard Jungle* (1955), *To Sir with Love* (1967), and *Stand and Deliver* (1988) that also deal with the interface of schooling and the harsh realities of inner city life, *Dangerous Minds* does more than simply narrate the story of an idealistic teacher who struggles to connect with his rowdy and disinterested students. *Dangerous Minds* functions as a dual chronicle. In the first instance, the film attempts to represent whiteness as the archetype of rationality, "tough" authority, and cultural standards in the midst of the changing racial demographics of urban space and the emergence of a resurgent racism in the highly charged politics of the 1990s. In the second instance, the film offers viewers a mix of compassion and consumerism as a pedagogical solution to motivating teenagers who have long given up on schooling as neither relevant nor meaningful to their lives. In both instances, whiteness becomes a referent not only for rearticulating racially coded notions of teaching and learning but also for redefining how citizenship can be constructed for students of color as a function of choice linked exclusively to the marketplace.

Providing an allegory for both the purpose of schooling and the politics of racial difference as they intersect within the contested space of the urban public schools, *Dangerous Minds* skillfully mobilizes race as an organizing principle to promote its narrative structure and ideological message. Black and Hispanic teenagers provide the major fault line for developing classroom pedagogical relations through which whiteness, located in the authority of the teacher, privileges itself against the racially coded images of disorder, chaos, and fear. The opposition between teacher and student, white and nonwhite, is clearly established in the first few scenes of the film. The opening sequence, shot in grainy monochrome, depicts a rundown urban housing project teeming with poverty, drug dealing, and imminent danger. Against this backdrop, disaffected black and Hispanic children board a school bus that will take them to Parkmont High School and out of their crime and drug-infested neighborhoods. This shot is one of the few in the film that provides a context for the children's lives; the message is

clear: the inner city has become a site of pathology, moral decay, and delin-
quency synonymous with the culture of working-class black life. Featuring a hip
hop music score that includes artists such as Coolio, Sista, and Aaron Hall, the
soundtrack is present only as a backdrop to the film.

While the driving beat of hip hop reinforces the gritty urban realism that
provides a tidy summation of these kids' everyday lives, it is completely ignored
as a cultural or pedagogical resource for learning about their histories, experiences, or
the economic, social, and political limits they face daily. Moreover, the musical
score's marginality to the plot of *Dangerous Minds* serves to reinforce the
right-wing assumption that rap music signifies black culture as a culture of
crime and violence. The soundtrack to this film stayed at the top of the charts
for weeks, providing a reminder of how black culture is commodified in the
dominant media.

Framed by a racial iconography and musical score that constructs minority
students as both the objects of fear and subjects in need of discipline and control, the audience is prepared for someone to take charge. Enter LouAnne Johnson, a good-hearted ingenue thrust into the classroom of "at risk" kids like a
lamb led to the slaughter.

A divorced ex-Marine, LouAnne Johnson turns up at Parkmont High to
student teach and finish her degree. She is immediately hired as an English
teacher in the "Academy School," a euphemism for warehousing students who are
considered unteachable. Dressed in frowzy tweeds and white lace, LouAnne
enters her class triumphant and full of high hopes to meet a room filled with
Hispanic and black kids who have brought the "worst" aspects of their culture
into the classroom. As music blares amidst the clatter of students shouting, rap-
ping, dancing, LouAnne is presented with a classroom in an inner city school
that appears to be disorderly and out of control. Leaving the safety of her white,
middle-class culture to teach in a cultural war zone teeming with chaos and potential danger, LouAnne Johnson is presented to the audience as an innocent
border crosser. Against this image of innocence and goodwill, white America is
provided with the comforting belief that disorder, ignorance, and chaos are always somewhere else—in that strangely homogenized, racial space known as
the urban ghetto.[23] Meeting LouAnne's attempt to greet them, the students respond with the taunting epithet, "white bread." Confused and unable to gain
control of the class, LouAnne is accosted by a male student who makes a mock-
ery of her authority by insulting her with a sexual innuendo. Frustrated, she
leaves the class and tells Hal, a friend who teaches next door, that she has just
met the "rejects from hell." He assures her that she can reach these students if
she figures out how to get their attention. These opening scenes work powerfully in associating black and Hispanic kids with the culture of criminality and
danger. These scenes also make clear that whiteness as a racial identity, embodied in LouAnne Johnson, is both vulnerable and under siege as well as the only

hope these kids have for moving beyond the context and character of their racial identities. In other words, whiteness as a racial identity is being constructed through the stereotypical portrayal of black and Hispanic kids as intellectually inferior, hostile, and childish, while whiteness is coded as a norm for authority, orderliness, rationality, and control.

The structuring principles at work in *Dangerous Minds* perform a distinct ideological function in their attempt to cater to white consumers of popular culture. Pedagogy performs a double operation as it is used in this film. As part of the overt curriculum, the film focuses on teaching in an inner city school and constructs a dominant view of race as embodied in the lives of urban black and Hispanic children. On the other hand, the hidden curriculum of the film works pedagogically to recover and mark the ideological and cultural values that construct whiteness as a dominant form of racial identity. Hollywood films about teaching have a long tradition, but rarely do such films merely use the theme of teaching as a pedagogical tool for legitimating a conservative view of whiteness as a besieged social formation; nor do they subordinate racial identities as a threat to public order. The conservative and ideological implications of how whiteness is constructed in this film can be seen through a series of representations.

The film tells us nothing about the lives of the students themselves. The audience is given no sense of their histories or experiences outside of the school. Decontextualized and dehistoricized, the cultural identities of these students appear marginal to the construction of race as an organizing principle of the film. Racial differences in this film are situated within the spatial metaphor of center and margins, with the children of color clearly occupying the margins. At the center of the film is the embellished "true story" of LouAnne Johnson, who not only overcomes her initial failure to motivate these students but also serves as a beacon of light by convincing them that who they are and what they know needs to be ditched if they are to become more civilized and cultured (and more white). Racial conflict in this context is resolved through a colonial model in which white paternalism and missionary zeal provide the inspiration for kids from deprived backgrounds to improve their character and sense of responsibility by reading poetry. The kids in this movie simply appear as a backdrop for expanding LouAnne's own self-consciousness and self-education, rather than providing an opportunity for understanding the coming of age of these city kids or how racism works in the schools and larger society. Whenever these kids do face a crisis regarding an unwanted pregnancy, the threat of violence, or dropping out of school, LouAnne invades their homes and private lives, using the opportunity to win the kids' allegiance or draw attention to her own divorce, physical abuse, or sense of despair. If any notion of identity occupies center stage, it is not that of the kids but that of a white woman trying to figure out how to live in a public space inhabited by racialized others.

The notion of authority and agency in *Dangerous Minds* is framed within a pedagogy of "tough love" that serves to mask how racial hierarchies and structured inequality operate within the schools and connect them to the larger society. Authority in *Dangerous Minds* is asserted initially when LouAnne Johnson shows up on the second day of class wearing a leather jacket and jeans. Reinventing herself as a military officer on leave, she further qualifies her new "tough" no-nonsense look by informing her students that she is an ex-Marine who knows karate. Suggesting that fear and danger are the only emotions they recognize as important, she crosses a racial divide by rooting her sense of authority in a traditionally racist notion of discipline and control. Once she gets the group's attention, she moves onto more lofty ground and begins the arduous task of trying to develop a pedagogy that is both morally uplifting and pedagogically relevant. Choice becomes for LouAnne the theoretical axis that organizes her classroom approach. First, on the side of moral uplift (complete with a 90s conservative, whitewashing of history), she tells her students that there are no victims in her class. Presumably, this is meant as a plea to rouse their sense of agency and responsibility, but it rings entirely hollow since LouAnne has no understanding of the social and historical limits that shape their sense of agency on a daily basis. Of course, some students immediately recognize the bad faith implicit in her sermonizing call and urge her to test it with a dose of reality by living in their neighborhood for a week.

Moreover, LouAnne appears to confuse her own range of choices, predicated, in part, on her class and racial privileges as a white person, with those of her students, even though they lack the power and resources to negotiate their lives politically, geographically, or economically with the same ease or options. She has no sense that choice springs from power and that those who have limited power have fewer choices. The subtext here reinforces the currently popular right-wing assumption that character, merit, and self-help are the basis on which people take their place in society. Of course, within a hierarchical and social structure organized by race, as well as economic power, gender, and other key determinants, whiteness emerges as the normative basis for success, responsibility, and legitimate authority. By suggesting that white educators can ignore how larger social considerations effect racial groups, the film relieves white privilege, experience, and culture of complicity with, if not responsibility for, racist ideology and structural inequalities.

Choice not only is trivialized in LouAnne's classroom, but it also provides the basis for a pedagogy that is as indifferent to the lives of poor inner city kids as it is demeaning. Relying on the logic of the market to motivate her kids, LouAnne rewards classroom cooperation with candy bars, a trip to an amusement park, and dinner at a fancy restaurant. Baiting students with gimmicks and bribes does more than cast a moral shadow on the pedagogical value of such an approach or on the teacher as a kind of ethical exemplar; it also makes clear how little LouAnne knows about the realities of her students' lives. Knowing little about the skills they need to survive, LouAnne is indifferent to their experiences, interests, or cultural resources. This becomes clear in three pivotal instances in the movie.

In the first instance, LouAnne attempts to motivate the students by giving them the lyrics to Bob Dylan's "Mr. Tambourine Man." Indifferent to the force of hip hop culture (though marketing executives appeared to know the draw and impact of hip hop on the film's audience in designing the soundtrack), her intervention into popular culture appears as nothing less than an act of cultural ignorance and bad pedagogy. But more revealing is her attempt to relate Dylan's lyrics to the most clichéd aspects of the students' culture—namely violence and drugs. Not only does she ignore the cultural resources and interests of her students, but she also frames her notion of popular culture in a text from the 1960s— almost twenty years before these kids were born. Rather than excavating the traditions, themes, and experiences that make up her students' lives to construct her curriculum, she simply avoids their voices altogether in shaping the content of what she teaches. Beneath this form of pedagogical violence, there is also the presupposition that whites can come into such schools and teach without theory, ignore the histories and narratives that students bring to schools, and perform miracles in children's lives by mere acts of kindness.

In LouAnne's romantic version of schooling and teaching, there is no sense of what it means to give urban youth survival skills. The teacher's ignorance is reflected in another scene when she visits the black grandmother of two black students missing from school for several days. The boys' grandmother has pulled them out of school, and LouAnne decides to reason with her to get the students back into her class. The grandmother meets her in the yard and refers to her as a "white-bread bitch." The grandmother is indignant over what the boys have brought home for homework and tells LouAnne that her boys have got bills to pay and that she should find some other poor boys to save. Regardless of the fact that Bob Dylan's lyrics are irrelevant to the kids' lives, the black grandmother is represented as an obstructionist. Yet, she is actually closer to the truth in suggesting that what LouAnne has passed off as useful knowledge will not help the boys survive life in the ghetto, nor will it change the conditions that give rise to urban squalor.

LouAnne's teaching is in actuality a pedagogy of diversion—one that refuses to provide students with skills that will help them address the urgent and disturbing questions of a society and a culture that in many ways ignores their humanity and well-being. These students are not taught to raise questions about the intellectual and cultural resources they need to address the profoundly inhuman conditions they have to negotiate every day. How to survive in a society, let alone remake it, is an important pedagogical question that cannot be separated from the larger issue of what it means to live in a country that is increasingly hostile to the existence of poor white and black kids in the inner cities. But LouAnne ignores these issues and offers her students material incentives to learn and in doing so constructs them as consuming subjects rather than social subjects eager and able to think critically in order to negotiate and transform the worlds in which they live. In one pivotal exchange, students ask LouAnne what reward they are going to get for reading a poem. She surprises her students and the wider audience by insisting that learning is its own best reward. In doing so, she switches her pedagogical strategy, completely unaware of the consequences or limitations of the marketplace pedagogy she has employed most of the semester.

LouAnne's sense of privilege also becomes evident in the boundless confidence she exhibits in her authority and moral superiority. She believes that somehow her students are answerable to her both in terms of their classroom performance and in terms of their personal lives; her role is to affirm or gently "correct" how they narrate their beliefs, experiences, and values. LouAnne takes for granted that she has an unquestioning right to "save them" or run their lives, without entering into a dialogue in which her own authority and purity of intentions are called into question. Authority here functions as a way of making invisible LouAnne's own privileges as a white woman, while simultaneously allowing her to indulge in a type of moralizing commensurate with her colonizing role as a white teacher who extracts from her students love and loyalty in exchange for teaching them to be part of a system that oppresses them.

The inability of LouAnne to enter into a dialogue with her students is apparent in two important interchanges with them. In one scene, LouAnne breaks up a fight between Emilio and some other students, then demands from Emilio a full explanation:

> LouAnne: "Was it worth it? You like to hit people? Why? You feel angry?"
> Emilio: "You're trying to figure me out. You going to try to psychologize me. I'll help you. I come from a broken home, and we're poor, okay. I see the same fucking movies you do."
> LouAnne: "I'd like to help you, Emilio."
> Emilio: "Thank you very much. And how you going to do that? You going to give me some good advice—just say no—you going to get me off the streets? Well forget it. How the fuck are you going to save me from my life?"

Emilio is trying to educate her, but LouAnne is not listening carefully. She assumes a moralizing posture that is totally indifferent to understanding the complex forces shaping Emilio's life. Nor can this great white hope consider that her students' histories and worldviews might be usefully incorporated into her pedagogy in order to teach kids like Emilio the skills they need to cope with the conditions and contexts of their surroundings. In another exchange, LouAnne takes Raul, a promising student, to a fancy restaurant because his group won a poetry contest. Not only is Raul uncomfortable in such a context, he tells LouAnne he bought an expensive leather jacket from a fence so he wouldn't humiliate himself and her because he wasn't dressed properly. LouAnne presupposes that Raul can cross with ease the same class borders to which she has access. There is also the suggestion that for working class kids such as Raul to succeed in life they need the cultural capital of white upper middle class people like herself.

Dangerous Minds functions mythically to rewrite the decline of public schooling and the attack on poor, black, and Hispanic students as a part of a broader project for rearticulating whiteness as a model of authority, rationality, and civilized behavior. The politics of representation at work in this film reproduces a dominant view of identity and difference that has a long legacy in Hollywood films, specifically Westerns and African adventure movies. As Robin Kelley points out, the popularity of many Hollywood films, especially the Western and African adventure genres, is as much about constructing whiteness as it is about demonizing the alleged racialized Other. He notes that within this racialized Hollywood legacy, "American Indians, Africans, and Asians represent a pre-civilized or anti-civilized existence, a threat to the hegemony of Western culture and proof that 'whites' are superior, more noble, more intelligent" (Kelley 1992, 1406). *Dangerous Minds* is an updated defense of white identity and racial hierarchies. The colonizing thrust of this narrative is highlighted through the image of Michelle Pfeiffer as a visiting white beauty queen whose success is, in part, rendered possible by market incentives and missionary talents.

Against LouAnne Johnson's benevolence and insight is juxtaposed the personality and pedagogy of Mr. Grandy, the black principal of Parkmont High. Grandy is portrayed as an uptight, bloodless bureaucrat; a professional wannabe whose only interest appears to be in enforcing school rules (Hollywood's favorite stereotype for black principals). Grandy rigidly oversees school policy and is constantly berating Johnson for bypassing the standard curriculum, generating nontraditional forms of teaching, and taking the students on unauthorized trips. As a black man in a position of leadership, he is depicted as an obstacle to the success of his charges and ruthlessly insensitive to their needs. When Emilio visits Grandy's office to report another student who is trying to kill him, Grandy orders him out because he failed to knock on the office door. After leaving the building, Emilio is soon shot and killed a few blocks from the school.

Racial politics in this film are such that black professionals come off as the real threat to learning and civilized behavior, and whites, of course, are simply there to lend support. In contrast to Grandy, Johnson's whiteness provides the racialized referent for leadership, risk taking, and compassion. This is borne out at the end of the film when the students tell her that they want her to remain their teacher because she represents their "light." In this context, *Dangerous Minds* reinforces the highly racialized, though reassuring, mainstream assumption that chaos reigns in inner city public schools and that white teachers alone are capable of bringing order, decency, and hope to the those on the margins of society.

Suturing Whiteness

Directed by David Siegel and Scott McGehee, *Suture* explores the location of identity within a dominant racial politics. Central to the politics of the film is the way in which it organizes the unfolding of its plot around two narratives. On the one hand, the directors use the discursive narrative, which develops through character dialogue and adopts the conventional form of the crime thriller. Set within a plot about murder and framed identity, *Suture* presents the story of two brothers, Vincent Towers and Clay Arlington. Under police investigation for killing his father, the rich and ruthless Vincent sets up a scheme in which he first plants his driver's license and credit cards in his working-class half-brother's billfold. He then convinces Clay to drive his Rolls Royce to the airport. Clay does not realize that Vincent has placed a bomb in the car that can be triggered by remote control through the car phone. Vincent waits until Clay leaves for the airport and with Clay sitting in the front seat, calls him, setting off the bomb. After the explosion, Vincent leaves town assuming that the police will mistake Clay for himself. Unfortunately for Vincent, Clay survives the explosion, though he has to undergo massive reconstructive surgery on his face. In fact, the damage to Clay is so extreme that the police and doctors who attend to Clay believe he is Vincent.

Clay survives the ordeal but is amnesiac and believes that he is Vincent. In fact, everyone who comes in contact with Clay believes he is Vincent. As Vincent, he undergoes psychoanalysis and repeated bouts of surgery and falls in love with Renee Descartes, a beautiful and renowned plastic surgeon. In the meantime, Clay's brother breaks into his old house to kill him but Clay shoots him first and disposes of his body. By the time he kills Vincent, Clay has regained his memory but refuses to either slip back into his old identity or to give up the identity and life he has assumed as his half-brother, Vincent.

What is so remarkable about *Suture* is that it is simultaneously mediated by a visual narrative that is completely at odds with the discursive narrative and unsettles the audience's role as "passive" spectators. Clay does not look anything like Vincent. In fact, Clay is black but is treated throughout the film as if he is white. In a scene fraught with irony and tension, Renee Descartes takes off Clay's bandages, and she tells him that he has a Greco-Roman nose, which allegedly proves that he isn't inclined to deviant behavior, like killing people.

Memory and identity in this film are fluid and hybridized rather than fixed and sutured. Black identity is presented as a social construction that cannot be framed in essentialist terms. Clay assumes all the markings of white experience and culture, and it is only the audience that is able to mediate his newly assumed cultural capital by virtue of his blackness. But there is more at work in this film than a critique of black essentialism, there is also the ironic representation of whiteness as both invisible to itself and at the same time the norm by which everything else is measured. That is, whiteness in *Suture* becomes the racial marker of identity, power, and privilege. Playing the visual narrative against the discursive narrative, *Suture* evokes a peculiar form of racial witnessing in which it exposes whiteness as an ideology, set of experiences, and location of privilege. But it does so not by trading in binaristic oppositions in which bad whites oppress good blacks, but by calling into question the racial tension between what is seen and what is heard by the audience. The discursive narrative in the film privileges language while denying the defining principle of race, but the visual narrative forces the audience to recognize the phenomenological rather than political implications of race, identity, and difference. As Roy Grundmann notes, "We initially want to jump out of our seats to scream at the characters who (mis?)take Clay for Vincent, especially upon such comparative 'evidence' as videos, photos, and a police lineup with a witness who knew Vincent" (Grundman 1994, 24). Racial difference, in this case, is defined entirely through a representational politics of visual imagery that assails both the liberal appeal to color-blindness and a power-evading, aesthetic of difference that reduces racial identities to lifestyles, marketing niches, or consumer products.

Rupturing the Hollywood cinematic tradition of presenting whiteness as an "invisible" though determining discourse, *Suture* forces the audience to recognize whiteness as a racial marker, an "index of social standing or rank" (Goldberg 1993b, 69). But in the end, *Suture* provides no means for framing whiteness outside of the discursive and visual politics of domination. The film's attempt to develop a representational politics certainly forces the viewer to demystify and debunk whiteness as invisible, outside of the modalities of power and identity, but it does nothing to develop a strategic politics that refuses to accept whiteness as a racial category the only purpose of which is closely tied to if not defined by shifting narratives of domination and oppression. This might explain why *Suture* eventually engages in a reductionistic moralizing by suggesting that Clay should be condemned for wanting to be white, doing so without really engaging whiteness in a more dialectical or critical fashion.

Toward a Pedagogy of Whiteness

Dangerous Minds and *Suture* offer contrasting narratives of race that can be used pedagogically to critically deconstruct both racial othering and whiteness as part of a broader discourse on racial justice. The incongruous juxtaposition of these two films opens up a pedagogical space for reading representations of whiteness as an ideology and site of power and privilege. Similarly, rupturing singular definitions of whiteness provides educators with the opportunity to construct more complex models for theorizing whiteness through a multiplicity of social relations, theoretical positions, and affective identifications.

Rather than being dismissed simply as a racist text by critical educators, *Dangerous Minds* should be read symptomatically for the ways in which it articulates and reproduces whiteness as a form of racial domination within the public space of the inner city classroom. Offering an unapologetic reading of whiteness as a trope of order, rationality, insight, and beauty, *Dangerous Minds* is an important pedagogical text for students to address how whiteness and difference are portrayed in the film, and how race shapes, consciously or unconsciously, their everyday experiences, attitudes, and worldviews. Pedagogically, the issue is not to force students into viewing *Dangerous Minds* as either a good or bad film but to engage the broader social conditions through which the popularity of the film has to be understood. One pedagogical task is to get students to think about how *Dangerous Minds* bears witness to the ethical and racial dilemmas that animate the larger racial and social landscape. Another is to get them to think about how this film reworks or affirms their own intellectual and affective investments as organized through dominant racial ideologies and meanings at work in this highly racialized text.

Students may offer a number of responses to a film such as *Dangerous Minds*. But given the popularity of the film, and the large number of favorable reviews it received in newspapers across the country, it is reasonable to assume that the range of readings available to white students will fall within a mix of dominant and conservative interpretations.[24] Rather than stressing that students are diverse readers of culture, it is important pedagogically to recognize that the issue of ownership and control of the apparatuses of cultural production places enormous limits on both the readings made widely available to students as well as on the popular context from which to understand dominant notions of racism. When racial difference does enter into classroom discussion, it more than likely will focus on the disruptive behavior that black and Hispanic students exhibit in schools, behavior that will often be seen as characteristic of an entire social group, a form of cultural pathology that suggests minorities are largely to blame for the educational problems they experience. Similarly, when whiteness is destabilized or critically addressed by students, it more than likely will be taken up within a power-evasive discourse in which white racism is often reduced to an act of individual prejudice cleanly removed from the messy contexts of history, politics, and systemic oppression.[25] This suggests that it is unlikely that white students will recognize LouAnne's pedagogy and insistence on the value of middle-class cultural capital as a racist attempt to teach black and Hispanic students that their own narratives, histories, and experiences are uncivilized and crude. And yet, however popular such dominant readings might be, they offer educators a prime pedagogical opportunity to interrogate and rupture their codes and ideologies. For instance, the ideological link between the privileging of white cultural capital and the ongoing degrading representation of the Other in Hollywood films about Africa, television sitcoms, or more recently in violent, black youth films may not be evident to students on a first reading of the film but certainly can become an object of analysis as various students in the class are provided with alternative readings.

At best, *Dangerous Minds* offers white students an opportunity to engage with a popular text that embodies much of what they generally learn or (mis)learn about race without initially putting their own racial identities on trial. When it is analyzed in conjunction with the viewing of *Suture*, a different set of claims about whiteness emerges that raises alternative possibilities for interrogating the relationship between whiteness, race, and racism. *Suture* presents a critical reading of whiteness as a dominant social and cultural construction and attempts through an unsettling visual narrative to reveal how whiteness wages symbolic violence through its refusal to name its defining mechanisms of power and privilege. In doing so, *Suture* forces students, especially white students, to consider problematizing the assumption that issues regarding race and racial politics are largely about blacks as a social group. The dominant defense of whiteness as a universal norm is visibly thrown off balance in this film and makes "whiteness" a racial category open to critique. In rupturing whiteness as a racially and politically neutral code, *Suture* provides a pedagogical opportunity for educators to talk about how white people are raced, how white experience is constructed differently within a variety of public spaces, and how it is mediated through the diverse but related lens of class, gender, and sexual orientation.

Played off against each other, the two films engage in a representational politics that illuminates whiteness as a shifting, political category whose meaning can be addressed within rather than outside of the interrelationships of class, race, ethnicity, and gender. In other words, the structuring principles that inform these films as they work intertextually provide a theoretical basis for challenging whiteness as an ideological and historical construction; it is precisely the tension generated between these films that invites entrance into a pedagogy that commences with what Gayatri Spivak refers to as "moments of bafflement" (Spivak 1990, 137). While such pedagogical tensions do not guarantee the possibility of

68   Chapter 2

recentering whiteness to render "visible the historical and institutional structures from within which [white teachers and students] speak" (Spivak 67), they do provide the pedagogical conditions for students and teachers alike to question and unlearn those aspects of whiteness that position them with the space and relations of racism.

While it is impossible to predict how students will actually react to a pedagogy of bafflement that takes whiteness and race as objects of serious debate and analysis, it is important to recognize that white students will generally offer enormous resistance to analyzing critically the "normative-residual space [of] white cultural practice" (Frankenberg 1993, 234). Resistance in this case should be examined for the knowledge it yields, the possibilities for interrogating its silences and refusals. Pedagogically, this suggests allowing students to air their positions on whiteness and race regardless of how messy or politically incorrect such positions might be. But there is more at stake here than providing a pedagogical space for students to narrate themselves, to speak without fear within the contexts of their own specific histories and experiences. Rather than arguing that students be simply allowed to voice their racial politics, I am suggesting that they be offered a space marked by dialogue and critique in which such positions can be engaged, challenged, and rearticulated through an ongoing analysis of the material realities and social relations of racism.

Needless to say, the issue of making white students responsive to the politics of racial privilege is fraught with the fear and anger that accompany having to rethink one's identity. Engaging in a pedagogy that prompts white students to examine their social practices and belief systems in racial terms may work to reinforce the safe assumption that race is a stable category, a biological given, rather than a historical and cultural construction. For instance, Ann Louise Keating points out that when teaching her students to interrogate whiteness critically, many of them come away believing that all whites were colonialists, in spite of her attempts pedagogically to distinguish between whiteness as the dominant racial and political ideology and the diverse, contingent racial positions white people take up (Keating 1995, 907).

In spite of the tensions and contradictions that any pedagogy of whiteness might face, it is imperative that teachers address the histories that have shaped the normative space, practices, and diverse relationships that white students have inherited through a legacy of racial privilege. Analyzing the historical legacy of whiteness as an oppressive racial force necessitates that students engage in a critical form of memory work while fostering less a sullen silence or paralyzing guilt and more a sense of outrage at historical oppression and a desire for racial justice in the present. Attempting to get students to think critically about racism and its systemic nature, Keating illuminates the problems she faced when attempting to get white students to interrogate or reverse their taken-for-granted assumptions about whiteness and racial privilege. She writes:

These reversals trigger a variety of unwelcome reactions in self-identified "white" students, reactions ranging from guilt to anger to withdrawal and despair. Instructors must be prepared to deal with these responses. The point is not to encourage feelings of personal responsibility for the slavery, decimation of indigenous peoples, land theft, and so on that occurred in the past. It is, rather, to enable students of all colors more fully to comprehend how these oppressive systems that began in the historical past continue misshaping contemporary conditions. Guilt-tripping plays no role in this process. (Keating 1995, 915)

However, Keating is not entirely clear on how educators can avoid guilt-tripping students or to what degree they are not to be held responsible (accountable) for their present attitudes within this type of pedagogy. Making whiteness rather than white racism the focus of study is an important pedagogical strategy. Analyzing whiteness opens up theoretical and pedagogical spaces for teachers and students to articulate how their own racial identities have been shaped within a broader racist culture and what responsibilities they might assume for living in a present in which whites are accorded privileges and opportunities (though in complex and different ways) largely at the expense of other racial groups. Yet, as insightful as this strategy may prove to be, more theoretical work needs to be done to enable students to critically engage and appropriate the tools necessary for them to politicize whiteness as a racial category without closing down their own sense of identity and political agency.

While both *Dangerous Minds* and *Suture* provide a pedagogical opportunity for students to see how dominant assumptions about whiteness can be framed and challenged, neither film addresses what it means to rearticulate whiteness in oppositional terms. Neither the portrayal of whiteness as a form of racial privilege nor its portrayal as a practice of domination necessarily establishes the basis for white students to rearticulate their own whiteness in ways that go beyond their overidentification with or desire to be "black" at the expense of their own racial identities.

All students need to feel that they have a personal stake in their racial identities, but one that allows them to assert a view of political agency in which they can join with diverse groups around a notion of democratic public life that affirms racial differences through a "rearticulation of cultural, social, and political citizenship" (Yudice 1995, 276-77). Linking identity, race, and difference to a broader vision of radical democracy suggests a number of important pedagogical considerations. First, students need to investigate the historical relationship between race and ethnicity. David Roediger is right in warning against the conflation of race and ethnicity by critical theorists, especially in light of a history of ethnicity in which white immigrants saw themselves as white and ethnic. According to Roediger, the claim to ethnicity among white immigrants, especially those from Europe, did not prevent them from defining their racial identities through the discourse of white separatism and supremacy (Roediger 1991, 181-98). In this case, white ethnicity was not ignored by such immigrants; it was affirmed and linked in some cases to the dominant relations of racism.

The issue of racial identity can be linked to what Stuart Hall has called the "new ethnicity."[26] For Hall, racial identities can be understood through the notion of ethnicity, but not the old notion of ethnicity that depends in part on the suppression of cultural difference and a separatist notion of white identity. Hall's attempt to rewrite ethnicity as a progressive and critical concept does not fall into the theoretical trap described by Roediger. By decoupling ethnicity from the traditional moorings of nationalism, racism, colonialism, and the state, Hall posits the new ethnicity as a referent for acknowledging "the place of history, language, and culture in the construction of subjectivity and identity, as well as the fact that all discourse is placed, positioned, situated, and all knowledge is contextual" (Hall 1996, 29).

Extending Hall's insights about ethnicity, I want to argue that the diverse subject positions, social experiences, and cultural identities that inform whiteness as a political and social construct can be rearticulated for students to recognize that "we all speak from a particular place, out of a particular history, out of particular experience, a particular culture without being constrained by [such] positions. . . . We are all, in that sense, ethnically located and our ethnic identities are crucial to our subjective sense of who we are" (Hall 1996, 29). In Hall's terms, "whiteness" cannot be addressed as a form of identity fashioned through a claim to purity or some universal essence, but as one that "lives with and through, not despite difference" (Hall 1990, 235).

Hall provides a theoretical language for racializing whiteness without essentializing it; he also argues correctly that ethnicity must be defined and defended through a set of ethical and political referents that connect diverse democratic struggles while expanding the range and possibilities of democratic relations and practices. Redefined within the theoretical parameters of a new ethnicity, whiteness can be read as a complex marker of identity defined through a politics of difference subject to the shifting currents of history, power, and culture. That is, whiteness can no longer be taken up as fixed, naturally grounded in a tradition or ancestry, but as Ien Ang claims in another context, must be understood as a form of postmodern ethnicity, "experienced as a provisional and partial site of identity which must be constantly (re)invented and (re)negotiated" (Ang 1995, 18). The notion of whiteness being in transit, hybrid, but at the same time grounded in particular histories and practices extends the political potential of Hall's new ethnicity thesis in that it provides a theoretical space for engaging racial identity as a fundamental principle of citizenship and radical democracy the aim of which is the "expansion of egalitarian social relations, and practices" (Mouffe 1992, 380).

The new ethnicity defines racial identities as multiple, porous, complex, and shifting and in doing so provides a theoretical opening for educators and students to move beyond framing whiteness as either good or bad, racially innocent or intractably racist. Whiteness in this context can be addressed through its complex relationship with other determining factors that usurp any claim to racial purity or singularity. At the same time, whiteness must be addressed within power relations that exploit its subversive potential while not erasing the historical and political role it plays in shaping other racialized identities and social differences. Unlike the old ethnicity, which posits difference in essentialist or separatist terms, Hall's notion of the new ethnicity defines identity as an ongoing act of cultural recovery, acknowledging that any particular claim to racial identity offers no guarantees regarding political outcomes. But at the same time, the new ethnicity provides a theoretical service by allowing white students to go beyond the paralysis inspired by guilt or the anxiety/fear of difference that fuels white racism. In this context, whiteness gains its meaning only in conjunction with other identities such as those informed by class, gender, age, nationality, and citizenship. For progressive whites, "crossing over does not mean crossing out" (Erickson 1995, 185). Whites have to learn to live with their whiteness by rearticulating it in terms that allow them to formulate what it means to develop viable cross relations, political coalitions, and social movements. Whites have to learn and unlearn, engage in a critical pedagogy of self-formation that allows them to be border crossers, crossing racial lines not to become black but so they can begin to forge multiracial coalitions based on an engagement rather than a denial of whiteness.

By positioning whiteness within a notion of cultural citizenship that affirms difference politically, culturally, and socially, students can take notice of how their whiteness functions as a racial identity while still being critical of forms of whiteness structured in dominance and aligned with exploitative interests and oppressive social relations. By rearticulating whiteness as more than a form of domination, white students can construct narratives of whiteness that both challenge and, hopefully, provide a basis for transforming the dominant relationship between racial identity and citizenship, one informed by an oppositional politics. Such a political practice suggests new subject positions, alliances, commitments, and forms of solidarity between white students and others engaged in a struggle over expanding the possibilities of democratic life, especially as it affirms both a politics of difference and a redistribution of power and material resources. George Yudice argues that as part of a broader project for articulating whiteness in oppositional terms, white youth must feel that they have a stake in racial politics that connects them to the struggles being waged by other groups. At the center of such struggles is both the battle over citizenship redefined through the discourse of rights and the problem of resource distribution. He writes:

This is where identity politics segues into other issues, such as tax deficits, budget cuts, lack of educational opportunities, lack of jobs, immigration policies, international trade agreements, environmental blight, lack of health care insurance, and so on. These are the areas in which middle and working-class whites historically have had an advantage over people of color. However, today that advantage has eroded in certain respects. (Yudice 1995, 276)

As part of a wider attempt to engage these issues, Yudice suggests that white youth can form alliances with other social and racial groups that recognize the need for solidarity in addressing issues of public life that undermine the quality of democracy for all groups. As white youth struggle to find a cultural and political space from which to speak and act as transformative citizens, it is imperative that educators address what it means pedagogically and politically to help students rearticulate whiteness as part of a democratic cultural politics. Central to such a task is the need to challenge the conventional left analysis of whiteness as a space between guilt and denial, a space that offers limited forms of resistance and engagement. For teachers, students, and others to come to terms with whiteness existentially and intellectually, we need to take up the challenge in our classrooms and across a wide variety of public sites of confronting racism in all its complexity and ideological and material formations. But most important, whiteness must provide a diverse but critical space from which to wage a wider struggle against the myriad of forces that undermine what it means to live in a society founded on the principles of freedom, racial justice, and economic equality. Rewriting whiteness within a discourse of resistance and possibility represents more than a challenge to dominant and progressive notions of racial politics; it provides an important pedagogical challenge for educating cultural workers, teachers, and students to live with and through difference as a defining principle of a radical democracy.

Notes

1. For an excellent analysis of the new work on whiteness, especially the historical approaches, see Erickson (1995). For more general treatments, see Macmillan (1995) and Stowe (1996).

2. Eric Lott cited in Stowe 1996, 76. Stowe's piece also serves as an overview and critical interrogation of the recent scholarship on whiteness.

3. This distinction is taken up in Frankenberg 1993, 7.

4. For example, see Scheurich (1993), and Sleeter (1993).

5. In this context, Stuart Hall is not talking about whites but blacks. It seems to me that his point is just as relevant for rearticulating whiteness as it is for debunking the essentialized black subject, though this should not suggest that such an appropriation take place outside of the discourse of power, history, inequality, and conflict. See Hall

1991a, 57. Pfeil raises a similar set of issues about white masculinity (Pfeil 1995, 3-4).

6. One exception worth noting is Keating.

7. For an excellent analysis of this issue, see Edsall and Edsall (1992).

8. On the meaning of the new racism and its diverse expressions, see Winant 1994. See also Giroux 1992.

9. I take up this issue in extensive detail in my *Fugitive Cultures: Race, Violence and Youth* (1996).

10. Kaus cited in Brenkman 1995, 34.

11. On the rise of right-wing groups in the United States, see Diamond (1995). On racism and right-wing movements, see Novick (1995). For a number of articles on the right-wing backlash, see Berlet (1995).

12. Both Richard Dyer and bell hooks have argued that whites see themselves as racially transparent and reinscribe whiteness as invisible. While this argument may have been true in the 1980s, it no longer makes sense as white youth, in particular, have become increasingly sensitive to their status as whites because of the racial politics and media exposure of race in the last few years. See Dyer (1998); and hooks (1992).

13. The sources documenting the growing racism in the dominant media and popular culture are too extensive to cite. Some important examples include Reeves and Campbell (1994); Fiske; Ferrell and Sanders (1995); Gray (1995); Dyson (1996); and Giroux (1996). For a summary of the double standard at work in the press coverage of rap music, see Jones and Deterline (1994).

14. For a brilliant analysis of the racial politics of *The Atlantic Monthly*, see Augnet (1996).

15. Fishkin 1995, 430. Fishkin provides an excellent analysis of the historical and contemporary work interrogating whiteness.

16 Some representative examples of recent scholarship on whiteness include: Roediger (1991 and 1994); hooks (1992); Winant (1994); Omi and Winant (1994); Ware (1992); Frankenberg (1993); Morrison (1993); Allen (1994); Pfeil (1995); Ignatiev (1995); and Ignatiev and Garvey (1996).

17. hooks 1990, 54. See also hooks's critique of Wim Wenders's film, *Wings of Desire* (1988) (165-71).

18. Cone cited in hooks 1992, 14.

19. Two excellent articles addressing the possibilities for rearticulating whiteness in oppositional terms are Jester (1992) and Yudice (1995). I have relied heavily on both of these pieces in developing my analysis of white youth.

20. I want to thank my colleague at Penn State University, Bernard Bell, for this insight (personal communication).

21. I think Houston Baker is instructive on this issue in arguing that race, for all of its destructive tendencies and implications, has also been used by blacks and other people of color to gain a sense of personal and historical agency. This is not a matter of a positive image of race canceling out its negative underside. On the contrary, Baker makes a compelling case for the dialectical nature of race and its possibilities for engaging and overcoming its worse dimensions while extending in the interest of a transformative and democratic polls.

22. See Snead (1994), especially chapter 10 (131-49). For an analysis of the importance of race in the broader area of popular culture, two representative sources include:

Dyson (1993) and Giroux (1996).

    23. On the localization of crime as a racial text, see Goldberg (1993a).

    24. For instance, see Glass (1995), Saillant (1995), and Chastain (1995).

    25. For example, in Frankenberg's study of white women, radical positions on race were in the minority; and in Gallagher's study of white college students, liberal and conservative positions largely predominated.

    26. Stuart Hall takes up the rewriting of ethnicity in a variety of articles. See especially the following: 1990, 1991a, 1991b, and 1996.

Works Cited

Allen, Theodore. 1994. *The Invention of the White Race*. London: Verso.

Ang, Ien. 1995. "On Not Speaking Chinese: Postmodern Ethnicity and the Politics of Diaspora." *Social Formations* 24: 118.

Augnet, Charles. 1996. "For Polite Reactionaries." *Transition* 6.1: 14-34.

Baker, Houston. 1992. "Caliban's Triple Play." In *Loose Canons: Notes on the Culture Wars*, ed. Henry Louis Gates, Jr. New York: Oxford University Press.

Baldwin, James. 1994. "On Being . . . And Other Lies." *Essence* 25: 90.

Bell, Derrick. 1992. *Faces at the Bottom of the Well: The Permanence of Racism*. New York: Basic Books.

Berlet, Chip, ed. 1995. *Eyes Right!: Challenging the Right-Wing Backlash*. Boston: South End.

Brenkman, John. 1995. "Race Publics: Civic Illiberalism, or Race after Reagan." *Transition* 5.2: 14.

Chastain, Sue. 1995. "Dangerous Minds No Threat to This Tough Teacher." *Times Union*, 13 August, G1.

D'Souza, Dinesh. 1995. *The End of Racism: Principles for a Multiracial Society*. New York: The Free Press.

Diamond, Sara. 1995. *Roads to Domination: Right-Wing Movements and Political Power in the United States*. New York: Guilford.

_____. 1996. *Facing the Wrath*. Monroe: Common Courage.

Dyer, Richard. 1998. "White." *Screen* 29.4: 44-64.

Dyson Michael. 1993. *Reflecting Black*. Minneapolis: University of Minnesota Press.

_____. 1996. *Between God and Gangsta Rap*. New York: Oxford University Press.

Edsall, Thomas Byrne and Mary D. Edsall. 1992. *Chain Reactions: The Impact of Race, Rights and Taxes on American Politics*. New York: Norton.

Erickson, Peter. 1995. "Seeing White." *Transition* 5.3: 166-85.

Ferrell, Jeff and Sanders, Clinton R., eds. 1995. *Cultural Criminology*. Boston: Northeastern University Press.

Fishkin, Shirley Fisher. 1995. "Interrogating 'Whiteness,' Complicating 'Blackness': Remapping American Culture." *American Quarterly* 47.3: 428-66.

Fiske, John. 1994. *Media Matters*. Minneapolis: University of Minnesota Press.

Frankenberg, Ruth. 1993. *The Social Construction of Whiteness: White Women, Race Matters*. Minneapolis: University of Minnesota Press.

Gallagher, Charles A. 1995. "White Reconstruction in the University." *Socialist Review* 94.1-2: 165-87.

Gates, David. 1993. "White Male Paranoia." *Newsweek*, 29 March, 48-53.

Giroux, Henry A. 1992. *Border Crossing*. New York: Routledge.

____. 1996. *Fugitive Cultures: Race Violence, and Youth*. New York: Routledge.

Glass, Jon. 1995. "'Dangerous Minds' Inspires Teachers." *Virginian Pilot*, 2 September, B1.

Goldberg, David Theo. 1993a. "Polluting the Body Politic: Racist Discourse and the Urban Location." In *Racism, the City and the State*, eds. Malcolm Cross and Michael Keith. New York: Routledge.

____. 1993b. *Racist Culture: Philosophy and the Politics of Meaning*. Cambridge: Blackwell.

Gray, Herman. 1995. *Watching Race*. Minneapolis: University of Minnesota Press.

Gresson, Aaron D, III. 1996. "Postmodern America and the Multicultural Crisis: Reading *Forrest Gump* as the 'Call Back to Whiteness.'" *Taboo* 1: 11-33.

Grundmann, Roy. 1994. "Identity Politics at Face Value: An Interview with Scott McGehee and David Siegel," *Cineaste* 20.3: 24.

Hacker, Andrew. 1992. *Two Nations. Black and White Separate, Hostile, Unequal*. New York: Scribner's.

Hall, Stuart. 1990. "Cultural Identity and Diaspora." In *Identity, Community, Culture, Difference*, ed. Jonathan Rutherford. London: Lawrence and Wishart.

____. 1991a. "Ethnicity: Identity and Difference." *Radical America* 13.4: 9-20.

____. 1991b. "Old and New Identities, Old and New Ethnicities." In *Culture Globalization and the World System*, ed. Anthony D. Ring. Binghamton: SUNY Press.

____. 1992. "Race, Culture, and Communications: Looking Backward and Forward at Cultural Studies." *Rethinking Marxism* 5.1: 10-18.

____. 1996. "New Ethnicities." In *Stuart Hall: Critical Dialogues in Cultural Studies*, eds. David Morley and Kuan-Hsing Chen. New York: Routledge.

Henry, William A, III. 1991. "Upside Down in the Groves of Academe." *Time*, 1 April, 66-69.

Herrnstein, Richard J. and Charles Murray. 1994. *The Bell Curve: Intelligence and Class Structure in American Life*. New York: The Free Press.

hooks, bell. 1990. *Yearning*. Boston: South End.

____. 1992. *Black Looks: Race and Representation*. Boston: South End.

Ignatiev, Noel. 1995. *How the Irish Became White*. New York: Routledge.

Ignative, Noel and John Garvey, eds. 1996. *Race Traitor*. New York: Routledge.

"The Issue." 1994. *New Republic*, 31 October 31, 9.

Jester, Diana. 1992. "Roast Beef and Reggae Music: The Passing of Whiteness," *New Formations* 118: 106-21.

Jones, Art and Kim Deterline. 1994. "Fear of a Rap Planet: Rappers Face Media Double Standard," *Extra* 7.2: 20-21.

Keating, AnnLouise. 1995. "Interrogating 'Whiteness,' (De)Constructing 'Race,'" *College English* 57.8: 901-18.

Kelley, Robin D.G. 1992. "Notes on Deconstructing the 'Folk'," *American Historical Review* 97.5: 140-48.

Macmillan, Liz. 1995. "Lifting the Veil from Whiteness: Growing Body of Scholarship

76 Chapter 2

Challenges a Racial 'Norm,'" *Chronicle of Higher Education*, 8 September, A23.

Morrison, Toni. 1993. *Playing in the Dark: Whiteness and the Literary Imagination.* 1992. New York: Vintage.

Mouffe, Chantal. 1992. "Feminism, Citizenship, and Radical Democratic Politics." In *Feminists Theorize the Political*, eds. Judith Butler and Joan Scott. New York: Routledge.

Nakayama, Thomas R. and Robert L. Krizek. 1995. "Whiteness: A Strategic Rhetoric," *Quarterly Journal of Speech* 81: 291-309.

Novick, Michael. 1995. *White Lies, White Power*. Monroe: Common Courage.

Omi, Michael and Howard Winant. 1994. *Racial Formations in the United States from the 1960s to the 1990s.* New York: Routledge.

Pfeil, Fred. 1995. *White Guys*. London: Verso.

Reeves, Jimmie L. and Richard Campbell. 1994. *Cracked Coverage: Television News, the Anti-Cocaine Crusade and the Reagan Legacy.* Durham: Duke University Press.

Roediger, David. 1991. *The Wages of Whiteness*. London: Verso.

_____. 1994. *Toward the Abolition of Whiteness*. London: Verso.

Saillant, Catherine. 1995. "School of Soft Knocks." *Los Angeles Times*, 11 October, B1.

Scheurich, James Joseph. 1993. "Toward a White Discourse on White Racism." *Educational Researcher* 22.8: 5-13.

Sleeter, Christine. 1993. "Advancing a White Discourse." *Educational Researcher* 22.8: 13-15.

Snead, James. 1994. *White Screens Black Images: Hollywood from the Dark Side.* New York: Routledge.

Spivak, Gayatri Chakrovorty. 1990. *The Post-Colonial Critic: Interviews, Strategies, Dialogues.* Ed. Sarah Harasym. New York: Routledge.

Stowe, David W. 1996. "Uncolored People: The Rise of Whiteness Studies," *Lingua Franca* 6.6: 68-77.

Ware, Vron. 1992. *Beyond the Pale: White Women, Racism, and History.* London: Verso.

Winant, Howard. 1992. "Amazing Grace." *Socialist Review* 75.19: 161-83.

_____. *Racial Conditions*. 1994. Minneapolis: University of Minnesota Press.

Yudice, George. 1995. "Neither Impugning nor Disavowing Whiteness Does a Viable Politics Make: The Limits of Identity Politics." In *After Political Correctness*, ed. Christopher Newfield and Ronald Strickland. Boulder: Westview.

3

Yes, Virginia, There Is an Answer

Houston A. Baker, Jr.

Nobody in this section of the country believes the old threadbare lie that Negro men rape white women. If Southern white men are not careful they will overreach themselves and public sentiment will have a reaction; a conclusion will then be reached which will be very damaging to the moral reputation of their women.

Ida B. Wells Barnett, 21 May 1892

As soon as Professor Anita Hill was in the dock at the Senate confirmation hearings on the nomination of Judge Clarence Thomas to the Supreme Court in 1991, anyone who had in the least allowed a black American woman's grammar to inform his or her hearing would not have been surprised that both Clarence Thomas and Anita Hill tried to find a "loophole of retreat." The phrase "loophole of retreat" belongs most decisively, in black women's expressivity, to Harriet Jacob's amazing nineteenth-century slave narrative, *Incidents in the Life of a Slave Girl*. The pseudonymous "Linda Brent," the work's winsome narrator, decides to secrete herself in a garret in her grandmother's house in a slaveholding community in order to deceive her master. From this virtually airless garret, she writes letters that are posted by a seaman friend, who dispatches them from the North to Linda's deceived master. The master is, thus, led to believe that his slave has escaped and traveled far away. The garret where

Brent executes these stratagems is labeled a "loophole of retreat."

Yet, what Brent actually accomplishes from a very tight space of maneuver is a cunning "literacy of resistance." However, though she is uncommonly effective in this literacy, she remains legally a slave. For the inexorable geographies of land in America are not easily re-mapped. White men in this law determined long ago and wrote the grammar of their determination in blood and southern horror that they and *only* they are real, and that: "There ain't nothing like the real thing, Baby."

Thus is constructed the law's imaginary in the United States. There can be only one Father, and "I am what I am." Yes, the eyes of Negroes had better be watching God, for in America, he is the definitive grammar book of transcendental signification.

But was sexuality always already at issue when the nomination of Clarence Thomas was announced to the press? Well, the judge's first photo opportunity came to us live from the president of the United States' bedroom in Maine. *The San Francisco Chronicle* editorial page on the day after the nomination asked if an appropriate caption for the bedroom photograph might read: "Sleeping with the Enemy?" In so many ways, the black man and woman are necessary inhabitants, aren't they, of the law's hunting/fishing/sporting-life bedrooms?

Think of Linda Brent, herself, who tells us in *Incidents in the Life of a Slave Girl* about the agonies thrust upon her when she was forced to have babies for an aristocratic southerner on his way to legislative office in Washington, D.C. Think of Anita Hill voicing herself up for Robert Bork and the Supremes. Remember the James Baldwin short story about the southern sheriff at home in his bedroom after a day of brutalizing a black male, telling his bed mate that he is going to do it to her "like a nigger." It would seem that Clarence Thomas was not unusual, then, and that, yes indeed, sexuality always has something grammatically to do with the "what matters" of "who speaks" in America.

Characteristically, it is Richard Wright who gets it roughly right. In American legal rites and white joint accords (i.e., who's got the biggest and best symbolism) the word to the black mother and brother alike is: "If you break the law of silence, you can't win!" It is the giant poster of State's Attorney Buckley in *Native Son* that casts this message over Bigger (ha!) Thomas's community.

A more vernacular site for the dynamics of American sexuality and law is offered by contemporary rap music, where we find the rapper Ice-T trying cannily to negotiate those dreaded geographies of the Fatherly law without tripping up. One of Iceberg's Syndicate (backup, sidemen, or posse) imploringly reminds, or cajoles, the Los Angeles rapper on his *OG* album of 1991: "Yo, ICE . . . we half-way through the album and we ain't had no sex rhymes." To which the icy OG responds: "Yo, man, like I really didn't wanna do none of that this year." Yet how is one—particularly a black ONE in America—going to avoid the LAW? Ice-T gives in and busts a mocking, parodic sex rhyme on his album.

Did Ice have a recourse? Was there help available? Is there an ally to be sought by the black ONE against the dread machinations of the LAW in America?

One thing we know from Virginia Lamp Thomas's encounter with *People* magazine (11November 1991) is that ole Sheriff John Brown is not likely to go down at the hands of white womanhood.

In her *People* magazine interview, Virginia Lamp Thomas has the look of the white women who attended Janie's murder trial in *Their Eyes Were Watching God*: "They wore good clothes," Janie reflects, "and had the pinky color that comes of good food. They were nobody's poor white folks" (Thomas 1991, 274). We learn from Virginia Lamp's interview that she "was brought up in Omaha, the youngest child of wealthy, well-connected parents" (Thomas, 1991, 108). In the *People* interview itself, Virginia seems at some moments to possess a dead-calm assurance about the bodies and desires of black women. At other moments, she seems naively silent about her own position in relation to the sexual politics of American law.

Now, her father was a real estate developer, and presumably (since he was "well-connected") he had brokering talents of his own. It would seem to me that a talent for chattel or property brokerage has been passed on to the daughter. In Virginia's case, it is not real estate that is grammatically brokered in the exchanges of her *People* encounter, but the bodies of black women.

Virginia obsessively lays hands/words upon black women's bodies and psyches, saying, for example, of Anita Hill: she "never got what she wanted . . . [from] my husband." Of the black Kathy Thomas (the judge's first wife), Virginia tells us that everything is harmonious; C.T., V.L., and Kathy, according to Virginia, "get along marvelously." But if the handling of the black bodies of Anita and Kathy seems only a mild form of brokerage, let us look at V.L.'s parting words on her first meeting with the judge.

The two partisans of the law share a cab to the airport after attending a conference on *affirmative action* (which both of them oppose). Leaving the cab, Virginia says: "I have some black female friends that I'd really like to put together with you."

"Put together"! What could Virginia's utterance possibly have meant in the economies of the law?

Is anyone reminded by all of this of Harriet Jacobs's Mrs. Flint (the master's wife), of whom Linda Brent says: "I pitied Mrs. Flint. She was a *second* wife, many years the junior of her husband; and the hoary-headed miscreant [Dr. Flint] was enough to try the patience of a wiser and better woman" (my italics).

Does anyone remember precisely what Mrs. Flint does when she knows that her husband has, shall we say, "legal designs" on the slave girl Linda Brent?

Listen: "She now took me [Linda] to sleep in a room adjoining her own.

There I was an object of her especial care, though not of her especial comfort, for she spent many a sleepless night to watch over me."

Mrs. Flint, in fact, feigns the voice (and desire) of her husband to try to get the slave girl to expose the workings of the law. Mrs. Flint is a woman obsessed, jealous, desirous (pace Hortense Spillers) of possessing/inhabiting/brokering the body of the black woman who is virtually in her bedroom. (Lord, what a tangled web Mrs. Flint weaves, when earnestly she attempts to deceive.)

So, Virginia's talk in the *People* encounter about a Christian, biblical, angelic "survival" of an ordeal by her and Clarence Thomas is—in its *au fond* instantiation—underwritten and grammatically controlled by the second wife's brokering ("putting together," as it were) of the black woman's body.

Is Virginia, though, omnisciently in control of her own white woman's control panel? Does she have the grammar of control down pat? Can she/will she "speak on it"?

Clarence Thomas is figured as a baffled, black male questioner at a key moment in the interview. "Virginia," says he, "Why are they trying to destroy me?" Virginia responds: "I couldn't answer him." Why? Because she did not know the answer? Or was it that she had enough grammatical control to refuse to focus and clarify the judge's pronoun usage?

I mean: Who is "they"?

It was not an amorphous or mysterious "they" who insisted on speech, but a young, beautiful, articulate black woman who never mentioned "destruction," only gross *harassment* by the LAW in blackface.

Anita Hill was, of course, the *uncanny* "return" that haunts the LAW with: "I will never leave you/I will never leave you alone." Anita Hill is *La Chat qui Pêche*.

Clarence was asking about that "third" woman—Ida, Rosa, Anita?—who always has an I/eye on the LAW. Perhaps, it is William Blake's eye of the four-fold visionary. And white women are, precisely, those who wish no part of this eye's recounted vision, since it is out of their control.

In a word, the white woman would just as soon not have the black woman signify on the provinces of white women's relationship to the LAW, their relationship, say, to sexuality and desire in the economies of lynch law.

A nineteenth-century example from the life of Ida Wells serves to illustrate. The white Frances Willard (head of the influential Women's Christian Temperance Union) responded to Wells's charges (captured in the epigraph to the present essay) that some white women may, in fact, share an agential role in the dynamics of American (lynch) law. Willard wrote as follows:

> It is my firm belief that in the statements made by Miss Wells concerning white women having taken the initiative in nameless acts between the races she has put an imputation upon half the white race in this country that is

unjust, and, save in the rarest exceptional instances, wholly without foundation. This is the unanimous opinion of the most disinterested and observant leaders of opinion whom I have consulted on the subject, and I do not fear to say that the laudable efforts she [Wells] is making are greatly handicapped by statements of this kind, nor to urge her as a friend and well-wisher to banish from her vocabulary all such allusions as a source of weakness to the cause she has at heart. (Wells Barnet, 1969, 71)

On one hand, I read Frances Willard as saying something akin to: "Shut up, or I'll have you bound over to the big court!" More charitably, I read her as a white, *well-connected* woman willfully misrepresenting Ida and playing a womanly possum vis-à-vis the implicit lynch law agency of white American womanhood.

It rather sounds, if one really thinks about it, like Willard is saying: "Mrs. Wells never got what she wanted."

What, precisely, is the "what" that white women seem so desperately to project on black women as their desire? Ultimately, Willard's discourse sounds very male and very legal: "If you break the law [of silence], you can't win!"

The fact that Willard's leadership of a temperance union is a "Christian" leadership does not allay my suspicions in the least. And Virginia Lamp Thomas's Christian allegorizing in her *People* interview—almost a century later—provokes the same suspicions. For the failure of Judge Thomas's second wife to answer the judge's question about a destructive "they" is, finally, a rejection by Virginia of black women's grammars and fourth-eye discourse. She is remarkably akin in this rejection to Frances Willard and Mrs. Flint. Now Ida Wells implicitly described the legal agency and necessary silences of white womanhood like that of Ms. Willard. Wells wrote:

If America would not hear the cry of men, women and children whose dying groans ascended to heaven praying for relief, not only for them but for others who might soon be treated as they, then certainly no fair-minded person can charge disloyalty to those who make an appeal to the civilization of the world for such sympathy and help as it is possible to extend. If stating the facts [as I have done] of these lynchings, as they appeared from time to time in the white newspapers of America—the news gathered by white correspondents, compiled by white press bureaus and disseminated among white people—shows any vindictiveness, then the mind which so charges is not amenable to argument. (Wells Barnett 1969, 80)

"Not amenable to argument." "Not amenable to argument." "Not amenable to argument." White women certainly are not amenable if the argument is a legal sighting and citing from the visionary, pronominal territories of the black woman's I-and-eye.

Chapter 3

What, then, must Virginia do? She must/does shut the kitchen blinds; kicks the media handlers out of her domestic temple. Summons "Steely Dan" Danforth for prayer and croissants. Virginia "could not answer," so she makes herself and her husband answerable only to the LAW—the transcendental "I am who I Am" himself. Or so she asserts in her *People* interview. Virginia might have constituted or figured for herself a newly born white woman's agency in the immemorially sordid provinces of American law. Instead, she summoned: John Danforth, God, and the Bible.

She decided, like Frances Willard or Mrs. Flint, to maintain her silent and silencing place in the geographies of the law. She thus, ironically, escaped in the television camera's very eye to the provinces of Providence.

When she was asked why her husband was so seldom at home, William Blake's wife is reputed to have said: "Mr. Blake spends much of his time in heaven." Virginia similarly escapes through the camera's eye into heaven during the hearings. She never even seemed to think about bringing the noise, or making herself amenable in any way, to the arguments of the black woman Anita Hill.

The concluding photo of the *People* interview features Virginia Lamp Thomas supine on a white sectional. Her head rests on the judge's right shoulder. His arm is around her. He is sitting almost terrifiedly upright. Together, Virginia and Clarence display an opened Holy Bible.

Who says Virginia does not understand how to provide an answer to Clarence's reputed question? The second wife's implicit portrayal of herself seems almost obscenely thin. I mean Virginia's Christian self-portrayal and silence seem, in the words of Ida Wells, a "threadbare lie" indeed.

Her feigned innocence evokes Ray Charles. In one of the Genius of Soul's funkiest classics about heterosexuality, the law, and the ceaselessly unanswered interrogatives of black fathers, he belts out: "Baby I got news, news for you/Somehow your story don't ring true!"

The truth of the LAW as it appears in the Virginia Lamp Thomas instance would seem to offer a fit coda for these brief reflections. This *truth* is both simple and complex, and it prevents the judge from living without a response. The question again: "Why are they trying to destroy me?"

Coda

Dear Virginia,
This has *long* been an American legal question for which the answer has always been, at least in some significant measure . . . you, yourself, are precisely the answer.

Works Cited

Jacob, Harriet. 1987. *Incidents in the Life of a Slave Girl*, ed. Jean Fagan Yellin. 1861. Cambridge: Harvard University Press.

Hurston, Zora Neale. 1979. Their Eyes Were Watching God. Urbana: University of Illinois Press.

Thomas, Virginia Lamp. 1991. *People Magazine*. 11 November: 108, 274.

Wells Barnett, Ida B. 1969. *On Lynchings: Southern Horror, A Red Record, Mob Rule in New Orleans*. New York: Arno Press and New York Times.

4

On Becoming an Ex-Colored Man: Postmodern Irony and the Extinguishing of Certainties in *The Autobiography of an Ex-Colored Man*

Neil Brooks

James Weldon Johnson's anonymously published 1912 novel *The Autobiography of an Ex-Colored Man* explores the phenomenon of those who were legally defined as "colored" passing as whites in American society. The unnamed first person narrator, who himself "passes," claims that in narrating the book he is engaged in an act of disclosure. His attempts to narrate a life of concealment and disguise produce a text that can only be understood through what it conceals, through the gaps and the unspoken. This lack of direct commentary has led many critics to discuss the work in terms of irony, but the very irreconcilability of that irony leads me to suggest that a more postmodern approach may help us understand the book's narrative position and the arguments concerning race and passing concealed within. This novel of passing cannot be fully explained by either straight or ironic reading, because in passing from "marginalized to center" from "other to being" from "signified to signifier," the narrative disallows all constructions that seek to map a stable center of self or other that the narrator might use as a guide in self-definition. Traditional irony is inadequate because it assumes a stable referent from which the ironic can be understood. This narrator can be better understood through a postmodern construction, such as those developed by Linda Hutcheon and, particularly, Alan Wilde.[1] I begin with a brief discussion of passing itself, which even today receives insufficient critical attention, and then develop a model of postmodern irony that can perhaps better clarify the relationship between the book's narrator, author, and message.

There is comparatively little in-depth contemporary historical or sociological writing on the subject of passing. Yet between 1880 and 1930 over a dozen novels were published with protagonists who passed. Narrative literature, by fictionalizing a very widespread activity, was the primary site of what little attention was accorded to a phenomenon nobody wanted to talk about. Narrative paradoxically becomes a political act in "speaking the unspoken," yet remains somewhat ineffective as social commentary by being removed to a realm of the merely fictional. But this, like every other simplistic dichotomy I will mention, also fails to address fully the horizon of the text's publication. Roxanna Pisiak suggests that narrative itself suffered under restrictive critical and publishing orthodoxies. Thus, the book was published as an anonymous "autobiography" because the text was too subversive to be presented even as fiction. In his own autobiography, *Along This Way* (1933), Johnson contends that he expected the text to be understood as a fiction, but on first publication much of the critical reception focused upon whether this was an actual or even a plausible account of a way of living in the United States. Some reviewers went so far as to denounce the book as a "vicious lie," since a black passing as white was to many simply an impossibility. But the relative lack of serious discussion about passing results not simply from the attitudes of those racists who believe in a clear and sharp distinction between black and white, but also from some black writers of the time who viewed those who passed as "sellouts" to the race. Similarly, many liberal thinkers did not and do not want to be reminded of the conditions that caused thousands of Americans to deny their heritage, their families, and in many cases their own identities, simply to gain access to the fundamental civil rights guaranteed by the Constitution.

Here are two passages from advertisements in nineteenth-century newspapers, which Charles Blockson quotes in his book *Black Genealogy* (1977). This from the *New Orleans Picayune*: "TWO HUNDRED DOLLARS REWARD— Ran away from the subscriber 18 November a *white negro man*, about 35 years old, height about five feet eight or ten inches, blue eyes, has a yellow woolly head, very fair skin." And this from the *Savannah Republican* in 1855: "Ran away from the subscriber, my negro man Albert, who is 27 years old, very white so much so that he would not be suspected of being a negro. Has blue eyes and very light hair." Blockson goes on to relate the story of Ellen Craft, who passed as a Southern planter while her darker-skinned husband acted as her servant. She traveled North, staying in all the finest hotels, and upon reaching Philadelphia resumed her true identity. Nevertheless, Maurice Evans in his 1915 volume

Black and White in the Southern States (published after *Ex-Colored Man*) concluded after much research that maybe perhaps a dozen people in the North had crossed the color line: "In the South I have never heard of such a thing nor do I believe it ever happens" (Evans 1915, 185). This comes from a man who in the introduction of his book insists his will be the first study to expose the truth concerning racial issues because he will remove emotion and be "scientific," with "facts observed and noted with scrupulous care, and no conclusion drawn until the body of data fully warrants it" (vi). Other studies use statistical "bodies of data," such as census figures, to show that substantial geographical drops in men and women defining themselves as "colored" or "mulatto" suggest that at least 2,600 men and women each year in the 1920s and 1930s could be accounted for only by a change in racial identity. Again these figures are themselves probably low, since those passing often would do all in their power to hide that fact. Children of "passers" may have never been told of their heritage. In 1948, *Time* magazine suggested that as many as five million Americans were passing.

But all these numbers I am citing and the very use of the term "passing" make a racial assumption—one must be either all white or all black—which, given the issues surrounding definitions of race, is relevant in that it carried great legal and social significance. In many states through the first half of our own century, this "all or nothing" attitude about race had legal authority, and Johnson's novel challenges this assumption. However, passing itself also is not as cut and dried as the above definition would imply. It would seem to propagate the view that black and white are two clearly separable and definable groups, and passing is when a member of one lives his life as a member of the other. However, as Pisiak succinctly puts it, "the split between 'white and black' in America is as unreliable as the narrator" (Pisiak 1993, 85). In fact, passing could be intentional or unintentional: intentional passing could be one time only for a specific purpose; occasional for convenience (dining, theater, travel); segmental (many African Americans earned their living in the white world but kept their personal lives in black society); and the permanent passing that the narrator of Johnson's novel is engaged in at the book's conclusion.[2] "Passing," then, does not simply refer to an impostor impersonating another racial group— "crossing the color line" as it was referred to—but rather to the physical manifestation of a psychological quest to understand oneself in a society where to be black was often not to have one consistent self but to have a double self—as described by W. E. B. Du Bois and others—or to have a multiplicity of selves—as does Johnson's narrator.

These various selves do not cohere to form a complete identity, because the contradictions within a society that, for example, wanted respectable, respectful, "free" citizens who, like slaves, could be denied basic human rights were utterly incongruous. But for the passer, such as Johnson's narrator, who has both black and white "selves," the contradictions themselves, not the resolution of those contradictions, paradoxically become his identity.

Most recent articles on the novel, to a greater or lesser extent, get around this paradox by speaking of irony in the novel. The narrator after many experiences concludes with a "Horatio Alger-like" success story in which the protagonist makes large sums of money, marries a beautiful white woman, and socializes in the highest circles of American society. We as readers, and intermittently the narrator himself, see this as ironic since we know he has rejected the heritage of his loving mother and embraced that of his absent, seemingly indifferent father. He has given up his attainable dream of being a great artist and is trapped in a social role as restrictive as any of those he rejects. Indeed, Lucinda Mackethan provides a fascinating reading of the text as an "inversion of the slave narrative" in which "the ex-colored man allows white value to cancel his self-hood" (Mackethan 1988, 141). The reverse slave narrative construction does tell part of the story, but such readings, as Stephen Ross has observed, tend "to see the irony as directed primarily *at* the narrator which gainsays the compassion with which Johnson treats his protagonist" (Ross 1974, 199). The narrator's "success," then, can be neither applauded nor dismissed, and the irony results from the utter lack of a normative standard by which to judge the ironic.

Near the beginning of his article "Irony in a Postmodern Age: Toward a Map of Suspensiveness," Alan Wilde gives "a baker's dozen of quotations" that he hopes will clarify the dilemmas of uncertainty the "postmodern subject" must face. Each of these quotations applies to various stages of Johnson's narrator's journey, but one from Donald Barthelme's "The Crisis" seems most fitting, particularly to the ending of the novel: "Yes, success is everything. Failure is more common. Most achieve a sort of middling thing, but fortunately one's situation is always blurred, you never know absolutely quite where you are. This allows, if not peace of mind, ongoing attention to other aspects of existence" (Wilde 1980, 4).

By this and the other quotations, Wilde seeks to show varying reactions to a postmodern milieu where, "in short, a world in need of mending is replaced by one beyond repair" (Wilde 1980, 9). The modernist "mending" is what the narrator himself has seen as his own project, but I agree with Pisiak and others who suggest that the narrator is not utterly unaware of what he seems inadvertently to reveal. And he is willing even to pay the price that his modernist construction of an ordered world demands. To quote Wilde again:

> the modernists demonstrably pay a price, namely the need to suffer the distance and detachment that are the inevitable corollary of an overly exigent sense of control and the special stigmata of modernist irony; or to put it differently, to endure unwillingly the estrangement of the self from the world it

seeks too urgently to shape and endow with meaning. (6)

This is part of the price the narrator of *The Autobiography of an Ex-Colored Man* believes he pays, but truly his cost is much higher than simply a decision to live in an ordered yet estranged world. For one thing, the artistic ideal of perfect, epiphanic moments that is a modernist response to chaos is unavailable to one who can never "fit all the pieces together" because some of them must be kept hidden away. The postmodern "turn of the screw" to the modernist irony of "detachment while imposing order" I see in the passer's continual and inescapable awareness of his own positioning of not just imposer but impostor. Indeed, the narrator does seek to remedy his isolation through the artwork he produces, his own narrative (the novel we read), in the opening chapter of which he says he is writing "out of a vague feeling of unsatisfaction" (Johnson 1965, 393) from which he is seeking relief. But he is unable to achieve any modernist closure. Rather, after telling the story of his success, he concludes with dissatisfaction, fearing that he has "sold his birthright for a mess of pottage" (511). This is not mere qualification of his success, or even equivocation, but rather an acknowledgment that despite his assertion of control as modernist narrator, he is unable to write his life to bring any modernist closure. Instead, his dilemma is what Wilde describes that of Oedipa Maas (in Thomas Pynchon's *Crying of Lot 49*) to be: "Modernist paradox gives way to postmodern quandary, to suspensiveness," and, for Oedipa, the state of "the true paranoid for whom all is organized in spheres joyful or threatening about the central pulse of himself" (Wilde 1980, 25). The narrator has created a world where all is organized around himself, but it can never be truly organized because the self he has placed at the center is as unstable as the external world he seeks to control.

The connection between the paranoid and the passer also seems quite apt. In passing, the narrator has chosen an existence in which at any moment his every construct could be taken away from him. Thus, I contend that we have here a storyteller trying to "pass" postmodern quandary as modernist irony.

Linda Hutcheon expresses many criticisms of Wilde's construction of postmodern irony that should also be considered in understanding the voice of the ex-colored man. Hutcheon particularly focuses on Wilde's phrase, "a world in need of mending is replaced by one beyond repair," asserting that "postmodernism works to show that all repairs are human constructs, but that, from that very fact, they derive their value as well as their limitation. All repairs are both comforting and illusory" (Hutcheon 1988b, 7). Many readings of Johnson's novel contend that the narrator has embraced "comfortable illusions," but the conflicted and unresolved nature of the text suggests rather that the narrator is at once embracing *and* critiquing those illusions.

Indeed, Hutcheon does specifically discuss African-American fiction as an important site of postmodern discourse, observing that "Black American Culture has been defined as one of 'double consciousness' in which black and white, master and slave cultures are never reconciled, but held in a doubled suspension" (Hutcheon 1988b, 44). But this very suspensiveness can in fact present a valuable contestatory position. Later she uses the example of Ishmael Reed's "Neo-HooDoo Manifesto" as a work that reveals that "those in power control history. The marginal and ex-centric, however, can contest that power, even as they remain within its purvey" (197). Reed challenges the existing system but also shows his own "insideness." By offering the "new totalizing narrative of Voodoo" but still seeming to believe in the "importance of the individual and other humanist notions," Reed, Hutcheon says, has produced "the kind of self-implicated yet challenging critique of humanism . . . that is typical of postmodernism. The position of black Americans has worked to make them especially aware of those political and social consequences of art, but they are still part of American society" (197). This conflicted positioning seems even more applicable to African Americans who pass. Certainly, the narrator of *The Autobiography of an Ex-Colored Man* constantly finds himself in the position of wanting to affirm the totalizing metanarratives of American humanism while daily struggling to escape some of the strictures those narratives placed on African Americans in the early part of this century. Consider his reflections after listening to a racist Texan cruelly denigrate all black Americans: "I was sick at heart. Yet I must confess that underneath it all I felt a certain sort of admiration for the man who could not be swayed from what he felt were principles" (Johnson 1965, 484). The narrator himself, of course, has no foundational principles from which he cannot be swayed, and this is the reason for both his success in society and his feelings of shame and failure.

In *The Politics of Postmodernism*, Hutcheon develops an even more compelling construction for my purposes here, when she discusses the Woody Allen film *Zelig*. In speaking of the American Jewish experience, she is again discussing a marginalized group in American society, members of which have often found it necessary to disguise their racial identity. The protagonist of the movie, which is also set in the early decades of this century, is known as "the human chameleon," and he takes on the characteristics of the people around him, whatever circumstances he might be in. Hutcheon notes, "As a Jew, Zelig has a special (and historically ironic) interest in fitting in, in being other than what he is—as we know from subsequent history" (Hutcheon 1988b, 109). Zelig goes on to become a "media monster," just as the ex-colored man becomes a "corporate monster," a real estate mogul making a fortune by buying run-down tenements and undoubtedly exploiting the black underclass he has ceased to recognize as his own relations. Hutcheon suggests that "the story of a self that changes constantly, that is unstable, decentered, and discontinuous, is a parody both of the traditionally filmic subject of realist cinema and also of the modernist searching for integration and wholeness of personality" (109). What Hutcheon says about "realist cinema" can easily be extended to the "realist novel," and her comments about Zelig as embodiment of the postmodern "subject" seem to apply directly to Johnson's narrator as well. Indeed, Johnson's alternative title for his novel was *The Chameleon*.[3]

This lack of stable identity is underscored by the protagonist remaining unnamed through the novel. Although we cannot simply dismiss the claims that the narrator's lack of a name is evidence of his failure to be a complete person, we can see namelessness as the narrator's attempt to avoid being labeled in any way that might restrict his ability to establish himself as an individual apart from socially defined categorizations. Throughout the book, we see a man arrogantly self-confident and individualistic to the point of blinding vanity regarding his personal accomplishment. Whatever job he takes, from rolling cigars in a factory to playing piano to speculating on real estate, the narrator claims to have become the "best" at the activity, envied by all around him. One of his childhood responses to being told he cannot be white is to assert his "self" and insist he can be. Hence, his passing is more than simply a material success. It is an assertion of his particular and personalized quest to overcome the barriers society has placed before him.

Nonetheless, the price he pays in missed opportunity for success is enormous, and when he wistfully admits that he is an ordinary white man who might have taken part in "work so glorious . . . as the making of history and a race" (Johnson 1965, 511), we can understand his failure. Yet, to do so completely is again to accept the dichotomy between black and white that the narrator's personality will not allow him to accept. Nor will society allow him to change. The birthright he traded is the same one John Walden abandons in Charles Chestnutt's passing novel, *The House behind the Cedars*. To John's childhood pleas that he is white, Judge Straight replies, "You are black . . . and you are not free. You cannot secure accommodations at an inn; you cannot be out after nine o'clock without a permit. If a white man struck you, you could not return the blow, and you could not testify against him in a court of law" (Chestnutt 1968, 168). Judge Straight goes on to describe the Dred Scott decision at some length, saying it concludes "that negroes are beings of an inferior order, and altogether unfit to associate with the white race either in social or political relations and have no rights a white man is bound to respect" (Chestnutt 1968, 169). This becomes eminently clear to Johnson's narrator when he witnesses a lynching, which makes him feel ashamed "that I belonged to a race which could be dealt with so" (Johnson 1965, 497) and spurs him to his life as an ex-colored man. The contradictions between this and the "glorious race" in which he could be a leader are simply unresolvable. Identity for the narrator demands a sort of external validation (a validation that is an act of hierarchical ordering), which is unavailable to him as a colored man in the United States. Benjamin Lawson asserts that the narrator "defines himself by loss . . . what he has chosen no longer to be" (Lawson 1989, 95). I would agree with Lawson, except for his choice of the word "chosen." This narrator cannot choose to be colored anymore than he has truly chosen to be white. He is neither; he is both. The tragedy is that society has chosen arbitrary categorizations, constructed a metanarrative of race that cannot be applied adequately to the personal narratives of its individual members.

The only nonhistorical character in the novel given a name (apart from nicknames and performers who have stage names) is the narrator's white patron's valet, Walter. This patron takes the ex-colored man to Europe, saying, "I'm going to Europe tomorrow . . . I think I'll take you along instead of Walter." In a book in which naming is so important, this one individual with a name seems incongruous. That, I would argue, is Johnson's point—the ex-colored man can never overcome the incongruity between "naming" and "identity." He passes as various things, but the passing itself becomes his story since he lacks any stable identity against which we can understand his masquerades. Walter has a name but can have his life completely disrupted, overturned without a second thought. Walter's is the untold story within *The Autobiography of an Ex-Colored Man*, he whose life the narrator appropriates. The irony here is again suspensive: since we know nothing of Walter to say why he gets a name, we can make no conclusions about the appropriateness of his being named. Rather, his life is a blank within the text, the space through which postmodern irony means. As Wilde argues: "Chary of comprehensive solutions, doubtful of the self's integrity, it [postmodern irony] confronts a world more chaotic (if chaos admits of gradations) than any imagined by its predecessors" (Wilde 1980, 7). As one of its predecessors, the world of the passer may in fact be as chaotic, as resistant to stability as this present-day postmodern world Wilde describes.

My appropriation of Johnson's novel is not an attempt to use it as a guide for making sense of our own age, but rather an attempt to show parallels between the structures of alienation of our own generation and those expressed in Johnson's novel, as a way to develop more fully our understanding of the novel. The novel shows us that the too-easy categorizations of reliable/unreliable, fictional/historical, personal identity/social role, and black/white are narratives telling incomplete and, in the narrator's case, uncompletable stories. His ironic stance derives from the fact that, as Maurice O'Sullivan observes, "he is a rebel violating the most sacred taboos of his time but a rebel who sees himself more as a confidence man than revolutionary" (O'Sullivan 1979, 62). He sees his life as a kind of "practical joke on society" (Johnson 1965, 393), and, at the end, he has discovered the most suitable identity for himself given his circumstances. Yet with his freedom from societal metanarratives of race comes the chaos of a disordered universe, which is also central to postmodern theory.[4] As I suggested earlier, the narrator seeks to write his life so as to bring some sort of modernist order and closure to his existence, but the text he seeks so desperately to control betrays the failures of such strategies to tell the story of the passer. Mackethan observes that "the effect of his attempt to keep very close control over his memory and its materials is to draw attention to his self-consciousness as a storyteller and more importantly, to his discomfort concerning the story" (Mackethan 1988, 140).

Narrating his "autobiography" is only the final step through which the ex-colored man "textualizes his life." The role literature and other antecedent texts play in the narrator's life also can be understood through postmodern theory. Hutcheon divides postmodern irony into two categories:

> What postmodernism also seems to signal is irony—irony in two senses: in a formal sense, that is, as ironic intertextuality or more simply parody; and in a more ideological sense, in which the postmodern speaks with a forked tongue, using and abusing, inscribing and subverting at the same time the cultural dominants within which it inevitably works. (Hutcheon 1988a, 63)

We have seen that second sense of irony in relation to the narrator's shifting identity, but *The Autobiography of an Ex-Colored Man* also uses intertexts in a complex and typically postmodern way.

As several critics have observed, the novel, in both form and content, owes much to the slave narrative tradition. Certainly, the use of the word "autobiography" in the title is a device to lend the book some sort of credibility not generally accorded to fiction. Further, like the slave narrative, the novel emphasizes the struggles of the protagonist to assert dignity in the face of oppression and thus to show the brutality of the oppressors. To this end Johnson at times employs the technique of slave narrative where "the more brutal the facts, often the more emotionless the relation of them" (Mackethan 1988, 127). The very narrative voice certainly owes more to the slave narrative than to any other African-American literary tradition. Eugene Levy even maintains that "Johnson was the first black writer to use the first-person narrator in fiction" (Levy 1973, 130). The book tells the tale of a free man aggressively asserting his individuality, yet trapped within a social system that denies him the rights of an individual. By structuring the story in a manner similar to the slave narrative, Johnson is able to demonstrate that the early twentieth century is not so very far removed from the early nineteenth century in terms of the opportunities accorded to African Americans.

Yet the novel does not really follow the primary structural pattern of the traditional slave narrative—the movement from servitude to freedom. In her study of *The Autobiography of an Ex-Colored Man* and Richard Wright's *Black Boy*, Mackethan refers to Johnson's book as an "inversion of the Slave Narrator's quest for voice" (Mackethan 1988, 123) and draws an important distinction between fiction and autobiographical narrative:

> While the strategy of slave narrators like Douglass and of autobiographical
> writers like Wright provide a "double 'I,'" as Olney calls it, a black fiction
> writer could create a "triple 'I'" . . . What this third voice could add most potently
> would be the effects of irony and independent vision. (125)

Mackethan goes on to argue that the novelist can assert a certain "mastery" of
the text through this voice and gives the example of *Invisible Man* before pro-
ceeding to her discussion of *The Autobiography of an Ex-Colored Man*. As important and compelling as her central arguments are, I think terms such as
"mastery" and "control," even "author," may be misplaced in relation to Johnson's text. Ellison does seem to gain the clear ironic perspective that Mackethan
refers to through his construction of the "Invisible Man" persona. The ex-
colored man, on the other hand, can only be understood through his simultane-
ous visibility and invisibility. He does not live underground; he lives next door.
He does not wage war with the Monopolated Light and Power Company; he
probably owns shares in it. To accept that he is only an African American who
has "sold out" is perhaps to deny one of the book's central purposes: to show
"the unreality and arbitrariness of race in America" (Lawson 1989, 94). The
narrator is an outsider to both white and black institutions precisely because he
has the skill to fit so easily into both. The book gives an inversion of the slave
narrative, but the inversion too is an arbitrary stance that cannot be consistently
maintained by either Johnson or his narrator.

   Mackethan suggests that Johnson himself can be found in the text in the
character of Singing Johnson, the blind preacher, to whom the narrator listens
toward the end of the novel.[5] She suggests that "surely James Weldon Johnson,
who wrote a very enlightening work entitled *The Book of American Negro
Spirituals*, is presenting his own mission through the ideal that he represents in
the figure of 'Singing Johnson'" (Mackethan 1988, 146). Singing Johnson is
presented in a much less ambiguous way than the narrator, and again Johnson
plays with antecedent literature by creating a traditional revival scene. However,
Levy points out that "in other works Black preachers are treated with contempt,
amusement, or condescension," whereas Johnson "deliberately tries to offset
this caricature" (Levy 1973, 138). Undoubtedly, Mackethan is correct in seeing
the insightful preacher as "the antithesis of the [spiritually] blind ex-colored
man" (Mackethan 1988, 146), but this does not lead to the conclusion that he
should serve as a role model for the narrator. The narrator can no more embrace
the values of Singing Johnson than the preacher can become a real estate
speculator. Rather, the intertextual allusions to preaching, rag-time songs, and
other aspects of black culture underscore the suspensive irony for both narrator
and reader. The narrator finds himself incapable of finding personal validation

as either a colored man or a white man. Yet he can be a "success" while living in any community. Johnson can then both question racial designations and simultaneously praise black accomplishments. The narrator's tragedy is not that he does not live up to the standard of Singing Johnson, whose own ability to keep the voice of his forefathers alive does resemble the abandoned project of the narrator, but that the narrator is only able to understand and accept his life when he stands apart from it and looks at it as a detached observer. When he describes his experience at the beginning of the revival meeting, he consistently characterizes the participants as "interesting" and "impressive" but stops short of allowing them to be "inspiring."[6]

This detachment leads the narrator to feel sometimes "that I have never really been a Negro, that I have been only a privileged spectator of their inner life" (Johnson 1965, 510). Positioning himself as a privileged spectator leads him to understand his own experiences as one would a story or a play, or, more specifically in the case of the narrator, a romance adventure. In his romantic conception of his life he can play the role of great hero that the racist American society denies him. His struggles to become a "success," and, more importantly, his descriptions of those struggles, belong more to the hero of a sentimental novel than to a slave narrative. For all its gestures toward realism, the book seems structured on the more refined fiction of the late nineteenth century. Robert Fleming suggests that "the narrator views himself in romantic terms, as a tragic hero whose flaw is the black blood he has inherited from his beloved mother" (Fleming 1971, 87). The political consequences of this are noted by Ross, who observes that even the narrator's excesses "are those associated with the correct sentiments of genteel fiction" (Ross 1974, 202). But eventually the narrator is "betrayed by a white, upper-class value system he cannot escape" (Ross 1974, 199). The "values" that the narrator learns through romantic fiction do not translate well to the narrator's life because his society does not value him for following the same path as the fictional heroes. Ross concludes that although we cannot ignore the weakness of the narrator, "we must be equally careful not to pile on his head the condemnation that Johnson rightly reserves for the psychological power of American whiteness" (Ross 1974, 210). Although Ross shows that power is transmitted through cultural productions and provides excellent analysis of how Johnson manipulates the text, he does not apply his argument fully to the narrator himself as "writing subject" within the text. Once again returning to the title of the work, by beginning as an "ex-colored man" the narrator acknowledges the distinction between himself and a "white man." Yet part of his motivation seems, as Ross discusses, to tell a "life story" that any white man, with simply a few details concerning race changed, could be proud to relate as his own. The associations with both slave narrative and genteel fiction serve to indicate the duality within the narrator, that in his own mind he has never passed because he utterly refuses to accept the false dichotomy that would categorize him.

This can be seen clearly when the narrator is compared with other passing characters such as those I have mentioned earlier—Chestnutt's John Warwick or Larsen's Clare Kendry. These characters fear exposure to such a degree that they are unable to distance themselves from the very racial distinctions they transgress. They accept that although society is wrong in its racist attitudes, they nonetheless are "blacks pretending to be white." The tragedy in both novels, and many other passing stories, is exposure. The tragedy of the ex-colored man is the impossibility of exposure. Even the act of publishing a biography really does nothing to jeopardize the world he has built for himself because the story he narrates is largely a romanticized version of his past and an elaborate justification of his present. The generic intertexts do not serve to provide this story a stable meaning, Rather, the book refuses to be simply slave narrative, aristocratic fiction, autobiography, or even passing novel. This complex intertextuality, which underscores the shifting identity of the narrator, does not keep the novel from expressing clear messages concerning race and passing but insists that part of that message, and certainly the irony, in *The Autobiography of an Ex-Colored Man* must remain suspensive, irresolvable.

Notes

1. In this paper I have quoted directly only from Wilde's essay, "Irony in the Postmodern Age," but my understanding of his argument is significantly informed by his book *Horizons of Assent: Modernism, Postmodernism, and the Ironic Imagination* (Johns Hopkins University Press, 1981), which also contains a slightly altered version of the *Boundary 2* article.

2. In Nella Larsen's novel *Passing*, the two principle characters are Clare Kendry, who has "crossed the color line," and Irene Redfield, who passes occasionally for convenience. The distinctions between the two characters clearly illustrate that no easy definition of the passer can exist.

3. In Johnson's autobiography, *Along This Way*, he speaks of the indecision he felt regarding the title of the book and whether to attach his name to the work. He writes, "I stuck to the original idea of issuing the book without the author's name and kept the title that had appealed to me first. But I have never been able to settle definitely for myself whether I was sagacious or not in these two decisions" (Johnson 1933, 238). Certainly publishing the book anonymously had the advantage of letting its circulation reflect the thematic message that easy categorizations are inappropriate to the world of the passer. The book was reviewed as fiction, autobiography, and even mystery story, with the reviewer seeking to "solve" the riddle of its authorship.

4. In some ways, by refusing to accept any restrictive identities, the narrator at the end of the novel becomes like that most famous of postmodern heroes, Pynchon's disintegrating Slothrop of *Gravity's Rainbow*.

5. Lawson, too, focuses on where Johnson might be giving us a more positive example to counteract the protagonist abandoning his dream. He suggests that Johnson's book of poems based on African-American preaching, *God's Trombones,* is Johnson's "acting out of the suppressed artistic instincts of the ex-colored man" (Lawson 1989, 97).

6. An important point related to the narrator's refusal to be inspired can be seen in his own reactions to literary texts. The novel contains within it much sociological comment and literary exegesis, interpretations of texts such as *Uncle Tom's Cabin* and *The Souls of Black Folks.* Lawson suggests that "the digressive polemics on race strike us as Johnson's" (Lawson 1989, 93), such as when the narrator deems that *Uncle Tom's Cabin* is a "fair and truthful panorama of slavery" (1989, 93). Rather than attributing such comments to Johnson, it may be better to accept that many people, black and white, feel a vested interest in accepting the narratives on those terms. Certainly the narrator does. What these "digressions" also evidence is that the narrator is much more comfortable finding his "truths" mediated through books, rather than the confusing and chaotic "truths" of his own experience. Ultimately, Johnson's novel demonstrates that "fair and truthful panoramas" such as *Uncle Tom's Cabin* or *The Autobiography of an Ex-Colored Man* or any postmodern novel must also be understood in terms of the "truths" they do not express.

Works Cited

Blockson, Charles L. 1977. *Black Genealogy.* Englewood Cliffs: Prentice-Hall.

Chestnutt, Charles. 1968. *The House Behind the Cedars.* Ridgewood: Grange.

Evans, Maurice S. 1915. *Black and White in the Southern United States.* New York: Longmans, Green.

Fleming, Robert E. 1971. "Irony as Key to Johnson's *The Autobiography of an Ex-Colored Man.*" *American Literature* 43: 83-96.

Hutcheon, Linda. 1988a. "Complicity and Critique: The Canadian Postmodern." In *Essays in Canadian Irony*, ed. Linda Hutcheon. Toronto: Robarts Centre for Canadian Studies Working Paper Series 88-F02.

_____. *A Poetics of Postmodernism.* 1988b. New York: Routledge.

_____. *The Politics of Postmodernism.* 1989. New York: Routledge.

Johnson, James Weldon. 1933. *Along This Way.* New York: Viking.

_____. 1965. *The Autobiography of an Ex-Colored Man. Three Negro Classics.* New York: Avon.

Larsen, Nella. 1993. *Passing.* Salem: Ayer.

Lawson, Benjamin Sherwood. 1989. "Odysseus's Revenge: The Names on the Title Page of *The Autobiography of an Ex-Colored Man.*" *Southern Literary Journal* 21: 92-99.

Levy, Eugene. 1973. *James Weldon Johnson: Black Leader/Black Voice.* Chicago: University of Chicago Press.

Mackethan, Lucinda. 1988. *"Black Boy* and *Ex-Colored Man*: Version and Inversion of the Slave Narrator's Quest for Voice." *College Language Association Journal* 32: 123-47.

O'Sullivan, Maurice. 1979. "Of Souls and Pottage: James Weldon Johnson's *The Auto-*

biography of an Ex-Colored Man." *College Language Association Journal* 23: 60-70.

Pisiak, Roxanna. 1993. "Irony and Subversion in James Weldon Johnson's *The Autobiography of an Ex-Colored Man.*" *Studies in American Fiction* 21: 83-96.

Pynchon, Thomas. 1965. *The Crying of Lot 49.* New York: Harper and Row.

Ross, Stephen M. 1974. "Audience and Irony in Johnson's *The Autobiography of an Ex-Colored Man.*" *College Language Association Journal* 18: 198-210.

Wilde, Alan. 1980. "Irony in the Postmodern Age: Toward a Map of Suspensiveness." *Boundary* 2.9: 5-46.

5

The Veils of the Law: Race and Sexuality in Nella Larsen's *Passing*

Corinne E. Blackmer

When Nella Larsen, then a prominent young writer of the Harlem Renaissance, published her second and final novel, *Passing,* in 1929, the Supreme Court's "separate but equal" interpretation of the equal protection clause of the Fourteenth Amendment in *Plessy v. Ferguson* (1896) had been law for over thirty years. *Plessy* turned on the issue of the constitutionality of so-called Jim Crow laws, which mandated racially-segregated facilities for whites and "coloreds" throughout the South. Homer Plessy, a resident of Louisiana who described himself as "seven-eighths Caucasian and one-eighth African blood" (*Plessy* 1896, 1138), was forcibly ejected, after he refused to leave voluntarily, from the first-class, whites-only section of a railroad car in his home state. Declaring that "the mixture of colored blood was not discernible in him, and that he was entitled to every recognition, right, privilege, and immunity secured to the citizens of the United States of the white race," Plessy argued that the Louisiana law violated his constitutional rights of habeas corpus, equal protection, and due process. The Supreme Court denied the validity of this reasoning on several counts, among them that various state laws forbade interracial marriage on the grounds, as the state of Virginia later argued unsuccessfully before the Court in *Loving v. Virginia* (1967), that "Almighty God created the races white, black, yellow, malay and red, and he placed them on separate continents. . . . The fact that he separated the races shows that he did not intend for the races to mix."[1] Second, in an egregious instance of conceptual blurring of categories of persons that implied, without submitting the proposition to local scrutiny, that white males were intrinsically more "adult" and "able" than nonwhites or women, the Court argued that most states had established "segregated" schools "for children of different ages, sexes and colors, and . . . for poor and neglected children" (*Plessy* 1141).[2] The Court avoided responsibility for promoting institutional racism and established the constitutionality of de jure segregation by stating that "the assumption that the enforced separation of the two races stamps the colored race with a badge of inferiority . . . is not by reason of anything found in the act, but solely because the colored race chooses to put the construction upon it" (1143). It made an invidious distinction between the cultural and political rights of whites and "coloreds" on the basis of the intrinsic "reasonableness" of long-established cultural practices.[3] Writing for a majority of seven, Justice Henry Brown allowed that while the "officers" empowered to judge racial identity by outward appearances might conceivably err in their judgment, the "object of the [Fourteenth] amendment was undoubtedly to enforce the absolute equality of the two races before the law, but in the nature of things it could not have been intended to abolish distinctions based upon color, or to enforce social, as distinguished from political, equality, or a commingling of the two races upon terms unsatisfactory to either" (1140).[4]

In the fifty-eight years between *Plessy* and the Court's landmark decision in *Brown v. Board of Education of Topeka, Kansas* (1954), which declared separate public facilities based on race "inherently unequal," many African-American authors pursued an actively critical engagement with the convoluted and contradictory terms of racial identity and identification set forth in *Plessy*. On the one hand, African-American letters faced the onerous burden of proving the cultural worth of black culture to an often doubting, condescending, and largely white audience. On the other hand, the legal decision and the Social Darwinism underlying it provided an unwelcome opportunity to thematize the willful ignorance and blindness informing racial segregation by exploring how racial stigmas were not founded in the "natural" superiority or inferiority of the races but rather constructed through historical prejudices and arbitrary (often illusory) social distinctions. Moreover, since *Plessy* not only denied the long if publicly unacknowledged history of interracial sexual unions (which had produced, among others, Homer Plessy as subject) but also strengthened existing miscegenation statutes by forbidding the social commingling of the races, narrative treatments of interracial sexual unions featuring characters who "passed" racially became an ideal vehicle through which to explore the inevitable intersection of racism (and, in some cases, sexism) with sexual taboos.

Seen in the light of the legal and cultural assumptions informing its production, Larsen's *Passing*, the curious plot of which has thus far eluded satisfactory analysis, becomes a searching exploration and critique of the aesthetic, narrative, and ideological incoherences that confronted Larsen as an urbane African-American woman author who eschewed racial separatism and nineteenth-century "racial uplift" rhetoric—which might in part explain why she abandoned her promising literary career after writing this novel.[5] Indeed, *Passing*, a relatively late example of this topos of American writing, represents both an original reconfiguration of and a commentary on more conventional plots of racial passing, which typically center on a psychologically and culturally divided "tragic mulatto" figure, in such novels as James Weldon Johnson's *The Autobiography of an Ex-Colored Man* and Jessie Fauset's *Plum Bun*, among others. While these novels offer trenchant critiques of institutional racism, they also emphasize the heavy personal costs of crossing over the "color line," and thus in some measure reinforce the consequences of racial division in an equally separatist "national" literature. *Passing*, in contrast, stresses the interpretive anxieties and sexual paranoias that make convention-bound people reluctant to allow others the freedom to travel freely throughout the many worlds, identities, and sexualities of American society. Larsen's novel not only explores a legally fraudulent *interracial* union in the marriage between Clare Kendry and John Bellew, but also subtly delineates the *intraracial* sexual attraction of Irene Redfield for Clare, while the former projects her taboo desires for Clare onto her husband Brian. Ironically, Brian Redfield, who the text implies might be homosexual, evinces no sexual interest in women, but Irene nonetheless begins to suspect that Brian and Clare are conducting an illicit, clandestine affair. Since the term "passing" carries the connotation of being accepted for something one is not, the title of the novel serves as a metaphor for a wide range of deceptive appearances and practices that encompass sexual as well as racial passing. Focused principally on the operation of chance and accident as well as on the epistemological crises of unknowability that result from self-silencing and self-repression, Larsen's novel ostensibly "passes" for a conventional narrative of racial passing.

The story is narrated from the point of view of Irene Redfield, a light-skinned, middle-class African-American woman who disdains passing and is married to a successful doctor, too dark to pass, by whom she has had two sons. Irene, although self-consciously proud of her African racial heritage, has internalized the separate but equal dictum of *Plessy* as well as the ideology of bourgeois morality, both of which lead to a notable prudishness on her part and an obsessive attention to seemingly miniscule distinctions of caste and class. The well-regulated surface of her existence is shattered, however, by the unexpected arrival of Clare Kendry, a light-skinned African-American woman from Irene's long-forgotten childhood past who has, through a combination of personal adventurousness and familial mishaps, ended up marrying John Bellew, a prosperous white businessman who knows nothing of her racial identity and by whom she has had a daughter. Hence, these once intimate childhood friends are simultaneously separated and tethered together, so to speak, by the divergent strategies they have adopted as adults to cope with their racial identities and their options to pass racially. The fact that they are, like Homer Plessy but unlike the vast majority of their fellow African Americans, sufficiently light-skinned to pass marks them out as relatively privileged and distinctive individuals, ideally situated to both embody and expose the Janus-like duplicity of social arrangements that divide the races according to "discernible" outward appearances and, hence, "inner nature."

Larsen connects the arbitrarily segregated lives of these two married women by having them meet accidentally in the rooftop restaurant of a Chicago hotel, where they are not in company with their husbands, and where Irene, in this instance, has resorted to passing to escape a sweltering heat wave. Clare's chance meeting with her long-lost childhood friend instigates a potent desire in her, described in an effusive letter intertwining romantic and racial longings for Irene, to escape the isolated life of deception and secretiveness forced on her by passing:

> For I am lonely, so lonely . . . cannot help longing to be with you again, as I have never longed for anything before; and I have wanted many things in my life. . . . You can't know how in this pale life of mine I am all the time seeing the bright pictures of that other that I once thought I was glad to be free of. . . . It's like an ache, a pain that never ceases. (Larsen 1992, 174)

These profound if, significantly, somewhat inarticulate yearnings to return to the conditions of her childhood, before she and Irene "fell" into the self-divided condition of adult women, culminate in her decision, near the end of the narrative, to abandon her husband and child and return home to Harlem. As Clare's plans to reassume her earlier identity as an unmarried African American crystallize, Irene convinces herself, with inconclusive evidence at best, that Clare actually intends to steal her husband, Brian, a discontented if wittily urbane man who expresses periodic disgust with United States racism and who cherishes a dream, actively suppressed by Irene, of emigrating with his family to Brazil. In the denouement, which again takes place on a rooftop, Clare, Irene, and Brian assemble for a party hosted by a couple ironically named the Freelanders. John Bellew, who, unbeknownst to everyone save Irene, has accidentally discovered the racial identity of his wife by running into Irene with a woman too dark to pass, bursts into the apartment. Before the scene can develop beyond Bellew's initial reaction of pained horror and outrage, Irene "accidentally" pushes Clare from the window, and she falls to her death. In the end, Clare—whose death, the text indicates, is interpreted and dismissed by the authorities as an accident or suicide—becomes a poignant symbol of the victory of de jure segregation and narrow social conformity over integration and self-creation, and thus a symbol of the eclipse of the potential of both Irene as an independent woman and the Harlem Renaissance as an artistic movement:

> Gone! The soft white face, the bright hair, the disturbing scarlet mouth, the dreaming eyes, the caressing smile, the whole torturing loveliness that had been Clare Kendry. That beauty that had torn at Irene's placid life. Gone! The mocking daring, the gallantry of her pose, the ringing bells of her laughter. (Larsen 1992, 272)

Given the unconventional nature of this plot, which conjoins Larsen's interest in the operation of contingency and accident with her use of an unreliable narrator, earlier critics have judged *Passing* an artistic failure that represents an uneasy admixture of public issues of race and racial passing with the more private ones of sexual jealousy. The gender bias of this critique is not difficult to detect, and subsequently several African-American feminist critics focused on Larsen's use of irony to critique, through the character of Irene Redfield, conventional bourgeois notions of feminine propriety and racial identity and identification (see Fuller 1971, Youman 1974, Ramsey 1976, Tate 1980, and Christian 1980). In her 1986 introduction to the reissue of Larsen's *Quicksand* and *Passing*, moreover, African-American feminist Deborah E. McDowell broke from (and, in some senses, extended) these critical interpretations in an atmosphere that, influenced most prominently by Alice Walker's *The Color Purple* and Audre Lorde's essays and poems, gave new importance to issues of lesbian sexuality in African-American literature. Treating *Passing*'s ostensible concern with racial passing as a rhetorical cover, McDowell contended that the novel's apparent inconsistencies resulted from Larsen's actual concern with exploring the taboos against lesbian desire. According to this analysis, the novel "superficially" concerns passing for white and related issues of racial loyalty, but "underneath the safety of that surface is the more dangerous story—though not named explicitly—of Irene's awakening sexual desire for Clare" (McDowell 1986, xxvi).

This interpretation elucidates many of the otherwise quixotic motives that impel the narrative and serves in part to explain Irene's highly contradictory and volatile reactions to Clare as instances of what Patricia Juliana Smith has termed "lesbian panic," which finally impels Irene to destroy her friend in order to prevent disclosure, perhaps even to herself, of her taboo sexual desires.[6] Nevertheless, McDowell's analysis, which in effect *substitutes* sexual for racial passing, both dehistoricizes and somewhat mischaracterizes the text, in which lesbian desire becomes an aftereffect, or, perhaps more accurately, an inevitable corollary of racial panic and the *sexualization* of socially taboo racial contacts in an environment governed by the legal and cultural presumptions of *Plessy*. In a narrative centered on the emotionally charged relations between two light-skinned African-American women, both of whom hold the secret of Clare's racial identity as an intimate and potentially explosive bond between them, their friendship also becomes fraught with secret sexual fantasies as the mysterious and alluring Clare becomes for Irene both an exotic object and a projection of her profound dread of and taboo desires for sexual pleasure, worldly experience, independence from men, and escape from the narrow conventions of the marriage plot. Clare's legally proscribed liberation from the constraints of racial identity configured through marriage implies, for Irene, the equally terrifying possibility of liberation from those of "feminine" and heterosexual propriety as well. Irene may be intensely curious about—and, indeed, both desirous and envious of—the capacity of an "exotic" person like Clare to resist or evade the forces of domination, but her fear of freedom eventually impels her to act much like a Social Darwinist, and thus to force this representative of sexual and racial exoticism to lose the battle for survival.

Although Larsen, in 1929, uses the term "passing" to connote *both* racial and sexuality masquerading, the recent shift in criticism from issues of racial to sexual passing can itself be historicized, for passing now refers almost exclusively to the self-protective disguise of identity practiced by lesbians and gays in a society presumed and enjoined to be universally heterosexual. Moreover, homosexuals continue to occupy both in law and culture an analogous if not parallel position to that held by the minority of African Americans under *Plessy* who were sufficiently light-skinned to pass for white and thus to hide their "innate" inferiority. The differences are significant inasmuch as the vast majority of African Americans under *Plessy* could not (or chose not to) pass for white, whereas the vast majority of lesbians and gays do pass for, and are assumed to be (unless declared otherwise), heterosexual. The similarities between the groups are equally compelling, however, inasmuch as when Larsen wrote *Passing*, blackness and homosexuality were both held to be stigmas that disqualified the bearers of these labels from freedom from undue social burdens and equal protection under the Constitution. For Irene Redfield and Clare Kendry, the social deployment of the hidden knowledge of racial identities (and homosexual desires) in contexts presumed to be universally white (and heterosexual) takes a form uncannily similar to what Richard D. Mohr calls "The Secret," or that informal community contract of complicity and deception that characterizes the epistemological regime of the majority of lesbian and gay lives (Mohr 1992a, 30).[7] That Larsen inextricably intertwines both forms of secrets, like both forms of passing, indicates her interest in stressing the interrelationship of racial identification and homoerotic desire. That tragedy ensues in *Passing* once Irene Redfield misinterprets her own attraction for Clare

Kendry, however, also clarifies the complex cultural and historical precedents of recent Supreme Court decisions that, deploying the hatred of homosexuals as an "invisible" fulcrum, have developed a mode of historically based legal reasoning that threatens to erode relatively recent extensions of constitutional protections to both women and racial minorities.

Since the late 1930s, the Supreme Court has identified several considerations for determining which governmental classifications require "heightened scrutiny" under its three-tier equal protection analysis of the Fourteenth Amendment: (1) whether the discrimination is unjustifiable or invidious; that is, based on an obvious, immutable, or distinguishing trait that frequently bears no relation to the ability to contribute to society; (2) whether the class historically has suffered from purposeful discrimination; and (3) whether the class lacks the political power necessary to obtain protection from the political branches of government. But most courts have ignored purposeful historical discrimination and lack of political power and have simply concluded, without supporting authority, that heightened scrutiny is inapplicable in cases involving lesbians and gays, because homosexuality is not an "immutable characteristic."[8] The very mode of framing this debate as one of a voluntary decision between heterosexual (i.e., "moral") behavior on the one hand and homosexual (i.e., "immoral") behavior on the other is itself deeply homophobic, as it assigns arbitrary values to the intrinsically neutral category of sexual orientation. This debate has, moreover, encouraged some scientific researchers to ascertain a biological basis for homosexual identity to meet the legal criterion for equal protection.[9] By framing the issue in biological terms that implicitly regard homosexuality as a "crime against nature" and reducing the cultural dimensions of homosexual identity to criminal "acts," the courts have thus far evaded a broader ethical debate concerning the right to privacy, which "embodies the moral fact that a person belongs to himself and not others nor to society as a whole."[10] Therefore, the present laws of the United States give force to societal homophobia by defining lesbians and gays, as they once defined African Americans and women, as objects of contempt and lesser mortals who have a fundamentally different (and inferior) "nature" from other human beings, and thus do not deserve equal protection under the law.

The fact that the law offers no protection for sexual orientation has forced most homosexuals to adopt costly and self-damaging strategies of secrecy and self-disguise, just as, before the Court's adoption of "heightened scrutiny" of racial classifications, Clare Kendry passes racially and adopts similarly destructive deceptions to elude recognition by American society. The peculiarly exposed condition of homosexuals has also obscured the fact that whereas race, gender, alienage, and illegitimacy can, like sexual orientation, be changed or concealed, these former conditions have, in recent times, been defined as "immutable characteristics" and thus compel heightened scrutiny by the courts.

For these reasons, Kurt D. Hermansen has recently argued that "immutable characteristic" not be treated as a presumably biological category defined through history, culture, and politics, but rather in reference to a particularly reprehensible form of discrimination inflicted on minorities qua minorities:

> While one might be able to alter or conceal traits such as race, gender or sexual orientation, that change can only occur at a prohibitive cost to the average individual. The court only looks to the immutable traits, which are central, defining traits of personhood, which one may alter only at the expense of significant damage to one's identity. In this context, sexual orientation fulfills the requirement that the identifying trait be immutable. (Hermansen 1992, 174)

Nevertheless, even if the courts refuse to grant sexual orientation the status of an "immutable characteristic," they must make the more important decision as to whether the perpetuation of social stigmas against homosexuals constitutes a legitimate state interest. In *Palmore v. Sidoti* (1984), for example, the Supreme Court held that a white father could not sue for custody of the child he had had with his divorced wife, a white woman who had remarried an African American man, on ground that social recrimination against a mixed-race marriage would inevitably damage the child. In this case, the Supreme Court ignored the high-tier equal protection analytic it had set out for itself, because that analytic, which holds that promoting the welfare of children constitutes a compelling state interest, would have resulted in giving custody of the child to the father. Making no explicit reference to race, the Court held that while social prejudices may be outside the reach of the law, "the law cannot, directly or indirectly, give them effect." The principle in *Palmore*, if neutrally considered, holds that the perpetuation of stigmas does not constitute an acceptable means by which the state can carry out its interests. Hence, in *City of Cleburne v. Cleburne Living Center* (1985), the Court, quoting *Palmore*, struck down zoning laws that gave effect to fears and biases over having a group home for the mentally challenged nearby, even though the Court refused to broaden its equal protection analytic by holding that discriminations against the mentally challenged were "suspect" or "quasi-suspect."[11]

One year later, however, in *Bowers v. Hardwick* (1986), the Supreme Court not only refused to see but also pointedly denied the relevance of *Palmore* or *Cleburne* for gays and lesbians and upheld the constitutionality of a Georgia sodomy law on the grounds that "sodomy was a criminal offense at common law and was forbidden by the laws of the original thirteen States when they ratified the Bill of Rights," and that the law expressed a legitimate state purpose in that it promoted "morality," which the Court defined simply as "majority sentiments about . . . morality." The second dissenting opinion, written by Justice

John Paul Stevens and joined by Justices William J. Brennan and Thurgood Marshall, pointed out not only that the original sodomy statutes had applied neutrally both to heterosexuals and homosexuals, and married and unmarried persons, but also that "at one point in the 20th century, Georgia's law was construed to permit certain sexual conduct between homosexual women even though such conduct was prohibited between heterosexuals" (Bowers 1989, 2857).[12] Since the Court had previously established that a state may not prohibit sodomy (here defined as anal intercourse or cunnilingus) between married couples in *Griswold v. State of Connecticut* 381 U.S. 479 (1965) or between unmarried heterosexual couples in *Eisenstadt v. Baird* 405 U.S. 436 (1972) the Court had to establish why the selective enforcement of the statute against the class of homosexual persons constituted a compelling state interest. By disdaining to advance an adequate rational basis for this selective enforcement, the dissent strongly implied that the *Bowers* majority had, ironically, transformed homosexuals into a "suspect class." Moreover, Justice Harry Blackmun, as if to underscore the majority's unprincipled departure from presumably settled legal precedents, noted in his dissenting opinion the "almost uncanny" parallels between *Bowers* and *Loving v. Virginia* (1967), in which the petitioners employed biblical doctrine (as well as majority opinions regarding morality) to show that "traditional Judeo-Christian values" proscribed interracial marriage.[13]

By employing arguments from biblical morality and social custom to deprive lesbians and gays of equal protection, the *Bowers* decision also places women and African Americans in greater jeopardy, as the rights of both these groups are guaranteed, as *Passing* amply illustrates, by relatively recent extensions of constitutional law rather than long-standing tradition. Indeed, Richard D. Mohr has argued persuasively that *Bowers* stood behind the Court's subsequent decision in *City of Richmond v. J. A. Croson* Co. 488 U.S. 469 (1989), which crippled municipal and state affirmative action programs by establishing the fundamental rights of white people, much as *Bowers* upheld the fundamental rights of heterosexuals (or, more accurately, the ill-defined class of nonsodomites). In *City of Richmond*, Mohr notes, the Court held that state and municipal minority set-aside programs are unconstitutional under the equal protection clause because racial classifications made with respect to whites are as "suspect" as those made with respect to blacks:

> If, as per Bowers, it is those actions that are by tradition socially averred that are the actions that are performed by right, then it is the people whose privileges are by tradition socially averred who have those privileges as a matter of right. It is the history and tradition of white privilege that converts the privileges into white rights. Thus, the style of reasoning specifically developed to deny rights to lesbians and gay men is now used to restrict legal

protections afforded to other minorities and to enhance majority privilege. (Mohr 1992, 72-73)

The peculiarly insidious manner in which social prejudice against lesbians and gays is employed to undermine the basis of civil rights protections, perhaps most notably for African-American women, is exhaustively illustrated in *Passing*, where Irene Redfield's sexual and racial panic transforms her into the unwitting instrument and reinforcer of social prejudices and legal prohibitions designed to keep women and African Americans in place. Charles R. Larson has recently used biographical evidence to suggest that Larsen's marital difficulties with her husband, Elmer Imes, a professor of physics at Fisk University who subsequently became romantically involved with a white woman, are reflected in the plot of *Passing*, where Irene suspects her husband of infidelities with Clare and, like the latter, becomes a woman with unspeakable "secrets" after she destroys her rival. While Larson describes with great insight the mind of an intensely suspicious, rather cloistered woman who does not fully understand the story in which she becomes implicated as the central narrative consciousness, this critic's "heterosexualization" of the narrative not only ignores the fact that Larsen's marital difficulties and divorce occurred after the publication of *Passing*, but also reprises the humiliating public scandal that Larsen subsequently endured in 1932, when the *Baltimore Afro-American* conflated Larsen with her fictional character Clare Kendry and suggested that the former "jumped" from the window in the wake of her discovery of her husband's affair with a white woman.[14]

Passing is not fictionalized autobiography so much as it is acute social observation of her artistic peer community, for Larsen fashioned herself as a writer in the context of the Harlem Renaissance, most of whose major figures were both racial and sexual minorities.[15] In addition, Larsen dedicated *Passing* to her literary sponsors, Carl Van Vechten and Fania Marinoff, the white patrons and promoters of the Harlem Renaissance. Since Van Vechten actively sponsored lesbian and gay modernist writers such as Gertrude Stein and Ronald Firbank in addition to African American authors such as Larsen (whose novels he helped get published by Alfred Knopf), her imbrication of the issues of racial and sexual "passing" can be seen as both an appeal to her potential audience and literary colleagues and an informed critique of socially conservative African Americans like Irene Redfield, whose understandable desire to gain marginal acceptance and security in American society under *Plessy* compels her to imitate the prejudices of the dominant society. Unfortunately and tragically, Irene reinforces her identity as an American by destroying an African-American woman much like herself in outward *appearance* and thus diminishes, through ignorance, perceived necessity, and limited moral agency, the value and meaning of her own selfhood.

Given the secrecy and duplicity enjoined upon Clare and the self-deception unwittingly practiced by Irene, neither woman can, in any sense, be considered a morally exemplary or self-consistent character. Within these intractable limitations, however, Larsen explores the crucial distinctions between Clare's highly self-conscious rhetorical deployments of the fictions of race and Irene's unself-conscious internalization of the dictum of *Plessy*. While Clare becomes adept at subverting expectations and eluding capture through selective shape shifting and camouflage, Irene has a self-divided consciousness both as an African American and a woman, for she believes she can gain security and meaning solely through marriage and ignore the larger implications of living in a racially divided and segregated society. While Irene finds Clare's refusal of her own "feminine" ideal of self-effacement, self-denial, and service to men proof of her selfish, immoral, and "catlike" disposition (Larsen 1992, 173), the example of Clare's nonconformity not only invokes her reluctant admiration but also eventually shatters her illusions of the inviolability and "sanctity" of masculine propriety and power. Moreover, Larsen makes the point about Irene's sexual attraction to (and fear of) Clare, and the defiant bid for freedom she represents, in two crucial scenes that represent an extremely detailed and, I would argue, intentional representation of the epistemological uncertainties attending both racial and sexual passing. In the first, both forms of passing are inextricably imbricated through projections of exoticism, while the second illustrates that the social predicaments faced by African Americans who pass are structurally analogous to those faced by homosexuals who pass.

The first occurs in the initial encounter between Irene and Clare, which sets the stage for the action that follows, which takes place in a rooftop tearoom of the Drayton Hotel in Chicago. Significantly, Irene is away from her home in New York City, not in company with her husband, and therefore "free" to exercise the option of passing for white to escape a heat wave. Once settled in this unfamiliar environment, Irene's attention becomes riveted on a "sweetly smelling" woman wearing a "fluttering dress of green chiffon [with] mingled pattern of narcissuses, jonquils, and hyacinths" (Larsen 1992, 176) that associates her with familiar topoi of feminine artifice and French exoticism. Her aura of illicit sexuality is heightened, moreover, by her brief appearance with a white man, neither her husband nor a mere platonic friend, whom the woman swiftly if gracefully dismisses from her company. Since this scene takes place in a hotel, an acute reader might surmise that this woman is an expensive mistress or prostitute, although the text, narrated from Irene's characteristically discreet and unobservant point of view, does not comment further. Instead, Irene openly admires the woman's dress, "her dark, almost black, eyes," her "wide mouth like a scarlet flower against the ivory of her skin," and her "odd sort of smile" (177), which Irene interprets as hovering between sexual provocation and self-assurance. Conscious, at last, that she has been staring at this woman, she is even more disconcerted when the stranger, in turn, stares back at her, like "one who with the utmost singleness of mind and purpose was determined to impress firmly and accurately each detail of Irene's features upon her memory for all time" (178).

Ironically, although Irene cannot determine what she sees when she gazes at this alluring woman, or what the woman sees when she gazes at Irene, in reality she looks at someone who very much resembles herself in outward appearance, indicating that Irene, at least when alone, does not see herself as an African American (or an exotic woman). Racial identification (and self-identification) is, Larsen hints, a matter of context and social convention. As if to underscore Irene's limited self-knowledge and fear of self-disclosure when confronted with her mirror image in another woman, she begins to question her own outer appearance and suspects this woman might unmask her racial identity, an anxiety uncannily similar to that an unconscious lesbian would experience in company with another suspected lesbian to whom she found herself unaccountably attracted. Although Irene experiences "a small inner disturbance, odious and hatefully familiar" (Larsen 1992, 178), she promptly dismisses her fears of racial disclosure, as "white people were so stupid about such things" and "always took her for an Italian, a Spaniard, a Mexican, or a Gypsy" (178). In this context, Irene's fear of racial exposure both parallels and masks her fear of sexual exposure, particularly to herself. Irene, however, automatically assumes that the woman staring at her must be white, suggesting that Irene regards this stranger as possessing an ineffable power over her, which, on the one hand, distances them, but on the other, draws them together in an ineluctable bond of mutual attraction and fascination. In this instance, then, racial invisibility camouflages all other modes of recognition, enabling Irene to deny what she sees and finds compelling about this mysterious woman.

At this point, however, the stranger approaches and, with grace and warmth, unmasks herself as Irene's long-forgotten childhood friend, Clare Kendry. Having experienced life on both sides of the color line, and thus expert at distinguishing reality from conventional appearances, Clare immediately recognizes Irene on a personal and historical rather than an abstract or "exotic" level. She launches into a picaresque account of the accidents and misadventures that have befallen her since the death of her white father (which, ironically, removed her from the black community) and that have resulted in her perpetrating a legal fraud by marrying a white man who knows nothing of her racial identity. By the end of this story, Irene, whose experience has been far more limited and uniform than Clare's, and who already projects a certain taboo exoticism on her friend, longs to ask Clare how she sustains her racial masquerade, but, with her customary propriety, finds herself "unable to think of a single question that in its context or its phrasing was not too frankly curious, if not actually impertinent" (Larsen 1992, 187). In other words, the intimate details of how Clare passes for white are inappropriate questions for a "proper lady" to ask, and Irene therefore retains an essential ignorance regarding Clare that becomes increasingly fraught with danger as the narrative progresses. On the other hand, Clare's knowledge of the profundity of others' capacities for self-deception and the complexity of her own experience has obviated temptations on her part to exoticize or primitivize others. Nevertheless, the manner in which the accidents of her personal history have made her unacceptable in both the white and African-American worlds becomes illustrated in the next major scene of the novel, after Clare convinces a highly reluctant Irene to attend an afternoon tea party in her apartment.

Clare and Irene are joined by Gertrude, a childhood friend of both women who has pursued yet another social configuration of racial identification inasmuch as, like Irene, she does not pass for white, although she, like Clare, has married a white man. In this context, Irene, unaccustomed to being out of place, feels both outnumbered and defensive, while Clare, with her almost ludicrous attention to environmental disguise, has decorated her sitting room in dark browns and blues to obscure the sharp visual distinctions between white and black. This masquerade of interior decor serves to further ironize the problematics of racial identity and identification when Clare's husband arrives to "rescue" them from a stilted conversation that has devolved into embarrassing banalities and heavy silence. John, with no hint of self-consciousness, refers to his wife, whom he affectionately complains has become "darker" since their marriage, by the nickname "Nig," but then complains viciously about the "niggers" he reads about in the newspapers. Larsen reveals the limits of knowledge conveyed through language when compared with the ambiguities of perception inherent in experience, since the difference between marital love and racial animus comes down to the syllable "ger." In launching into an ignorant and bigoted attack on blacks in the company of three African-American women passing for white, this scene replicates with remarkable accuracy the social dynamics experienced by closeted lesbians and gays when in company with people who, presuming everyone to be heterosexual (or, perhaps more insidiously, shaming those suspected of being "queer" into silence), openly attack or ridicule homosexuals.

Clare, however, seemingly determined to make her friends admire her recklessness and share the intense contradictions of her day-to-day life, almost goads her husband into displaying his dangerous blindness, as if this humiliating spectacle will finally expose the speciousness of her own rationales for passing. In reality, her friends can hardly enjoy the presumed superiority of their insight into the real state of affairs, since their knowledge leaves them powerless in the face of Bellew's privileged and voluble ignorance. Therefore, this strategy places Clare and her friends in an ironic double bind, since they must modulate between secret knowledge and the social presumption of whiteness. As in the analogous case of lesbians and gays, if they defend blacks against his racist slander, they might expose themselves as the very people Bellew attacks, and thus jeopardize Clare's marriage and social masquerade. In effect, this scene reveals to the women their limited moral agency in providing them the untenable choices between silent complicity and exposure. Thus, the question of what loyalty to race, to sex, or to Clare might mean in this context is impossible to determine, since any valid description of reality depends on the articulated language of personal history and experience rather than obscure *appearances* offered visually. Yet this carefully crafted visual illusion eloquently demonstrates the limits of passing and thus dramatizes the inescapable moral conundrums that finally impel Clare to leave her husband and return to Harlem.

Unfortunately, this scene does not have the intended effect on Irene, who feels justifiably enraged over her powerlessness in the face of Bellew's bigotry and thus adamantly resists acknowledging the full dimensions of Clare's predicament. Since Irene, like society at large, is unwilling to assume responsibility for her knowledge, in any sense, of Clare Kendry, Clare becomes for Irene a sign for the intractable social and moral dilemmas attendant on *Plessy*. Significantly, however, although Irene vows never to see Clare again and dismisses her lingering "sense of panic" (Larsen 1992, 212) by projecting onto Clare the abstract offense of racial disloyalty, she cannot for long repress the profound attraction she feels for Clare as an exotic woman sufficiently daring to violate the conventions of American society, particularly since her successful defiance represents a potential model for Irene herself. Thus, although Irene on one level shuns and condemns Clare, on another level her attraction redoubles when Clare, exercising her formidable will against the force of circumstance, arrives uninvited and unwanted at Irene's home. Once Clare breaks into the "sanctum" of Irene's private bedroom and "drop[s] a kiss on [Irene's] dark curls" (224), Irene's distance and aversion transform almost magically into admiration and desire for intimacy: "Looking at the woman before her, Irene Redfield had a sudden inexplicable onrush of affectionate feeling. Reaching out, she grasped Clare's two hands in her own and cried with something like awe in her voice: 'Dear God! But aren't you lovely, Clare!'" (225).

The quasi-sexual gallantry of this encounter is reinforced when Clare comments suggestively that, in asking the post office for letters from Irene that never arrived, she had felt sure that "they were all beginning to think that I'd been carrying on an *illicit love affair* and that the man had thrown me over" (Larsen 1992, 225, italics mine). Since virtually all of Clare's affairs are, in some measure, illicit, and Irene feels constrained by her sense of decorum not to probe into the truth, the remainder of the text details the intense ambivalences Irene experiences through her realization that Clare, "in spite of her determined selfishness . . . was yet capable of heights and depths of feeling that she, Irene Redfield, had never known. Indeed, never cared to know" (226).

Indeed, once Clare threatens to return to Harlem and thus to transform from an exotic dream into a familiar reality, Irene seems impelled to associate Clare's bid for freedom and self-creation with her husband Brian's long deferred dream of escaping to Brazil. At last, in a kind of interpretive desperation, Irene conflates Clare and Brian in her imagination as potential "runaways" and imagines that she is really involved in a rather mundane plot of marital infidelity. While it is perfectly true that Clare, as the scene in the Drayton Hotel implies, is far from a conventionally moral woman, there is no tangible evidence to suggest that she plans to secure her position in Harlem society by stealing Brian from Irene. In fact, Irene's determination to make Brian's dream of Brazil die constitutes the first in a series of destructive longings for stability and order that culminate in her determination to destroy Clare as the embodiment of her own socially, racially, and sexually transgressive desires. The remaining narrative is played out against a backdrop of Irene's increasingly pronounced extremes of physical attraction and moral aversion for her exotic friend. Aware of the racial and sexual masquerades enjoined upon the characters by *Plessy,* Irene decides that she must maintain her social respectability and economic security at any cost, even if "only by the sacrifice of other things, happiness, love, or some wild ecstasy that she had never known" (Larsen 1992, 234). As she fears that "if Clare were freed," anything might happen" (268), she acts in the guise of a Social Darwinist compelled, as it were, to vanquish Clare as an instance of an exotic culture that, however seductive and admirable, must fall before the "superior" forces of American civilization. In removing Clare, however, Irene also eliminates the possibility of her own freedom from the shackles of the racial and sexual conventions that imprison her.

While the strategies of self-disguise and masquerade Clare employs are far from ideal, they represent viable means of survival and self-transformation under conditions that temporarily limit her moral agency as she fashions an identity that allows her greater autonomy and self-determination. Tragically, Clare is not permitted to complete this journey or force the other characters in the novel to confront their ignorance or drop their self-protective disguises. Thus, a novel by an ostensibly heterosexual author forcefully critiques censorship and self-repression as well as the conventional narrative paradigms that compel her, through the agencies of Irene Redfield and John Bellew, to destroy anyone who resists these stifling social and artistic conventions. Hence, through the destruction of Clare Kendry, Larsen also suggests the intractible artistic limits that confronted her in this, her second and final novel. Accordingly, the social and legal dimensions of racial segregation and sexual "panic" are neither separable nor tangential issues in *Passing.* Rather, they are central in an innovative narrative that posits a choice between a racially divided and moralistic model of social and artistic decorum ultimately enforced by John Bellew and his like, and an integrated and *worldly* model that challenges not only the lingering separatist traditions of *Plessy v. Ferguson* but also the willful ignorance and sexual paranoia embodied in its contemporary legal analogue, *Bowers v. Hardwick.*

Notes

1. The Court not only held that the invidious racism of Virginia's law violated the equal protection clause of the Fourteenth Amendment, but also stated that "the freedom to marry has long been recognized as one of the vital personal rights essential to the orderly pursuit of happiness by free men" [*Loving v. Virginia* 388 U.S. 1 (1967) 11].

2. Specifically, the Court treats age (as well as poverty and neglect) as if it were parallel to the categories of race and sex. States can thus establish different schools on the basis of race and sex using the same "principle" used to establish separate elementary, junior, and high school facilities.

3. In this instance, the Court applied the standard of "reasonableness" to the Fourteenth Amendment, and found that "in determining the question of reasonableness, [the Court] is at liberty to act with reference to the established usages, customs, and traditions of the people, and with a view to the promotion of their comfort, and the preservation of the public peace and good order" (*Plessy* 1896, 1143).

4. In his lone dissenting opinion, Judge Harlan noted prophetically that "the judgment this day rendered will, in time, prove to be quite as pernicious as the decision made by this tribunal in the Dred Scott Case" (*Plessy* 1896, 1146).

5. After the publication of *Passing*, Larsen received a Guggenheim Fellowship (the first awarded to an African-American woman) to write her third novel, *Mirage*, which was to focus on the intersections of Latin, Anglo, and African-American cultures, but she never finished the project. She subsequently returned to her earlier career as a nurse, and some critics, notably Charles R. Larson, have speculated that the breakup of her marriage with Elmer Imes, in addition to the furor over Larsen's supposed plagiarism of a short story, "Sanctuary," caused her to retreat from writing.

6. Smith defines "lesbian panic" as "the disruptive action or reaction that occurs when a character . . . is incapable of confronting her own lesbianism or homoerotic desire." I thank her for access to her unpublished work ("And I Wondered If She Might Kiss Me" and "'Nothing Happened'").

7. In arguing in favor of outing, Mohr argues that "The Secret [that] currently binds the [gay and lesbian] community together is a commitment to a belief in the community's worthlessness. The very structuring principle of the community functions as a denial that the community exists—indeed, a denial that it should exist" (Mohr 1992b, 30).

8. In *Woodward v. United States* the Federal Circuit cited no authority in asserting that "members of recognized suspect or quasi-suspect classes, e.g., blacks or women, exhibit immutable characteristics, whereas homosexuality is primarily behavioral in nature" (1989, 1076). In *High Tech Gays v. Defense Industry Security Clearance Office,* the Ninth Circuit repeated this language almost verbatim, asserting that "homosexuality is not an immutable characteristic; it is behavioral and hence is fundamentally different

from traits such as race, gender, or alienage, which define already existing suspect and quasi-suspect classes" (1990, 573).

9. In "Homosexuality and Biology," gay scientist Chandler Burr marshals the growing if highly contested evidence for the biological basis of homosexual orientation, and concludes by noting that while opponents "discern in the biological quest the seeds of genocide . . . the spectre of the surgical or chemical 'rewiring' of gay people, or of abortions of fetal homosexuals who have been hunted down in the womb. . . . Five decades of psychiatric evidence demonstrates that homosexuality is immutable, and nonpathological, and a growing body of more recent evidence implicates biology in the development of sexual orientation" (Burr 1993, 65). Burr realizes, however, that scientific research can provide no antidote to the misuse of science in a homophobic society. For this reason, the struggle for gay rights must ultimately rest on "fundamental questions involving human rights, human freedom, and human tolerance." See also Halley, who contends, arguing against legal strategies that seek to secure rights for sexual minorities by tethering homosexuality to the legal discourse of "immutable characteristics," that the supposed homogeneity of the category "heterosexual" needs to be exposed as an intrinsically incoherent, self-contradictory legal fiction.

10. Quoted from Justice Blackmun in his dissenting opinion in *Bowers v. Hardwick* (1986), who quoted Justice Stevens quoting Fried, *Correspondence*, 6 Phil. & Public Affairs (1977): 288-89, in his concurring opinion in *Thornburgh v. American College of Obstetricians & Gynecologists*, 476 U. S., at 777, n. 5, 106 S. Ct. at 2187, n. 5. While the right to privacy has come under attack recently as an appropriate legal strategy for securing rights for sexual minorities, it is important to remember that, while privacy and secrecy can overlap, they are nonetheless distinct entities. A disclosure of sexual orientation does not violate privacy since such a disclosure reveals nothing about private sexual acts or activities between consenting adults.

11. The decision of the Court in *Cleburne* not to decide the case on heightened equal protection scrutiny indicates that the Court (perhaps with lesbians and gays in mind) wants to delimit the class who can claim suspect or quasi-suspect status. The Court refused to deem the mentally retarded a quasi-suspect class because doing so would make it "difficult to find a principled way to distinguish a variety of other groups who have perhaps immutable disabilities setting them off from others, who cannot themselves mandate the desired legislative responses, and who can claim some degree of prejudice from at least part of the public at large. . . . We are reluctant to set out on that course, and we decline to do so."

12. Justice Stevens cites *Thompson v. Alredge*, in which the Georgia Supreme Court held that the sodomy statute referred to anal intercourse and did not prohibit lesbian activity. In *Riley v. Garrett*, moreover, the Georgia Supreme Court held that the same statute did not prohibit heterosexual cunnilingus. The current Georgia statute under consideration in *Bowers* provides that "[a] person commits the offense of sodomy when he performs or submits to any sexual act involving the sex organs of one person and the mouth or anus of another," (*Bowers* 1989, 2849). Stevens also refers to the definition of sodomy given in May: "Sodomy, otherwise called buggery, bestiality, and the crime against nature, is the unnatural copulation of two persons with each other, or of a human being with a beast. . . . It may be committed by a man with a man, by a man with a beast, or by a woman with a beast, or by a man with a woman—his wife, in which case, if she

consents, she is an accomplice." While Justice Stevens points out the wide historical variability of sodomy statutes, neither of the two dissenting opinions mentions that English common law had never specifically applied to lesbian sexuality. The decision in *Bowers* to group lesbians under "homosexual sodomy" is thus a very new social construction of sexual taboo with very little history or tradition to support it.

13. See *Loving v. Virginia.* Justice Blackmun notes that in *Loving* as in *Bowers*, the petitioners "relied heavily on the fact that when the Fourteenth Amendment was ratified, most of the States had similar prohibitions [against sodomy and miscegenation, respectively]."

14. In some senses, Larson's introduction can be seen as a direct response to McDowell's earlier introduction to *Quicksand* and *Passing.* Larson never refers to McDowell's introduction, underplays Larsen's feminist concerns, and makes no mention of the possibility that *Passing* might depict female (or male) homoerotic desire. Larson quotes the headlines from three articles in the *Baltimore Afro-American*: "Fisk Professor Is Divorced by N.Y. Novelist"; "Friends Think Love Cooled While Wife Wintered in Europe"; and "Recall 'Jump' from Window" (Larson 1992, xvi-xvii).

15. Eric Garber notes that many of the leading figures of the Harlem Renaissance— for example, Bruce Nugent, Langston Hughes, Wallace Thurman, Countee Cullen, Claude McKay, Alain Locke, Bessie Smith, Gertrude "Ma" Rainey, Ethel Waters, Josephine Baker, Alberta Hunter, and Gladys Bentley—were gay, lesbian, or bisexual.

Works Cited

Burr, Chandler. 1993. "Homosexuality and Biology." *Atlantic* 271.3: 47-65.

Christian, Barbara. 1980. *Black Women Novelists: The Development of a Tradition, 1892-1976* Westport: Greenwood.

City of Cleburne v. Cleburne Living Center, Inc. 473 US 433, 488. 1985.

Fuller, Hoyt. 1971. Introduction to *Passing*, by Nella Larsen. New York: Collier.

Garber, Eric. 1989. "A Spectacle in Color: The Lesbian and Gay Subculture of Jazz Age Harlem." In *Hidden from History: Reclaiming the Gay and Lesbian Past*, ed. Martin Bauml Duberman, Martha Vicinus, and George Chauncey, Jr. New York: Dutton.

Halley, Janet E. 1991. "Misreading Sodomy: A Critique of the Classification of 'Homosexuals' in Federal Equal Protection Laws." In *Body Guards: The Cultural Politics of Gender Ambiguity*, ed. Julia Epstein and Kristina Straub. New York: Routledge.

Hermansen, Kurt D. 1992. "Analyzing the Military's Justification for its Exclusionary Policy: Fifty Years Without a Rational Basis." *Loyola of Los Angeles Legal Review* 26: 35.

High Tech Gays v. Defense Industry Security Clearance Office. 895 F.2d 563. 1990.

Larsen, Nella. 1992. *An Intimation of Things Distant: The Collected Fiction of Nella Larsen.* Ed. and intro. Charles R. Larson. New York: Anchor.

Larson, Charles R. 1992. Introduction to *An Intimation of Things Distant: The Collected Fiction of Nella Larsen.* New York: Doubleday.

Linda Sidoti Palmore v. Anthony J. Sidoti, 104 S. Ct. 1879. 1984. *Supreme Court Reporter.* St. Paul: West, 1987. 1879-83.

Loving v. Virginia, 388 U. S. 1, 87 S. Ct. 1817, 18 L. Ed. 2d 1010. 1967.

May, J. 1893. *The Law of Crimes* 203. 2nd. ed.

McDowell, Deborah E. 1986. Introduction to *Quicksand* and *Passing*, by Nella Larsen. New Brunswick: Rutgers University Press.

Michael J. Bowers v. Michael Hardwick, 106 S. Ct. 2841. 1986. *Supreme Court Reporter* St. Paul: West, 1989. 2841-59.

Mohr, Richard D. 1992a. "Black Law and Gay Law." In *Gay Ideas: Outing and Other Controversies.* Boston: Beacon.

_____. 1992b. "The Outing Controversy." *Gay Ideas: Outing and Other Controversies.* Boston: Beacon.

Plessy v. Ferguson. The Supreme Court Reporter 16. St. Paul: West, 1896.

Ramsey, Priscilla. 1976. "A Study of Black Identity in 'Passing' Novels of the Nineteenth and Early Twentieth Century." *Studies in Black Literature* 7 (Winter): 1-7.

Riley v. Garrett. 219 Ga. S. E. 2d 367. 1963.

Smith, Patricia Juliana. 1992. "And I Wondered If She Might Kiss Me: Lesbian Panic in Postmodern British Women's Fiction." Paper presented at MLA Convention 28 December. New York City.

_____. "'Nothing Happened': Lesbian Panic and the Disruption of Narrative." Ph.D. diss., University of California, Los Angeles.

Tate, Claudia. 1980. "Nella Larsen's *Passing:* A Problem of Interpretation." *Black American Literature Forum* 14 (Winter): 142-46.

Thompson v. Alredge. 187 Ga. 467, 200 S. E. 799. 1939.

Woodward v. United States. 871 F.2d 1068. 1989.

Youman, Mary. 1974. "Nella Larsen's *Passing*: A Study in Irony." *College Language Association Journal* 18 (December): 235-41.

II

VOICE

6

"A Woman Speaks . . . I am Woman and Not White": Politics of Voice, Tactical Essentialism, and Cultural Intervention in Audre Lorde's Activist Poetics and Practice

Brenda Carr

Audre Lorde—self-defined African-American, feminist, lesbian, poet—is an uppity woman. She talks back, speaks out, uses language as a crucial means of intervention in a sociocultural field structured by systemic inequities—sexism, racism, classism, and heterosexism. Because her strategic invocations of identity are implicitly problematized by her multiple positioning, Lorde's practice of poetic cultural intervention provides a context for me to engage the question of essentialism under debate in the feminist and broader theoretical communities. As well, Lorde's figuring of "voice" and "silence" as central to her activist poetics and practice in such works as *The Black Unicorn* (1978) compels me to meditate on the meanings and politics of these terms within (overlapping) aesthetic, feminist, political, and academic contexts.

In her 1969 essay "The Aesthetics of Silence," Susan Sontag defines modernist avant garde art and literary practice by structural silences that frustrate interpretation and, in this way, act as a form of aggression against the would-be receiver. While poststructuralists now celebrate these same tendencies toward indeterminacy, what is crucial for me is Sontag's inadvertent indication that the aesthetics of silence intersects a discourse of mastery: "an exemplary decision of this sort (for silence) can be made only after the artist has demonstrated that *he possesses genius and has exercised that genius authoritatively*" (Sontag 1969, 7, my emphasis). This begs the question of what cultural assumptions and privileges underpin the genius construct. Sontag further discloses that an aesthetics of silence is also implicated in a dream of a transcendant "ahistorical condition": "the advocacy of silence expresses a mythic project of total liberation . . . of the artist from himself, of art from the particular artwork, of art from history, of spirit from matter, of the mind from its perceptual and intellectual limitations" (15-18).

When this conception of an ahistorical aesthetics of silence is counterpointed with the art practice of members from oppressed groups, silence within "project[s] of total liberation" takes on an entirely different meaning. *AIDS Demographics*, a book on AIDS activist art, features a poster designed by the AIDS Action Network, ACT UP, in 1986. It reads in bold print capitals **"SILENCE = DEATH,"** while the small print makes the conditions of this silence explicit: "Why is Reagan silent about AIDS? What is really going on at the Center for Disease Control, the Federal Drug Administration, and the Vatican?" (Crimp and Rolston 1990, 30, 31). Silence here marks the site of oppression. Conversely, speaking out is the sign of and, often, a literal means of intervention in oppressive systems. This equation between speaking out and acting up, voice and public visibility, has been central to twentieth-century activism that coheres around group identity formation—for example, the black power, women's liberation, and gay pride movements. Such agency is contingent on finding a communal voice opposed to what Jo Spence calls "structured and structuring silences"(Spence 1990, 8).[1] In counterpoint, strategic silence (quite different from voicelessness) as a strategy of resistance is not to be overlooked. As a kind of antivoice, what Trinh T. Minh-ha calls "a mode of uttering, and a response in its own right," such loud silence only "gains a hearing" in concert with "other silences"—coalition rather than solo silences (Minh-ha 1989, 83).

Translating such linkage of voice and "hearing" into a literary context raises the suspect equation of voice with identity, presence, authority, and intentionality. While I do not think that recent questions can or should be dismissed, I agree with Jeanne Perreault's sense that these categories must be renegotiated when considering a writer such as Lorde, whose cultural authority is always already provisional: "only if 'voice' or 'presence' is assumed to be that of the most profound of authorities, indeed, a voice/presence not limited by social or political conditions, is it necessary to detach it from writing" (Perreault 1988, 4). I would extend Perreault's observations on the gendered voice to the inscription of any marginated subjectivity, so that I see those who write "resistance literatures" of all kinds (gays, lesbians, people of color, working class) as writing to strategically assert "presence" and cultural authority, to assert agency through self-defined sociosymbolic practices.[2] It is instructive in such a retake on "voice/presence" to ask why and how authorial voice signifies differently within diverse critical and cultural discourses. For example, how might various cultural privileges contextualize Roland Barthes's "The Death of the Author" (1977) and Michel Foucault's "What is an Author" (1984)?[3] It also seems to me that "intention" in the context of marginated writing is as much a function of the actual author-outside-the-text as it is of the text, the historical moment, or interpretative activation by the reader, although never fully recoverable as a key to unlocking *the* ideal meaning. Specifically, I see Lorde's invocation of her "voice/presence" as a provisional assertion of strategic authority; she "intends" to intervene in the symbolic order with her alternative signifying practice. Such an authority de-authorizes those with capital A/Authority and opens up the cultural space for others speaking.[4]

Within the (sometimes) intersecting activist and literary contexts, who is made visible by voicing also involves privilege. The limited universal implied by the "unified" voice of protest in liberation movements has frequently been based on an exclusion of certain of their constituents. For example, white middle-class women have tended to speak for all women, black middle-class men for all blacks, white middle-class gay men for all gays and lesbians. Invoking voice as cultural intervention in the public realm, then, has the attendant danger of exclusion based on certain privileges. It is relevant at this juncture to consider the politics of my own invocation of Lorde's black lesbian female voice in the institutionally empowered frame of an academic journal. Writing across the differences of my white and heterosexual subject positioning, I seek to negotiate the problematics that ensue when the "other voice" is appropriated, spoken for by well-intentioned liberalism, legitimated by a cultural majority. Feminist standpoint theorists such as Donna Haraway call for an embodied knowledge formation that opens up possibilities for ethical conversations accountable to asymmetrical power relations. I conceive of my theorized close readings of Lorde's work as a provisional textual exchange, a "partial translation" across the knowledge gaps of our differences, in which I am responsible to the intersecting and contradictory privileges and oppressions that frame my speaking. I see my writing, then, as an answer to her urgent call that we "not hide behind the mockeries of separations that have been imposed upon us" and that we "bridge some of those differences between us, for it is not difference which immobilizes us, but silence" (Lorde 1984e, 43, 44). In that journey towards bridging, I am willing to risk mistakes. I have faith that there are now enough strong Afra-American voices in the cultural room—Lorde's, Alice Walker's, bell hooks's, Hortense Spillers's, Mae Henderson's, and Barbara Christian's, for example— that they will speak back.[5] I welcome that. A Canadian Metis writer, Maria

Campbell, notes that "when you admit you're a thief, then you can be honourable" (Campbell and Griffiths 1989, 112). Those of us writing across difference from variously privileged subject positions are always already inside the activity of appropriation. I think we have mistakenly attempted to theorize strategies that locate us outside of appropriation when silence affords the only "pure" means. While I see strategically chosen silences as necessary in specific situations, as Lorde indicates, this is not always productive. I am seeking here to find ways toward what might be termed an honorable appropriation that takes cultural humility and self-reflection as a starting place for negotiating a horizon of what Mae Henderson envisions as "a multiplicity of 'interested readings' . . . entering into dialogic relationship with other 'interested readings'" (Henderson 1989a, 162).[6]

* * *

Feminists who see "coming to voice" as a sign of female self-determination participate in what thinkers such as Linda Alcoff have called "cultural feminism," which aims to facilitate women's liberation through the recovery of women's history, tradition, and culture (Alcoff 1988, 411). Feminist self-critique in the 1980's focused on calling those with unquestioned investment in this project to accountability. For example, a focus on (universal) female culture and history tends to obscure pressing questions of which specific women's culture and history are celebrated—typically, that of white middle-class heterosexual women, like myself, to the exclusion of others. Further, such celebrations have frequently focused on what are perceived as innate female qualities such as nurturing, which is seen as being naturally derived from women's biological capacity to be mothers. Belief in a "natural" or given "femininity" does not account for the social equation between "maternal" and "feminine." As well, it erases differences between and among women. For example, other cultures may not privilege the nurturing function in women the way that ours does, and some women within our culture may not identify with the maternal model.

Thinkers such as Mary Daly and poets like Adrienne Rich, now identified as cultural feminists, often become whipping girls for social-constructionist feminists such as Alcoff, who dismiss their emphasis on reconstructing female culture as dangerously essentialist (Alcoff 1988, 411).[7] Interestingly, Alcoff recuperates Audre Lorde, whose invocations of the black female voice and emphasis on poetry as the vehicle for social change also seem to imply an essential black female identity. However, for Alcoff, Lorde's location within a "simultaneity of oppressions . . . resists essentialist exclusions" (412). I find the dismissal of Rich as one of feminism's bad girls and the recuperation of Lorde as the new good girl on the block to be a strange move when they are close friends who publicly acknowledge the deep affinities between their cultural projects.[8] To dismiss Rich involves ignoring evidence from her earliest feminist thought that contradicts a totalized essentialism, as well as freezing her in a single historical moment rather than following her theory-in-process to the increasingly sophisticated and antiessentialist positioning of her writing in the eighties.[9] On the other hand, to recuperate Lorde as a "pure" antiessentialist is to suppress the unruly signs of her location within cultural feminism, such as when she self-identifies as "a Black woman warrior poet" (Lorde 1984e, 41-42) or invokes "the goddess" (Lorde 1988, 101). I dwell on the strange case of Alcoff's reading of Rich and Lorde because it may provide a cautionary tale for feminist theory and practice. Essentializing essentialist tendencies or suppressing them is still locked into a binary economy. It seems to me more productive to identify and negotiate the contradictions of strategic or provisional essentialism that I see as operative in both their works and to question whether "cultural feminism" is as monolithic a concept as recent theory has constructed it to be.

The possibility of a strategic essentialism is theorized first by Gayatri Spivak in a 1984 interview with Elizabeth Grosz. Rather than protecting "theoretical purity" by refusing to take a stand against anything, Spivak calls for a "strategic choice" of privileging feminist practice over theory (Spivak and Grosz 1990, 11-12). In a second interview from a 1989 special issue of *differences* on "Another look at Essentialism," she doubles back on her analysis to remind us that "a strategy suits a situation, a strategy is not a theory" (Spivak and Grosz 1990, 127). In this way, she implements deconstruction's "most serious critique . . . the critique of something that is extremely useful, something without which we cannot do anything" (Spivak and Grosz 1990, 129). Teresa de Lauretis in "Taking the Risk of Essentialism" and Diana Fuss in *Essentially Speaking* also argue for similarly contradictory practices of strategic essentialism. These women suggest that the charge of essentialism is not necessarily grounds for dismissing projects identified with cultural feminism. Instead, in the context of identity politics, they revalue tactical deployment of seemingly essentialist notions such as female voice or identity as a strategy of intervention in oppressive systems (Fuss 1989, 20). What Spivak, de Lauretis, and Fuss are renegotiating is not belief in a biologically determined female essence or core attributes that can be objectively discovered through observation, but rather a paradoxical conceptual essentialism or "classificatory fiction," self-consciously framed as a product of language, which is no less powerful for being fictional (Fuss 1989, 4-5). I would suggest that agency is, in fact, impossible without the "enabling fictions" accommodated by such a refigured essentialism. Invocations of identity, then, facilitate agency through the formation of coalitions from which demands for change in the name of women (or other marginated groups) can be made. One way to deploy such a tactical feminist essentialism is to account for the ways in which gender or sexual difference is in a constant state of interanimation with the elements of class, physical ability, race, ethnicity, nationality, and sexual orientation, among other "identity" markers (de Lauretis

1990, 133). For example, when a black lesbian woman such as Lorde writes from her complex subject positioning, she cannot separate the strands of gender, race, and sexual orientation, except in a kind of dance, where one element temporarily shifts to the foreground as the other fades to the rearground of inscription. Gloria T. Hull points to Lorde's multivalent subject construction as her "tricky positionality" or "ceaseless negotiation of a positionality from which she can speak" (Hull 1989, 159, 155). For feminist thinkers and writers, there are times, however, when it may be strategically necessary to foreground (temporarily) "gender" through addressing overlapping positionalities, those intersecting aspects of women's experience that afford a provisional "standpoint" from which to gain knowledge and to engage in collective liberatory struggle (de Lauretis 1990, 139).[10]

* * *

At the intersection of multiple oppressions, Audre Lorde risks essentialism to affirm her own speaking and call other black lesbian women's voices from silence. In bell hooks's terms, "for women within oppressed groups . . . coming to voice is an act of resistance" (hooks 1989, 12). African-American female literary acts of talking back to the powers extend the boundaries of the category identified by Barbara Harlow as "resistance literature" from the "Third World" context of liberation struggles to the North American context of liberation struggles on multiple and intersecting fronts. Following Mae Henderson's provocative model of "discursive diversity," I will engage Lorde's "dialogic of differences" and "dialectic of identity" through theorized close readings of poems from *The Black Unicorn* intertextually glossed by her essays (Henderson 1989b, 17, 20). Such "speaking in [other] tongues," according to Henderson, marks Afra-American signifying practices, which dialectically testify to their various communities of affiliation and dialogically challenge the "hegemonic dominant" and "'ambiguously (non)hegemonic' discourses" (Henderson 1989b, 20). Speaking both "*inter*culturally" and "*intra*culturally" (Henderson, "Speaking" 25), Lorde theorizes the relationship between her discursive practice and sociocultural agency in two essays—"Poetry is not a Luxury" and "The Transformation of Silence into Language and Action"—written in 1977, the year she was diagnosed with breast cancer and underwent a mastectomy.

Facing her own mortality, Lorde was brought to a sense of "urgent clarity" about the need to break the cultural silences around her identity not only as a woman, but also as a black and a lesbian. She gives this account of her reasons for publicly naming herself at an October 1985 talk she gave in East Lansing, Michigan:

> first off I identified myself as a Black Feminist Lesbian poet, although it felt
> unsafe . . . because if there was one other Black Feminist Lesbian poet in

isolation somewhere within the reach of my voice, I wanted her to know she was not alone. I think a lot about Angelina Weld Grimke, a Black Lesbian poet of the Harlem Renaissance, who is never identified as such, when she is mentioned at all . . . I often think of [her] dying alone in an apartment in New York City in 1958 while I was a young Black Lesbian struggling in isolation at Hunter College, and I think of what it could have meant in terms of sisterhood and survival for each of us to have known of the other's existence. (Lorde 1988, 73)

Breaking silences, for Lorde, involves self-naming and offering her identity to facilitate building communities through which future action is made possible.

Audre Lorde's primary venue for coming to voice is poetry. While socialist feminists often critique cultural feminists' emphasis on aesthetic productions as being divorced from the material conditions of women's lives, Lorde asserts the opposite in her essay "Poetry is Not a Luxury":

> For women, then, poetry is not a luxury. It is a vital necessity of our existence. It forms the quality of light within which we predicate our hopes and dreams toward survival and change, first made into language, then into idea, then into more tangible action. Poetry is the way we help give name to the nameless so it can be thought. (Lorde 1984c, 37)

Here, Lorde speaks in the name of women, brings gender to the fore as the basis of the coalition she envisions. For her, coming to voice in poetry provides women with "illumination," a "spawning ground for the most radical and daring of ideas." Challenging the formalist binarism (evidenced in the Sontag essay) between the aesthetic and the historical/political, Lorde also reminds us of how the visionary is integral to liberation struggles. Alternative sociocultural realities are birthed in the realm of the imagination as Martin Luther King's "I have a dream" speech indicates. While the word "visionary" is often used negatively to mean idealistic and unpractical, it also means to have discernment and wisdom. Visionary thought, as Lorde suggests, is theory at its best, formulating future possibility, opening up the questions that can be asked.

Lorde implements her theory of visionary activism in a literary context in *The Black Unicorn*. Throughout the volume, she equates the pain of "having to live a difference that has no name" with voicelessness (Lorde 1988, 57): "the pain of voiceless mornings / voiceless kitchens I remember / cornflakes shrieking like banshees in my throat" (25). The volume is redolent with instances of the poet/speaker in the acts of vocalizing, laughing, singing, drumming, screaming—in short, making sounds that mark her responses to the specific conditions of her life. Frequently, Lorde invokes musical or oratorical forms such as the litany, dirge, eulogy, ballad, and lullaby with such titles as "A Litany for Survival" and "Woman/Dirge for Wasted Children." These signal her affiliation with African expressive culture. For instance, "A Litany for Survival" makes use of the African call-and-response pattern to give poetic shape to Lorde's theorizing of the relationship between fear, silence, and invisibility in contrast to courage, coming to voice, and visibility. This poem occupies an intersection of Western and African traditions, so that the Western liturgical form of the litany or antiphonal prayer is resonant with the African call and response structure. By repeating the lines "for those of us" at the beginning of stanzas one and two with the variant "for all of us" at the end of stanza two, the poet/speaker establishes the litany framework:

> For those of us who live at the shoreline
> standing upon the constant edges of decision
> crucial and alone
> for those of us who cannot indulge the passing dreams of choice
> who love in doorways coming and going
> in the hours between dawns
> looking inward and outward
> . . . .
> For those of us
> who were imprinted with fear
> like a faint line in the middle of our foreheads
> learning to be afraid with our mother's milk (31)

Through phrasal repetition, the speaker signals her inclusion in a community, marked by the collective pronouns "us" and "we"; but uncharacteristically for Lorde, the communal identity is not distinctively specified. Because of this, the poem seems to gesture toward the universal. There are, however, several indicators that the members of this community affiliate around determinately intersecting oppressions. When the poet/speaker equates a future with bread in the children's mouths in stanza one, she signals that this community is not economically privileged. Further, "heavy-footed" in stanza two, with its military and masculinist associations, suggests gender oppression. Lorde also invokes figures of liminal or in-between spaces in the opening stanza with the phrases "at the shoreline," "upon the constant edges of decision," "in doorways," "looking inward and outward." These signify the community's peripheral status. Such a spatial construction may also signal heterosexist oppression of lesbians, "who cannot indulge/ the passing dreams of choice/ who love in doorways coming and going."[11]

However, such readings of the indicators of this communal subject positioning are somewhat speculative unless "A Litany for Survival" is read intertextually with other poems from *The Black Unicorn* and essays from the same period. A purely formalist reading of such a poem in isolation from its contexts is an abdication of the responsibility that attends reading across different subject positionings, although this is an issue I can only gesture toward here.[12] Because an ethically responsible contextualized reading accounts for the particular communities invoked in the poem, it uncloses the notion of the lyric as a bounded text, a private voice speaking in a closed frame. Phrases and concepts circulate between the poem and a resonant essay (one of many possible sociodiscursive contexts). "The Transformation of Silence into Language and Action" was originally delivered at the 1977 MLA "Lesbian and Literature Panel" and originally published in *The Cancer Journals*, written during Lorde's experience with breast cancer. Her near death caused her to realize that safety in silence is a false illusion. In "A Litany for Survival," by cataloging and ultimately playing a reversal on a litany of fears that block speech-acts of resistance, she enjoins other black women to come to voice despite silencing fears:

> when we are loved we are afraid
> love will vanish
> when we are alone we are afraid
> love will never return
> and when we speak we are afraid
> our words will not be heard
> nor welcomed
> but when we are silent
> we are still afraid.
> So it is better to speak
> remembering
> we were never meant to survive. (Lorde 1988 32)

A moving intertext from "The Transformation of Silence into Language and Action" marks the specific communities signaled by the ambiguously unmarked pronoun "we" in the poem:

> In the cause of silence, each of us draws the face of her own fear—fear of contempt, of censure, or some judgment, or recognition, of challenge, of annihilation. But most of all, I think, we fear the visibility without which we cannot truly live. Within this country where racial difference creates a constant, if unspoken, distortion of vision, Black women have on one hand always been highly visible, and so, on the other hand, have been rendered invisible through the depersonalization of racism. Even within the women's movement, we have had to fight and still do, for that very visibility which also renders us most vulnerable, our Blackness. For to survive in the mouth of this dragon we call America, we have had to learn this first and most vital lesson—that we were never meant to survive. Not as human beings. And neither were most of you here today, Black or not. And that visibility which makes us most vulnerable is that which also is the source of our greatest strength. Because the machine will try to grind you into dust anyway,

whether or not you speak. We can sit in our corners mute forever while our sisters and our selves are wasted, while our children are distorted and destroyed, while our earth is poisoned; we can sit in our safe corners mute as bottles, and we will still be no less afraid. (Lorde 184c, 42)

In this excerpt, which explicitly equates coming to voice with cultural visibility, Lorde seems to speak first in the name of generic woman: "each of us draws the face of her own fear." However, it soon becomes clear that she is speaking specifically in the name of black women, to and for them from within their shared experience of racism. In this way, she problematizes the notion of a generic "woman" for the women's movement by reminding us that sexual difference can never be the only explanation for unequal power relations. Similarly, when she ends her poem "A Woman Speaks" with the declaration "I am woman and not white," Lorde brings the black woman to what bell hooks calls the "speaking center," while shifting a white academic woman such as myself to the rearground (Lorde 1988, 15).

Survival is defined in terms of race as well as gender. However, as soon as Lorde invokes the nominal essentialism of her racial identity as it intersects with gender in the essay, she undercuts this as a stable point of location by gesturing back toward the universal to include her audience members at large in the group who were never meant to survive. In this way, Lorde speaks in "diverse known tongues" (Henderson 1989, 22), negotiates multiple axes of community affiliation, in a manner that suggests the possibility of a provisionalized universal around which coalitions of "corresponding differences" may be formed (Marlatt 1990, 189). Reading Lorde's poem intertextually with the essay facilitates a dance of readings, a "dialogics of difference," in which multiple communities of response may be ethically accounted for after the primary community of black lesbian women is honored.

Lorde's voicing of African-American female identity works to refigure intersecting Eurocentric and sex/gender signifying systems. In fact, provisionalizing a universal subject position may be seen as one of the projects of the entire volume, as the title poem "Black Unicorn" indicates. Lorde invokes and reframes the unicorn seduction narrative from Western folklore, for while the unicorn is always white and (implicitly) male, her unicorn is black and female. Such a representational shift asks us to question our assumption that Western culture is universal by foregrounding the connection between cultural formations and positioning in such identity factors as race and gender. Further, Lorde strategically appropriates and refigures the dominant iconography of the phallic horn; inverted, it is the marker of female sexual power: "it is not on her lap where the horn rests/ but deep in her moonpit/ growing" (Lorde 1978, 3). Such reformulation of the sexual economy is even more prominent in other poems, where the geography of desire is explicitly lesbian. Fundamentally, "The Black

Unicorn" meditates on the need for opening up the representational frame as a sphere of activism. Like the unicorn of lore, the black unicorn is "not free," but she is also not the willing captive of desire; she is imprisoned by false versions and reifications of her identity, "mistaken for a shadow or symbol." As a figure of resistance, the black unicorn signals that this volume will negotiate an activist intervention in dominant cultural formations.

Another way Lorde renegotiates exclusionary signifying systems is by drawing on African myths and traditions, specifically those from Dahomey and the Yoruba cultures of Western Nigeria, which Lorde found transplanted to her mother's Grenadian context. In poems such as "Dahomey," she borrows stories and key figures from this alternative tradition, but provides a glossary at the back of *The Black Unicorn* that positions the reader as a student of West African culture. Such poems engage non-African readers in a process of reformulating received notions of a "universal" literary tradition. In "Dahomey," Lorde speaks from the intersections of gender and race to improvise on the primacy of female figures in the Dahomean myths:

> It was in Abomey . . .
> . . . where I found my mother
> Seboulisa
> standing with outstretched palms hip high
> one breast eaten away by worms of sorrow (Lorde 1978, 10)

Seboulisa here signifies multiply—as a Goddess in the Dahomean pantheon known as "The Mother of Us All" or "Creator of the Universe," as one of the Amazon warrior women marked by their missing breast (who are indigenous to Dahomean myths), and as a self-representation for the activist poet/speaker who reframes her mastectomy as a sign of empowerment.

In the last stanza, Lorde renegotiates the cult of divination centering around Shango, God of Thunder. While traditionally in this cult women were priestesses and oracles who interpreted the sacred writings or "fas" of Seboulisa, in Lorde's version Shango is usurped by the priestess who takes on his property of thunder as the sign of her oracular speech: "Thunder is a woman with braided hair/ spelling the fas of Shango." There is a crucial conflation of speaking voices and locations in this stanza for it begins with the third-person assertion "thunder is a woman," but shifts midway to the first person: "Bearing two drums on my head I speak/ whatever language is needed to sharpen the knives of my tongue." Time frames and cultural frames collapse as a Dahomean priestess is conflated with an African-American poet who speaks dialogically with forked tongue the multiple languages necessary to address the shifting contexts of race and gender, among other axes of subjectivity. Further, female linguistic power is figured as "sharpening the knives of my tongue," so that language is conceptualized as the weapon of the activist poet.

In "The Transformation of Silence into Language and Action," Lorde states: "Perhaps for some of you here today, I am the face of one of your fears. Because I am woman, because I am Black, because I am lesbian, because I am myself—a Black woman warrior poet doing my work—come to ask you, are you doing yours?" (Lorde 1984e, 41-42). Here and elsewhere, Lorde's insistence on multiple self-naming implicitly problematizes the politically necessary invocation of the seemingly essentialist descriptors "woman," "Black," and "lesbian." In another of her poems, the poet/speaker declares "I am lustful now for my own name . . . I seek my own shapes now " (Lorde 1978, 62). Within her creative/critical activist project, voicing and naming as self-invention are interchangeable. But it is, finally, Lorde's self-naming as lesbian that I want to engage, for this is an axis of subjectivity that is frequently elided in critical discourses, feminist or otherwise. It is the wounding of this absence that Lorde addresses in her poem "Scar" as it intersects with other woundings along race and gender lines. She addresses the poem to the women "who burn/ me at midnight/ in effigy . . . laughing me out of your skin/ because you do not value your own" (Lorde 1978, 48). This ritual expulsion marks another site of cultural wounding for the poet/speaker. It is only later in the poem that the reason for her derision by and excision from the Afra-American community is revealed: her self-identification as lesbian poses a threat to the heterosexual codes imbricated with female gender positioning. Parallel to the way she problematizes the category "woman," Lorde's interrogation of heterosexism and homophobia in the black community problematizes the assumption of a monolithic African-American female identity or tradition. Naming the absence of kinswomen through negation—"I will have no mother no sister no daughter/ when I am through"—Lorde interrogates intersecting constructions of gender and sexuality. In stanza three, she figures subsumption of black female identity under that of the male (in the heterosexual couple) as a scene of self-mutilation:

> see how the bones are showing
> the shape of us at war
> clawing our own flesh out
> to feed the backside of our masklike faces
> that we have given the names of men. (Lorde 1978, 48)

Figured as violent self-negation or cannibalism, female erasure behind the mask of the male family name results in wars within and between women at the site of (homoerotic) contradictions to heterocentric encoding.

In stanza six, Lorde further probes the wounded experience of female deselfing within the heterosexual economy by ventriloquizing the voice of a prostitute:

Come Sambo dance with me
pay the piper dangling dancing
his knee-high darling
over your wanting under your bloody
white faces come Bimbo come Ding dong
watch the city falling down down
down lie down bitch slow down nigger
so you want a cozy womb to hide you
to pucker up and suck you back
safely
. . . .
look me up
I'm the ticket taker on a queen
of roller coasters
I can get you off
cheap. (Lorde 1978, 49-50)

Here, the poem stages a collision between the racialized signs "Sambo" and
"nigger" and the gendered sign "bitch" to further interrogate the intersecting
zones of race, gender, and sexuality. In this ironized direct address to the multiracial consumers of the female body/commodity, the subject of address first
appears to be Sambo, the figure of the African-American male frozen in a children's book racist stereotype, but the pronoun "your" shifts multiply to refer to
the "white faces," who are similarly cartooned as "Bimbo" and "Ding Dong."
Desire of possession emanates from both positions, just as the vocal imperative
"lie down bitch" may. However, the subject of address shifts from the multiple
to the singular with "slow down nigger," a command to the Sambo figure that
seems to derive from the speaker/prostitute. The line following is enjambed
through nonpunctuation, so that the "you" who wants a "cozy womb" to hide in
would seem to refer to the figure of the "nigger." Such use of the racist terms
and signs for the African-American male within this skin-trade context inserts
sex/gender positioning into a scene of racial oppression. Lorde here suggests
that male sex consumption is an attempted escape from the pain of racism, so
that there is, as the repetition in the lines "watch the city falling down down/
down lie down bitch slow down nigger" suggests, a downward spiral of dehu-
manization.

However, Lorde frames this ironized mimicry of the African-American
sex/gender (victim) position between two stanzas that present an alternative
construction. In the preceding stanza (five), Lorde repeats, as a refrain, the lines
that witness the absence of family women for the poet/speaker, while affirming
a new community of affiliation:

        I have no sister no mother no children
        left
        only a tideless ocean of moonlit women
        in all shades of loving
        learning the dance of open and closing
        learning a dance of electrical tenderness
        no father no mother would teach them. (Lorde 1978, 49)

This passage provides a figure of lesbian community that transgresses and re-formulates the code of the nuclear family and the positioning of women within that social order. Lorde's essay "Uses of the Erotic: the Erotic as Power" helps contextualize a sharp shift in tone and subjectivity between the utopian dance of moonlit women in this stanza and the prostitute's dance in stanza six. Lorde theorizes a distinction between the pornographic, defined as "plasticized sensa-tion" devoid of feeling, and the erotic, which signifies deep feelings of joy shared with another physically, intellectually, and emotionally (Lorde 1984f, 56). From engaging capacity for shared joy, Lorde theorizes "erotic knowledge" as an "empowering" tool, a "lens through which we scrutinize all aspects of our existence" and by which we measure quality of life (57).[13] Erotic knowledge thus becomes a tool for critical interrogation of all the forms of "anti-life" or oppression that Lorde speaks out against (Lorde 1988, 130).

        While Lorde reformulates our cultural understanding of the erotic as purely sexual, she does not desexualize it in either the essay or poem intertexts. She in fact reinserts it into a specifically lesbian context. The dance of electrical ten-derness, then, in stanza five provides a figure for what Lorde theorizes in her essay as "women-identified women brave enough to risk sharing the erotic's electrical charge . . ." (Lorde 1988, 59). The final stanza of "Scar" constructs a sexual-ized figure of lesbian eroticism who also speaks back to the plasticized figure of the prostitute in the preceding stanza:

        This is a simple poem
        sharing my head with dreams
        of a big black woman with jewels in her eyes
        she dances
        her head in a golden helmet
        arrogant
        plumed
        her name is Colossa
        her thighs are like stanchions
        or flayed hickory trees
        embraced in armour
        she dances
        slow earth-shaking motions
        that suddenly alter

and lighten
as she whirls laughing
the tooled metal over her hips
comes to an end
and at the shiny edge
an astonishment
of soft black curly hair. (Lorde 1978, 50)

This fantasized figure is marked by her armor as an Amazon, reclaimed as a lesbian precursor from Dahomian mythology. However, Lorde conflates and conflicts signifying systems by naming her Colossa. Here, on the representational horizon she constructs a "big black woman" as a cultural sign that can only be read as talking back to that giant figure of the Western patriarch—the Colossus of Rhodes.[14] Further, in lines such as "her thighs are like . . . flayed hickory trees," she appropriates the figural strategies deployed in the Song of Solomon to displace the culturally and divinely sanctioned heterosexual economy with that of the homoerotic. As she challenges systems of signification encoded with race and gender norms in other poems, Lorde transgresses literary and cultural norms for sexuality. The surprise ending that discloses Colossa as naked from the waist down to focus on the "astonishment of soft black curly hair" constructs a black lesbian eroticism that asserts self-determined agency.

By framing the prostitution stanza in "Scar" with the lesbian erotic "dance of electrical tenderness," Lorde remarks the wounds of gender, race, and sexuality as potential sites of transformative cultural practice. The poem as an explication of a "scar" has particular resonance within the context of enslavement history. As Hortense Spillers notes, for African Americans the scar is a sign encoded in this history, along with other marks of tortured flesh—"lacerations, woundings, fissures, tears . . . openings, ruptures, lesions, rendings, punctures." Bearing witness to the scar, as Lorde does, returns us to the "flesh" as a "primary narrative," "that zero degree of social conceptualization that does not escape concealment under the brush of discourse" (Spillers 1987, 67). Slippage occurs between the term *scar*, the mark of wounding in the flesh that, as Spillers notes, "contemporary critical discourse" can "neither acknowledge or discourse away," and the scar as a trope for "an interiorized violation of body and mind" (68). By constructing an inside/outside reversibility between the enfleshed wound and the wounded body, Lorde suggests a powerful equivalency between interior violence at the level of the symbolic and violence materialized in the flesh. It is not, however, with the self-cannibalized victim at war with herself that she identifies her own subject position. Rather, through alternative figures of black, female, lesbian subjective agency, she talks back to and on the place of wounding.

Finally, to understand the complexity of Lorde's discursive praxis it is crucial to attend to the ways in which she problematizes liberatory reclamation of

African-American, female, and lesbian linguistic agency, as she does in "Power." In this poem, she self-reflexively meditates on the responsibilities that attend the privilege of coming to voice. As an exercise in self-critique, the poet/speaker poses herself a disturbing riddle in the opening stanza:

> The difference between poetry and rhetoric
> is being
> ready to kill
> yourself
> instead of your children. (Lorde 1978, 108)

Meditating on various abuses of power, she negotiates the potentially destructive poetic articulation of her outrage at the acquittal of a white policeman who murdered a ten-year-old black child by constructing, in stanza two, a surrealistic allegory in which the poet/speaker rhetorically objectifies and so vampirizes the murder victim:

> I am trapped on a desert of raw gunshot wounds
> and a dead child dragging his shattered black
> face off the edge of my sleep
> blood from his punctured cheeks and shoulders
> is the only liquid for miles . . .
> my mouth splits into dry lips
> without loyalty or reason
> thirsting for the wetness of his blood
> as it sinks into the whiteness
> of the desert where I am lost
> without imagery or magic
> trying to make power out of hatred and destruction (Lorde 1978, 108)

From within the allegorized desert space of white culture, Lorde engages the difficult question she articulates elsewhere: "how do you reach down into threatening difference without being killed or killing?" (Lorde 1984a, 107). She answers it through violent self-displacement in the last stanza of "Power." Here, the poet/speaker construction shifts abruptly across gender and age lines to the subject position of a teenaged African-American male whose unfocused rage is externalized in the act of raping an 85-year-old white woman:

> I have not been able to touch the destruction within me.
> But unless I learn to use
> the difference between poetry and rhetoric
> my power too will run corrupt as poisonous mold
> or lie limp and useless as an unconnected wire
> and one day I will take my teenaged plug

and connect it to the nearest socket
raping an 85-year-old white woman
who is somebody's mother
and as I beat her senseless and set a torch to her bed
a greek chorus will be singing in 3/4 time
"Poor thing. She never hurt a soul. What beasts they are." (Lorde 1978, 109)

A "dialogics of identity" is nowhere more painfully evidenced than in this poem. As a female, the poet/speaker would be outraged at the rape, beating, and murder of the elderly woman, but as an African American she cannot accept the "expert" witness of a twentieth-century "greek chorus" that unself-consciously perpetuates the racist cycle of violence endemic to Western culture by typifying her people as "beasts." While the Greek chorus, ironically constructed as singing glibly in time to "The Blue Danube," provides one example of corrupt and irresponsible rhetoric, the poet/speaker engages her own similar capacity. Her answer to the opening riddle about the difference between poetry and rhetoric involves a kind of linguistic death in which she displaces her black, lesbian, female subject position with that of the black male rapist in order to confront and take responsibility for her (potentially) destructive rage. Such a move also implicitly provisionalizes monolithic construction of the lyric voice and its attendant authority. The difference between poetry and rhetoric, Lorde suggests, is a de-authorized responsible use of voice that is constantly provisionalized by radical openness to self-questioning. In this way, the metapoetic process of the poem negotiates a self-reflexively engaged protest poetry that does not vampirize its own subjects, as the poet/speaker imagines herself doing in the earlier surrealistic allegory, or reverse the paradigm of oppression in "trying to make power out of hatred and destruction."

In antithesis to the Greek chorus that reduces the complexities of race and gender construction framing the violent drama evoked in the last stanza of "Power," Lorde allows herself (and her readers) no unconflicted response. Her strategic location at the site of contradiction between her femaleness and her blackness functions as a sign of her positioning at a crossroads of intersecting and mutually determining subject markers. The "tricky positionality" mobilized here and in the other poems and essays may be seen as a parable of the way in which multiple elements interanimate and destabilize any subject position. Putting pressure on the fracture points within and between subject positions may facilitate Lorde's project of "bridging differences" for collective agency. Subjectivity, even for socially empowered persons, can be read as a contradictory site of privilege and lack. At a 1989 conference on "Women in America: Legacies of Race and Ethnicity," Lorde enjoined her hearers to identify those places of overlapping subjectivity ("read the words of women who have written things that can be crossed with who you are") within the project of accounting for "the

powers of our differences": "we have different legacies; we have different powers. We must use our differences in order to reach the goals we share" (Lorde
1989, 18). Text-reader transactions across multiple differences operate as what Mae
Henderson terms "a multi-metalevel negotiation of hegemonic and nonhege-
monic discourses and positionalities" (Henderson 1989a, 157). Gloria T. Hull
suggests that it is those persons constituted as "radically-situated subjectivities"
who are best able to hear and be challenged by Audre Lorde's project (Hull
1989, 168). Such "ideal readers" and hearers are those who, I contend, strategically inhabit the unstable border places of identity: they practice a "dialectic of
identity with those aspects of self shared with others," while responsibly hearing
the "dialogics of difference" that may constitute them as the culurally hegemonic other (Henderson 1989b, 18).

    In the poems and essays cited above, Lorde slides between the particular
and the universal and takes the risk of deploying essentialism to call the multiple
constituents of the women's, black, and lesbian communities to vocal acts of
responsible cultural intervention upon which agency is contingent. In this way,
she practices what Gayatri Spivak calls "deconstructive homeopathy," or deconstruction of "identity by identities," a strategy that does not refuse identity
but problematizes it as a stable home (Spivak and Rooney 1989, 130). A dance
of "difference and identity" not only structures and problematizes the speaking
voice activated within the text, but also invokes a similarly decentered scene of
subjects reading, theorizing, and doing. The emphasis in recent feminist theory
on the need to deploy a provisional strategic essentialism situates us at the trans-
active border between literary/cultural texts and social texts, reminds us that
what is at stake is justice for social subjects—real bodies in a lived world.
Lorde's invocation of identity within the intersecting communities of women,
lesbians, and African Americans risks essentialism "in the name of something
that must be done" (Lorde 1988, 130). Such a strategy will never be theoretically pure, but it can be kept honest by practicing a "persistent critique" of what
we cannot live without (Spivak 1990, 93). Audre Lorde knew risk taking in the
flesh, refusing traditional medical intervention and living with liver cancer from
1984 until December 1992. Her long walk in the valley of the shadow lent a
particular urgency to her need to "speak out . . . against the many forms of anti-
life surrounding us" (Lorde 1988, 130). That potent poetic witness will continue
to re-sound, calling other voices into action.[15]

Notes

    1. Nancy S. Love identifies voice as a metaphor for a feminist "political epistemol-
ogy" or "power/knowledge regime." Such "allocentric perception" signals a shift from
the classical equation between knowledge and the mastering gaze (Love 1991, 86, 91).

2. In tracing an African-American genealogy of "voice," Henry Louis Gates, Jr., notes that "recording an authentic black voice" was the means for transforming the Anglo-European colonizing view of the enslaved African from "brute animal" to human being (Gates 1986, 11-12). While "voice" was imbricated with racialist/racist constructions, it seems to me that such circumscription has been displaced within contemporary liberatory discourses of empowerment through self-definition and communal affiliation marked by voicing.

3. Cheryl Walker renegotiates such poststructuralist theories by calling for "reanimation of the author" through reading for the traces of her "life-text" as one strand in the textual weave. She situates this within a "politics of author recognition," a strategy that she reads out from the practice of feminist theorists acknowledging the "authorship" of other feminists (Walker 1990, 553). In *Reclaiming the Author*, Lucille Kerr reads Spanish-American fiction for the contradictory ways in which even metafictional texts both perform the author's demise and reinscribe this figure. Rather than a "stable solution" to the problem of the author, she proposes "reading around a dialogue of figures in a competition that cannot be settled" (Kerr 1992, 25).

4. Thanks to Adeena Karasick for suggesting the notion of voice as a provisionalized play of strategic authority that de-authorizes within specific literary-cultural contexts.

5. Anthologies edited by Barbara Christian, Cheryl Wall, and Henry Louis Gates, Jr., for example, provide a powerful testament to the formation of African-American feminist critical discourses.

6. I am grateful to the women of the Simone de Beauvoir Institute at Concordia University for challenging me further to theorize appropriation of (different) voices and to Terry Goldie for his insights on this problematic.

7. My argument, then, is not with the necessity of critiquing essentialist and universalist constructions of "woman," but with the way in which this charge becomes the "bullet" in a kind of feminist murder mystery. See Mohanty for an unmasking of the Anglo-European ethnocentrism behind Western feminist invocations of universal sisterhood and the resultant colonizing analyses of "third world women." For an Anglo-European critique, see Elizabeth V. Spellman's analysis of the way "generic 'woman' functions in feminist thought in much the way the notion of generic 'man' functions in Western philosophy" (Spellman 1988, ix).

8. See, for example, the Lorde/Rich interview in *Sister Outsider*.

9. Although Alcoff does acknowledge that Rich "has recently departed from this position and in fact begun to move in the direction of the concept of woman I will defend . . . in her *Blood, Bread, and Poetry*," she sidelines this significant observation in a footnote (Alcoff 1988, 408).

10. While I do not advocate a return to an ethos of global sisterhood that erases difference by analyzing gender through the normative lens of the Anglo-European non-poor woman, Patricia Hill Collins points to the value of theorizing the intersections of subdominant epistemologies or contextualized standpoints. She notes that "the search for the distinguishing features of an alternative epistemology used by African-American women reveals that values and ideas that Africanist scholars identify as being characteristically 'Black' often bear remarkable resemblance to similar ideas claimed by feminist scholars as being characteristically 'female.' This similarity suggests that the material

conditions of oppression can vary dramatically and yet generate some uniformity in the epistemologies of subordinate groups" (Collins 1989, 756-57).

11. Thanks to Sue Schenk for pointing out that my earlier reading of possible identity markers elided the encoding of closeted lesbian existence.

12. See my work-in-progress "Texts in Contexts: Toward an Ethics of Reading and Writing Across Difference."

13. While this (1970s radical feminist) opposition of the pornographic to the erotic is problematic in its construction of reified and artificial categories, Lorde's reformulation and expansion of the erotic as a basis for theorizing agency is innovative and should not be dismissed.

14. Interesting comparisons may be made between Sylvia Plath's different interrogation of this sign of Western patriarchy in her poem "The Colossus."

15. I am grateful to the Social Sciences and Humanities Research Council of Canada for their generous postdoctoral funding and wish to thank Carol Farber, Elizabeth Harvey, and Dorothy Nielsen, and members of my 1989-90 Contemporary Poetry class and Sue Schenk's African-American Women Writers class.

Works Cited

Alcoff, Linda. 1988. "Cultural Feminism Versus Post-Structuralism: The Identity Crisis in Feminist Theory." *Signs* 13: 405-36.

Barthes, Roland. 1977. "The Death of the Author." In *Image-Music-Text*, trans. Stephen Heath. New York: Hill and Wang.

Belenky, Mary Field, et al. 1986. *Women's Ways of Knowing: The Development of Self, Voice, and Mind*. New York: Basic.

Campbell, Maria, and Linda Griffiths. 1989. *The Book of Jessica: A Theatrical Transformation*. Toronto: Coach House .

Christian, Barbara. 1985. *Black Feminist Criticism: Perspectives on Black Women Writers*. New York: Pergamon.

Collins, Patricia Hill. 1989. "The Social Construction of Black Feminist Thought." *Signs* 14.4: 745-73.

Crimp, Douglas, and Adam Rolston. 1989. "The Essence of the Triangle or, Taking the Risk of Essentialism Seriously: Feminist Theory in Italy, the U. S., and Britain." *difference*: 3-37.

____. 1990. *AIDS Demographics*. Seattle: Bay.

De Lauretis, Teresa. 1990. "Eccentric Subjects: Feminist Theory and Historical Consciousness." *Feminist Studies* 16 (Spring): 115-50.

Foucault, Michel. 1984. "What is An Author?" In *The Foucault Reader*, ed. Paul Rabinow. New York: Pantheon.

Fuss, Diana. 1989. *Essentially Speaking: Feminism, Nature & Difference*. New York: Routledge.

Gates, Henry Louis, Jr. 1986. "Writing 'Race' and the Difference It Makes." In *"Race," Writing, and Difference*, ed. Henry Louis Gates. Chicago: University of Chicago Press.

____, ed. 1990. *Reading Black, Reading Feminist*. New York: Meridian.

Grosz, Elizabeth. 1989. "Sexual Difference and the Problem of Essentialism." *Inscriptions* 5: 86-101.

Haraway, Donna. 1988. "Situated Knowledges: the Science Question in Feminism and the Privilege of Partial Perspective." *Feminist Studies* 14.3: 575-99.

Harlow, Barbara. 1987. *Resistance Literature*. New York: Metheun.

Henderson, Mae Gwendolyn. 1989a. "Response" to Houston A. Baker, Jr.'s "There is No More Beautiful Way." In *Afro-American Literary Studies in the 1990's*, ed. Houston A. Baker, Jr. Chicago: University of Chicago Press.

____. 1989b. "Speaking in Tongues: Dialogics, Dialectics, and the Black Woman Writer's Literary Tradition." In *Changing Our Own Words: Essays on Criticism, Theory, and Writing the Black Women*, ed. Cheryl A. Wall. New Brunswick: Rutgers University Press.

hooks, bell. 1989. "'When I Was a Young Soldier for the Revolution': Coming to Voice." In *Talking Back: Thinking Feminist. Thinking Black*, ed, bell hooks. Boston: South End.

Hull, Gloria T. 1989. "Living on the Line: Audre Lorde and Our Dead Behind Us." In *Changing Our Own Words: Essays on Criticism, Theory, and Writing the Black Women*, ed. Cheryl A. Wall. New Brunswick: Rutgers University Press.

Kerr, Lucille. 1992. *Reclaiming the Author: Figures and Fictions from Spanish America*. Durham: Duke University Press.

Lorde, Audre. 1978. *The Black Unicorn*. New York: Norton.

____. 1984a. "An Interview: In Audre Lorde and Adrienne Rich." In *Sister Outsider*, Audre Lorde. Trumansburg: Crossing.

____. 1984b. "My Words Will Be There." In *Black Women Writers (1950-1980): A Critical Evaluation*, ed. Mari Evans. Garden City: Anchor/Doubleday.

____. 1984c. "Poetry is Not a Luxury." *Sister Outsider*. Trumansburg: Crossing.

____. 1984d. "Revolutionary Hope: A Conversation between James Baldwin and Audre Lorde." *Essence* (4 December): 72-74, 129-30, 133.

____. 1984e. "The Transformation of Silence into Language and Action." *Sister Outsider*. Trumansburg: Crossing.

____. 1984f. "Uses of the Erotic: The Erotic as Power." In *Sister Outsider*, ed. Audre Lorde. Trumansburg: Crossing.

____. 1988. *A Burst of Light*. Ithaca: Firebrand.

____. 1989. "Women, Power, and Difference." *Sojourner* 15 (November): 18-19.

Love, Nancy S. 1991. "Politics and Voice(s): An Empowerment/Knowledge Regime." *differences* 3.1: 85-103.

Marlatt, Daphne. 1990. "Difference (em)bracing." In *Language in Her Eye/Writing and Gender/Views by Canadian Women Writing in English*, ed. Libby Scheier et al. Toronto: Coach House.

Minh-ha, Trinh T.. 1989. *Woman, Native, Other*. Bloomington: Indiana University Press.

Mohanty, Chandra. 1991. "Under Western Eyes: Feminist Scholarship and Colonial Discourses." In *Third World Women and the Politics of Feminism*, eds. Chandra Mohanty, Ann Russo, and Lourdes Torres. Bloomington: Indiana University Press.

Perreault, Jeanne. 1988. "'That the pain not be wasted': Audre Lorde and the Written Self." *A/B: Autobiography Studies* 4 (Fall): 1-16.

Plath, Sylvia. 1968. "The Colossus." In *The Colossus and Other Poems*. New York:

Vintage.

Smith, Valerie. 1989. "Black Feminist Theory and the Representation of the 'Other.'" In *Changing Our Own Words: Essays on Criticism, Theory, and Writing the Black Women*, ed. Cheryl A. Wall. New Brunswick: Rutgers University Press.

Sontag, Susan. 1969. "The Aesthetics of Silence." In *Styles of Radical Will*. New York: Farrar.

Spellman, Elizabeth V. 1988. *Inessential Woman: Problems of Exclusion in Feminist Thought*. Boston: Beacon.

Spence, Jo. 1990. "Identity and Cultural Production." *Views* (Summer): 8-11.

Spillers, Hortense. 1987. "Mama's Baby, Papa's Maybe: An American Grammar Book." *Diacritics* (Summer): 65-81.

Spivak, Gayatri, with Elizabeth Grosz. 1990. "Criticism, Feminism, and the Institution." *The Post-Colonial Critic: Interviews, Strategies, Dialogues*. Ed. Sarah Harasym. New York: Routledge.

Spivak, Gayatri. 1990. "On the Politics of the Subaltern: Interview with Howard Winant." *Socialist Review* 3: 81-97.

Spivak, Gayatri, with Ellen Rooney. 1989. "In a Word. Interview." *differences* 1.2: 124-56.

Wall, Cheryl A., ed. 1989. *Changing Our Own Words: Essays on Criticism, Theory, and Writing by Black Women*. New Brunswick: Rutgers University Press.

_____. 1990. "Taking Positions and Changing Words." In *Changing Our Own Words: Essays on Criticism, Theory, and Writing the Black Women*, ed. Cheryl A. Wall. New Brunswick: Rutgers University Press.

Walker, Cheryl. 1990. "Feminist Literary Criticism and the Author." *Critical Inquiry* 16: 551-71.

7

The Hybrid Terrain of Literary Imagination: Maryse Condé's Black Witch of Salem, Nathaniel Hawthorne's Hester Prynne, and Aimé Césaire's Heroic Poetic Voice

Mara L. Dukats

> Literature is not only fragmented, it is henceforth shared. In it lie histories and the voice of peoples.
>
> Édouard Glissant, *Caribbean Discourse*

"Women have no mouth," claims a Cameroon proverb (Schipper 1985, 20). The corollary to such "common knowledge" is, of course, that women, by their very nature, cannot speak. Against this image of woman's essential silence, feminist writing has historicized and contextualized woman's absence and her enforced voicelessness. Charting the arduous journey from silence into speech, feminist writing has literally written women into existence and given a forum to words that have gone unheard. Thus, Carole Boyce Davies and Elaine Savory Fido argue that "the concept of voicelessness necessarily informs any discussion of Caribbean women and literature" (Davies and Fido 1990, 1). Voicelessness, as these authors claim, means not only the "historical absence of the woman writer's text," but also the "inability to express" and the "silence" of "articulation that goes unheard" (Davies and Fido 1990, 1). This same voicelessness surrounds the absent and silenced text of Tituba Indian, a Barbadian slave woman whom Maryse Condé "ressurects" in the novel *I, Tituba, Black Witch of Salem*.[1] The novel reconstructs the life of Tituba, sold in Barbados to the Reverend Samuel Parris, and brought to the American colonies to serve his family. Alleged to have bewitched the minister's daughter and his niece, causing the children severe fits of hysteria, and initiating the accusations, interrogations, and executions of the Salem witches, Tituba has become inseparably linked with the beginning of this notoriously odious chapter of American history.

Presented as Tituba's first-person narrative that Condé, as "author," has transcribed, *I, Tituba*, responds to the historical absence of Tituba's own narration of her life. As narrator in Condé's novel, Tituba emphasizes the fact that there is no written record of her existence: "I can look for my story among those of the witches of Salem, but it isn't there" (Condé 1992, 149). Indeed, Tituba experiences this deliberate omission and silencing as "a violent feeling of pain and terror" (110).

Halfway into the narrative, Condé has inserted extracts from Tituba's official deposition—the one safely deposited for posterity in the Essex County Archives in Salem, Massachusetts. Ironically, this recontextualization of Tituba's interrogation and of the words that she is recorded as having spoken serves to underscore her voicelessness—her lack of access to a voice at the very moment when she is called on to speak.

Tituba's confession, inserted into the narrative in the form of four pages of transcribed excerpts from the documents of her deposition, functions as the official text against which Condé's Tituba speaks and defines herself anew. *I, Tituba*, is a retelling of history with Tituba as the first-person narrator and Condé as the scribe. This collaborative response to the "racism of the historians" (Condé 1992, 183) is thus a literal writing-into-being of an historically effaced woman.

Although historical reality is the basis for *I, Tituba*, Condé's narrative claims neither to be "history" nor to constitute "historical truth." As Condé has said:

A historian is somebody who studies the facts, the historical facts—somebody who is tied to reality, somebody who is tied to what actually happens. I am just a dreamer—my dreams rest upon a historical basis. Being a black person, having a certain past, having a certain history behind me, I want to explore that realm and of course I do it with my imagination and with my intuition. But I am not involved in any kind of scholarly research. . . . For me Tituba is not a historical novel. Tituba is just the opposite of a historical novel. I was not interested at all in what her real life could have been.

I had few precise documents: her deposition testimony. It forms the only historical part of the novel, and I was not interested in getting anything more than that. I really invented Tituba. (Condé 1990, 200-201)

Filling in the blank spaces of lost history is thus not the primary focus of Condé's novel. Rather, it marks out a space for Caribbean woman's presence on the literary landscape by exposing her historical marginalization. Condé's explicit affirmation of the collaborative nature of *I, Tituba*, is not so much a technique of postmodernist fiction or magical realism as it is the assertion of the extent and duration of confinement and the surreal efforts necessary to move out of voicelessness. By incorporating and revisiting the canonized texts of Aimé Césaire and Nathaniel Hawthorne, Condé reclaims Tituba's presence as a shaping force, as a background against which both the Caribbean hero and the American heroine took form.

Giving voice to a silenced Tituba, Condé recontextualizes her trial and the text of her deposition. Resituating this official text to the core of her novel, Condé allows Tituba a new hearing. Although these literary techniques clearly give Tituba a new visibility and force us to rethink the ways in which the past has been discursively constructed, the focus of my discussion is the way in which Condé's text rethinks literature itself.

Arguing for the hybridity of cultural processes, traditions, and formations, several contemporary theorists have advanced a view of culture as "a multivalent weave of dominant, residual, and emergent strands that are often in tension with one another" (Fraser 1992, 18).[2] This view of culture necessarily implies a reconceptualization of agency and a rethinking of the ways in which the "dominant" is itself defined and conditioned by the residual and emergent. In this view, "dominant" culture is no longer a closed and exclusive totality, but rather, a complex web of both hegemonic and counterhegemonic forces. What I would like to suggest in the following discussion is that dominant culture shares with literary imagination its hybridity.

Condé's mélange of historical and literary texts makes Tituba a symbolic presence that enables a revision of literary imagination, by which I mean the set of perceptual constructs within which a writer thinks, works, and creates at any given time. Literary imagination is a hybrid terrain, meaning not only that it is made up of a weave of diverse strands, but, more importantly, that within this hybrid terrain there are elements that are invisible, overshadowed, and suppressed. Moreover, these effaced elements often provide the enabling conditions for "dominant" cultural constructs and thereby manifest themselves as shaping forces, albeit unacknowledged ones. Condé's *I, Tituba*, brilliantly illustrates ways in which literary texts reclaim unacknowledged and effaced agency, thus reconceptualizing the processes of cultural formations and revealing the interrelational terrain, or hybridity, of literary imagination.

Similar to the concept of hybridity is that of *métissage*, defined by Françoise Lionnet as a concept that "allow[s] us to think *otherwise*" and "bypass the ancient symmetries and dichotomies that have governed the ground and the very condition of possibility of thought . . . in . . . Western philosophy" (Lionnet 1989, 6). In her theoretical work, Lionnet has used the concept of *métissage* to suggest a radical revision of the ways in which identity, culture, and counterhegemonic practices have been conceptualized.

In "*'Logiques métisses'*: Cultural Appropriation and Postcolonial Representations," for example, Lionnet sets forth the argument that the "ground upon which contemporary global culture can begin to be understood" is made up of the "processes of adaptation, appropriation, and contestation that govern the construction of identity in colonial and postcolonial contexts" (Lionnet 1992/93, 101). Lionnet's quarrel with the way that the relationship between the colonized culture and the hegemonic system has generally been conceptualized is that it has emphasized only the subjugation, assimilation, and passivity of the colonized and has failed to assess the "transformative" processes and the "appropriative techniques" with which the colonized culture has actively "delegitimated" cultural hegemony and refuted the "paradigm of exoticism and/or victimization" (103-16). The "patterns of influence" between the colonized culture and the hegemonic system are "never unidirectional," but rather, "mutual and reciprocal" (103), argues Lionnet, quoting Toni Morrison: "Afro-American culture exists and though it is clear (and becoming clearer) how it has responded to Western culture, the instances where and means by which it has shaped Western culture are poorly recognized or understood" (102).

In *Playing in the Dark,* Toni Morrison takes up this very argument, claiming that black slavery created "a playground for the imagination" (Morrison 1990, 38) of early American writers. Contrary to the conventionally accepted "knowledge" that "traditional, canonical American literature is free of, uninformed, and unshaped by the four-hundred-year-old presence of, first, Africans and then African-Americans in the U.S." (5), argues Morrison, the Africanist presence has provided the "arena for the elaboration of the quintessential American identity" (44) and furnished the major themes of American literature. This corresponds to what Lionnet, in the above-mentioned article, calls the "global mongrelization or *métissage* of cultural forms" (Lionnet 1992/93, 101). Lionnet's and Morrison's focus on the unacknowledged agency of historically marginalized voices in the shaping of dominant tradition points to the Africanist other as the effaced, enabling force behind such classics as *The Scarlet Letter.* Correspondingly, *I, Tituba* should be read not primarily as a countertext to historical lacuna, but rather, as a text that conceptualizes Tituba as the effaced and unacknowledged presence that conditions the construction of the canonized texts that it interrogates.

Set within the brutal, patriarchal, racist societies of New England and Barbados during the late seventeenth century, when collective hysteria was sweeping the villages of Massachusetts into a cruel witch-hunt and the slave trade was growing in intensity, *I, Tituba* presents itself as a corrective for historical oblivion—an explicit response to the "intentional or unintentional racism of the historians" (Condé 1992, 183) who have excluded Tituba from their accounts of the trials and executions of the alleged witches of Salem. As narrator, Tituba senses the cruelty of this effacement, this "injustice" (110), but knows that she will be immortalized in the hearts of her people, existing as the vital force that ignites revolt and sustains the dream of freedom.

This oppositional or revolutionary Tituba presents the other of the Tituba we have come to know via our history texts—the West Indian slave who, under torture, confessed that she had submitted to Satan's control and had tormented children. Condé's Tituba focuses on her enforced voicelessness. Forced to deny her self and to affirm her subjugation to a masculine power, she assumes the identity that her oppressors design. "Well spoken, Tituba. You understood what we expected of you" (Condé 1992, 106), Samuel Parris says after her interrogation. In response, Condé's Tituba can only acknowledge, to herself, the violent self-negation of her confession: "I hate myself as much as I hate him" (106).

Interestingly, this text of silenced history becomes a text that returns to other literary texts, and specifically to two that have been canonized as points of origin for their respective literary traditions. If Nathaniel Hawthorne's *The Scarlet Letter* has been regarded as the "true beginning of American prose fiction" (Bloom 1986, 8), Aimé Césaire's "Notebook of a Return to the Native Land" has been canonized as a "fundamental" or "sacred" text (Condé 1993, 126) that has given rise to all subsequent Francophone Caribbean literature. Although Condé herself has acknowledged both the literary and political significance of Césaire's "Notebook" (see *Cahier* and *La poésie*), she takes issue with the way that it has been canonized, specifically, with the way that its reception has led to prescriptive "orders" for Antillean literature, stifling its creativity and perpetuating the oblivion and incomprehension of women writers of the West Indies (Condé 1993, 122-34).

I, Tituba, thus takes the events at Salem as a backdrop for the exploration of the ways in which Tituba's silenced narrative has been incorporated into canonized texts and, more significantly, for an exploration of the ways in which this silenced text has functioned as an enabling or conditioning force for canonized texts. Condé's *I, Tituba*, illustrates both what Lionnet calls the "*métissage* of cultural forms" and what Morrison identifies as the "compelling and inescapable" (Morrison 1990, 46) ways in which unacknowledged presence shapes the texture of canonized literature.

If "Africanism is the vehicle by which the American self knows itself as not enslaved, but free; not repulsive, but desirable; not helpless, but licensed and powerful; not history-less, but historical; not damned, but innocent; not a blind accident of evolution, but a progressive fulfillment of destiny" (Morrison 1990, 52), in short, if a negatively valued Africanism enables the construction of a positive American identity, then similarly, within the context of the witch trials of Salem, and within Condé's narrative, Tituba is the vehicle by which Puritan identity reestablishes itself as powerful, righteous, and innocent.

Tituba's "confession," the text of her deposition testimony, is the only historical document that Condé has at her disposal. The text of the novel is Tituba's second confession, and as Condé states in the epigraph, it contains her "endless conversations" with Tituba, conversations during which Tituba revealed things "she had confided to nobody else." This "second" and "private confession" (which is not really a confession at all, but rather, a coauthored life story resulting from a presumed and intimate woman-to-woman dialogue), in which Tituba claims her own identity with the words "I, Tituba," is countered by the first public confession, in which Tituba strives to follow Hester's recommendations and give the magistrates "their money's worth" (Condé 1992, 99), describing to them exactly what they believe, even if it has nothing to do with the truth. Hester thus advises Tituba to legitimate the beliefs of her persecuters, and not without good reason, because, by law, the life of a witch was spared if she confessed. By confessing, then, Tituba escapes death, yet legitimates the authority of her oppressors.

If, after her public confession, Tituba hates herself because she has acquiesced and affirmed an identity that her oppressors have constructed for her, she nonetheless has also spoken a truth that Condé's novel unearths centuries later. *I, Tituba*, is the text that allows Tituba to say to her oppressors, "You created me; you constructed and imposed a false identity upon me, but now that I have found a space in which I can speak openly, I am able to reveal not only my true self, but, as well, the ways in which I have shaped you and the ways in which I have informed your view of yourself." Tituba is thus able to illustrate what might forever have remained unacknowledged.

Condé narrates the way that the American literary imagination has "played in the dark" and the way that the "dark and abiding presence" now reclaims its role as "mediating force" (Morrison 1990, 46) through a rewriting of Hester Prynne, the heroine of the "quintessential American novel" (Baym 1986, xxv), *The Scarlet Letter*. If for Morrison the "imaginative encounter with Africanism enable[d] white writers to think about themselves" (Morrison 1990, 51), for Condé, the imaginative encounter between Tituba and Hawthorne's Hester Prynne enabled Condé to think about the way that her heroine, Tituba, had enabled Hawthorne to produce the "true beginning of American prose fiction." Condé thus returns to this canonized "absolute point of origin" (Bloom 1986, 8) to reclaim Tituba's part in this origin and to reaffirm Tituba's presence in what inevitably becomes a "wider landscape" (Morrison 1990, 3) and a more hybrid lineage than heretofore imagined.

When asked about her incorporation of Hester Prynne in *I, Tituba*, Condé has replied:

First of all I like the novel *The Scarlet Letter* and I read it often. Second, it is set in roughly the same period as *Tituba*. Third, when I went to Salem to visit the village, the place where Tituba used to live, I saw the house of Nathaniel Hawthorne, the House of the Seven Gables . . . meaning there was a link between Tituba and Nathaniel Hawthorne. (Condé 1992, 202)

Condé's oblique answer refuses any comment on Hester, and rather than drawing a link between herself and Hawthorne,[3] Condé forges a link between the voiceless Tituba and Nathaniel Hawthorne, the white male writer who, "with the publication of *The Scarlet Letter* . . . was instantly elevated to the position of the nation's foremost man of letters" (Baym 1986, xxi).

This gesture is, on the one hand, ironic, since it implies that although Tituba was as much alive and real as Hawthorne, she was silenced for centuries and could not become a "writer" until the 1986 collaboration with Maryse Condé. The linking of Tituba and Hawthorne also comments on the way that popular imagination is formed and preserved. If Tituba's traces have been entirely erased from Salem, and Maryse Condé's trip to the village is a return to a place that might somehow stir her imagination or speak to her intuitively, the House of the Seven Gables physically imposes itself on the visitor, reinforcing what has already been immortalized in the popular imagination and canonized in the American literary tradition. Condé's connection between Tituba and Hawthorne thus has a trifold effect: first, it reveals an effacement; second, it reclaims Salem as a shared terrain; and third, it reappropriates "the imaginative and historical terrain upon which early American writers journeyed" as a terrain "shaped by the presence of the racial other" (Morrison 1990, 46).

It is no surprise, then, that Tituba is more present in the imaginative terrain, in literature,[4] than in "historical" documents. In her search for a "folk heroine of the West Indies" (Condé and Clark 1989, 129), Condé revisits the American literary tradition, returning to the scarlet letter, the signifier of Hester Prynne's infamy.

The opening scene of *The Scarlet Letter* recounts the visual display of Hester's body in the marketplace. Rather than appearing disgraced, however, Hester emerges from the prison "marked with natural dignity and force of character" (Hawthorne 1960, 54), proudly displaying her elaborately and artistically embroidered letter A. As one of the spectators remarks, Hester has made "pride" out of "punishment" (56). By embellishing the letter that is to mark her with ignominy, Hester transforms the sign into a complex and ambiguous symbol—one that signifies both Puritan control and domination and the refusal and delegitimation of this control.

Likewise, *I, Tituba,* Tituba's autobiographical narrative, is the embellishment of a text (Tituba's deposition testimony) that signifies Tituba's guilt. Like Hester Prynne, Tituba refutes her subjugation by reappropriating, transforming, and signifying on a text intended as an unambiguous assertion of her fault. There is thus an alliance between Tituba and Hester, a connection Condé imagines and narrates as the sisterhood and friendship between two victimized women.

Although it is unlikely that Hester Prynne is Hawthorne's intentional embodiment of an Africanist presence, I would like to suggest that the "invisible mediating force" (Morrison 1990, 46) behind Hester is the Africanist presence, as formulated by Morrison. Indeed, Morrison has argued that "even, and especially, when American texts are not 'about' Africanist presences or characters or narrative or idiom, the shadow hovers in implication, in sign, in line of demarcation" (46-47). Hence, Morrison contends that the Africanist presence acts "[a]s a metaphor for transacting the whole process of Americanization, while burying its particular racial ingredients" and "may be something the United States cannot do without" (47). By drawing a parallel between Tituba and Hester, Condé's text unburies this "racial ingredient," deciphering and making visible the complex workings of literary imagination. As Morrison says:

> For American writers . . . th[e] Africanist other became the means of thinking about body, mind, chaos, kindness, and love; provided the occasion for . . . the contemplation of freedom and of agression; permitted opportunities for the exploration of ethics and morality, for meeting the obligations of the social contract, for bearing the cross of religion and following out the ramifications of power. (47-48)

Following this argument, then, the Africanist other enabled, or made conceivable, the exploration of the issues central to *The Scarlet Letter.* Condé's novel thus not only fills a gap in the search for legendary Caribbean women, but also reclaims the Africanist presence as a shaping force in canonical American literature.

In her rewriting of Hawthorne's Hester Prynne, Condé retains some of Hester's defining characteristics—such as the blackness of her physical traits—but, on the whole, creates an altogether different Hester. Whereas Hawthorne's Hester gives birth to Pearl and lives according to what she feels is her maternal duty—to "conform with the most perfect quietude to the external regulations of society" (Hawthorne 1960, 163)—Condé's Hester hangs herself in prison, before the birth of her child. Although Hawthorne's Hester contemplates suicide and infanticide, and although she is deeply critical of her society, she contents herself with a life of meditation, without investing her thought in action. If it weren't for Pearl, however, Hester might have attempted "to undermine the foundations of the Puritan establishment" (163-64).

In a sense, Tituba's return to Barbados and her decision to carry her child to term can be read as her attempt to be like Hawthorne's Hester Prynne. In Hawthorne's text, the scarlet letter becomes legendary, assumes different meanings as time goes on, and, in the end, is even looked upon "with reverence" (Hawthorne 1960, 261). Society denies Tituba such luxury—in Barbados she is still "the black witch of Salem," and she is hanged, pregnant with child. *I, Tituba* thus emphasizes the issue of agency. Whereas Hawthorne's Hester chooses not to speak (to conceal the identity of Chillingworth and Dimmesdale), Tituba is silenced. Although Condé's Hester is not to be envied, she is the author of her own death, unlike Tituba and unlike Abena.

As Harold Bloom has noted, "every reader of *The Scarlet Letter* comes to feel a great regret at Hester's unfulfilled potential. . . . Certainly we sense an unwritten book in her, a story that Hawthorne did not choose to write" (Bloom 1986, 8). On another level then, we might read Tituba's participation in the slave revolt as an attempt to fulfill Hester's revolutionary potential. Back in Barbados, Tituba dreams of raising her yet unborn daughter in a different world. Nonetheless, the revolt she helps plan and carry out is unsuccessful. What *I, Tituba*, suggests, then, is that Tituba, by reason of her race, is in a no-win situation. She can neither be redeemed nor live out her life in tranquility like Hawthorne's Hester. She can neither successfully undermine the system that oppresses her nor author her own death. Curiously, then, if the Africanist presence generates the imaginative terrain for Hawthorne's narrative, when we paint Hester black, then *The Scarlet Letter*, as we know it, becomes inconceivable. Condé's text thus unearths this necessary camouflaging of the Africanist presence.

In the explicit rewriting of its own ending, however, the narrative allows us to envision an empowered Tituba. *I, Tituba*, is not only a rewriting of Tituba's life, but also a rewriting of her fictional death. Although the novel ends with Tituba at the gallows, the epilogue allows Tituba to speak once again and to claim that her story really "has no end" (Condé 1992, 175). In this purely imaginative terrain of the "Epilogue," Tituba becomes a revolutionary and a mother by choice. Whereas *The Scarlet Letter* allows us to sense in Hester the unwritten book that Hawthorne chose not to write, *I, Tituba*, allows us to sense in Tituba an unwritten book that was denied expression.

If Hawthorne's heroine is one point of reference for Tituba, the Caribbean hero is another. Kathleen Balutansky has argued that "for contemporary women writers, imagining and representing fully autonomous Caribbean women seems paradoxical, especially when the governing symbol for the Caribbean condition remains that of Caliban" (Balutansky 1992, 29). Condé's claim that the text before us is the product of conversations between two women separated by three centuries of time allows Tituba to transcend time and signify on Aimé Césaire's "Notebook of a Return to the Native Land," in particular its Calibanesque parthenogenesis. In terms of emplotment and imagery, Tituba's narrative echoes the

"Notebook," inviting comparison between a text that gives voice to a forgotten and silenced black heroine and a text that has become inseparably linked with the origins of Antillean negritude. If Césaire's negritude renewed awareness in black culture and black identity, Condé's novel implies that this was largely a "male" identity, but an identity that obtained its insurrectional force from its own conscious or unconscious inscription of woman's experience.

Whereas the hero of the "Notebook" is an anonymous male who comes to embody the universal voice of his people, Tituba's story is the personal account of the life of an outcast. Unlike the male hero, who is able to establish fraternity with his people, the heroine is a solitary figure whose revolt remains circumscribed by the limits society imposes on her gender. After her mother is hanged for having defended herself against the sexual aggression of her master, Tituba voices her impotence, alluding to the fact that Césairian heroism is inaccessible to her:

> Oh yes, I should have liked to unleash the wind like a dog from his kennel so that the white Great Houses of the masters would be blown away over the horizon, to order a fire to kindle and fan its flames so that the whole island would be purified and devastated. But I didn't have such powers. I only knew how to offer consolation. (Condé 1992, 141)

As argued by Janice Lee Liddell, the archetypal Caribbean woman is the "good mumma," and women are so constrained by this image that they can only be "something else" if the "mother spirit" is present in that "something else" (Liddell 1990, 321). When Tituba returns to her island with a sense of revolt against injustice and finds herself pregnant again, even Man Yaya and Abena equate Tituba's maternity with her *nature*: "Well, this time you can't do away with it! Your real nature has spoken!" (Condé 1992,158). Indeed, Tituba's revolt is articulated within the maternal context, indicating that it is only possible where the "mother spirit" is clearly evident. Thus, she is asked to "disarm" (Condé 1992, 163) Christopher, being the only one who can do so, as she is carrying his child.

The turning points of Tituba's life—her rebirth into the world when her shackles and chains are smashed to pieces, the return to her island, her sacrificial offering and unsuccessful revolt—ironically echo the emplotment of Césaire's "Notebook." Upon their return, both Tituba and Césaire's hero are struck by the stench and ugliness of their native land. Tituba laments:

> my island did not exactly deck itself out to greet me. . . . The streets were churned with muddy water in which men and beasts were splashing. . . . How ugly my town was! Small. Petty. A colonial outpost of no distinction, reeking with the stench of lucre and suffering. (Condé 1992, 141)

Echoes of Césaire's "mute," "inert," and "sprawled-flat" town, the "hungry Antilles . . . pitted with smallpox" and . . . "stranded in the mud" like a "bedsore on the wound of the waters" (Césaire 1983, 35) immediately come to mind. Although the poetic voice in the "Notebook" bemoans the "restrained con-flagration of the morne" and the "sob gagged on the verge of a bloodthirsty burst" (Césaire 1983, 37), his "male thirst" allows the hero to overcome voice-lessness and become "the mouth of those calamities that have no mouth" (45). Tituba's narrative, on the other hand, is punctuated with the screams of women, yet these are screams that go unheard and, ultimately, communicate to no one.

Tituba's voicelessness becomes all the more evident with the incessantly muted screams that cannot but echo back to Césaire's text and its development of an ever-more resounding and self-affirmative voice. As she witnesses the hanging death of Goody Glover, for example, Tituba recalls: "I *screamed*, and the more I *screamed* the more I felt the desire to *scream*. To *scream* out my suf-fering, my revolt, and my powerless rage" (Condé 1992, 49, my emphasis). This "powerless rage" later becomes the scream of her aborted child. When she learns of Hester's suicide, Tituba identifies herself with a screaming fetus who fights not for life, but for death:

> I *screamed* down the door of my mother's womb. My fist broke her bag of waters in rage and despair. I choked and suffocated in this black liquid. I wanted to drown myself. . . . Mother, will our torture never end? If this is how things are, I shall never emerge into the light of day. I shall remain crouched in your waters, deaf, dumb, and blind, clinging like kelp to your womb. I shall cling so tightly you'll never expel me and I shall return to dust without you, without ever having known the curse of day. Mother, help me! (Condé 1992, 111, my emphasis)

Whereas the male hero is able to "forc[e] the vitelline membrane that separates [him] from [him]self" (Césaire 1983, 57), to give birth to himself, to imagine a "yet undared form" issuing from "man's unfathomable sperm" (Césaire 1983, 67), and to claim an identity, Tituba's text is marked with impotence.

It is particularly with the metaphors of blood and birth that the heroine's text returns to the hero's poem as a native to an alien land. The blood of revolt, so prominent in the "Notebook," becomes, in Tituba's text, the blood of the violated woman. This blood precariously unites Tituba and her mistress, Eliza-beth Parris, when Samuel Parris strikes the two women. It is the blood of aborted birth, the black stinking blood of the sacrificial rabbit, which unites with Tituba's own blood as she wounds herself with the knife she uses to slit the rabbit's belly. The puddle of blood at her feet reminds Tituba of Yao's words, which echo, not surprisingly, the words of the "Notebook": "Our memory will have to be covered in blood. . . . Our memories will have to float to the surface like water lilies" (Condé 1992, 165).

The irony of the use of Césaire's "Notebook" as subtext is compounded when Tituba is called on to command to the elements. Compared to the male sorcerer, Tituba, the tortured and misunderstood *sorcière*, has no alchemic or metamorphic powers. Unlike the male hero-narrator, she is "nothing but a common Negress" (Condé 1992, 155). The question she asks as her narrative draws to a close—"Do I have to go on to the end?" (166)—emphasizes the difference between her muffled dissent and the powerful, rising, and climactic poetic voice that closes Césaire's "Notebook."

Voicelessness—so crucial an issue for an understanding of Caribbean women's creativity (Davies and Fido 1990, 1)—is deeply tied to historicity and to the reconstitution of black women's history. As Angela Davis has said in her foreword to the translation of *I, Tituba*:

> As Condé offers to Tituba the possibility of filling the silence and voids with voice and presence, we who are Tituba's cultural kin experience the possibilities of our own history. . . . And when Tituba takes her place in the history of the Salem witch trials, the recorded history of that era—and indeed the entire history of the colonization process—is revealed to be seriously flawed. (Davis 1990, xii)

Because voicelessness as suppressed history and unacknowledged agency is so central an issue in Tituba's life story, the very fact of presenting the possibility of her narrative is empowering. Not only does Tituba's voice participate in the reconstruction of the suppressed history of black women and challenge the ways that the past has been encoded, but it also reveals the presence of subdued voice in canonized literary texts.

As Ann Armstrong Scarboro points out, "Condé does not merely retell Tituba's story; she recreates it to new purposes" (Scarboro 1992, 213). Condé's recreation of Tituba's life allows the silenced heroine to intervene in the canon by proposing a revision of the way that we read texts. Tituba subverts the canon not by replacing some texts with others, but by articulating the need for alternative reading practices. By encoding the hybrid terrain of literary imagination, the narrative offers an alternative perspective on the enabling and formative conditions of canonized texts. *I, Tituba*, also suggests a renewed awareness of the complexity of cultural formations and the way that the discursive features of a text actively revise, transform, and establish interrelations that in turn lead to the revaluation of power and the renegotiation of social relations.

Notes

1. All textual references to Condé's *Moi, Tituba* are from Richard Philcox's translation (*I, Tituba*).
2. I borrow this formulation from Nancy Fraser, who uses it in her introduction to *Revaluing French Feminism* to define "two antithetical conceptions of culture," the other being the view that culture is "monolithically phallocentric, everywhere instantiating the same hierarchical binary oppositions and eternally repressing feminine difference" (Fraser 1992, 17-18).
3. A link for which there are clear grounds: both authors claim to have found "evidence"—in Condé's case, the deposition, in Hawthorne's, the scarlet letter—that marks their respective heroines and inspires the narratives created about them, both of which deal thematically with guilt, confession, silence, and retribution.
4. Jeanne Snitgen gives the following list: Henry Wadsworth Longfellow's *Giles Corey of the Salem Farms*, William Carlos Williams' *Tituba's Children*, Arthur Miller's *The Crucible*, and Ann Petry's *Tituba of Salem Village* (Snitgen 1989).

Works Cited

Balutansky, Kathleen M. 1992. "Creating Her Own Image: Female Genesis in *Mémoire d'une amnésique* and *Moi, Tituba sorcière. . . .*" *L'Héritage de Caliban*. Ed. Maryse Condé. Guadeloupe: Jasor.
Baym, Nina. 1986. *The Scarlet Letter: A Reading*. Boston: Twayne.
Bloom, Harold. 1986. Introduction to *Nathaniel Hawthorne's The Scarlet Letter*, ed. Harold Bloom. New York: Chelsea.
Césaire, Aimé. 1983. "Notebook of a Return to the Native Land." In *The Collected Poetry*, trans. Clayton Eshleman and Annette Smith. Berkeley: University of California Press.
Condé, Maryse. 1978a. *Cahier d'un retour au pays natal: Césaire: analyse critique*. Paris: Hatier.
____. 1978b. *La poésie antillaise*. Paris: Nathan.
____. 1986. *Moi, Tituba, sorcière . . . Noire de Salem*. Paris: Mercure de France.
____. 1989. "'Je me suis réconciliée avec mon île'/'I Have Made Peace with My Island': Une interview de Maryse Condé/An Interview with Maryse Condé." With VèVè A. Clark. *Callaloo* 12 (Winter): 85-133.
____. 1992a. "An Interview with Maryse Condé." With Ann Armstrong Scarboro. Afterword to *I, Tituba, Black Witch of Salem*, trans. Richard Philcox. Charlottesville: University Press of Virginia.
____. 1992b. *I, Tituba, Black Witch of Salem*. Trans. Richard Philcox. Charlottesville: University Press of Virginia.
____. 1993. "Order, Disorder, Freedom, and the West Indian Writer." *Yale French Studies* 83: 121-35.
Davies, Carole Boyce, and Elaine Savory Fido. 1990. "Introduction: Women and Litera-

ture in the Caribbean: An Overview." In *Out of the Kumbla: Caribbean Women and Literature*, ed. Carole Boyce Davies and Elaine Savory Fido. Trenton: African World.

Davis, Angela Y. 1978. Foreword to *I, Tituba, Black Witch of Salem*, trans. Richard Philcox. Charlottesville: University Press of Virginia.

Fraser, Nancy. 1992. Introduction to *Revaluing French Feminism: Critical Essays on Difference, Agency, and Culture*, ed. Nancy Fraser and Sandra Lee Bartky. Bloomington: Indiana University Press.

Hawthorne, Nathaniel. 1960. *The Scarlet Letter*. Ed. Harry Levin. Reprint 1850. Boston: Houghton.

Liddell, Janice Lee. 1990. "The Narrow Enclosure of Motherdom/Martyrdom: A Study of Gatha Randall Barton in Sylvia Wynter's *The Hills of Hebron*." In *Out of the Kumbla: Caribbean Women and Literature*, ed. Carole Boyce Davies and Elaine Savory Fido. Trenton: African World.

Lionnet, Françoise. 1989. *Autobiographical Voices: Race, Gender, Self-Portraiture*. Ithaca: Cornell University Press.

_____. 1992/93. "*'Logiques métisses'*: Cultural Appropriation and Postcolonial Representations." *College Literature* 19.3/20.1 (October/February): 100-120.

Morrison, Toni. 1990. *Playing in the Dark: Whiteness and the Literary Imagination*. Cambridge: Harvard University Press.

Scarboro, Ann Armstrong. 1992. Afterword to *I, Tituba, Black Witch of Salem* by Maryse Condé. Trans. Richard Philcox. Charlottesville: University Press of Virginia.

Schipper, Mineke. 1985. "Women and Literature in Africa." In *Unheard Words: Women and Literature in Africa, the Arab World, Asia, the Caribbean and Latin America*, trans. Barbara Potter Fasting. London: Allison and Busby.

Snitgen, Jeanne. 1989. "History, Identity and the Constitution of the Female Subject: Maryse Condé's Tituba." In *Black Women's Writing: Crossing the Boundaries*, ed. Carole Boyce Davies. Frankfurt: Holger Ehling.

8

The Black Voice and the Language of the Text: Toni Morrison's *Sula*

Biman Basu

One of the most significant developments in the African-American tradition has been the formation of a class of intellectuals (scholars, critics, writers), a formation shot through and through with conflict both within and without. The conflict, on one hand, is between African-American and American culture, and on the other, between this class of intellectuals and the "people," the "masses." The conflict, in both its productive and traumatic force, may, in fact, be seen as propelling the trajectory of the African-American intellectual and expressive enterprise. Even the terms used to understand this phenomenon offer ample evidence of the centrality of conflict in the works of African-American writers: double consciousness, dialogics of difference/dialectics of identity, simultaneity of oppression/discourse, immersion and ascent, roots and routes, anchorage and voyage, and so on.

The centrality of this concern in cultural analysis cannot be elided when we shift our focus to literary studies. While this conflict is operative in practically all African-American writing, the focus here is on the tradition of black women's fiction, specifically as it appears in Toni Morrison's *Sula*. In terms of narrative strategy, black women writers have negotiated this conflict by manipulating what we have traditionally called point of view and, by extension, voice. This mobilization of voice enacts the conflict between cultures. At another level, however, African-American women's fiction has produced, from within, profound philosophical reflections on language itself.

Perhaps one of the most significant, and early, contributions to the study of voice in African-American fiction is John Wideman's "Defining the Black Voice in Fiction." He calls our attention to "the colonial interface of two language cultures—one written, literary and the other oral, traditional" (Wideman 1977, 81). The former is invested with a legitimating authority in the form of a "literary frame" that functions as a legitimating device: "the literary frame was a mediator, a legitimizer" (81). Furthermore, "the frame implies a linguistic hierarchy, the dominance of one language variety over all others" (81).

As a result of "the colonial interface," narrative strategy in black fiction involves a negotiation with the literary frame and its linguistic hierarchy. Different writers have, of course, intervened in this hierarchy in different ways, and, as Wideman suggests, the specific modes of this intervention, in fact, provide a continuum along which African-American literature may be charted (Wideman 1977, 79-80). As Henry Louis Gates has demonstrated most vigorously, Zora Neale Hurston's "oxymoronic oral hieroglyphic" (Gates 1988, 215) constitutes her specific mode of intervention. Gayl Jones intervenes in such a way that, as Wideman asserts, "the frame has disappeared" (Wideman 1977, 81).

Although Wideman later concedes that "black speech cannot escape entirely the frame of American literary language" (Wideman 1977, 82), the significant point is that we can observe a continuum in black women's fiction in which orality ruptures the fabric of the literary text; oral syntax implodes the literary voice. And although we might also concede that strictly, if somewhat fastidiously, speaking, "oral literature" is a "strictly preposterous term" (Ong 1982, 11), black women's fiction not only contains a substratum of oral residue but also actively communicates an oral/aural and tactile experience; that is, it manipulates and redistributes the sensory configuration of the literary experience. One of the ways it does so is through its concern with voice.

The concern with voice is intimately connected in black women's fiction with the nature of language, specifically with the written word itself. Limiting ourselves to an analysis of these concerns in *Sula*, we might articulate, albeit rather schematically, two rival claims of language. The first, which privileges the signifier and is perhaps best represented by Michel Foucault's method, has been immensely productive in literary and cultural studies and, for specific historical reasons that we need not consider here, in minority studies generally. Foucault does not, of course, remain intractable at the level of the signifier, but in the momentum of his method, particularly in certain aspects of his archaeology, traces of which are unmistakably carried over into his genealogy, one notes the loss of agency, the sense of being inexorably determined by a set of discursive regularities. At one point in his critique of Foucault, Habermas probes into these regularities, or into the regulation of these regularities, and forces us to acknowledge "'the strange notion of regularities which regulate themselves'" (Habermas 1992, 268). While Foucault's work has unquestionably been productive, the general methodological ascendancy of discourse analysis has fostered what one critic refers to as an "exorbitation of language" (Ahmad 1992, 6); and some African-American scholars have reacted against the textual orientation of African-American literary studies.[1]

As an alternative to this textualization, different groups have articulated different emphases, all of which aim to free literary studies from a somewhat rigid textuality. At the level of literature, the study of the relationship of the literary text to culture in general is a productive one even if, at times, the insistence on the nontextual in literary study seems to move in the direction of attempting to liberate literature from letters. At the level of language, representation may mark the epistemological limits of access, and yet representation itself seems constantly to be disfigured by unrepresentability. Even if one acknowledges that there is, at a certain level, no getting away from representation, marks of the nonrepresentational continue to leave their traces in the text. At the same time, even if one acknowledges that there is, at a certain level, no getting away from metaphysics, tentative excursions into metaphysics run the risk of being recuperated into essentialisms; and the charge of essentialism, which in some quarters has reached a ridiculously petulant pitch, remains, nevertheless, a serious one.

In *Sula*, Toni Morrison doggedly pursues these possibilities of language. She has, in her nonfiction, made her intentions clear. She asserts that "in Afro-American literature itself the question of difference, of essence, is critical" (Morrison 1989b, 11). She then asks, "What makes a book Black? The most valuable point of entry into the question of cultural (or racial) distinction, the one most fraught, is its language—its unpoliced, seditious, confrontational, manipulative, inventive, disruptive, masked and unmasking language. Such a penetration will entail the most careful study, one in which the impact of Afro-American presence on modernity becomes clear and is no longer a well-kept secret" (11).

Her observation about the black impact on modernity is profound, and this has been and continues to be read and demonstrated in various ways. For the purposes of this paper, however, it is her overwhelming emphasis on language that is important. Her response to the question, "What makes a book black?" is tautological: what makes a book black is its black language. We may also provisionally note that her insistence that the black "difference," the black "distinction," is its "essence"; its "presence" constitutes a move toward a metaphysics of race. Having observed these general directions of her comments, however, one also needs to observe that the black language of the black text, as cultural/racial index, is "the one most fraught," and the "entry," the "penetration," into this language "will entail the most careful study."

Characteristically, Morrison proceeds by exclusion and by analogy, by describing those traits that do not define black literature or, rather, by rejecting those definitions imposed by others, and by drawing an analogy with music. In an earlier interview, attempting to define "what makes a book 'black,'" she says, for example, "The only analogy I have for it is in music," and a little later, "I don't have the vocabulary to explain it better" (McKay 1983, 427). It has perhaps become all too easy to read in some of Morrison's comments a dangerous essentialism and a retrograde politics. Yet, these same comments may point toward that oral syntax that implodes the literary voice and, more generally, toward that element of the nonrepresentational, of excess, of grotesquerie that finds its embodiment in Sula. In the same interview cited above, Morrison makes a pertinent remark: "There was an articulate literature before there was print. There were griots. They memorized it. People heard it. It is important that there is sound in my books—that you can hear it, that I can hear it" (427).

The question of a defining, distinctive voice also crystallizes into a specifically technical problem of narrative strategy, that of point of view. And Morrison is heir to this concern in the tradition of black fiction. She seems, for example, altogether dissatisfied with her handling of point of view in her first novel, *The Bluest Eye*. She says she fails "to secure throughout the work the feminine subtext" and "the shambles this struggle became is most evident in the section on Pauline Breedlove where I resorted to two voices, hers and the urging narrator's, both of which are extremely unsatisfactory to me" (Morrison 1989b, 23). On *Sula*, Morrison is particularly terse about the opening: she says she is "embarrassed" by it and "despises" it (23-27). She calls it the "valley man's guidance," his "door" into "the territory."

The construction of this "valley man's" door, this discursive, authenticating,[2] introductory "literary frame," involves the opposition between "the nightshade and blackberry patches," the "two words of darkness in 'nightshade,'" indicating "Sula's double-dose of *chosen* blackness and *biological* blackness" (Morrison 1989b, 26). Further, Sula is "quintessentially black, metaphysically black, if you will, which is not melanin and certainly not unquestioning fidelity to the tribe" (25). In the next sequence of terms, Morrison moves from "metaphysically black" to "dangerously female": "She is new world black and new world woman extracting choice from choicelessness, responding inventively to found things. Improvisational. Daring, disruptive, imaginative, modern, out-of-the-house, outlawed, unpolicing, uncontained and uncontainable. And dangerously female" (25). Sula represents "the complex, contradictory, evasive, independent, liquid modernity" that "ushers in the Jazz Age" (26).

It is perhaps already clear that if we juxtapose what Morrison has to say about language and about Sula, or about the blackness of black language and Sula's blackness and femaleness, we find a compelling coincidence. We find direct repetition and echoes in "disruptive," "unpoliced/unpolicing," "inventive/improvisational/imaginative" and "seditious/outlawed"; the syntactically repeated closing of each sequence, "masked and unmasking" and "uncontained and uncontainable." In her descriptions of language and of Sula (i.e., in her remarks on representation and subjectivity) Morrison returns to the concept of modernity, a concept heavily sedimented with a subtext of blackness and femaleness. And, finally, she ends in both cases with the "only analogy" with music and, specifically, with "the Jazz Age."

Morrison, then, is clearly preoccupied not only with the technical considerations of point of view but also with the question of representation itself. It is as if she would have Sula become the figure of music in the text. When Morrison attempts to define the blackness of black language, she has, as we have observed, no vocabulary for it but relies on an analogy with music. So, too, when she attempts to describe Sula's blackness and femaleness. Sula, then, becomes the figure of language itself. More specifically, however, she seems to function as the figure of the semiotic in the text. She is the semiotic constituent of the symbolic, or the symbolically represented semiotic. In this sense, the collaborative effort between the narrator and Sula produces the voice of the text. This helps to explain the extreme ambivalence with which Sula is represented, the constant slippages and shifts between voices, and, most importantly here, the duet enacted in the scene of Sula's "mounting to orgasm" between narrator and character, a duet, a collaboration between the unconstituted and yet inalienably constitutive semiotic and the symbolic.

Without reference to these concerns, it is not possible to understand certain key passages in *Sula*, or, specifically, four passages that we might arrange in a sequence. For convenience of reference, we will designate these as Sula's response to the "pathos of the black male," the "cosmic grotesque," the by now often quoted "orgasmic 'howl,'" and the "mounting to orgasm" as Sula makes love to Ajax. Critical references to these passages are generally inadequate. Some are interesting but limited; others are couched in superlatives but offer little commentary. The last passage, for example, is called "the novel's most spectacular passage" (Homans 1983, 193) and is cited for its "stunning language of poetic metaphor" (Henderson 1989, 33) but little else.

These passages, moreover, have not been understood in their interconnectedness, in the way they function as a specific configuration of moments that describe a specific movement in the text. These four passages function in pairs. The first two are presented in direct discourse, spoken by Sula, to Jude and Nel respectively. They are Sula's response to a black male and a black female text constructed by her two interlocutors. We might also note that while the first may convincingly be read as Sula's speech, the second is difficult to read as such. This progressive invasion of the narrator's voice into the character's speech continues in the third passage, where direct quotations are abandoned and the narrator frankly describes the "orgasmic 'howl.'" The final passage, with the typographical assistance of interspersed italicized lines, enacts a collaboration of voices, a duet—a strategy that Morrison has used in her first novel and returns to at the end of *Beloved*.

These passages can be clarified by some of Bakhtin's ideas about the grotesque.[3] Above all, and in spite of his almost unrestrained eulogization of the folk, the consistency with which he grounds his analysis in the folk offers a useful, if obvious, parallel to African-American literary theory. In fact, he asserts that the folk sense of the grotesque is not entirely recuperable in the literary text. It is born only at the "confines of languages" because "it is impossible to overcome through abstract thought alone, within the system of a unique language, that deep dogmatism hidden in all forms of this system" (Bakhtin 1984, 472).

The intractable quality of the grotesque (which, of course, Bakhtin nevertheless tracks for some five hundred pages) leads Bakhtin into another pertinent area of our discussion, that of orality. He emphasizes the marketplace form of Rabelais's language. In a remarkable resemblance to what Morrison says about her own writing, Bakhtin designates the Rabelaisian grotesque image as "a vivid and dynamic 'loud' image" a "'loud' talking image" (Bakhtin 1984, 191). He associates the literary text, aside from some exceptional moments when the grotesque can emerge on the "confines of languages," with an atrophied sensuous perception of the world. This explains his assertion that "the nose and mouth play the most important part in the grotesque image of the body" and "the eyes have no part in these comic images" (316), an assertion that we will return to.

Two specific characteristics of the Bakhtinian grotesque need to be noted: its historical continuity and its embodiment in the material, though not the individual, body.[4] The grotesque embodies a specific conception of time, which is historical and materialist; this time defines a horizontal continuity of the "ancestral body" (Bakhtin 1984, 367) that defeats the gloomy eschatological time of a vertically constructed medieval hierarchy (363). Further, this regenerative aspect of the grotesque attaches primarily to the "bodily lower stratum," but the grotesque body is also not one that is carefully demarcated and separate. It is one that stresses continuity and those parts that can be anatomically projected and penetrated: "All these convexities and orifices have a common characteristic; it is within them that the confines between bodies and between the body and the world are overcome" (317).

If the content of the grotesque image is one of continuity and materiality, its method relies on subversion and enumeration, anatomical or otherwise. Its movement is subversive and transgressive: "Down, inside out, vice versa, upside down, such is the direction of all these movements. All of them thrust down, turn over, push headfirst, transfer top to bottom, and bottom to top, both in the literal sense of space, and in the metaphorical meaning of the image" (Bakhtin 1984, 370). And the enumerations, relying on excess and hyperbolization, and close to an oral folk world, "still have something of the nature of proper nouns" (457) that "are as yet insufficiently neutral and generalized" (458). They are "nearer to appellations" "as yet not disciplined by the literary context and its strict lexical differentiation and selection" (462). The language of the marketplace in Rabelais is "grammatically and semantically isolated from context and is regarded as a complete unit, something like a proverb" (16).

The passage we have designated the "pathos of the black male" is schematic to the point of caricature:

> White men love you. They spend so much time worrying about your penis they forget their own. The only thing they want to do is cut off a nigger's privates. And if that ain't love and respect I don't know what is. And white women? They chase you all to every corner of the earth, feel for you under every bed. I knew a white woman wouldn't leave the house after 6 o'clock for fear one of you would snatch her. Now ain't that love? They think rape soon's they see you, and if they don't get the rape they looking for, they scream it anyway just so the search won't be in vain. Colored women worry themselves into bad health just trying to hang on to your cuffs. Even little children—white and black, boys and girls—spend all their childhood eating their hearts out 'cause they think you don't love them. And if that ain't enough, you love yourselves. (Morrison 1989a, 103-4)

The passage is constructed of five units: white male, white female, black female, children, and black male. The first two images, explicitly sexual and violent, are double-faced, ambivalent. They are historical images and stereotypes recalled and submitted to a subversive gaze, turned inside out, inverted, and rendered grotesque. The first is of a lynching, of castration. The prevailing justifications behind this were attached to the subhuman, racially transgressive black phallus. The gaze of the grotesque, however, makes clear that the source of this threat lies not so much in black desire as in white fear and impotence—"so much time worrying about your penis they forget their own." The juxtaposition of the two images, passivity and dominance, evokes an unmistakable, if obsessive, homoeroticism. It is the collision of "forget their own" and "nigger's privates" within the image itself that is the condition for the emergence of Sula's grotesque: "And if that ain't love and respect."

The second image is closely related to the first. It is that of the "rape of the white woman," that vehicle of cultural purity sullied by the uncontrolled libidinal transgression of black desire. But this, too, is subverted by "the rape they looking for," in fact, "search[ing]" for. Thus, the image of a racially transgressive black male sexuality collides with the white female fantasy of the exotic and prodigious superpotent black phallus. The next two images, by comparison, are truncated—one sentence each, compared to the four and five in the first and second—but they, too, evoke historical and social conditions meant, by Sula, to demonstrate that the black male is "the envy of the world." These images blend the historical figures of the roving black male, the abandoned black female, and the personage of the benevolent "Uncle Tom."

What is significant about these images is not only that they are drawn from a fund of historical experience, but also that they have been historicized. That is, they are drawn from a specific historical and sociological body of knowledge, constructed and disseminated by the social sciences. Further, they function with "something of the nature of proper nouns"; they exert a sheer appellative force. Each image here is a "complete unit," and the serialization of such units exerts a formal pressure on content. The unit is wrenched from a disciplined and disciplinary context, is "semantically isolated," and inverted to yield a grotesque image.

The second passage, we will remind ourselves, is presented in direct quotations, spoken, or even better delivered, spectacularly by Sula, on her deathbed, presumably moments before her death:

> After all the old women have lain with the teen-agers; when all the young girls have slept with their old drunken uncles; after all the black men fuck all the white ones; when all the white women kiss all the black ones; when all the guards have raped all the jail-birds and after all the whores make love to their grannies; after all the faggots get their mothers' trim; when Lindbergh sleeps with Bessie Smith and Norma Shearer makes it with Stepin Fetchit; after all the dogs have fucked all the cats and every weathervane on every barn flies off the roof to mount the hogs . . . then there'll be a little love left over for me. (Morrison 1989a, 145-46)

It is constructed of eight units, punctuated by semicolons, in one sentence. All the units begin with the subordinating "after" or "when," some packing two clauses separated by a coordinating "and," and the series leads up to the culminating "then." The subordinators thus do not introduce hierarchy into the syntax; in fact, the subordinators coordinate, linking the units in the paratactic style of oral speech.

The first two units are organized by the opposition between youth and age, the second two by that between black and white. Further, the morphology of the paired units is chiasmic, in the first, "old-teen-young-old," in the second, "black-white-white-black." The principle is that of inversion, of "inside out," which does not aggravate the oppositions but rather posits a continuity between polarities. This series of eight units does not, however, proceed in a coherently linear syntax. The first structuring principle, youth and age, for example, is already contaminated by the incestuous "girls" and "uncles." Rather, the organizing dynamic of the series is a spiraling into the anarchic grotesque. In the next two units, we have a bizarre coupling of crime and punishment, of criminals and the custodians of culture, or, of law and lawlessness. These two units also transgress sexual boundaries in their movement toward homosexuality and incest. The seventh unit, maintaining a white-black polarity, makes clear the sheer appellative force of all the units by its simple enumeration of proper nouns. But it is the last unit that is most spectacular in its embodiment of the grotesque. The weathervane that "flies off the roof to mount the hogs" is unleashed from all referential burden and strains toward an ontologically other embodied in the grotesque.

In these two passages, images function as linguistic units, or perhaps as semiotic units. While they are not entirely detached from the plot, their attachment is tangential. They are "isolated from context" and function as "complete units" in themselves. They may even, in a sense, be considered impediments to the plot. They appear in a rupture of the text, in a semiotic convulsion that asserts the primacy of the prediscursive. They are, in Bakhtin's words, "as yet not disciplined by the literary context." And while the assertion of orality in a literary text must seem like a gross violation of "strict lexical differentiation and selection," one must note that it is precisely through these linguistic units, and their detachment from the literary context, that the images and their syntax assert the sensory matrix of an oral world.

Both passages celebrate the sheer material abundance of the body and of language, one embedded in the other, one that both threatens and impels the other. Keeping in mind Bakhtin's twin emphases on the materiality of the body and the word, we can observe a tension between narrator and character, particularly in the second passage, the "cosmic grotesque." It is as if the semiotic, in rebellion, would conduct a continual raid on the symbolic function, would turn it back into itself and rupture the symbolic structuring. Embedded in the symbolic structure, the figure of the semiotic disfigures the symbolic. This is language continually invoking its other or, more specifically here, invoking the grotesque body of the community. The series of images presents a chain of signifiers, always straining toward freedom from a semantic grid, always pointing toward another chain of signifiers, an impossible chain of coupling bodies. The series, seeming to arrive at a referential point of attachment, eludes that point through a loophole in a process of continual deferral, always invoking the continuous body of the communal grotesque.

This image of the grotesque body of the community is clarified in our third passage, a passage that has received some significant critical commentary[5] but needs to be situated in relation to the sequence of passages that is the focus here. When Sula

> began to assert herself in the [sexual] act, particles gathered in her like steel shavings drawn to a spacious magnetic center, forming a tight cluster that nothing, it seemed, could break. . . . But the cluster did break, fall apart, and in her panic to hold it together she leaped from the edge into soundlessness and went down howling, howling into a stinging awareness of the endings of things: an eye of sorrow in the midst of all the hurricane rage of joy. (Morrison 1989a, 123)

   This passage occurs in a sequence of approximately eight dense paragraphs
after Sula's break with Nel and after the communal condemnation of Sula. In
other words, it is a moment of meditative isolation. In this sequence of paragraphs, two images dominate, that in which Sula "went down howling" and that
of her "free fall" into the "snake's breath," a "full surrender to the downward
flight" (Morrison 1989a, 120). Further, the "breath of the snake" represents the
members of the community, and unlike Sula, Nel is driven back by "the flick of
their tongues." The "snake's breath," however, cannot be read as representing
individual members of the community. Sula is, after all, the town pariah. If she
gives herself to the community, she certainly does not do so according to any
moral design.
   At this point, it is useful to remind ourselves that Bakhtin is extremely careful, even to the point of what at times one senses is an anxiety-ridden redun-
dancy, to underline throughout his study that the grotesque body is not the individual, biological body; it is not the "subjective grotesque," but the "ancestral
body," "precisely the historic, progressing body of mankind" (Bakhtin 1984,
367). Sula, then, gives herself to the "free fall" into the "breath of the snake,"
that is, into the "gaping mouth" of the historic, progressing, grotesque body of
the community, a mouth that, according to Bakhtin, is "the most important of all
human features for the grotesque": "It dominates all else. The grotesque face is
actually reduced to the gaping mouth" (317). It may also be worth noting here
that even though Bakhtin cannot entirely endorse Victor Hugo's interpretation of
the grotesque, he is quite taken by Hugo's image of the grotesque, "of a serpent
inside man; 'these are his bowels'" (126). And Sula is, of course, in one reading
(significantly, Jude's), marked by "a copperhead over her eye" (Morrison 1989a,
103).
   That Sula does not "belong" to the community is quite clear. She cherishes
her "postcoital privateness," she goes "down howling" into "soundlessness" and "the
death of time and a loneliness so profound the word itself had no meaning"
(Morrison 1989a, 123). The community that Morrison represents here, however,
is complex and ambivalent.[6] It is both nourishing and devouring. And while the
relationship between Sula and the community is marked by mutual antagonism,
she is not separate from it. In fact, she is integral to it.[7] Far from seeking nourishment from the members of the community, Sula gives herself to a collective,
ritual, devouring.
   In other words, the community is projected here in the terms of the grotesque. Disregarding a vertically constructed hierarchy, Sula "falls" or goes
"down howling" into the grotesque space of a horizontally constructed continuity, a continuity that is not that of an abstract eternal but a historical, materialist,
bodily continuity. This is also the logic of the grotesque that underlies the con-

struction of the passage we have referred to as the "orgasmic grotesque." The linguistic units, in their paratactic syntax, uprooted from their literary context, exerting their sheer appellative force, represent this continuity. Similarly, Sula, devoured in the gaping mouth of the serpent, inhabiting an interiority, is simultaneously penetrated and inhabited by the serpent. The "breath of the snake" and the "copperhead over her eye" are integrated in the logic and syntax of the grotesque.

The last passage we will examine here has received both the least critical attention and the most uncritical appreciation. We have noted, in Bakhtinian terms, the function, on the one hand, of appellations and proper nouns, of appellative force and pronominalizations and, on the other, of the lower bodily stratum in the three passages above. This method has underscored the materiality of the word and of the body, and these two come together in this last passage as Sula, penetrating her lover's body, would tear into the sign, would turn it inside out in a grotesque act that is both violent and regenerative. It is an act of mutilation, dismemberment, and death, but it is also one of remembrance and regeneration.

Sula would "return to the state anterior to discourse" (Foucault 1972, 48), a state that is anterior to symbolic capacity. She would "reach out to and touch" this anteriority "with an ungloved hand" (Morrison 1989a, 121). What Foucault discourages in his analysis of discourse is precisely what Sula wishes to do, "to pierce through its density [of discourse] in order to reach what remains silently anterior to it" (Foucault 1972, 47).

The passage, a lyrical representation of "the drift of her flesh toward the high silence of orgasm," follows in its entirety:

If I take a chamois and rub real hard on the bone, right on the ledge of your cheek bone, some of the black will disappear. It will flake away into the chamois and underneath there will be gold leaf. I can see it shining through the black. I know it is there. . . .

How high she was over his wand-lean body, how slippery was his sliding sliding smile.

And if I take a nailfile or even Eva's old paring knife—that will do—and scrape away at the gold, it will fall away at the gold, it will fall away and there will be alabaster. The alabaster is what gives your face its planes, its curves. That is why your mouth smiling does not reach your eyes. Alabaster is giving it a gravity that resists a total smile.

The height and the swaying dizzied her, so she bent down and let her breasts graze his chest.

Then I can take a chisel and small tap hammer and tap away at the alabas-

ter. It will crack then like ice under the pick, and through the breaks I will see the loam, fertile, free of pebbles and twigs. For it is the loam that is giving you that smell.

She slipped her hands under his armpits, for it seemed as though she would not be able to dam the spread of weakness she felt under her skin without holding on to something.

I will put my hand deep into your soil, lift it, sift it with my fingers, feel its warm surface and dewy chill below.

She put her head under his chin with no hope in the world of keeping anything at all at bay.

I will water your soil, keep it rich and moist. But how much? How much water to keep the loam moist? And how much loam will I need to keep my water still? And when do the two make mud?

He swallowed her mouth just as her thighs had swallowed his genitals, and the house was very, very quiet. (Morrison 1989a, 130-31)

The passage, as we have observed, enacts a duet between narrator and character. The italicization, while keeping the voices separate, paradoxically marks their complicity. It alternates between Sula's "voice," using first and second person—with Sula "speaking" to her lover, Ajax, while reaching orgasm—and the narrator's voice using third person. The instruments she uses to reach into Ajax's anterior self, that is, a self anterior to representation, progress from a chamois to a nail file/paring knife to a chisel and tap hammer or, by metaphorical extension, an ice pick. What she uncovers, or discovers, similarly progresses from black (skin) to gold leaf to alabaster to loam. When Sula "rub[s] real hard," "scrape[s] away," and "tap[s] away," Ajax's skin "disappear[s]" or "flake[s] away," his gold "fall[s] away," and his alabaster "crack[s]" or "breaks." In terms of sensory perception, Sula progresses from "planes" and "curves" to "smell" to "feel," that is, from visual to olfactory to tactile perception. We may represent these progressions schematically:

Chamois ⟹ Nail file/Paring knife ⟹   Chisel/Tap hammer

Rub   ⟹ Scrape ⟹   Tap
Black (skin)⟹ Gold leaf ⟹   Alabaster   Loam
Flakes   ⟹ Falls   ⟹   Cracks

The moment of high literacy is marked by the sovereignty of the eye. After all the reservations and qualifications have been taken into account, the experience of literacy unequivocally privileges the sense of sight, and yet the passage, quite equivocally, moves away from sight to tactility, or from the isolation of sight to an altered sensory matrix. And while this movement need be neither nostalgic nor apocalyptic, as it often seems to be in Marshall McLuhan, for example, the trajectory of the sensory apparatus is toward the increasingly tabooed senses, a progression/retrogression that culminates in the "gaping mouth": "He swallowed her mouth just as her thighs had swallowed his genitals." Thus the body turns a cartwheel, the apparatus of speech and the abdomen,[8] the mouth and the genitals, are rotated in a grotesque affirmation of language and the body. This entire movement, this collaboration of voices, moves toward the aphasic, the "high silence of orgasm," toward "soundlessness": "and the house was very, very quiet."

In addition to the weaving of voices, the altered sensory matrix, the rotated bodily hierarchy, the passage also establishes an ambivalence about life and death, a reciprocity between desire and death. It vigorously brings together the embodiment of death, Shadrack, and the perfect lover, Ajax. The narrator's voice observes, "How high she was over his wand-lean body, how slippery was his sliding sliding smile." Ajax's "slipping, falling smile" (Morrison 1989a, 129), his "sliding sliding smile," resembles the "flake away," the "fall away," of the different layers of his being. Further, his smile and his "velvet helmet of hair" (129) are described in the terms of Shadrack's experience on the battlefield. Shadrack watches as "the soldier's head disappeared under the inverted soup bowl of his helmet," and the body of the "headless soldier" ran on "ignoring altogether the drip and slide of brain tissue down its back" (8). A description of sexual fulfillment is rendered in terms of death.

The metaphor of uncovering not only brings together the battlefield and the site of sexual fulfillment, but it also affirms the affinity between Shadrack and Sula in what Sula supposes is their complicity in Chicken Little's death. Shadrack had once offered Sula a word of "comfort": "he had said 'always,' so she would not be afraid of the change—the falling away of skin, the drip and slide of blood, and the exposure of bone underneath" (Morrison 1989a, 157). When Sula lyrically strips away the different layers of Ajax's being, she is engaged in a potentially deadly act. These different layers "fall away" in a way resembling the headless soldier's "falling away of skin."

Death, in this passage, is a real death, not to be trivialized, but it is not a final death. It is a creative death, a "pregnant death." This is reinforced by Sula's death, immediately preceding which the text tells us that "she might draw her legs up to her chest, close her eyes, put her thumb in her mouth and float . . . down until she met a rain scent and would know the water was near, and she would curl into its heavy softness and it would . . . wash her tired flesh always" (Morrison 1989a, 149). The foetal position indicates Sula's return to infancy, to the watery womb of a prediscursive plenitude, which, as the words "curl into its heavy softness" suggest, is the plenitude of the amniotic fluid. In the passage itself, the oblique reference to Egyptian creation myths and the references to soil, loam, and mud, on the one hand, and to water, on the other, that is, earth and water, male and female principles, suggest creation and procreation.

In this passage, several boundaries are placed under erasure, boundaries between voices, between sensory and bodily hierarchies, between life and death. The body becomes a cipher in a matrix of signifiers, a surface that Sula would penetrate, a site where "the confines between bodies" are placed under erasure. The bodily lower stratum and the gaping mouth, the genitals and the mouth, are rotated and aligned in the topography of the grotesque body. The mouth and the womb are reciprocally and simultaneously devouring and nourishing. The boundaries between bodies begin to disintegrate as skin "falls away," as flesh is "torn" from the face (Morrison 1989a, 136), and interiority and exteriority are no longer strictly demarcated but defined in a continuity.

The figuration of death and desire in the passage denies and rejects the somber finality of death. The novel, in general, is saturated with death, and Sula herself is often participant or observer in these deaths. The text, however, seems to sustain its representation of Sula as a figure of the constitutive element of language, an element that is "uncontained and uncontainable." In this sense, in terms of its language, the text offers what is perhaps its most playful and "disruptive" moment in Sula's death. At this point, the novel gives the slip to the grim reaper, its language offers what Bakhtin calls the "gay loophole" (Bakhtin 1984, 454): "Sula felt her face smiling. 'Well, I'll be damned,' she thought, 'it didn't even hurt. Wait'll I tell Nel'" (Morrison 1989a, 149). Far from a metaphysically conceived finality, or a moralistically stipulated justification, Sula's words represent an affirmation of life, irreverent, "outlawed," intractable.

Morrison's concern with orality and literacy, with interiority and exteriority, and with voice and language is certainly not anomalous, and we may turn to the work of several black women for the relevant intertextual relations. The most compelling in its uncompromising preoccupation with these concerns, however, is Zora Neale Hurston's *Their Eyes Were Watching God*. As a remarkable instance of intertextuality, one passage in particular deserves attention for its relation to the passage examined above:

> She had found a jewel down inside herself and she wanted to walk where people see her and gleam it around. But she had been set in the market-place to sell. Been set for still bait. When God had made The Man, he made him out of stuff that sung all the time and glittered all over. Then after that some angels got jealous and chopped him into millions of pieces, but still he glittered and hummed. So they beat him down to nothing but sparks but each little spark had a shine and a song. So they covered each one over with mud. And the lonesomeness in the sparks make them hunt for one another, but the

mud is deaf and dumb. Like all the other tumbling mud-balls, Janie had tried to show her shine. (Huston 1965, 138-39)

The similarities between this passage and that from *Sula* are perhaps not immediately apparent. One may initially, however, associate the "jewel," the "glitter," the "spark" and "shine," on the one hand, with the "sparkle or splutter" that is rubbed down to a "dull glow" in Nel (83) and, on the other, with the "gold leaf" Sula can see "shining through the black." The word "mud" may also remind one of Sula's last question, *"And when do the two make mud?"* Missy Dehn Kubitschek, in *Claiming the Heritage*, observes that "This irreverent, edited, and conflated variation of *Paradise Lost* and several Egyptian myths emphasizes both the mud and the shine" (57). Janie can be free, can become "an active agent," only by accepting both the shine and the mud, only by accepting her "existential responsibility" (56). The intertextual connection between the passages is perhaps most striking in their references to the Egyptian creation myths. We may represent this passage diagrammatically:

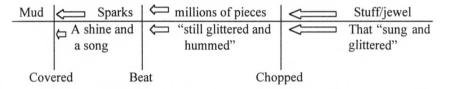

Mud ⇐ Sparks	⇐ millions of pieces	⇐ Stuff/jewel
⇐ A shine and a song	⇐ "still glittered and hummed"	⇐ That "sung and glittered"
Covered	Beat Chopped	

The process here is one that progressively diminishes the original jewel. The jewel that sung and glittered is chopped into millions of pieces that still glittered and hummed. These pieces are beaten into sparks, but they still have a shine and a song. These sparks are then covered with mud, but in their "lonesomeness," they still "hunt for one another."

The process described in *Sula* is precisely the reverse of that in *Their Eyes*. If, in *Sula*, we witness an interiorization, here we observe an exteriorization. In *Sula* we move toward an uncovering or discovering; in *Their Eyes* we witness a covering. Even if the direction of the movement in both passages is different, toward an interiority and toward an exteriority, both passages deploy a method to engage the central condition of absence. The condition is one of having been plucked from a plenitude, of dislocation and diminishment, and the method deployed is one of resistance. Janie and Sula, then, are both nourished by the memory of a prediscursive universe, one that precedes the symbolic order. They both wish to recreate this universe.

In the latter, however, the "mud" is "deaf and dumb," and the human element is reduced to "sparks," which, to be sure, because of their "lonesomeness," "hunt for one another." Thus the method deployed against diminishment is relational, but it is a relation at the level of essence. In the former, in contrast, the "mud" is elemental and bodily. It is creatively constituted in a careful combination of water and soil/loam. In other words, the human element is defined in terms of existence, in terms of the materiality and (pro)creative possibilities of the cosmic body of the grotesque.

All four passages from *Sula* that we have examined here may be exorbitant in their celebration of the signifier; they may seem to strain toward unrepresentability, to be unleashed from referentiality. But in every instance this momentum is harnessed and reined in by an insistence on the materiality of the word, the word rigorously, even strenuously, embodied. This dialectic between the abstract and the concrete, the idealist and the materialist, provides a crucial impetus for the language of the text. The word finds a local habitation in the body at the same time as the body, or the trajectory of desire, penetrates and inhabits the word. And while the body is the historic, progressing, grotesque body of the black community, the word, here, is the oral word of black speech. This is the orality that ruptures the language of the black text.

This is also the orality that alters the sensory configuration of the literate and literary experience. The orality of black speech, by invading the language of the black text, continually resists a sterile and aestheticized textuality which, ironically enough, itself risks being recuperated into a sort of technicist essentialism—in what we have noted as a privileging of the signifier. In resisting this sort of textualization, however, the text simultaneously risks being recuperated into other types of essentialisms. This conflict between orality and textuality accounts for the uneasiness we may feel in trying to situate novels such as *Sula* in contemporary critical discussions about language. This is also Toni Morrison's mode of intervention in the "linguistic hierarchy" of the "literary frame"; but more generally, African-American literature, in defining the black voice in fiction, responds, resists, and modifies the hierarchy of the literary frame.

Notes

1. See, for example, Paul Gilroy (1993).

2. For a study of authenticating devices in African-American literature, see Robert Stepto (1979).

3. Even if *Sula* is not really Rabelaisian, certain aspects of his analysis are useful for an understanding of these passages. Bakhtin can also be somewhat disturbing, as, for example, in his rather limited observation that the "age of discovery" in general provided a positive propellent to the development of the European Renaissance grotesquerie (Bakhtin 1984, 271-72). While it is certainly permissible, even required, that a writer define his/her area of study, to write, in the twentieth century, of how colonialism served to develop a particular genre, and to write about it with no qualification, is to remain within the reductive parameters of a Eurocentric scholarship.

4. Two images, among others, deserve attention: that of pregnant hags and that of a

stutterer. Of the first, Bakhtin comments that "It is pregnant death, a death that gives birth" (25), a comment that he repeats tirelessly throughout the book. The second, bringing together the bodily lower stratum and the word, insisting on the materiality of the word, is that of a stutterer who cannot pronounce a word till Harlequin "rushes head forward and hits the man in the abdomen" and "The difficult word is 'born'" (Bakhtin 1984, 304). Bakhtin comments that "the stutterer enacts a scene of childbirth" (308), and "the entire mechanism of the word is transferred from the apparatus of speech to the abdomen" (309).

5. Although Mae Henderson persuasively argues that the howl represents the irruption of the presymbolic into the symbolic, the "breaks" in the dominant discourse (Henderson 1989, 33), Margaret Homans reminds us repeatedly that these representations achieve their status, ironically, by "representing their skepticism about representation" and by "the ambiguity entailed in the representation of unrepresentability" (Homans 1983, 205).

6. For the general responses of black women novelists to the nationalist aesthetic and their particular responses to the nationalist representation of community, see Madhu Dubey (1994)..

7. Mae Henderson, for example, comments that "the community closes ranks against [Sula] who transgresses the boundaries prescribed for women" (Henderson 1989, 28).

8. See Mikhail Bakhtin (1984, 309, 373).

Works Cited

Ahmad, Aijaz. 1992. *In Theory: Classes, Nations, Literatures*. London: Verso.

Bakhtin, Mikhail. 1984. *Rabelais and His World.* Bloomington: Indiana University Press.

Dubey, Madhu. 1994. *Black Women Novelists and the Nationalist Aesthetic.* Bloomington: Indiana University Press.

Foucault, Michel. 1972. *The Archaeology of Knowledge*. New York: Pantheon.

Gates, Henry Louis Jr. 1988. *The Signifying Monkey: A Theory of African-American Literary Criticism*. New York: Oxford University Press.

Gilroy, Paul. 1993. *The Black Atlantic: Modernity and Double Consciousness.* Cambridge: Harvard University Press.

Habermas, Jurgen. 1992. *The Philosophical Discourse of Modernity*. Cambridge: MIT Press.

Henderson, Mae. 1989. "Speaking In Tongues: Dialogics, Dialectics, and the Black Woman Writer's Literary Tradition." In *Changing Our Own Words*, ed. Cheryl A. Wall. New Brunswick: Rutgers University Press.

Homans, Margaret. 1983. "'Her Own Very Howl': The Ambiguities of Representation in Recent Women's Fiction." *Signs* 9.2: 186-205.

Hurston, Zora Neale. 1965. *Their Eyes Were Watching God*. Chicago: University of Illinois Press.

Kubitschek, Missy Dehn. 1991. *Claiming the Heritage: African-American Women Novelists and History*. Jackson: University Press of Mississippi.

McKay, Nellie. 1983. "An Interview With Toni Morrison." *Contemporary Literature* 24.

4 (Winter): 413-29.
Morrison, Toni. 1989a. *Sula.* New York: Knopf.
_____. 1989b. "Unspeakable Things Unspoken: The Afro-American Presence in American Literature." *Michigan Quarterly Review* 28.1: 1-34.
Ong, Walter J. 1982. *Orality and Literacy: The Technologizing of the Word.* London: Methuen.
Stepto, Robert. 1979. *From Behind the Veil: A Study of Afro-American Narrative.* Urbana: University of Illinois Press.
Wideman, John. 1977. "Defining the Black Voice in Fiction." *Black American Literature Forum* 11: 79-82.

III

HISTORY

9

From the Far Side of the Urban Frontier: The Detective Fiction of Chester Himes and Walter Mosley

Robert Crooks

Western Frontier and Urban Frontier

> They draw a line and say for you to stay on your side of the line. They don't care if there's no bread over on your side. They don't care if you die. And . . . when you try to come from behind your line they kill you.
>
> Richard Wright, *Native Son*

Frederick Jackson Turner's 1893 essay, "The Significance of the Frontier in American History," marked a watershed for the European-American version of the history of North America.[1] By 1890 the western frontier as a geographical space had disappeared, and "the frontier" as signifier was now cut adrift, its attachment to past, present, and future conceptual spaces a matter of debate. Indeed, for Turner himself the signifier slides significantly, sometimes figuring as a place where European-American settlement or colonization of North America ends, but also as a conceptual space, a shifting no-man's-land between European- and Native-American cultures, and finally, ideologically, as a

175

"meeting point between savagery and civilization" (Turner 1920c, 3).[2]

Other conceptual and spatial divides along ethnic and racial lines emerged almost simultaneously with the western frontier, however, and were available to absorb and transform its conceptual significance. The most obvious was that between European and African Americans embodied in the codes, economy, and practices of slavery and subsequent segregation. Such lines of segregation became particularly sharp and contested in urban settings, thanks to the close proximity of sizable communities formed along racial lines, often subject to differential treatment in terms of urban development, availability of credit, school funding, policing, and so forth. It is this urban manifestation of frontier ideology, and particularly the textual space opened up by crime fiction for an articulation of that frontier from its "other" side, that will concern me here.

Turner suggests, in an inchoate way, the need for and function of the particular ideological formation that drew a line between "white" civilization and "Indian" savagery, a term for which "black" criminal chaos could easily be substituted. Noting that there was not one frontier, but rather a trading frontier, a farming frontier, a military frontier, a railroad frontier, and so forth, he also notes that the various frontiers did not coincide geographically, nor in the economic interests that constructed them (Turner 1920c, 10-15). In an attempt to account for the assumed ideological unity of the (European-American) United States, Turner maps these differences onto a progressive cultural history stretching from the savage prehistory of Indian lands in a linear development to the industrial metropolitan centers of the East. Ignoring the lack of fit between this mapping and the uneven developments of various frontiers, Turner identifies the Indians as the unifying factor that transformed the various frontiers, their regulation, and their histories into a unity by posing a "common danger" of absolute otherness (15).

It is difficult to reconcile this distinctive unity produced by common danger with Turner's invocation of the western frontier as the factor that transformed the European colonists into Americans: "The American frontier is sharply distinguished from the European frontier—a fortified boundary running through dense populations. The most significant thing about the American frontier is, that it lies at the hither edge of free land" (Turner 1920c, 3).[3] On the one hand, Turner conceives of the frontier as the near edge of a wilderness of free resources, providing what he would later call a "safety valve" inhibiting the reproduction of the European class tensions between owners of the means of production and labor (Turner 1920b, 279-80; 1920d, 320). In this sense the ideological work of the frontier was the production of individualism—meaning both individual liberty and individualized entrepreneurial competition—as an alternative to class politics (Turner 1920c, 30). On the other hand, the frontier as a producer of unity is precisely a "fortified boundary" dividing "civilization" from "savage" others, a consolidating interpretation that rescues a racialized sense of national identity from the threat of anarchic individualism.

The role of individualism in this racializing and naturalizing of the frontier, translating it from a site of cultural contestation and ideological struggle into an expanding boundary of civilization, is overdetermined. First, the ideology of individualism romanticizes capitalist competition, displacing collective machinations with an image of a "fair fight" between free individuals. Second, as Richard Slotkin points out, early frontier narratives depicted figures such as Benjamin Church and Daniel Boone as "the lone white man among tribes of Indians," even though "both men dealt with the Indians as agents for large land companies" (Slotkin 1985, 65). Produced by a familiar trope of individualizing the European-American self against collectivized others, the "lone white man" would be a recurring image suggesting that the struggle of European Americans against the wilderness was not even a "fair fight," but rather a heroic battle against the odds. Third, in conjunction with the representation of the far side of the frontier as vacant wilderness, capitalist competition (including that with Native Americans for land and resources) could be concealed behind images of individual entrepreneurs—whether farmers, traders, trappers, or prospectors—taming a "nature" divested even of collectivized Native-American subjects, bringing it within the pale of culture. Finally, the ideology of individualism could mediate between the narratives of men against the wilderness and the experiences of the European-American colonists of the frontier as a site of ideological struggle between different cultures. A continuous stream of diatribes against "Indianization" and the motif of the "good Indian," prominent in frontier narratives from Cooper through Zane Grey to the *Daniel Boone* television series, have helped in a variety of ways to reconcile a racially defined oppression with ideologies of egalitarianism and tolerance by posing frontiersmen and Indians as individuals free to choose European-American civilization over Indian savagery.

These various meanings and functions of individualism are not mutually compatible or equally operative in every moment of discourse. Such disjunctions are a consequence of contradictions that emerge in the ideological negotiation of material encounters between cultures or emergent micro-cultures.[4] The ability of Turner to move discursively back and forth between "Indian lands" and "free lands," or to rewrite complex modalities of capitalist competition as a progressive history inscribed seamlessly across the continent, demonstrates the possibility and necessity of evading such contradictions through the ideological isolation of discourses.[5] In geographical terms, the western frontier was a battlefront in a territorial war that was articulated within various struggles over issues including race, the structuring of the state, and the proper use of land and resources. Because such war could not be justified according to prevailing ethics or law, it was necessary to isolate discursively the colonization of territory from the battle between civilization and savagery by converting "the idea of racial propensities into a rationale for wars of extermination" (Slotkin 1985, 54).

From the European-American perspective, then, the frontier wars were not wars of conquest, for the assertion of authority by the U.S. government to make legal claim to land occupied by Native Americans was tantamount to redefining Native Americans themselves as foreign intruders to be eradicated. Through this redefinition, the "Indian Question" was discursively linked to the "Slavery Question." At the same time that the European-American frontier was being pushed westward, a new and distinctively American "science" of craniometry was developing an "objective" method for differentiating among races (see Jeffries 1992, 156).

Such work in racial "science" not only helped to justify the continuation of slavery and the war on Native Americans, but also helped determine the shape of the eventual "solutions" to those problems. Though the complete extermination of Native Americans and the mass transportation of black Americans "back" to Africa had many proponents, the compromise solution was collective oppression and exploitation facilitated by racial segregation, the containment of Native Americans and Native-American culture on reservations, and the similar containment of African Americans through various forms of segregation.

This partitioning refocused the frontier ideology, which continued to map cultural and racial divisions, but in geographical terms now denoted relatively fixed lines of defense for the purity and order of European-American culture. Such lines became particularly charged in cities such as New York, Chicago, and Los Angeles, where population densities and the size of minoritized communities threaten individualist ideologies, since the collective experience of exploitation lends itself to collective resistance or rebellion. Thus, the meaning of the other side of the frontier, in the shift of focus from its western to its urban manifestation, has been partly transformed: no longer enemy territory to be attacked and conquered or vacant land to be cultivated, it now constitutes in mainstream European-American ideologies pockets of racial intrusion, hence corruption and social disease to be policed and contained—insofar as the "others" threaten to cross the line.

Like the association of individualism with European-American manifest destiny, the association of black urban communities in particular with the criminal side of the urban frontier has historically been overdetermined. Many of the African Americans migrating to the cities were forced to seek housing in and then to remain in the poorest areas of the cities by discriminatory practices in housing, as well as in the workplace and schools (see, for instance, Glasgow 1980, ch. 4 and 5). Furthermore, as Homer Hawkins and Richard Thomas point out:

Most northern white policemen not only believed in the inferiority of blacks but also held the most popular belief that blacks were more criminally inclined by nature than whites. . . . For decades, white officials in northern cities allowed vice and crime to go unpoliced in black neighborhoods. This non-protection policy had the effect of controlling the development of black community by undermining the stability of black family and community life. (Hawkins and Thomas 1991, 75-76)

Police indifference to black-on-black crime has been frequently noted in all regions of the United States.[6] and persists to such an extent that Rita Williams exaggerates little, if at all, when she says that "African Americans know they can murder each other with impunity and absolutely no one will care" (Williams 1993, 115).

Inadequate policing of intracommunity crime, the saturation of black communities with liquor and gun stores, and gentrification supplement strategies of containment with strategies of eradication and displacement (on gentrification see Smith 1991, 108-14). If the war of extermination and deterritorialization goes largely unrecognized, it is because the urban frontier works more through hegemony[7] than openly repressive force. All Americans can watch the physical and economic "self-destruction" of black communities on the nightly news, and conservative African-American intellectuals can be co-opted into chastising blacks for failing to take responsibility for "their own" problems and the disintegration of their communities.[8] Meanwhile the urban frontier serves the same purpose for capitalism as did the western frontier and the European colonial frontiers in general: the production of relatively cheap resources, including labor.

Though specific techniques of oppression and exploitation have changed, then, the frontier ideology remains largely intact, though displaced. Individualism in particular remains crucial in disguising a site of ideological struggle as a line of defense against crime and chaos or the boundary of advancing modernization or "urban renewal" or "revitalization," and for disarming collective resistance. Hegemony works through negotiation, though, and resistance does exist, in however fragmented forms. In the remainder of this essay I consider one mode of resistance from the far side of the frontier, the emergence of African-American detective fiction, a popular form that has the capacity both to represent and to enact resistance in social and literary terms.

Crime Fiction and the Racial Frontier

And it wasn't just this city. It was any city where they set up a line and say black folks stay on this side and white folks on this side, so that the black folks were crammed on top of each other—jammed and packed and forced

into the smallest possible space until they were completely cut off from light
and air.

Ann Petry, *The Street*

Cultural historians like Slotkin and Alexander Saxton have argued persuasively
that the hard-boiled American detective is a direct descendant of nineteenth-
century frontier heroes such as Natty Bumppo, liminal figures who crisscross
the frontier, loyal to European-American society but isolated from it through
their intimate involvement with Native American others.[9] Indeed, Saxton sees
the rapid emergence of the dime-novel detective in the late 1880s partly as a
consequence of the closing of the frontier and a corresponding "credibility gap .
. . between the occupational activities of [real contemporary miners and
cowboys] and the tasks that western heroes were expected to perform" (Saxton
1990, 336). Critics of detective fiction—Cynthia Hamilton's recent *Western and
Hard-Boiled Detective Fiction in America* is the most elaborate and thorough
account—have likewise traced the lineage of the American adventure hero
through the hard-boiled detectives of Dashiell Hammett and Raymond Chandler
and beyond, without, however, paying much attention to the fate of the
"frontier" in that passage.

The importance of that genealogy is indisputable, I think, particularly for
considering the ideological and cultural work of hard-boiled crime fiction. The
emphasis on the figure of the adventure hero, largely apart from the rest of the
hard-boiled urban world, has on the other hand been something of a critical red
herring encouraged by the rhetoric of the fiction itself. Hard-boiled fiction,
possibly more than any popular formula, has been overwhelmingly dominated
by the individualism that is crucial to frontier ideology, in that it allows
recuperation of the outlaw frontier hero who, in Slotkin's suggestive reading, is
represented as renewing European-American civilization through acts of
violence that at once transgress and defend its symbolic and geographical
boundaries (Slotkin 1988, 81-106 and *passim*). Though particular discourses do,
of course, construct particular subject positions, their most important ideological
work lies not in the construction of individual subjects but rather in matrices of
subject relations within a conceptual space. For that reason, we need to look
beyond particular characters in adventure fiction to the dynamic spaces, the
intersubjective matrices, constructed by those fictions.

Given the overdetermined association of African Americans and crime in
everyday life and the representations of that association as a natural result of
essential racial characteristics, one might expect black crime and racial conflict
to play a more central role in hard-boiled detective fiction, which more often
deals with white law and white deviance.[10] That this is not the case seems partly
a consequence of the transformation of the frontier from a movable western
boundary into a relatively fixed partitioning of urban space. An overt war of

extermination requires that the other side be represented, if in distorted or fantasmatic form. Sustained oppression, which is a covert war of extermination largely by ideological remote control, benefits more from sanctioned ignorance. Nevertheless, there are occasionally references to a racial frontier at the extreme edge of society that marks the ultimate frontier, the absolute boundary of the "order" of the familiar, as in this passage from Mickey Spillane's *One Lonely Night*:

> Here was the edge of Harlem, that strange no-man's-land where the white mixed with the black and the languages overflowed into each other like that of the horde around the Tower of Babel. There were strange, foreign smells of cooking and too many people in too few rooms. There were the hostile eyes of children who became suddenly silent as you passed. (1951, 134)

This frontier dividing Harlem from the rest of Manhattan is represented from its far side in Chester Himes's novel of the same period, *A Rage in Harlem* (also known as *For Love of Imabelle*), as Jackson, the central character, on the verge of escape after a harrowing flight from the police, suddenly realizes that he has left Harlem and is "down in the white world with no place to go . . . no place to hide himself" (Himes 1989, 137). He turns back to face certain capture rather than go on. Himes does more than simply affirm the existence of the border, however: he explores its meaning as an ideological concept marking the exercise of white hegemony. In doing so he offers a conception of crime never more than tentatively articulated in European-American detective novels by acknowledging an "underworld" that is "catering to the essential *needs* of the people" (49; my emphasis), perhaps not in ideal fashion but in a manner necessitated by the character of the socioeconomic system. A good deal of criminal activity in this fiction is a result of the U.S. economy's partitioning through segregation. Crime itself, then, is a potentially resistant practice.

Viewing crime as part, rather than the breakdown, of a cultural system, Himes and, more recently, Walter Mosley construct a complex picture of crime and detection as a negotiation of cultural needs and values, operating within the black American subculture as a critique of white racial ideologies. Referring repeatedly and explicitly to the complex politics of race and class in the United States, they seek to disentangle justice and morality from white hegemony, fighting exploitation and violence within black communities while also attacking a social system that engenders crime. In short, they resist the assimilation of the far side of the frontier as "chaos" and "evil," favoring a conception of the frontier as a site of ideological struggle for rights and privileges between two American microcultures.[11]

The general grounds for such struggle are perhaps best summed up by Himes, commenting on "The Dilemma of the Negro Novelist in the U.S.A.":

"Of course, Negroes hate white people, far more actively than white people hate Negroes. . . . Can you abuse, enslave, persecute, segregate and generally oppress a people, and have them love you for it? Are white people expected not to hate their oppressors?" (Himes 1972, 398-99). Whatever differences there might be on specific details, Himes and Mosley agree in affirming the need for African-American opposition to oppression and in rejecting the privilege of white supremacist ideology to diagnose and prescribe remedies for the situation of African Americans.

Self-policing of a community, even an oppressed one, is not necessarily complicitous with the oppressive order, of course, or at least not completely so. As I indicated earlier, crime within an oppressed community may be a form of resistance, but it is also a part of the larger, macrocultural economic and social structure. In the United States that means crime is exploitative, for it acts out the imperatives of capitalist competition in a particularly unfettered manner. Therefore, as Manning Marable has pointed out, in relatively poor African-American communities, like those of the Himes and Mosley novels, "the general philosophy of the typical ghetto hustler is not collective, but profoundly individualistic. . . . The goal of illegal work is to 'make it for oneself,' not for others. The means for making it comes at the expense of elderly Blacks, young black women with children, youths and lower-income families who live at the bottom of the working class hierarchy" (Marable 1983, 64). It is because of their need to resist the manifestations of individualist competition as criminal entrepreneurship that Himes's police detectives and Mosley's private investigator work in their own communities.

Aside from that common ground, however, the novels of the two series differ considerably, and these differences intersect in complicated ways with the construction of the urban/racial frontier in the two series. These constructions in turn reflect the contradictions produced by ideological struggle between differing American microcultures. A dominant ideology tends to be self-sustaining, thanks to its greater access to means of reproduction such as educational systems and mass communication media. Nevertheless, dominance and its reproduction can never be complete, never attend adequately to every extracultural force operating through travel, migration and immigration, international economic transactions, and so forth, or to every gap that develops in the intracultural social formation through uneven development. On the other hand, the pervasiveness of dominant ideologies tends to fragment and disperse the force of other microcultural modes of ideological resistance. Resistance is therefore always under pressure, faced with an incessant need to escape from or relocate itself within a space defined by the dominant microculture.

Michel de Certeau's *Practice of Everyday Life* still offers perhaps the most exhaustive attempt to theorize this locating of resistance, by positing two logical possibilities. *Strategic* resistance finds its space outside the domain of the dominant by attaching itself to an alternative, fully constituted ideology that exists elsewhere. *Tactical* resistance, on the other hand, works within the space of the dominant, exploiting the contradictions within that space as opportunities arise, but unable to hold on to what is gained in the tactical moment (de Certeau 1984, 34-39). The novels of Mosley and Himes can be usefully read as narratives representing, respectively, strategic and tactical resistance. To read the novels this way, however, also raises questions about the dichotomy de Certeau constructs, suggesting a more complicated relation between strategies and tactics.

Resistance in *representational* practices, of course, cannot operate in a straightforward manner. Fictional narratives in particular raise the question of the use of representation for resistance, since the diegetic world constructed by a narrative has an ambiguous, if necessary, relation to the world of everyday practice. Furthermore, representation of resistance need not itself be a resistant practice (mainstream media coverage of the Los Angeles uprising in 1992 offers the most blatant recent demonstration). Therefore, in what follows I will separate questions of representing resistance from the manner of representation, in this case narration.

Representing Resistance

> "Detectives Grave Digger Jones and Coffin Ed Johnson reporting for duty, General," Pigmeat muttered.
> "Jesus Christ!" Chink fumed. "Now we've got those damned Wild West gunmen here to mess up everything."
>
> Chester Himes, *The Real Cool Killers*

Representation and enactment of resistance to white hegemony is central to the detective fiction of both Himes and Mosley. In discussing these issues, I consider the two writers in reverse chronological order for two reasons. In terms of representation, Himes's police detectives occupy a more complex and ambiguous ideological space. In terms of enactment, Himes's formal experimentation, especially in *Blind Man with a Pistol,* possesses a more radical potential than anything in Mosley's writing to date, though the latter also suggests directions for resistance unexplored by his precursor.

Unlike detective characters ranging from Mike Hammer to Kinsey Millhone, who despite many differences all bend the law only to better uphold it, Mosley's Easy Rawlins readily and unrepentantly acknowledges having been on the "wrong" side of the law himself. His detective work is described as being for the community and outside the white system of law, often performed on a barter basis and for people who "had serious trouble but couldn't go to the police" (Mosley 1991, 5) because they themselves are already of material necessity living on the fringes, if not outside, of the law: "In my time I had done work for the numbers runners, church-goers, businessmen, and even the police. Somewhere along the line I had slipped into the role of a confidential agent who represented people when the law broke down" (Mosley 1992, 17). This strategic position of "confidential agent" is justified partly on the grounds that an African American could not both work for the police and remain part of the community. Speaking of Quinten Naylor, a black cop who figures in the second and third novels, Rawlins says that he "got his promotion because the cops thought that he had his thumb on the pulse of the black community. But all he really had was me. . . . Even though Quinten Naylor was black he didn't have sympathy among the rough crowd in the Watts community" (Mosley 1992, 18-19).[12]

Within the narratives as a whole, the division between a communal African-American order and white law proves tenuous. Mosley's first three novels turn on problematic intersections of the white and black communities of Los Angeles, focusing on figures who traverse the unstable interstice between: Daphne Monet/Ruby Hanks, an African-European-American ("passing" for a white woman) who likes the Central Avenue jazz clubs and black lovers; Chaim Wenzler, a Jewish member of the American Communist Party who works in and for the black community; Robin Garnett, a rich young white woman who has rebelled against her family and upbringing by becoming a stripper and prostitute in Watts under the name of Cyndi Starr. And in each case, Easy Rawlins is pressed into detective work by forces from the white world as well: racketeer DeWitt Albright, who plays on Easy's need for quick mortgage money after losing a job *(Devil in a Blue Dress*, 1990*)*; the IRS and FBI, who threaten to prosecute him for tax evasion *(Red Death*, 1991*)*; the L.A. police, who threaten to pin a series of murders on his friend Mouse *(White Butterfly*, 1992*)*. More important than these connections with the white community, however, is Easy Rawlins's discovery that there is no simple way to work for order and justice in his African-American community when what counts as "order" and "justice" are defined, at least in part, by a dominant white supremacist ideology. Rawlins does not share the common illusion of the privileged, that such terms can be defined outside of ideology. He observes frequently that all people act according to what they perceive to be their own best interests. That leaves open, however, the question of whether a community that is systematically disempowered by a dominant ideology can produce a coherent strategic resistance.

Mosley's second novel, *A Red Death*, addresses the question most directly. At the beginning of the story Rawlins is summoned by an IRS investigator for tax evasion. Technically the charge is valid, because Easy failed to report as income $10,000 that he acquired illegally, though in his own view legitimately, in *Devil in a Blue Dress*. FBI Agent Craxton then offers to help Rawlins cut a deal with the IRS, provided that he helps them get damaging information about Chaim Wenzler, a Polish Jew who survived the Holocaust and is a member of the Communist Party in the U. S. Craxton appeals to Easy's patriotism, positing an alliance between them through an explicit statement of urban frontier logic: "the Bureau is a last line of defense. There are all sorts of enemies we have these days. . . . But the real enemies, the ones we have to watch out for, are people right here at home. People who aren't Americans on the inside" (Mosley 1991, 50). Easy doesn't trust Craxton, insists that he will do the job only because he has no choice, and tells us that his own feelings about communism are "complex" because of the alliance between the Soviet Union and the United States during the war and Paul Robeson's professionally disastrous connections with Russia (47). However, he doesn't actually challenge Craxton's construction of the frontier between real Americans and un-Americans. Instead he dismisses the idea of communist activity in the African-American community and insists that he will help the FBI get Wenzler but won't work against his "own people" (53).

The rest of the narrative shows that any attempt to define such an internal frontier that aligns black and white interests against a common un-American enemy leads to unresolvable contradictions. Wenzler himself proves to be a sympathetic figure who works in the black community because of the links he sees between his own experience as Jew in Poland and that of African Americans (Mosley 1991, 91).[13] His main activities involve charitable work that Rawlins supports and aids. Furthermore, Wenzler's connections within the black community make any attempt to isolate him as an object of investigation impossible. Partly as a result of Rawlins's work, two black women and a black minister get murdered in addition to Wenzler, and Rawlins finds himself having to investigate the Garveyite African Migration group.

In short, Easy finds no reason to aid the FBI's investigation except his own economic interests, and he feels increasingly guilty about that. What is most interesting about the novel in ideological terms, however, is the response he works out to that guilt. One might expect that, seeing the impossibility of sharing the collective interests of the white-dominated U.S. government, Rawlins would decide between the two models for African-American opposition offered by Wenzler's Communist Party and the African Migration group. Both, after all, draw on oppositional ideological formations, one drawn along class lines, the other along racial and cultural ones. Mosley uses an appeal to individualism to validate Easy's rejection of both collective positions. In each case Easy appeals to Jackson Blue, who might be described as the paradigmatic organic intellectual of Mosley's mid-twentieth century Watts. Jackson expresses his own rejection of the Migration agenda in terms of the cultural gap between Africa and African Americans: "We been away too long, man" (Mosley 1991, 184). Shortly thereafter Easy echoes Jackson's rejection of the Migration movement himself, but with a crucial difference: "I got me a home already. It might be in enemy lands, but it's mine still and all" (190). Unlike Jackson's argument on grounds of collective, microcultural differences, Easy appeals to the imperative of individual property interests.

Jackson rejects communism on similar grounds of an unbridgeable difference of *collective* interests. While admitting that the communist economic agenda coincides with the interests of African Americans, he reduces the question of the Communist Party in America to the blacklist, and says that whites will eventually get off the list, but the situation of blacks will remain the same (Mosley 1991, 197-98). Again Easy's rejection of collective action soon follows, based again on individual interests rather than microcultural ones: "It wasn't political ideas I didn't care about or understand that made me mad. It was the idea that I wasn't, and hadn't been, my own man. . . . Like most men, I wanted a war I could go down shooting in. Not this useless confusion of blood and innocence." (203)

The position reflected here aligns Easy with the individualist ideology that has crucially underpinned conservative frontier American politics, which helps explain why he is unable to reject the FBI's new frontier account of real and unreal Americans even though he distrusts Craxton. The positing of "American" as a collective cultural and ideological identity stands in direct contradiction with the notion that what makes one American is precisely radical "individuality." That contradiction has enabled the frontier ideology, in both its western and urban manifestations, to link an egalitarian political rhetoric with systematic aggression against Native Americans on the one hand, and with the systematic underdevelopment of black America meticulously documented by Marable on the other. Given the demand of political expediency, frontier ideology sometimes serves the establishment of national boundaries or internal partitions on the basis of an essentialist racial ideology that hierarchizes individuals by group identifications. At other times, however, and in other geographical or cultural terms, the idea that all people are free individuals is used to argue that they fall on either side of the frontier lines through their own bad choices or personal failings. The logic of individualism coupled with that of nationalism and patriotism thus permits systematic and collective cultural aggression and oppression to be passed off as a policing action against one bad Indian like Cochise or Crazy Horse or Geronimo, or as the legitimate surveillance of a dangerous black leader like Martin Luther King or Malcolm X—or a communist like Wenzler. That Easy Rawlins falls into line with the ideology that claims that he can be his own man seems to confirm the accusation made by his friend Mouse: "You learn stuff and you be thinkin' like white men be thinkin'. You be thinkin' that what's right fo' them is right fo' you" (Mosley 1990, 205). Thus it is on very shaky ground indeed that Easy chides the black police officer Quinten Naylor: "You one'a them. You dress like them and you talk like them too" (Mosley 1991, 154).

The trajectory of Easy's particular negotiation of the contradictions of

American culture can be traced, I think, to a lesson he learns from DeWitt Albright in the first novel of the series: "You take my money and you belong to me. . . . We all owe out something, Easy. When you owe out then you're in debt and when you're in debt then you can't be your own man. That's capitalism" (Mosley 1990, 101). There is no necessary linkage between capitalism and white supremacist ideology, but just as racism can serve the interests of capitalism by ideologically fragmenting classes, so too can a capitalistic individualism undermine collective resistance to racism. Various sympathies notwithstanding, Easy's actions are structured by the drive to accumulate wealth, which drives wedges between him and the South Central community. At the end of *White Butterfly,* Easy announces his move to a section of West Los Angeles that "[m]iddle-class black families had started colonizing" (Mosley 1992, 271). Significantly absent from the text is the recognition of the way this geographical sectoring of classes in the capitalist metropolis splits the interests of African Americans as a minoritized community—a phenomenon well understood by Bob Jones in Himes's *If He Hollers Let Him Go*: "When you asked a Negro where he lived, and he said on the West Side, that was supposed to mean he was better than the Negroes who lived on the South Side; it was like the white folks giving a Beverly Hills address" (Himes 1986a, 48). Instead, Easy's casual use of the "colonizing" metaphor suggests the subordination of collective interests to the exigencies of white capitalism, which undermines strategic resistance organized around either class or community.

As police detectives, on the other hand, Chester Himes's Grave Digger Jones and Coffin Ed Johnson align themselves explicitly with the existing power structure, while nevertheless enacting a tactical resistance within that system. Although they ostensibly solve crimes, the solutions often turn out to be plausible but false ones. These solutions satisfy the white legal establishment, but also work to rid Harlem of committed criminals while sparing others, often "squares" who have gotten involved in crime through a desperate need for money, and offering them incentives to avoid further crime. Usually these fortunate survivors, such as Jackson and Imabelle in *A Rage in Harlem* (1989c) or Sissie and Sonny in *The Real Cool Killers* (1988c), marry at the end of the novels. In addition, Jones and Johnson's position within the law enforcement structure allows them to critique it directly, which they do most frequently by pointing out the roots of black crime in economic exploitation by whites.

Nevertheless, they take their orders and carry them out. As insiders, Grave Digger and Coffin Ed cannot mount any consistent resistance to white oppression. Rather, in the way that de Certeau cogently recognizes, they seize opportunities where they arise, never working directly against the interests of the police department, but twisting situations and police procedures in such a way as to subvert them and turn them to the use of the Harlem community.

Such tactical resistance proves as difficult to define and sustain as the strategic resistance attempted by Easy Rawlins, however, and that difficulty seems implicitly addressed by a trajectory that can be traced through the Grave Digger/Coffin Ed series. The pattern involves the way in which crime and policing, the relation between the two, and between the two and the Harlem community, are conceived.

As I pointed out earlier, a passage in the first novel of the series radically defines crime not as a deviation from, but rather as an integral part of the U.S. economy, catering to "essential needs" of people that are not satisfied through "legitimate" business, or at least not satisfied uniformly, given the various kinds of inequalities that are also integral to the U.S. economy and culture. And far from standing in simple opposition to one another, the police and the organized crime system are also bound by economic relations. Himes's detectives are said to take "their tribute, like all real cops" (Himes 1989c, 49), and as Coffin Ed succinctly puts it, "Crime is what pays us" (Himes 1988a, 100). Nonetheless, the novels insist on an order, a standard of tolerable or legitimate action, and that requires drawing a line, constructing a frontier. The passage on crime and the police in *A Rage in Harlem* reveals some of the contradictions that ordering raises, even within Himes's radical redefinitions:

> [Grave Digger and Coffin Ed] took their tribute, like all real cops, from the established underworld catering to the essential needs of the people— gamekeepers, madams, streetwalkers, numbers writers, numbers bankers. But they were rough on purse snatchers, muggers, burglars, con men, and all strangers working any racket. And they didn't like rough stuff from anybody else but themselves. (Himes 1989c, 49)

Aside from the complicated question of what constitutes "essential needs" or legitimate access to "rough stuff," the inclusion of "strangers" in the list of those who cross the line of legitimacy is a particularly troubling one given the line drawn by whites that establishes all blacks as strangers outside Harlem. Jones and Johnson themselves, by working for the white police, make themselves strangers both in and outside Harlem. The novels themselves acknowledge this tenuous position. Early in *The Heat's On,* Coffin Ed notices residents of a white-occupied apartment building watching them, and remarks, "They think we're burglars," to which Grave Digger replies, "Hell, what else are they going to think about two spooks like us prowling about in a white neighborhood in the middle of the night?" (Himes 1988b, 16). In *Blind Man with a Pistol* a black woman appeals to the two for help when white policemen try to arrest her unjustly, and Grave Digger is forced to respond: "Don't look at me . . . I'm the law too" (Himes 1989a, 59).

Theoretically, the problem is one that de Certeau's *The Practice of Everyday Life* manages consistently to evade or finesse: since even dominant cultures are riven by ambiguities and contradictions emerging in the gap between ideologies and practices, how exactly is tactical resistance to be distinguished from complicity, or to put it in terms that Himes might more likely use, how is justice to be distinguished from injustice?

Himes's novels themselves seem aware of this problem and try to address it by gradually shifting the position of Jones and Johnson from one of tactical to one of strategic resistance. The claim that the two take their tribute from the underworld like all the rest of the cops is reversed in later novels, and in *Blind Man with a Pistol* they are described as martyrs for the cause of honesty: "Now after twelve years as first-grade precinct detectives they hadn't been promoted. Their raises in salaries hadn't kept up with the rise of the cost of living. They hadn't finished paying off their houses. Their private cars had been bought on credit. And yet they hadn't taken a dime in bribes (Himes 1989a, 97)." It is from this position of unshakable honesty that Coffin Ed can ask, in *The Heat's On*, "Is everybody crooked on this mother-raping earth?" (Himes 1988b, 146). The immediate point of such passages seems to be the moral superiority of the two over the rest of the police force, yet the passages also work to legitimate Jones and Johnson's access to acceptable violence in Harlem on the same moral grounds. Thus, Himes emphasizes the distance Grave Digger and Coffin Ed place between themselves and the Harlem community, a distance he otherwise tries to mitigate through occasional encounters between the detectives and acquaintances from their childhood. In effect, then, the resistant position of the detectives is established in terms of the individualist ideology that Mosley resorts to, because the legitimacy of Jones and Johnson's liberties with the law rests entirely on their individual moral quality, and has nothing to do with the inadequacy of the law itself. Collective resistance to a system of law and order based on collective oppression is therefore undermined altogether and the black detective located on what has been the good white side of the frontier all along. The project of collective opposition to a white supremacist culture succumbs to the fantasy of being one's own man.

Yet neither Himes nor Mosley embraces individualism unambiguously. *Blind Man with a Pistol* maps the end of multiple trajectories of the Harlem detective series, and where the career of Jones and Johnson leads to an ideological cul de sac, the narrative turns instead back to the Harlem community itself for a model of effective resistance. Indeed, the story is one of continual frustration for Grave Digger and Coffin Ed. They are forbidden by their superiors to use their prized pistols, forbidden to solve the murders that occur, and instead ordered to determine who's responsible for a series of riots in Harlem. The detectives offer one culprit themselves—Lincoln, who "hadn't ought to have freed us if he didn't want to make provisions to feed us" (Himes 1989a, 135)—and they receive another answer from Michael X, a Black Muslim leader— "Ask your boss, if you really want to know . . . he knows" (174). Other culprits are produced by the narrative as a whole: an earnest but stupid integrationist organizer named Marcus Mackenzie; the leader of a Black Jesus movement named Prophet Ham, whose motives seem dubious; Dr. Moore, a racketeer who uses a Black Power movement as a front; and finally, a blind man with a pistol.

This multiplication of suspects, and the failure of the detectives to narrow the list to one guilty party, as the detective formula demands, suggests that the individualist question posed is the wrong one altogether. Instead the novel suggests that riots are caused by a conjuncture of various personal interests with a general atmosphere of frustration, resentment, and hatred. The parable of the blind man with a pistol that forms the narrative's conclusion, displacing the conventional tying up of loose ends in the district attorney's office, is important in this regard. Superficially, the tale suggests that riots are caused by blind anger lashing out randomly. There is a crucial, though implicit, connection between this episode and the rest of the novel, however. Though the blind man starts shooting his pistol because of a complex misunderstanding and hits all the wrong targets, the one certain condition of possibility for the event is his fear and hatred of white people, which is produced by the dominant racial ideology of the United States. It is the same ideology that creates the crowds necessary to turn an individual cause or scam into a riot, that allows Michael X to say with confidence, "Ask your boss, he knows" who's starting the riots, and impels Grave Digger to respond, "You keep on talking like that you won't live long" (Himes 1989a, 175).

The turn away from individualist ideology, which permits right and wrong to be sorted out in terms of intrinsically good and bad guys, is manifested in other ways as well. For the first time in the series, Grave Digger and Coffin Ed have serious and repeated disagreements, not about facts or procedures in a specific case, but about their own role in general. Here's a representative passage, from a scene in which the detectives question a witness, a white woman named Anny:

> "You changed your race?" Coffin Ed interrupted.
> "Leave her be," Grave Digger cautioned.
> But she wasn't to be daunted. "Yes, but not to your race, to the human race."
> "That'll hold him."
> "Naw, it won't. I got no reverence for these white women going 'round joining the human race. It ain't that easy for us colored folks."
> "Later, man, later," Grave Digger said. "Let's stick to our business."
> "That is our business." (Himes 1989a, 68)

In this reconsideration of their business, the detectives and the narrative itself suggest that the answer to the linked problems of racism and crime may not lie with them at all, but rather in collective resistance within the black community. In the earlier *Cotton Comes to Harlem*, a back-to-Africa movement is dismissed as a scam through which hustlers con the squares of Harlem, much in the same way that the Brotherhood, Black Jesus, and Black Power movements are dismissed in *Blind Man with a Pistol*. The Black Muslims also figure briefly in *Cotton Comes to Harlem* (114-16) and are not subject to the same satirical treatment, but neither are they dealt with in more than a passing way. However, Grave Digger and Coffin Ed's ultimate engagement with the Black Muslims in *Blind Man with a Pistol*, an alternative ending that immediately precedes the concluding parable, is marked by startling departures from character on the part of the detectives. For the first time in the series, their engagement with another character is free of both irony and paternalistic condescension. Having chafed at orders not to use their pistols throughout the novel, here they volunteer to surrender them as a gesture of their goodwill toward Michael X. And when Michael X does agree to talk to them, they listen with astonishing seriousness and humility to the man described unequivocally as "the master of the situation" (174).

I take the gesture of offering to hand over their pistols to be particularly significant because of the way it alters the position of the detectives constructed in *A Rage in Harlem* through the words "they didn't like rough stuff from anybody else but themselves" (Himes 1989c, 49). This early position reproduces a dominant definition of legitimate access to violence. The gesture of laying down arms, while not reversing that definition, at least marks a refusal on the part of Jones and Johnson to uphold it actively.

The novel doesn't explicitly endorse the Black Muslims or lay out in any detail an effective oppositional strategy. Indeed, as I noted above, Grave Digger's last words to Michael X are a grim prediction of an imminent and violent death. In addition, sexual integration is tentatively held up earlier in the novel as the ultimate solution to racial inequality (Himes 1989a, 64-65). I will not pretend to resolve the question of whether the proper form of black American resistance is tactical or strategic, terms that in this case coincide roughly with integrationist/assimilationist and black nationalist agendas. The merits and weaknesses of each of these projects have been widely debated, and the problems are perhaps best summed up by Michele Wallace (citing Harold Cruse's *The Crisis of the Negro Intellectual*) in "Doing the Right Thing":

> black political philosophy has always seesawed between an integrationist/assimilationist agenda and a cultural nationalist agenda. . . . Integrationism always ends up being an embarrassment to its black supporters because of the almost inevitable racism and bad faith of its white supporters; they are willing to "integrate" with a small portion of upper-class blacks only if the masses of poor blacks are willing to remain invisible and

powerless. Cultural nationalism, on the other hand, has conventionally taken
refuge in a fantasy of economic and political autonomy that far too often
compounds its sins by falling into precisely the trap of bigotry and racism
(against gays, women, Jews, "honkies," and others) it was designed to
escape. (Wallace 1990, 110)

Aside from the problems, though, integrationism and separatism need to be seen
not in simple opposition to one another, but rather in triangulation with the
ideology they resist, that of old or new frontier capitalist individualism. Thus
far, Mosley's series, at the level of representation, has examined that
triangulation and opted for individualism, viewing the collective possibilities of
integration or separatism as they inevitably look from the individualist position:
as individual choices amounting to something like voluntary club membership.
Himes's series, on the other hand, finally leaves the triangulation as exactly that,
an unresolved tension pulling the community of Harlem in different directions.

Mosley gestures toward a critique of individualism in a different way, by
elaborating Easy's place within a community. His relationships with other
characters such as Jackson Blue, Mouse, and EttaMae are not merely glyphs that
naturalize the authority of the central figure, as in most detective series, but
rather change in significant connection to events of the narratives—Easy makes
friends, loses them, feels the conflicts among his own various interests and ties
acutely enough not to set himself on a moral pedestal. As a result, those other
characters attain a complex subjectivity that allows us to measure Easy's own
limitations, making room for ironies at the level of textual narration if not at that
of the first-person narrator.

Himes's critique of individualism depends also on redefining crime again in
Blind Man with a Pistol. Michael X implies that Harlem's crime is not a self-
sustaining economy, as was suggested in *A Rage in Harlem*, and that the
ultimate profit goes to the white community outside. In those terms, the
irreducibly collective form of "crime," rioting, that preoccupies the novel also
invalidates the individualist premises of American justice and law enforcement
systems. Walter Mosley's series seems headed toward similar ends, since the
historical trajectory of his series so far suggests that Easy Rawlins will
eventually confront the Watts riots of 1965, just as *Blind Man with a Pistol*
obviously alludes to the Harlem riots of 1964. The difference between the two
series in their relation to the individualism central to frontier ideology extends
beyond representations of crime and detection or policing, however. The
Harlem series and Mosley's three novels employ quite different strategies of
narrational enunciation that have implications as well for their relation to the
urban frontier.

Enacting Resistance: Himes, Mosley, and Narration

It was a Black-Art bookstore on Seventh Avenue dedicated to the writing
of black people of all times and from all places. . . .
"If I had read all these books I wouldn't be a cop," Coffin Ed said.
                                   Chester Himes, *Blind Man with a Pistol*

Like most kinds of fiction aimed at a mass market, detective fiction generally
has been fairly conventional in most formal terms. Although the detective story
trades heavily on enigmas, withheld information, misdirection, and confusion,
readers can generally depend on the detective to finally put all the scattered
pieces in place to construct a single, accurate account of events. Walter
Mosley's novels are no exception, assuming perhaps the most common form for
hard-boiled detective novels since Raymond Chandler began the Philip Marlowe
series: a first-person narrative told by the detective. Though any narrative form
can be manipulated to various ideological ends, this form lends itself to an
individualist stance, especially in a formula where the central question might be
articulated as, Who has the one true version of the story? The ideological
frontiers that the detective novel generally constructs, between good and evil or
justice and injustice, tend to get drawn around the figure of the narrating
detective trying to negotiate a path of honesty in a corrupt world. Easy Rawlins
agonizes over his own shortcomings and ethical blind spots—letting himself be
manipulated into betraying his friends and community in *A Red Death,* forcing
his wife to have sex against her will in *White Butterfly,* and so forth. He still
seems to emerge, in his own accounts, as the most scrupulous and decent of the
erring humans mired in the blindness of their cultural situations. In this respect
Rawlins is hardly distinguishable from Philip Marlowe, Mike Hammer, or
Kinsey Millhone, though as I suggested above, his meticulous placing within a
community works against the monological form of the detective's narration, and
perhaps will undermine it altogether as the series continues.

Chester Himes offers no such vision of community micropolitics, but on the
other hand, he established himself as a formal innovator in the field of popular
crime fiction from the beginning. In what seems an ingenious tactical response
to the problem of writing novels set on the far side of the urban frontier, he
rejected the convention of centering the novel in the perspective of the
detectives, instead combining the narrational forms of the hard-boiled detective
novel with that of criminal adventure narratives such as James M. Cain's
Double Indemnity (1989) or, to stretch definitions a bit, his own *If He Hollers
Let Him Go* (1986a) and *Lonely Crusade* (1986b). All the novels begin with so-
called crimes and criminals, and the detectives often aren't introduced until
several chapters into the narrative. Subsequently the point of view tends to shift

back and forth, with some additional shifting on both sides of the law/crime divide. The limitations of each perspective are emphasized through a sprinkling of observations such as "[Coffin Ed] hadn't discovered any lead to Uncle Saint, so he didn't know there were already three others dead from the caper" (Himes 1988b, 127). No single character ever acquires complete knowledge of the events of the novels. The conventional aim of the detective novel, to restore or uphold an order we are asked to accept as legitimate, and that of the conventional aim of the criminal adventure thriller, to test the order but finally to succumb or be reconciled to it, are displaced by a negotiation that never leaves an established order entirely dominant or unquestioned.

This mixing of genres tends to subvert the adamant insistence of crime fiction on the accessibility of "truth" to an individual perspective and its containment within a single coherent narrative. Such resistance to a dominant fictional mode is still limited, nonetheless, by established conventions of reading. Setting the detective story against the criminal adventure story does not simply consign meaning and truth to a site of contestation. Rather, both narrative points of view are subordinated to that of the overarching narration that assures readers of getting a true account, even if it is denied to any diegetic subject. *Blind Man with a Pistol* carries narrational innovation further, however, in a way that undermines the assurance of single, stable meaning.

As narratologists such as Seymour Chatman have argued, narrative discourse as such depends on a double time scheme, in which we can distinguish an order of diegetic events from the order in which those events are narrated (Chatman 1978, 62-63). We need not have a complete account of the events told, but conventional narrative depends on a stable narrational time to ensure that such a complete account is available in principle. Cutting between different scenes of action, different sets of characters, different points of view, and so forth, is acceptable even without explicit transitions, so long as we have the impression that a unique spatial and temporal relation between all the events could at least possibly be reconstructed.

Blind Man with a Pistol flouts these conventions. It is impossible to tell how many riots occur, or when they occur in relation to other events of the novel. There are repetitions of names and features of characters without a clear indication in some cases of whether the same character is reappearing or whether another happens to have the same feature. There are italicized interludes whose relation to the rest of the story seems to vary considerably. For the most part events seem organized according to a clear temporal order only within specific episodes.

This narrative disorder threatens the possibility of conventional narrative closure (aside from the fact that no closure is offered even nominally within some of the particular subplot sequences). If we nevertheless finish the novel and try to make sense of it, we are forced to seek some other principle of unity than temporal sequence of events connected through a limited set of characters. What offers itself instead, I think, is a thematic coherence linking various episodes. And the point of that alternative mode of coherence, I think, is that the problems of racism and oppression cannot be thought through in the personal, individualistic terms that conventional narrative offers, but rather in terms of collective practices that invisibly link disparate individual stories. In other words, a novel such as *Blind Man with a Pistol* reproduces ideological linkages as rhetorical ones, and therefore renders at least potentially visible in fiction what is generally concealed in the practices of everyday life in the United States.

This is only textual play, perhaps. But the frontier remains powerful as the text of American destiny, fixing it in a genre of expansionist adventure and natural cultural dominance. The erosion of generic boundaries may then be crucial to eroding the urban frontier. From frontier adventure tales to Proposition 187, the text of the frontier has been most effective in its capacity to construct a single cultural enemy on which to build a fantasy of a unified American people pursuing a linear national narrative. The disruption of narrative exemplified in Himes's *Blind Man with a Pistol* may offer one effective strategy for disrupting the frontier narrative itself in a way that lays bare its ideological underpinnings and internal contradictions. Mosley's digressions into the micropolitics of community and between communities pull at the seams of the detective narrative in another way, undermining the traditional generic reassurance that the good guys and bad guys can be sorted out, and disrupted order reestablished. Pursuing this trajectory, investigating the genre as much as the crimes, may lead toward and beyond the achievement of *Blind Man with a Pistol,* toward multiple stories that produce irreducibly multiple culprits. A radical rewriting of the frontier might thus be an overdue rewriting of Turner's thesis, insistently restoring the frontier's fragmentation that he was at pains to conceal.

Notes

1. I am grateful to Bob Winston, Mike Frank, and Kalpana Seshadri-Crooks, as well as four anonymous readers for *College Literature,* for valuable critical comments on earlier versions of this essay. I should also note a general indebtedness to the work of Marxist and postmodern geographers such as Neil Smith, Derek Gregory, David Harvey, and Edward Soja, whose works inform my theoretical framework.

2. The civilization/savagery opposition and the racial characterization of the frontier was, of course, partly an inheritance from and parallel development to ideologies of European colonialism. A detailed discussion of the relation between the development of the European-American ideology of racial and cultural difference I am discussing here and its European colonialist counterparts is beyond the scope of this essay. For a useful

psychological analysis of self/other oppositions in colonialist ideology, see the introduction and conclusion in JanMohamed (1983, 1-13, 263-83). For an acute description of spatial partitioning of colonialist settlements that closely parallels that of U.S. cities, see Fanon 1968, 38-39.

3. Part of the confusion of Turner's essay results from his avoidance of the obvious comparison of the western frontier to European *colonialist* frontiers, which results, I think, from his determination to affirm a clear economic and ideological break between Europe and the United States. In later essays he approaches, without quite reaching, a recognition that "frontier conditions" had been but a localized sector of European colonialist capitalism.

4. For a difficult but useful analysis in discursive terms of such ideological negotiations, see the work of Homi Bhabha (esp. "Signs Taken for Wonders" [1985] and "Articulating the Archaic" [1990]) on ambivalent signification in the interstices between cultures.

5. I am using the term "isolation" in roughly Freud's sense, as a mechanism through which two ideas, acceptable in themselves but not in combination, remain accessible to consciousness but isolated from one another by repression or absence of any associative paths of connection (see Freud 1959, 45-48, 89-90). For a more elaborate discussion of ideological mechanisms of isolation, see Crooks 1993.

6. See, for example, Marable 1983, 113. The phenomenon has been so widespread as to be obvious even to a demonstrably racist novelist such as Raymond Chandler (1940, 11).

7. Throughout this essay I use the term "hegemony" in Gramsci's sense of domination that works by eliciting the consent to be dominated from subordinate groups (Gramsci 1971, 210 and *passim*).

8. Judith Butler, in an essay on the first Rodney King trial, acutely analyzes a particular instance of white racist interpretive strategies that transform violence against African Americans as self-inflicted (Butler 1993, 20).

9. See Saxton 1990, 331-38 and Slotkin, "The Hard-Boiled Detective Story" (1988). Bethany Ogdon critiques the focus on the descent of hard-boiled fiction from frontier adventure narratives on the ground that it tends to obscure specificities of the later genre (Ogdon 1991, 72-73). Ogdon's objections are aimed at a critical methodology focusing on motifs or archetypes, rather than questions of genealogy, however. Her own provocative reading of relations between hard-boiled fiction and fascist ideology is compatible with the present essay, if one acknowledges homologous relations between fascist and frontier ideologies.

10. There is considerable ethnic coding of law and crime, but mostly involving the stereotypically more and less "civilized" European immigrants. Orientalism of the sort found in Hammett's *Maltese Falcon* and Chandler's *Big Sleep* is not uncommon also.

11. While dealing here with issues of race and, to a lesser extent, of class, I have paid little attention to those of gender. That would require a much longer essay, which I hope to undertake in the future. I would, however, point out that Himes's novels seem to me blatantly misogynist and Mosley's at least highly problematic in the way they construct gender roles and relations. Interestingly, Mosley's Easy Rawlins becomes increasingly self-conscious about gender relations in *White Butterfly,* and it is the novel's attention to conflicts between Easy's relation to his wife and the conventional

masculinist trajectory of his detective work that offers the strongest challenge in Mosley's work to the identity of the detective fiction genre, which I will discuss in the final section of this essay.

12. Ellis Cashmore, in "Black Cops Inc." (1991), points out that such assumptions of natural microcultural affinities were commonly made in the early assigning of African-American police officers.

13. Easy Rawlins himself makes the same connection in *Devil in a Blue Dress*: "many Jews . . . understood the American Negro; in Europe the Jew had been a Negro for more than a thousand years" (Mosley 1990, 138).

Works Cited

Bhabha, Homi K. 1985. "Signs Taken for Wonders: Questions of Ambivalence and Authority under a Tree Outside Delhi, May 1817." In *"Race," Writing, and Difference*, ed. Henry Louis Gates, Jr. Chicago: University of Chicago Press.

____. 1990. "Articulating the Archaic: Notes on Colonial Nonsense." In *Literary Theory Today*, ed. Peter Collier and Helga Geyer-Ryan. Ithaca: Cornell University Press.

Butler, Judith. 1993. "Endangered/Endangering: Schematic Racism and White Paranoia." In *Reading Rodney King/Reading Urban Uprising*, ed. Robert Gooding-Williams. New York: Routledge.

Cain, James M. 1989. *Double Indemnity*. 1936. Reprint, New York: Vintage.

Cashmore, Ellis. 1991. "Black Cops Inc." In *Out of Order? Policing Black People*, by Ellis Cashmore and Eugene McLaughlin. New York: Routledge.

Cashmore, Ellis and Eugene McLaughlin. 1991. *Out of Order? Policing Black People*. New York: Routledge.

Certeau, Michel de. 1984. *The Practice of Everyday Life*. Trans. Steven Rendall. Berkeley: University of California Press.

Chandler, Raymond. 1988. *Farewell, My Lovely*. 1940. Reprint, New York: Vintage.

Chatman, Seymour. 1978. *Story and Discourse: Narrative Structure in Fiction and Film*. Ithaca: Cornell University Press.

Crooks, Robert. 1993. "Reopening the Mysteries: Colonialist Logic and Cultural Difference in *The Moonstone* and *The Horse Latitudes*." *LIT: Literature, Interpretation, Theory* 4: 215-28.

Fanon, Frantz. 1968. *The Wretched of the Earth*. Trans. Constance Farrington. New York: Grove.

Freud, Sigmund. 1959. *Inhibitions, Symptoms and Anxiety*. Trans. Alix Strachey. Rev. and ed. James Strachey. New York: Norton.

Glasgow, Douglas G. 1980. *The Black Underclass: Poverty, Unemployment and Entrapment of Ghetto Youth*. New York: Random House.

Gramsci, Antonio. 1971. *Selections from the Prison Notebooks*. Ed. and trans. Quintin Hoare and Geoffrey Nowell Smith. New York: International.

Hamilton, Cynthia. 1987. *Western and Hard-Boiled Detective Fiction in America: From High Noon to Midnight*. Iowa City: University of Iowa Press.

Hawkins, Homer, and Richard Thomas. 1991. "White policing of Black Populations: A History of Race and Social Control in America." In *Out of Order? Policing Black*

198   Chapter 9

People, by Ellis Cashmore and Eugene McLaughlin. New York: Routledge.
Himes, Chester. 1972. "Dilemma of the Negro Novelist in the U. S. A." In *New Black Voices: An Anthology of Contemporary Afro-American Literature*, ed. Abraham Chapman. New York: Mentor.
_____. 1986a. *If He Hollers Let Him Go*. 1945. Reprint, New York: Thunder's Mouth.
_____. 1986b. *Lonely Crusade*. 1947. Reprint, New York: Thunder's Mouth.
_____. 1988a. *Cotton Comes to Harlem*. 1965. Reprint, New York: Vintage.
_____. 1988b. *The Heat's On*. 1966. Reprint, New York: Vintage.
_____. 1988c. *The Real Cool Killers*. 1959. Reprint, New York: Vintage.
_____. 1989a. *Blind Man With a Pistol*. 1969. Reprint, New York: Vintage.
_____. 1989b. *The Crazy Kill*. 1959. Reprint, New York: Vintage.
_____. 1989c. *A Rage in Harlem*. 1957. Reprint, New York: Vintage.
Jameson, Fredric. 1981. *The Political Unconscious: Narrative as a Socially Symbolic Act*. Ithaca: Cornell University Press.
JanMohamed, Abdul R. 1983. *Manichean Aesthetics: The Politics of Literature in Colonial Africa*. Amherst: University of Massachusetts Press.
Jeffries, John. 1992. "Toward a Redefinition of the Urban: The Collision of Culture." In *Black Popular Culture*, ed. Gina Dent. DIA Center for the Arts Series on Discussions in Contemporary Culture 8. Seattle: Bay.
Marable, Manning. 1983. *How Capitalism Underdeveloped Black America*. Boston: South End.
Mosley, Walter. 1990. *Devil in a Blue Dress*. New York: Pocket.
_____. 1991. *A Red Death*. New York: Pocket.
_____. 1992. *White Butterfly*. New York: Norton.
Ogdon, Bethany. 1991. "Hard-Boiled Ideology." *Critical Quarterly* 34.1: 71-87.
Petry, Ann. 1946. *The Street*. Boston: Houghton Mifflin.
Saxton, Alexander. 1990. *The Rise and Fall of the White Republic: Class Politics and Mass Culture in Nineteenth-Century America*. London: Verso.
Slotkin, Richard. 1985. *The Fatal Environment: The Myth of the Frontier in the Age of Industrialization 1800-1890*. New York: Atheneum.
_____. 1988. "The Hard-Boiled Detective Story: From the Open Range to the Mean Streets." In *The Sleuth and the Scholar: Origins, Evolution, and Current Trends in Detective Fiction*, ed. Barbara A. Rader and Howard G. Zettler. New York: Greenwood.
Smith, Neil. 1991. Contribution to discussion on "Housing: Gentrification, Dislocation and Fighting Back." In *If You Lived Here: The City in Art, Theory, and Social Action* (A Project by Martha Rosler), ed. Brian Wallis. Dia Art Foundation Discussions in Contemporary Culture 6. Seattle: Bay.
Spillane, Mickey. 1951. *One Lonely Night*. 40th Anniversary Edition. New York: Signet.
Turner, Frederick Jackson. 1920a. *The Frontier in American History*. New York: Henry Holt.
_____. 1920b. "Pioneer Ideals and the State University." In *The Frontier in American History*. New York: Henry Holt.
_____. 1920c. "The Significance of the Frontier in American History." In *The Frontier in American History*. New York: Henry Holt.
_____. 1920d. "Social Forces in American History." In *The Frontier in American History*.

New York: Henry Holt.
Wallace, Michele. 1990. "Doing the Right Thing." *Invisibility Blues: From Pop to Theory*. London: Verso.
Williams, Rita. 1993. "To Live and Die in L. A." *Transition* 59: 110-19.
Wright, Richard. 1993. *Native Son*. New York: Harper Collins.

10

"Building Up from Fragments": The Oral Memory Process in Some Recent African-American Written Narratives

Helen Lock

Although the precise way in which memory functions is still open to question, especially in these days of contentious debate over repressed/coerced memory, a useful distinction can be made between the differing perceptions of the memory process generated by oral and by literate cultures. This distinction, and, more importantly, the possibility of mediating between these differing perceptions, has been extensively invoked by many writers of the African diaspora for whom the process of memory is a controlling narrative principle. Through memory, perceived in both oral and literate terms, they aim to reconstruct the absences and silences of oral history that are contained within the official written record.

This essay focuses specifically on recent African-American writers' revival, for this same purpose, of oral perceptions of the memory process within a literate/literary context and framework: the discussion will be centered primarily on three novels, Toni Morrison's *Beloved* (1987), Paule Marshall's *Praisesong for the Widow* (1983), and David Bradley's *The Chaneysville Incident* (1981). I choose these partly because of their broad familiarity as staples of college introductory courses in African-American literature, but also because—

superficially dissimilar as they are—they are representative of a generation of African-American literary artists whose sensibilities do not exclude orally constituted modes of thought. This is not by any means to suggest that they simply substitute an oral for a literate conception of memory, valorizing one and dismissing the other. To do so would be as exclusory as the process whereby written records dismiss much of oral history. Their aim, as African-American writers, is not to exclude either cultural tradition, but to energize the dialectic between them, by reasserting—through the medium of the written word—the value of an orally derived perception of the workings of memory. This perception, often obscured or debased during the ascendancy of literacy and literate thought in the twentieth century, provides a powerful alternative means of negotiating with the past.

Literate cultures characteristically consider memory to be a rational, intellectual process. Literate, text-oriented cultures that value empirical science and verifiable fact demand of memory that it adhere to rigorous standards of exactitude and verification. Because literates think in terms of a fixed original whose total recapitulation is not only possible but desirable, "objective, deliberate, and exact recall" thus becomes the privileged definition of memory. Despite its privileged status, however, verbatim recall is not the way memory functions naturally. Recall is in fact seldom exact, but "constructed or reconstructed from a few remembered details combined with an impression left by the original. Recallers think the result is actually a reproduction of what they have retained, whereas, in fact, it has been built up from fragments" (Cofer, Chmielewski, and Brockway 1976, 191). Although seldom attainable, exact recall is nevertheless the desired goal. Because of the general inability of the spontaneous or subjective memory process to recuperate a fixed original , therefore, it is not valued by literate societies as it is by oral cultures.

In *The Interface between the Written and the Oral* (1987), Jack Goody makes the important distinction "between exact recall (what psychologists often mean by 'memory') and creative reconstruction, which does not involve verbatim learning, or even imitation, but generative recall" (Goddy 1987, 180). Since oral cultures characteristically conceive of time more in cyclical than linear terms, the past is not experienced as a single fixed entity, repository of unchangeable facts or "truth"—a time irrevocably gone. Thus, it is recalled by memory into present consciousness not by an objective process whose results are subject to verification, but by "creative reconstruction."[1] Creativity, spontaneity, intuitiveness, and subjectivity all help to provide access, through memory, to a past that does not have to be—indeed, cannot be—monolithic.

In transitional periods during which oral cultures gradually achieve literacy, we find ambiguous attitudes toward the nature of memory. For example, Frances A. Yates's *The Art of Memory* (1966—this is still the best-known and most authoritative book on the subject, though now joined by Carruthers 1990) described the elaborate memory arts that reached their zenith during the European Renaissance, when predominantly oral societies were becoming increasingly literate. That these arts contained components of both oral and literate conceptions of memory is made clear in a recent essay by Paul Sharrad, which discusses the acknowledged debt of contemporary Caribbean writer Wilson Harris's fiction to the art of memory as Yates defines it (and as Sharrad interprets Yates's definition): "[D]espite its drive to fix everything . . . it is flexible, open to rearrangements, additions, deletions, in the light of cumulative feedback. . . . [It is] a system which is not solely or even primarily devised as a rationalistic attempt to encompass material reality" (Sharrad 1995, 101). Sharrad shows the relevance and value of this mediation to the postcolonial writer whose society is undergoing a related transition: in the struggle for national self-definition, a response to the past that includes both the rational memory process and "creative reconstruction" enables the writer to look through and then beyond the written colonial record, to a "subjective, tentative deconstruction of dominating presence to show the shadows of reconstructions from absence" (97).

A similar imperative informs the work of many recent African-American writers, although with a different emphasis. In the transitional period during which African Americans achieved literacy, especially in the early twentieth century, the powerful oral tradition continued to flourish, thanks both to the ambiguity of attitudes toward literacy characteristic of such periods, and to varying degrees of ambivalence among African Americans about adopting the dominant culture's most privileged form of expression.[2] As it evolved, African-American literature continued to look to the oral tradition, not just for its expressive forms, but for access to a past not preserved in literary form. But then, as both literacy itself and the African-American literary tradition become more firmly entrenched, so inevitably do literate definitions of the proper use of memory to access the past. This becomes especially problematic when the past in question—particularly as it pertains to slavery—becomes subsumed in the collective unconscious because it is too painful to confront directly. The linear conception of time characteristic of the literate memory process, which fixes the past unchangeably, reinforces this resistance to confrontation, because it demands that the past remain static, never to be revisited, reconfigured, or transcended. In response to this impasse, many recent African-American written narratives have sought to propose an alternative approach to the past, by foregrounding the functioning of oral memory both thematically and structurally: not to recall a fixed original or a singular truth, but to reconstruct and regenerate (inter)subjectively many kinds of truth. This approach ultimately enables participation in, as well as preservation of, the past, and provides the potential for its transformation and the exorcism of its pain.

Perhaps the clearest and best-known example can be found in Toni

Morrison's *Beloved* (1987). Through her central character, Sethe, Morrison coins the neologism "rememory," and implies that rememory is to be understood differently from the conventional (literate) definition of memory. It puns on the fact that to "re-member" something is to perform the act of reassembling its members, thus stressing the importance to the memory process of creative reconstruction. Rememory, in fact, evokes the more intuitive oral memory process, which both defines the characters' negotiations with the past and provides the novel's narrative and structural principle. Yet it does so within the context of a highly sophisticated literary framework.

Rememory, as Sethe expresses it, is both subjective and intersubjective: "'Someday you be walking down the road and you hear something or see something going on. So clear. And you think it's you thinking it up. A thought picture. But no. It's when you bump into a rememory that belongs to someone else'" (Morrison 1987, 36). Rather than a solipsistic "remembering subject," Morrison envisions a remembering community of overlapping and interlocking, sometimes interdependent, consciousnesses. Rememory is also premised on a cyclical understanding of time: "'Where I was before I came here, that place is real. It's never going away. Even if the whole farm—every tree and grass blade of it dies. The picture is still there and what's more, if you go there—you who never was there—if you go there and stand in the place where it was, it will happen again; it will be there for you, waiting for you'" (36). "Place" is important to the visual orientation of memory, just as it was to the many *ars memorandi* Yates described, which advised memorizing ideas by associating them with different parts of physical structures.[3] Here, though, the focus is on the power of the spirit of place to evoke visual memory—again, both subjectively and intersubjectively: "'Places, places are still there. If a house burns down, it's gone, but the place—the picture of it—stays, and not just in my rememory, but out there, in the world'" (35-36).

Rememory, however, does not put the same premium as literate memory on the objectivity required to achieve exact recall of a fixed and verifiable original. The "truth" of the past to which rememory provides access does not take a fixed, singular form, and has different implications in the present for all those— Sethe, Denver, Paul D, Stamp Paid, Baby Suggs, the women who converge on 124 at the end, and many others—who participate in the re-membering, and by doing so, re-participate in a past that they now experience differently. In a 1987 television interview, Toni Morrison described the novel as presenting "the cumulative effect of memory and of . . . deliberately forgetting." For Sethe, in particular—whose name echoes Lethe, the mythical river of forgetfulness— *re*memory provides the key to unlocking, and ultimately transforming, a past her rational memory has repressed.

The re-membering that will enable the elements of the past to be collectively and creatively reconfigured is reflected in the structure of the narrative itself, which proceeds by "building up from fragments," shifting between present time and different points in the past as seen from multiple perspectives.[4] As Philip Page explains, "One word, detail, or image drops into their consciousness and reminds them of some part of their buried pasts. Cautiously, they relive the memory, rethinking and sometimes retelling it bit by bit, then dropping it, only to circle back to it later, with or without purpose" (Page 1992, 36). As this process unfolds—parts of the same story are reconstructed from different points of view, new details emerge before a coherent interpretive framework can be established, and all the while Sethe is "[c]ircling [Paul D] the way she was circling the subject" (161)—perplexed readers find themselves in the position of having to join the re-memberers in the act of creative reconstruction.

To extract individual meaning from the narrative, readers must enact the oral memory process by piecing together fragments, suggestions, hints, to make a whole that can never be precisely the same in each case—since one man's evocative detail is another woman's insignificant trifle—and would be diminished if it were. Morrison makes it clear that the story to be reconstructed can only be generated subjectively and intuitively, and thus cannot take a final, definitive form: "To make the story appear oral, meandering, effortless, spoken—to have the reader feel the narrator without identifying that narrator, of hearing him or her knocking about, and to have the reader work with the author in the construction of the book—is what's important" (Morrison 1984, 341). This complex literary text achieves its purpose, in other words, by evoking orally derived thought processes.

Each of the characters likewise re-members the story differently, though interconnectedly, according to their different needs—Denver, for example, collaborates with Beloved "to create what really happened" (Morrison 1987, 78), the focus of which is the story of her own birth. For Sethe, the need is critical: first, to confront, finally, the horror of the past that her rational memory has repressed and that she has been "circling," avoiding,"beating back the past" (73). But then, more importantly, she needs to re-member it. The rational memory of "what really happened" is not the whole story. When she relives the crucial scene at the end, it is through the fragmented sensory and emotional perceptions of her nonrational memory, as she confronts the man who "is coming for her best thing. She hears wings. Little hummingbirds stick needle beaks right through her headcloth into her hair and beat their wings. And if she thinks anything, it is no. No no. Nonono" (262). Through rememory, the past is reconfigured. This visceral reenactment enables Sethe to see past the "facts" and place the blame for her daughter's murder where it belongs, exorcising at least part of the guilt (and, finally, the ravenous Beloved herself).

History is not repeated in this reenactment, but transformed, and it is this transformative power of rememory that enables Morrison ultimately to use her novel to make restitution not just to Sethe and Beloved, but by extension to all the "[d]isremembered and unaccounted for" (Morrison 1987, 274) of the past—the "sixty million and more" of her headnote. The written text of *Beloved* is their memorial, supplying a voice to a silence in the oral tradition, a silence containing stories too horrible to tell ("It was not a story to pass on" [274]). The use of rememory as narrative principle, then, enables *Beloved* to mediate between past and present realities, blurring the distinction between them and re-membering the disremembered.

Although it stands as a paradigmatic example of this narrative approach to memory, *Beloved* is not its original (and will not be its final word). Among many other examples that might be discussed, one of the most pertinent is Paule Marshall's *Praisesong for the Widow* (1983), in which the protagonist, Avey Johnson, re-members her life, undoing what it has become and reconnecting it to what she had not consciously realized it was, so that past and present lives are transformed. Like *Beloved*, the story is "built up from fragments," in this case as Avey gradually makes connections (and is guided by others to make connections) among her fragmented memories, and between these memories and her present experiences, eventually reconstructing herself as Avatara—an avatar of all the past and present consciousnesses that have contributed to the making of Avey Johnson.

Avey's transformation is set in motion by a series of apparently unconnected and inexplicable sensory prompts. The overheard sound of patois in Martinique, for example, "had fleetingly called to mind the way people spoke in Tatem long ago" (Marshall 1983, 67), which in turn prompts the dream of her father's great-aunt Cuney, trying to coax and then drag Avey back to that Landing at Tatem from which the Ibos walked across the water back to Africa. Upon awakening, Avey retains the physical sensations of the fight that ensued (in front of her suburban neighborhood), as she resisted being pulled from the sophisticated, affluent life she had been conditioned to value, back to a life that values the nonmaterial and nonrational, and is powerfully connected to its past. Cuney's grandmother had identified so strongly with her Ibo ancestors' rebellion that while her body might be in Tatem, "her mind was long gone with the Ibos" (39), but in the dream her descendant and namesake manifests different priorities: "Did [Cuney] really expect her to go walking over to the Landing dressed as she was? . . . With her hat and gloves on? And her fur stole draped over her arm? Avey Johnson could have laughed, the idea was so ridiculous" (40), though it is not long until "[h]er amusement began to give way to irritation" (41). That she has not fully embraced the values of her shallow suburban life, however, becomes clear the day after the dream, when the mere sight of a rich parfait causes an unshakeable physical discomfort, a feeling of surfeit, which is the first clue to her subconscious dissatisfaction with a life overloaded with materialism and luxury but lacking spiritual sustenance, especially that which a reconnection with her ancestral past could bring her.

Thenceforth, after she abruptly leaves the cruise ship for reasons ill-defined even to herself, and embarks on a different journey that will eventually lead her to Carriacou with Lebert Joseph, Avey finds her memory constantly leading her in unexpected and unwilled directions. Her conscious, rational memory ceases to function: "[A]lthough she strained in her mind to see the [dining] room and the familiar objects there"—her silver, crystal, and china, the chandelier—"their reassuring forms refused to emerge. Instead she kept seeing with mystifying clarity the objects on display in the museum in the town of St. Pierre . . . which she had visited three days ago in Martinique" (Marshall 1983, 83)—objects that, bearing the scars of a volcanic eruption, are powerful reminders of the fragility and impermanence of affluent societies. Although her deliberate memory refuses to function, however, her spontaneous memory responds to a multiplicity of sensory stimuli by evoking seemingly random scenes from different points in the past: the feel of the milling crowd on the wharf, for example, their "colors and sounds" (187), remind her of her daughter's home movie, of her trip to Ghana, and then of her own childhood boat rides up the Hudson. Then the memory of the excited anticipation of the boat ride in turn evokes memories of Tatem, watching the communal ecstasy of the Ring Shout with Cuney, who had been excluded from it in punishment for "crossing her feet" (33).

Gradually, as the narrative of fragmented memories and sensations unfolds, the underlying pattern begins to emerge. Memories of the Ring Shout and of the boat ride are linked by "the same strange sensation" of

> hundreds of slender threads streaming out from her navel and from the place where her heart was to enter those around her. . . . Then it would seem to her that . . . the threads didn't come from her, but from them, from everyone on the pier, including the rowdies, issuing out of their navels and hearts to stream into her. . . . While the impression lasted she would cease being herself . . . instead, for those moments, she became part of, indeed the center of, a huge wide confraternity. (Marshall 1983, 190-91)

It is these connections, these "slender threads," that have been reaching out of the past to tug at her visceral memory, prompted by her subconscious need to re-member both her individual and her communal identity: her need is to reconnect not only with others in her immediate past, but also with all the earlier consciousnesses, the "pantheon of most ancient deities" (Marshall 1983, 127) that dwell inside herself (just as in Avey's delirium Rosalie Parvay contains all the significant women of Avey's past [217], and Lebert Joseph[5] contains an "endless array of personas" [243]). Her rememory, then, will again be both subjective and intersubjective; it is evoked and shaped both by herself and others.

Ultimately, Joseph reenacts Cuney's role in the dream by taking Avey's wrist and pulling her back toward the past. She feels "as exhausted as if she and the old man had been fighting" (Marshall 1983, 184), but this time offers less resistance, and allows herself to be taken on a journey that begins with a physical purging and ends with spiritual enrichment. The journey to the island (and here the spirit of place is again important: rather than "an actual place," the island seems "[s]omething conjured up perhaps to satisfy a longing and a need" [254]) in turn reenacts a more distant, ancestral memory—the Ibos's journey home—so that when Avey finally enters the dance in remembrance of the ancestors, she feels, like the Ibos, "as if the ground under her was really water" (248): she is not simply remembering, but reexperiencing. The ancestors join the dance with the living: "Kin, visible, metamorphosed and invisible, repeatedly circled the cleared space together" (239). As the boundaries of time and place are erased, Avey again feels the "slender threads" of connection, as the dance is metamorphosed into the Ring Shout, and she feels reborn, "with her entire life yet to live" (249); her fellow dancers salute the deities resurrected inside her, as she re-becomes the Avatara of her past, but in a new, revitalized form.

Here too, then, rememory is transformative, as Avey plans to return home to a different life and tell her story to those "lacking memory" (Marshall 1983, 225), to transmit orally the story of the Ibos to rising generations. Marshall makes clear that the power of this kind of memory lies in its differentiation from conventional memory, which makes sharp distinctions between past and present, and which uses concepts such as "history" to consign people, places, and events irrecoverably and unchangeably to the past. Significantly, Avey's husband Jay, source of her material affluence, was renowned for his "photographic memory" (92)—the epitome of exact recall. But oral, intuitive memory can evoke

> feelings that were beyond words, feelings and a host of subliminal memories that over the years had proven more durable and trustworthy than the history with its trauma and pain out of which they had come. After centuries of forgetfulness and even denial, they refused to go away. The note was a lamentation that could hardly have come from the rum keg of a drum. Its source had to be the heart, the bruised still-bleeding innermost chamber of the collective heart. (244-45)

Like Sethe, Avey had been subject to forgetfulness and denial. Like Sethe, rememory enables her to reconstruct the past, recover and reconnect with what is important, reject mistakes and injustices, and finally remake herself differently—not just as an individual, but as a feeling part of "the collective heart."

History, "with its trauma and pain," is problematic in these texts precisely because it *is* painful: painful in its exclusions from the written historical record—the silences that *Beloved* seeks to fill—and painful in its isolation in an immutable past of so many whom the present wishes to claim and revitalize, an isolation that is the source of the sense of loss articulated by the "lamentation" Avey Johnson hears issuing from the collective heart.[6] The linear time of history fixes their fate unchangeably, and precludes the transformative impulse of rememory, by denying the reciprocal interaction of past and present. David Bradley's *The Chaneysville Incident* (1981), a final example, directly addresses this issue: in this novel, a young history professor discovers he can only find meaning in his family's and community's past by abandoning the established methods of historical inquiry, and relying instead on a creative reconstruction that enables him to actively enter into and connect himself to that past, transforming the possibilities for his future.

John Washington's journey is both physically and spiritually a return to the site of his Pennsylvania childhood, initially to attend the deathbed of his father's (and his) old friend Jack. John's life has become completely disconnected from this milieu—"I knew nothing about the Hill any longer, I had made it my business not to know" (Bradley 1981, 17)—but on his arrival at the Hill, the power of the spirit of place begins to evoke initially unwilled memories: "[S]uddenly, inexplicably, I was curious, and so I thought for a moment, pulling half-remembered facts from the back of my mind" (17). His reunion with Jack revives other half-buried memories, of his own childhood and of his father, Moses Washington, and of the attempt he had made as a child to research his father's history and discover the truth about his mysterious death. The attempt had been a failure, because "I could not imagine. And if you cannot imagine, you can discover only cold facts, and more cold facts; you will never know the truth" (152). Now the adult John makes another attempt, his curiosity as a historian piqued by the fact that his father had left him a trail to follow.

In his will, Moses had bequeathed to John all his "books and records," which are not to be relinquished "'until you have examined all volumes, including personal memoirs'" (Bradley 1981, 204). So John again attempts to decipher the written record, noting and organizing key points on index cards, which he shuffles hopelessly, failing to find connections—the trail leads him only to more "cold facts," and no closer to Moses Washington himself. He only begins to make progress when he departs from the cards and begins to talk: when he abandons the written record and begins to imaginatively reconstruct the story orally, in creative interaction with his audience, his white girlfriend, Judith (a process similar to Denver and Beloved's collaboration).[7] By thinking as a member of the collective heart, and not as a detached historian, he can reconstruct intuitively a story that takes him beyond the documented facts, beyond individual memories, beyond Moses Washington himself, and toward a personal interaction with the past of his ancestors.

The novel's narrative structure reflects this progress from fragmented "facts" toward imaginative connection. At the beginning, John is so disconnected from his family and background that his father is referred to only as "Moses Washington," without explanation. As in *Beloved*, readers find themselves in the position of trying to make their own connections, as John's narrative ranges from the present to different points in the past—prompted, for example, by memories sparked by his talks with Jack, memories of the visceral experience of hunting, or those prompted by the sight of Moses' folio—and interspersed with digressions on historical matters. This nonlinear narrative movement suggests (among other things) John's difficulty in giving a coherent shape to his memories, and in connecting them with his new discoveries.

But then gradually the initially self-sufficient first-person narrative begins to admit other voices: firstly Jack's lengthy tales about Moses Washington, then the voices of the Judge, Judith, and others, and ultimately the voices in the mind of the runaway slaves led by John's ancestor, C. K. Washington. These voices in the wind, which have been present throughout the story (disguised in the beginning as the hum in the telephone wires, for example), and which John finally opens himself to hear, are, in Klaus Ensslen's words, "a motif which transcends rational analysis and historical quest and thereby helps to lift John's cognitive endeavor to a more imaginative and magical level where story opens into myth and assumes instinctual and somatic overtones that point away from the criteria generally accepted in Western culture, seeking connection with other cultural norms" (Ensslen 1988, 288). John cannot consciously summon these voices ("'You can't hear them if you try. Don't try. Just listen'" [Bradley 1981, 411]), but by allowing them to speak through him, he becomes able to enter imaginatively into the story, to make an intuitive connection with his ancestors by mentally reliving their (hi)story.

The end of John's physical journey, like Avey Johnson's, marks a return: he stands on the same spot where C. K. and the runaway slaves died their heroic deaths, and where Moses reenacted their deaths through his own, in a ritual rejoining of his ancestors. The voices in the wind, which John realizes how to hear after remembering Jack's hunting advice about the necessity of intuition and identification with one's quarry ("'Quit tryin' to figure where he's at an' jest follow him" [Bradley 1981, 410]), give him access to years of family and community memories, which he uses to re-member the story of the fates of Moses and C. K. It is not the definitive version—in the absence of the "cold facts" of history there can be no definitive version, but, as John discovered, if he has *only* cold facts as material, there can be no version at all. The story can only become coherent and meaningful to him if he reconstructs it without regard to rational analysis, and lets it tell itself, relive itself, through him, in all its evocative detail ("that was how he found them, how he heard them, panting in the mist" [419])—if he lets it join him empathetically to the ancestral community.

And at the end, when he burns the index cards on which the cold facts were inscribed, he sees the transformative possibilities of the story he has creatively reconstructed, not just for the shape of the past, but for the future: "[A]s I dropped the match to the wood and watched the flames go twisting, I wondered if . . . someone would understand. Not just someone: Judith" (Bradley 1981, 450). There is one last potential reenactment: Judith's emulation of the white miller Iiames, who, by imaginatively identifying with the runaway slaves enough to bury them according to "who loved who" (449), transcended centuries of racial conflict and antagonism. The tensions of John's relationship with Judith can be similarly transcended, if she chooses to forget history and make that empathetic leap into transformative rememory.

The narratives just discussed[8] use the workings of the intuitive, nonrational memory to reconstruct a past that the rational memory has often chosen not to confront because of its "trauma and pain." Thus, these narratives do not seek its exact, accurate recuperation. Instead, they illustrate how the memory process of creative reconstruction can re-member the fragments so as to transform the past and its implications, and to give it new life in the present. As Sharrad says in the article mentioned earlier, "The very fallibility of memory [in the literate sense] involves us in *mutual* reconstruction beyond solipsistic enclosure" (Sharrad 1995, 106; his emphasis): just as the past was shaped by many consciousnesses, many (including the reader's) contribute in different ways to its reshaping, and become active participants in stories resurrected from the grave of history. The felt need for this liberation back into the living world is, ultimately, the impulse for these novels' liberation of the oral memory process as literary narrative principle: the written text can serve to evoke all the many potential "truths" of all the unwritten stories.

Notes

1. "[I]n functionally oral cultures the past is not felt as an itemized terrain, peppered with verifiable and disputed 'facts' or bits of information. It is the domain of the ancestors, a resonant source for renewing awareness of present existence, which is itself not an itemized terrain either" (Ong 1982, 98).

2. As Bernard W. Bell explains, "[T]o cope with the complexities of their socialized ambivalence, to reconcile the tensions of their double-consciousness, the most intellectually capable and economically fortunate middle-class blacks borrowed Eurocentric forms of culture. . . . In contrast, the black majority . . . by virtue of their exclusion from full participation in the systems of the larger society were more inclined toward the alternative of the continuation and revitalization of residually oral Afrocentric forms of culture" (Bell 1987, 14-15).

3. The sixteenth-century Memory Theater of Giulio Camillo, as described by Frances Yates (Yates 1966, ch. 6), is a good example.

4. Walter Ong demonstrates that this kind of nonlinear, nonobjective structure is characteristic of oral narratives: "memory, as it guides the oral poet, often has little to do with strict linear presentation of events in temporal sequence" (Ong 1982, 147).

5. Karla Holloway identifies Lebert Joseph as "the incarnation of [Avey's] ancient Ibo ancestors" (Holloway 1982, 118), but he is also an incarnation of the trickster god Papa Legba (as his name suggests), clearly identified by his characteristic positioning at the crossroads with his stick, and by his shape-shifting (232-33).

6. Arnold Rampersad has well expressed the necessity for this pain to be overcome: "Only by grappling with the meaning and legacy of slavery can the imagination, recognizing finally the temporality of the institution, begin to transcend it" (Rampersad 1989, 123).

7. Klaus Ensslen notes the similarity of *Chaneysville*'s structure also to Faulkner's *Absalom, Absalom!* but with a salient difference: "[W]hile Faulkner's narrators tend to become victims of their obsessive investigations into the past by getting hopelessly entangled in it, Bradley dramatizes the quest for a coherent history as instrumental in a positive reconstruction of self and community" (Ennslen 1988, 287).

8. Others might include Morrison's *Song of Solomon* (1977), Ishmael Reed's *Mumbo Jumbo* (1972), Sherley Anne Williams's *Dessa Rose* (1986), and John Edgar Wideman's *Damballah* (1981). For this approach to memory as especially characteristic of African-American women's writing, see Holloway 1992.

Works Cited

Bell, Bernard W. 1987. *The Afro-American Novel and Its Tradition.* Amherst: University of Massachusetts Press.

Bradley, David. 1981. *The Chaneysville Incident.* New York: Avon.

Carruthers, Mary. 1990. *The Book of Memory.* Cambridge: Cambridge University Press.

Cofer, Charles N., Donna L. Chmielewski, and John P. Brockway. 1976. "Constructive Processes and the Structure of Human Memory." In *The Structure of Human Memory*, ed. Charles N. Cofer. San Francisco: Freeman.

Ensslen, Klaus. 1988. "Fictionalizing History: David Bradley's *The Chaneysville Incident.*" *Callaloo* 11.2: 280-96.

Goody, Jack. 1987. *The Interface Between the Written and the Oral.* Cambridge: Cambridge University Press.

Holloway, Karla F. C. 1992. *Moorings and Metaphors: Figures of Culture and Gender in Black Women's Literature.* New Brunswick: Rutgers University Press.

Marshall, Paule. 1983. *Praisesong for the Widow.* New York: Dutton.

Morrison, Toni. 1984. "Rootedness: The Ancestor as Foundation." In *Black Women Writers (1950-1980): A Critical Evaluation*, ed. Mari Evans. Garden City: Anchor.

_____. 1987. *Beloved.* New York: NAL.

Ong, Walter J. 1982. *Orality and Literacy: The Technologizing of the Word.* New York: Methuen.

Page, Philip. 1992. "Circularity in Toni Morrison's *Beloved.*" *African American Review*

26.1: 31-39.
Rampersad, Arnold. 1989. "Slavery and the Literary Imagination: Du Bois's *The Souls of Black Folk.*" In *Slavery and the Literary Imagination*, ed. Deborah E. McDowell and Arnold Rampersad. Baltimore: Johns Hopkins University Press.
Sharrad, Paul. 1995. "The Art of Memory and the Liberation of History: Wilson Harris's Witnessing of Time." *Callaloo* 18.1: 94-108.
Yates, Frances A. 1996. *The Art of Memory.* Chicago: University of Chicago Press.

11

Reconstructing Kin: Family, History, and Narrative in Toni Morrison's *Beloved*

Dana Heller

In "Reading Family Matters," Deborah E. McDowell narrates the on-going controversy surrounding a small but outstanding group of black female writers and critics' accusations that these writers are fracturing the image of an already besieged black American nuclear family. The complaint, which has been registered in the news media and academic journals, suggests that these writers—Toni Morrison among them—have betrayed the black family by failing to shoulder responsibility for restoring to it an image of wholeness and unity. Admittedly, McDowell observes, the "family romance is de-romanticized in writings by the greater majority of black women," whose portraits of domestic life do not simply paint Norman Rockwell in black, but rather seek out the distinct voices of black women, themes appropriate to their experience within the nuclear family, and narrative forms that place black women at the center of stories about family (McDowell 1989, 78). Consequently, reading and understanding black women's family narratives can present certain conflicts. For example, if we proceed from Marianne Hirsch's treatment of family romance as "an imaginary interrogation of origins" that "describes the experience of familial structures as discursive" (Hirsch 1989, 9), we see the unmistakable cultural bias towards Freudian principles, implicit in which is a notion of family structure already in place, and a notion of origin as ultimately knowable. However, the modern European definition of family plots has little relevance to a people displaced from their homeland, denied their claims to origin, separated from one another, forbidden their language, and refused participation in the dominant discursive economy to which they are subordinated. Regardless of where one stands on "family values," experienced readers of African-American fiction will rightly claim that the "de-romanticization" of the black family romance owes a great deal to the complex forms of economic and psychological oppression that black women and men have experienced both within the nuclear family and within the larger economic structure. In contemporary literature, this matrix of racism, sexism, and classism is registered in recurrent images of family violence, absent fathers, and woman-centered black families that function without the presence or support of men.

The cultural significance of these images, however, can be traced to a bigger picture of which contemporary family life is only a part. That picture *is* the historical processes of American social and economic development. Its organizing principle is racial oppression, or more specifically the dynamic of relations of domination perpetuated by the institutional enslavement of Africans who were brought to the American colonies as indentured servants as early as 1619.[1]

Toni Morrison's Pulitzer Prize-winning novel, *Beloved*, is a critical interrogation of family romance that examines the social deconstruction of African-American history and family life in the years before, during, and after the Civil War, when the United States became engaged in the project of "Reconstruction." More importantly for the purposes of my analysis, it is a novel centrally concerned with the need to rediscover or literally "re-member" the fractured stories of the past so that these stories might preserve lost culture and restore the familial and community bonds, which, although severely weakened by generations of enslavement, still function reciprocally to construct identity. As the novel demonstrates, it is these structures of narrative, these stories, that empower and unite the family.

While the reconstruction of family relations remains a central focus of *Beloved*, there is also significant stress placed on the need to dismantle the boundaries that separate family from community, private from public concerns. The novel brings about the gradual merger of those inside and those outside the haunted house at 124 Bluestone Road. Morrison suggests that a family closed off from caring relationships with nonkin is a family doomed to be consumed by the spirits of the unresolved past. As Sethe gives herself over more and more to Beloved's insatiable greed, a symbiotic union forms between the two that leaves Sethe starved and weak while Beloved grows fatter by the day. The women's withdrawal into 124, and into the reflective eyes of each other, is expressed in a series of interior voice passages that seem to blend together into one familial voice, although Morrison structures each section so that it must be read separately from the others, thus maintaining the integrity of individual consciousness within the triad.[2]

Beloved is a ghost story that challenges white-dominant culture's frame of reference for experiencing familial drama. Morrison's artistic narrative style, her merger of the powers of the past and the present, the living and the dead, the private sphere and the public sphere, unsettles the definitional boundaries of the Western European traditions of family romance and novelistic realism. In short, Morrison's critical project, like Hirsch's critical project on mother-daughter family romance, appears to take "as its point of departure the intersection of familial structures and structures of plotting" (Morrison 1987, 3). But what has not been sufficiently explored, to my mind, is the extent to which the novel challenges the limits of narrative and familial systems in order to redefine the structures of African-American kinship and the structures of an African-American storytelling tradition as mutually determining.

Comparing families to mine fields, Mary Helen Washington writes: "We walk and dance through them never knowing where or when something or someone is going to explode" (Washington 1991, 1). Indeed, there has been—and still is—much to say about the explosive mother-daughter relationships depicted in *Beloved*.[3] But what need be acknowledged are the actual shapes that familial representations take within historically specific communities of women, and the forms that make communication—even explosive communication—possible between generations separated by the brutality of a slave-labor economy that places the value of a dollar above the value of human life.

The central event of Morrison's intricately woven narrative is a brutal act of infanticide: After sending her three children ahead to safety, Sethe escapes from a Kentucky plantation known as Sweet Home. In flight, she gives birth to a daughter and arrives with the new infant at 124 Bluestone Road, a house situated near Cincinnati, Ohio. With her four children, her mother-in-law, Baby Suggs, and the attentive local community, Sethe experiences twenty-eight days of freedom before the sadistic master of the plantation, a man known as Schoolteacher, catches up with her. When she sees his wagon approaching the house at Bluestone Road, Sethe takes her children to the shed out back and in a desperate effort to protect them—to put them all someplace where they'd be safe—she attempts to kill them, although ultimately there is only time to cut the throat of her eldest daughter, who bleeds to death in her arms.

Schoolteacher returns to Kentucky empty-handed. Sethe survives with her remaining children, two sons and the new infant, Denver, named after a white girl who stopped to soothe Sethe's wounds and help her deliver during the escape. After serving a sentence in prison, Sethe returns to 124 where she, Baby Suggs, and Denver withdraw into the house, rejected by the community, which stands in harsh and disbelieving judgment of what they perceive to be her brutal and inexcusable "crime." Sethe's two sons run away and Baby Suggs, once a great healer and spiritual leader of the local black community, retreats to her bed to slowly die. The house becomes violently haunted with the angry and confused spirit of the baby girl deprived of her mother's love and a chance to live.

Sethe and Denver continue to live with the restless spirit, in the house that glows red with rage and despair, until the day when Paul D, a former slave from the same plantation where Sethe was held, appears on the front porch of 124 after many years of aimless and sorrowful drifting. The narrative opens with his arrival, a moment that marks the beginning of a healing process for both him and Sethe. As they begin to recount to one another their lives, hardships, and mutual grief, they discover through the telling of these stories a connection to a past that must be confronted and exorcised if each is to have a future. Subsequently, the house begins to quake with the demanding spirit of loss that is the ghost-child, Beloved. Paul D rebukes the spirit, restores a momentary calm, and in the same instant realizes the dismal conditions under which Sethe and Denver have been living all these years.

One day, when Paul D, Sethe, and Denver return home from a local carnival, they find a young woman, fully dressed and wearing a broken-rimmed hat, sitting on a tree stump. When questioned about her circumstances and origins she says only that her name is Beloved. Beyond this she appears to have no memory, no history, and no identity. Without further interrogation, Sethe and Denver nurse Beloved back to health and gradually she begins recalling details and moments from the past that only a family member could possibly know about. Beloved demonstrates powerful need. At first, she craves anything with sugar. As her recovery progresses she becomes ravenous for information about Sethe's past. Storytelling thus becomes the treatment that Sethe administers to nurse Beloved back to strength.

The question Beloved's emergence occasions is two-fold: Is this young woman the ghost of the murdered child assuming human form? And, if she *is* the child returned from the dead, *why* has she returned, and what does she want? There is disagreement among critics concerning these questions, as well as the symbolic significance of the mysterious figure. While the majority agree that Beloved *is* a ghost, a visitor from the spirit world who makes visible the potent connection between the living and the dead, Deborah Horvitz has argued that she is a living being, an escaped slave who has been traumatized senseless, and upon whom Sethe projects her wish of reestablishing a bond with her murdered daughter.[4] Similarly, Rebecca Ferguson holds the opinion that *Beloved* is centrally concerned with women's role in maintaining the continuity of family life, though in a much broader sense, "through the protection of their children, their men and the community" (Ferguson 1991, 112). Consequently, for Ferguson, Beloved is more than the specific link between generations of women: "Beloved *is* above all a connection," she claims, "the reconnection with and restoring of all that was lost when [Sethe] was driven to kill her" (114).

The "connection" that Beloved represents is symbolized in Morrison's text by the bridge upon which Beloved claims she stood before finding her way to

124. In this way, Beloved is perhaps best understood as an embodiment of history held aloft by a foundation we call memory, a foundation that is shown to be partial and fragmentary. And indeed, history and memory, both individual and collective, are precisely the intertwining forces that construct, and at the same time threaten to destroy, the kinship group. It is my view that Beloved represents the family as well as the familial. She is as much the family Sethe, Denver, and Paul D have lost as she is all the families separated and dismembered under the slavery system. And the reason she comes back is the same as the reason that this novel had to be written: to understand. Beloved will remain the undoing of kinship structure until she reaches this understanding, and the way she reaches it is by demanding that the past be remembered through the gradual stitching together of stories. She *is* this need for stories, stories without which Sethe can never move forward, take hold of her life, her kin, and find the courage to love again.

As a study of the connection between the historical and the familial, *Beloved* is concerned with the healing of the black American family and the "reconstruction" of kinship structures. These structures had been violated by the cruel fact of family life under the slavery system: as enslaved Africans, women and men had no right to themselves, to one another, or to their children. Consequently, for Baby Suggs, "the nastiness of life was the shock she received upon learning that nobody stopped playing checkers just because the pieces included her children" (Morrison 1987, 23). Under the yoke of slavery, permeable and unstable kinship structures were often necessary so that parents could entrust their children to someone else if they were sold away or separated. Often, as a result, children were parented more by a community of caretakers than by their biological parents, and in this sense "family" came to mean a structure of relations capable of transcending blood kin to form an extended family including neighbors and friends. By necessity, "family" had to be structured in such a way as to include these "fictive kin," a communal network of caring individuals. *Beloved* explores this vital connection between the biological family and fictive kinship relations as necessary for blacks' survival, although contrary to the Freudian triad that has served as a prominent cultural reference point for conventional understandings of what family means.

In the cultural and economic redefinition of family life that followed upon the end of the Civil War and the gradual abolishment of the slavery system, many freed blacks were forced again to sacrifice their ties to family and community with their realization that their new "freedom" meant little more than abject poverty. Morrison describes this transitional period after the Civil War when freed blacks sought to reconstruct the pieces and fragments of the family and of themselves:

Odd clusters and strays of Negroes wandered the back roads and cowpaths from Schenectady to Jackson. Dazed but insistent, they searched each other out for word of a cousin, an aunt, a friend. . . . Some of them were running from family that could not support them, some to family; some were running from dead crops, dead kin, life threats and took-over land. Boys younger than Buglar and Howard; configurations and blends of families of women and children. (Morrison 1987, 52)

Karen E. Fields's argument that "the essence of slavery was the creation of free-standing individuals, not families or communities," provides a useful gloss to the above passage. "As units of commodity to be bought, sold, or put to use, individual slaves stood apart from any authoritative claim to human connection" (Fields 1989, 163). The economic institution of slavery destroyed black families not only by the forced separation of kin but also by the radical isolation and appropriation of the individual-as-merchandise.

Beloved's relentless need, her demand to be seen and heard, constitutes an outraged cry against this isolation. Her assumption of human form takes place at exactly the moment when Sethe, Denver, and Paul D begin to form some semblance of a communicative triad. "[Beloved] had appeared and been taken in on the very day Sethe and [Paul D] had patched up their quarrel, gone out in public and had a right good time—like a family" (Morrison 1987, 66). Beloved's arrival at this pivotal moment suggests both her desire to be included in this family-like group, and her infantile need to sever Sethe's new-found lifeline lest her memory be reconciled and her name forgotten. It is significant also that the ghost of the murdered child appears just as her mother returns from a carnival, her first "social outing in eighteen years" (46). The family bond that Sethe, Denver, and Paul D reestablish takes place in the context of a life-affirming ritual, a celebration of the continuous cycles of birth, decay, death, and rebirth. As they head toward the carnival they pass a lumberyard fence where "up and down . . . old roses were dying. . . . The closer the roses got to death, the louder their scent, and everybody who attended the carnival associated it with the stench of the rotten roses" (47). The possibility of a new life juxtaposed with the sickly sweet aroma of imminent death anticipates Beloved's image and the confrontation of the living and the dead that her arrival occasions.[5] Through her association of the carnival with the fetid roses Morrison evokes the fragile new freedom that Sethe experiences as the restoration of family and community.

However, implicit in this meditation on freedom is the burden of historical consciousness. It seems that the extent to which familial bonds can be mutually reclaimed by Sethe, Denver, and Paul D is the extent to which they mutually confront and interpret the past. The ghost of the murdered child loudly invites this opportunity, for as Ferguson notes, "what is commonly called the supernatural is also the manifestation of history" (Ferguson 1991, 113). In Beloved, the persistence of the supernatural signifies the black community's need to sustain a hold on its history, its identity, and especially its kin. Consequently, it should come as no surprise that Beloved's restless spirit is provoked by all expressions of human attachment and familial intimacy.

Beloved makes rigorous structural demands on readers and requires attention as close and exacting as Beloved herself requires from Sethe. The collective process of memory unfolds and is given shape with frequent tense shifts. The "action" of the novel alternates between past and present as fragments of stories, symbols, and codes are gathered and exchanged between characters. Also gathered are the different voices of all those who come into contact with the spirit of the murdered child. Individual identities begin to take shape as each character explores her or his relation to Beloved. Narrative point of view alternates through various re-memberings of the past. Imagistically dense stream-of-consciousness passages recall, in Beloved's voice, the experience of crossing the ocean by ship. Her references to what seems to be the "middle passage" merge with references to birth. The conflation of these images suggests a continuous process of being born into the past. The "dark place" Beloved recalls evokes in the same instant the safety of the mother's womb and the dismal bulk of the slave ships. The context of this passage is a series of first-person narratives similarly marked by opening declarations of affiliation to Beloved. The multiple points of view generated by generations of mothers and daughters seem to merge into one consciousness, yet at the same time they remain separate and autonomous voices. As the language and formal appearance of these passages become transformed into poetry, the women's voices blend and mirror each other in their cadences of speech, phrases, and metaphors. Kinship is thus shown to be held together by an economy of symbols, a web of language that—like the family—is dismembered and fractured.

In *Beloved*, family and language must be jointly reconstructed. Family is defined as a process of reading, a history of interpretive acts that are unique to each kinship group despite its ties to the larger cultural community. Claiming kin requires that one be able to share in a common language and read the symbols that constitute it. Under the system of slavery these fundamental structures of signification—the essential textuality of family—are suppressed, silenced, and even outlawed. When the signifying economies of enslaved Africans were rendered worthless, so were their cultures and identities. When the freedom to make and exchange meanings is denied, the freedom to form and claim family is denied. However, Morrison suggests that the victims of slavery managed to preserve kinship structures through the study and interpretation of alternative textual forms. In this way, *Beloved* is about the painful process of reestablishing familial literacy. This process necessitates the creation of an amalgam formed of diverse cultural symbols. Decontextualized units of signification that survive slavery by virtue of courage and/or memory are thus combined with new symbols adopted from the dominant culture in the piecing together of a language with which to affirm kinship bonds.

Throughout the novel there is emphasis on these alternative texts that covertly preserve family unity and values. Trees, for example, are a recurrent image that Morrison deploys to symbolize hope for the restoration of familial security. When Paul D escapes from his imprisonment for the murder of his white master, Brandywine, he is instructed by the Cherokee Indians to follow the blossoming tree flowers to the North and to freedom:

> "That way," he said, pointing. "Follow the tree flowers," he said. "Only the tree flowers. As they go, you go. You will be where you want to be when they are gone."
>
> So he raced from dogwood to blossoming peach. When they thinned out he headed for the cherry blossoms, then magnolia, chinaberry, pecan, walnut and prickly pear. . . . From February to July he was on the lookout for blossoms. When he lost them, and found himself without so much as a petal to guide him, he paused, climbed a tree on a hillock and scanned the horizon for a flash of pink or white in the leaf world that surrounded him. (Morrison 1987, 112-13)

When Paul D first encounters the dreadful scar on Sethe's back, the result of a brutal whipping, she describes it for him as Amy Denver had described it for her eighteen years earlier, as a chokecherry tree. At that moment it occurs to Paul D that what Sethe has on her back is

> nothing like any tree he knew because trees were inviting; things you could trust and be near; talk to if you wanted to as he frequently did since way back when he took the midday meal in the _elds of Sweet Home. Always in the same place if he could, and choosing the place had been hard because Sweet Home had more pretty trees than any farm around. His choice he called Brother, and sat under it. (21)

Morrison establishes an ironic connection between Paul D's invocation of fraternal intimacy and the brand that Sethe bears on her back as a relentless reminder of the perverse inhumanity that she was forced to endure. The scar on Sethe's back tells its own story, which Paul D reads as if he were deciphering braille. "He rubbed his cheek on her back and learned that way her sorrow, the roots of it; its wide trunk and intricate branches. . . . And when the top of her dress was around her hips and he saw the sculpture her back had become, like the decorative work of an ironsmith too passionate for display, he could think but not say, 'Aw, Lord, girl'" (17). Like Keats's Grecian urn, Sethe's scar holds the past frozen in time. Her body is the text upon which history has been written, and her only chance of reclaiming herself, for herself and her family, is to seize the power of interpretation, to suffer the past on her own terms.

The inscription on Sethe's back connects her to one of the few memories she has of her own mother. Sethe remembers that as a small child she was taught to recognize her mother by the brand with which she was marked as property:

> Back there she opened up her dress front and lifted her breast and pointed under it. Right on her rib was a circle and a cross burnt right in the skin. She said, "This is your ma'am. This," and she pointed. "I am the only one got this mark now. The rest dead. If something happens to me and you can't tell me by my face, you can know me by this mark." (Morrison 1987, 61)

In this way, Sethe is taught how to read kin, how to ascertain her own identity, and how to interpret the world around her. When Sethe asks her mother to "mark the mark on me too," she is immediately slapped across the face. Only years later does she understand why. To young Sethe, the cross within the circle is her family name, the only one she has ever been taught to recognize. Because she lacks this mark, she feels a lack of connection to her mother. But her mother knows what that brand really means in a system that commodifies, buys, and sells human life. It conveys the information that she is an extension of someone else's identity, a name that has become hers only as a result of profound dislocation, both external and internal.

The slap Sethe receives when she asks to be branded herself is meant to shock her into the recognition that, in a powerful sense, her people are not her people, and her beloved is not her beloved. My reiteration of the novel's biblical epigraph is meant to emphasize the essential fact that enslaved blacks were economically, psychologically, and *linguistically* blocked from passing on to future generations their names and symbolic orders. When Sethe begs for the brand, of course, she does not realize that she is asking to be given over to the system and marked as a piece of property. However, her mother's position is such that she can do no more than try to make passionately clear to Sethe the truth that Paul D echoes years later when he tells her, "You your own best thing, Sethe. You are" (Morrison 1987, 273). Thus, on an abstract level, Sethe's mother's violent expression of mother-love anticipates the violence that Sethe will eventually be driven to inflict on her own daughter: Both women attempt, in other words, to save their children from the mark of slavery, to put them someplace where they'll be safe.

When Sethe matures and chooses Halle to be her husband, Mrs. Garner, the wife of the self-styled "humanitarian" and master of Sweet Home, assumes the limited role of mother to Sethe. She gives her a pair of crystal earrings and turns a blind eye when Sethe steals some fabric to make herself a wedding dress. It is difficult not to see these small kindnesses as genuine acts, although it is equally difficult to ignore the fact that Mrs. Garner has far more to gain from her attachment to Sethe than Sethe does from her. Along these lines, Fields argues that "the mother-daughter relation [they] stitch together is inherently unstable because it cannot be upheld beyond the voluntary complicity of the two, and because nothing sustains it but their own separate desires." The relationship Mrs. Garner permits to exist between them is, in short, "a self-interested exchange" that joins slave-owner and slave together in a paradoxical alliance that is exploitative and yet contains rarefied elements of a genuine love and sense of connectedness (Morrison 1987, 165-66). Ultimately, Mrs. Garner's ministrations reflect the policy of her husband, who envisions Sweet Home as one thriving happy family, and himself the noble patriarch. This way, Garner promotes his superiority within the slaveholding community and indulges the fantasy that his "progeny" honor his authority, not because their lives are at stake, but because they are free to form attachments based on trust.

Schoolteacher represents an extreme embodiment of the logocentric assumption of the written word as constitutive of the domain of knowledge and truth. His fanatical abuses of power stress domination through the controlling authority of the logos. He symbolizes the distortions of knowledge that naturalize the "scientific" view that blacks are fundamentally inferior, perhaps even less human, than whites. In the name of education, he sustains and perpetuates an ideological construction—and here I refer to ideology in the Althusserian sense of its having a definite structural logic—of blacks as beasts of burden, as when Paul D is collared and given the bit. His assumed status as both master of the plantation and master of scientific discourse serve as his licence to conduct brutal experiments on Sethe, as when he instructs one of his nephews to hold Sethe down while the other nephew nurses at her breast.

Schoolteacher claims the discursive power to construct and withhold identity. Like Adam, he sees himself as the giver of the name; he sees the enslaved blacks, like the animals of Eden, as the passive recipients of the name. Here it is useful to reference Morrison's own meditation on the cultural devastation of this systematic hierarchy: "If you come from Africa, your name is gone. It is particulary problematic because it is not just *your* name but your family, your tribe. When you die, how can you connect with your ancestors if you have lost your name?" (qtd. in Rubenstein 1987, 153). Thus, one of the more radical gestures of the enslaved subject is the destabilization of the racist hierarchy through the courageous act of self-appropriation and self-naming. The slave, Joshua, enacts this subversion when he renames himself "Stamp Paid," thus signifying the extent of his sacrifice to the white man and his decision never to owe anything to anybody again.

Such signifying acts provide a basis, albeit fragile, for the establishment of an identity not dictated by the brands of slaveholders. The power of this connection, however, is experienced not simply in the rejection of the slave name, but in the exchange of stories that provide a context in which the name functions as an arbiter of history and identity. That Sethe's stories can only be related in pieces, rather than in grand narrative fashion, suggests that any strengthening of the boundaries of self, or of kinship ties, must proceed by self-conscious acts of construction. Neither genealogical coherence nor totalizing narratives are intrinsic to her knowledge of origin. The instability occasioned by this fractured sense of self is inherited by subsequent generations. This is certainly implied when Denver first attempts to learn the alphabet from Lady Jones. Her efforts are aborted when Nelson Lord confronts her with a question about her mother's crime. Significantly, the question comes when she is practicing how to write the letter "i." Unable to answer his question, Denver quits school just when she would have mastered the mark that denotes "self." She joins her mother, withdrawing into the haunted interior space of 124, leaving the little "i" and the written word behind.

Denver makes two important sacrifices when she walks out of Lady Jones's classroom. She surrenders her connection to the surrounding community, and so relinquishes its support. Also, she abandons her studies of the English alphabet and the written word, which, in the period of Reconstruction, represent freedom, whereas at Sweet Home they had meant certain death. The irony of this shift is doubled when we consider that by renouncing absorption into the dominant culture's logocentrism Denver also renounces the local community, which both she and her mother desperately need for nurturance and affirmation. Indeed, one of the salient themes of *Beloved* explores the vital correspondence between the establishment of the immediate familial "text" and the cooperation of the surrounding community. In a sense, Denver's attachment to family matters develops in accord with her embrace of the outside community. It is this mutually empowering exchange that finally makes it possible for Denver to "get a read" on her mother, and on the destructive voracity of her dead sister's spirit.

Toward the conclusion of the novel, when Beloved's ghost has been exorcised, Denver once again takes up the study of "book stuff" from Mrs. Bodwin, another white "schoolteacher." Denver's second bid for an education, and Paul D's concealed impulse to warn her—"Watch out. Watch out. Nothing in the world more dangerous than a white schoolteacher" (Morrison 1987, 266)— intersect to form a lethal possibility that Morrison subtly invites readers to consider: a "white" education may represent, for Denver, another form of enslavement to the master culture. While the formal institution of slavery may have become obsolete, the systematic structure of racial oppression and its denial of African culture, identity, and history continues in the socially and morally sanctioned institutions of education and language. Indeed, in this context, Paul D's inability to read the newspaper article describing Sethe's act of infanticide may suggest not that he has been deceived by Sethe, nor that he is ill-equipped to make sense of the world around him, but that the "literate" culture's interpretation of her act is, and by necessity should remain, far removed from his own. When he learns of the episode from Stamp Paid, Paul D struggles less with the moral implications of the slaying than he does with the need to comprehend Sethe's decision in the terms appropriate to his own read on the past that he and Sethe share, and the future they may yet have.

This is what Paul D himself realizes when he tells Sethe that "he wants to put his story next to hers" (Morrison 1987, 273). Given the novel's emphasis on stories as constitutive of familial bonds, these words can be understood as no less than a profound expression of a new configuration of family romance. It is here, at last, that Paul D is moved to claim kin, to commit to and honor not one woman, but the story they share. He thus enlists his participation in a mul-tivoiced process of deciphering and interpreting common experience. At last, Sethe's "story was bearable because it was his as well—to tell, to refine and tell again" (99).

What is paradoxical is that these stories are both life sustaining and toxic. In the immediate aftershock of the baby's murder, Baby Suggs hands Sethe her living infant, Denver, to nurse. Too late, Baby Suggs notices that Sethe's nipple is covered in blood: "So Denver took her mother's milk right along with the blood of her sister" (Morrison 1987, 152). In this powerful image, Morrison indicates that the post-Civil War black family was nourished by the combination of these essential elements: mother's milk, the blood of relations lost to the vio-lent reality of slavery, and the stories that are passed down to each subsequent generation, even if they require raising the dead. For to be denied these stories is as potentially debilitating as being denied food. Insofar as women have tradi-tionally been responsible for these domestic labors, *Beloved* confirms the belief set forth by Mary Helen Washington, that "women have been the caretakers in families, and that caretaking extends even to the stories of family history" (Washington 1991, 4).

Although some critics of the novel have focused attention on the conflict over Morrison's depictions of men as weak, absent, or violent, and her depic-tions of women as too passively dependent on the men who leave and/or abuse them, it is important to note, I feel, that in *Beloved* struggles between the sexes remain latent by comparison to the larger struggle between the white-dominant culture's interpretation of black history and the interpretations that blacks have pieced together from their own wealth of family stories and experiences. Al-though Sethe, Denver, and Beloved briefly form a version of the three-woman family that Morrison is alternately criticized and praised for, the women exclude male participation at the cost of Sethe's health and community support. At the same time, critics such as McDowell reference the line from the novel that reads, "They were a family somehow and [Paul D] was not the head of it," to show how Morrison validates the all-female household and undermines the patriarchal structure of the nuclear family (McDowell 1989, 79). My own reading of the novel agrees with McDowell's insofar as I would argue that Morrison affirms female strength and autonomy. However, I would argue this opposition is based on neither the portrayal of Sethe nor of Paul D, but on Morrison's portrayal of Denver, who in the end emerges as the unlikely hero of the novel.

My case can be made simply: Denver achieves heroic status in the novel because it is she who finally finds the courage and means to cross the boundary that divides home from the world, or the private family from the public sphere. It is Denver who reaches out to the community for help. In accomplishing this she demonstrates one of the central assumptions of the novel: the family cannot survive in isolation but requires the strength and protection of a much wider network of "kinfolk." By reestablishing this tie with the local community, Denver not only saves her mother's life but also engages the powerful presence of the "thirty women" whose arrival at the climactic conclusion of the novel helps drive Beloved from 124. In this way, Denver represents hope for the future.

However, this hope is contingent on maintaining a link to the past. By saving her mother, Denver reconnects spiritually with her father, Halle. Just as Halle works to buy Baby Suggs's freedom, Denver frees Sethe from enslavement to Beloved's ravenous appetite for the mothering she never had. Thus, while Sethe retains a tie to her father in name only, Denver retains a tie to Halle through heroic action. Both father and daughter make use of what resources they can muster—beating the odds in both instances—in the interests of securing a future, and both pay a dear price for this opportunity: Halle gives up five years of Sundays, ironically a day when families often visit. Denver puts an end to her sister's visitation, sacrificing their camaraderie, in favor of reestablishing the essential reciprocal tie that defines family as a network of "kinfolks."

Undeniably, Beloved's presence among the living prefigures their recognition of a communal loss that can only be mended by a communal effort to restore lost ties. But Beloved also functions as a persistent reminder of the unique loss suffered by each occupant of 124. Ultimately, what defines Beloved in the context of familial relationships that the novel explores is that she assumes the shape of something slightly different to all who embrace her. She is their worst fear and their most profound need combined. For Denver, who has suffered not only the loss of a sister's companionship but the judgment and neglect of the community as well, Beloved is the "interested, uncritical eyes of the other" (Morrison 1987, 118). To Paul D, Beloved is his "shame," or the utter depth of inhumanity and demoralization he experienced at Sweet Home when he was collared and given the bit. Beloved drives Paul D to reencounter this moment—which he has long since locked away in his heart—when she seduces him sexually and ultimately forces him out of the house. Beloved brings him face to face with his past by reducing him to a position of base functioning in which he is helpless. She thus "fixes" him, or literally takes possession of him, like the bit in his mouth and the concealed misery in his heart. As a result, Paul D abandons 124 and withdraws to the damp basement of a local church where, like Ellison's

Invisible Man, he descends underground for a time.

For Sethe, Beloved's return is an opportunity to do over again what she had not been able to do before: to be a mother, to forge the experiential connections known as family. But the past can neither be changed nor forgotten, only internally confronted and externally shared through the telling and exchanging of stories. So why then the echoing of the final line, "This is not a story to pass on"? Perhaps this is a warning that the cycle of separation and loss must not be repeated; paradoxically, however, it seems that the only way to prevent the repetition of such tragically severed human bonds is to transform loss into life through the creation of narrative. These stories are told and retold to reach some understanding of what may be lost, and how, so that freedom in its fullest sense may be attained. *Beloved* is a novel that reminds us that true "freedom," for the post-Civil War black family, was not freedom from the southern plantation, nor freedom by means of an emancipation proclamation, but freedom "to get to a place where you could love anything you chose" (Morrison 1987, 162).

Indeed, *Beloved* may not be a story to pass on, but it is a story that had to be told so that a healing process could begin, and so that family and community could be mutually restored. The process of restoration, like the making of myths, is a culturally specific process insofar as both are social constructs that no two persons will experience in precisely the same way. Morrison's novel asks us to consider the possibility that Sethe's impulse to infanticide—based on her own interpretation of history—is in its own context a valid act of courage and familial preservation. Sethe insists that all she wanted to do was put her baby someplace safe, and she did. For some families, there is a death that is safer than life, and there is a love powerful enough to bridge the distance.

Notes

1. I refer here to information provided by Erlene Stetson in "Studying Slavery: Some Literary and Pedagogical Considerations on the Black Female Slave" (1982, 71). For a more complete historical account of the black family under slavery and during the Reconstruction era see Gutman 1977.

2. In their spurious effort to contain all social and emotional exchange within the family unit, Sethe, Denver, and Beloved in some ways resemble family groupings depicted in other works by Morrison, for instance the Breedloves from *The Bluest Eye*, whom Rubenstein argues "survive at the very fringe of society, where the 'hem' begins to unravel," and where "economic destitution and psychic abjection undermine the very bonds that attach family members to one another and form the basis for community" (Rubenstein 1987, 129).

3. Deborah Horvitz, for example, has painstakingly described the novel's exploration of "matrilineal ancestry and the relationships among enslaved, freed, alive, and dead mothers and daughters" (Horvitz 1989, 157).

4. Horvitz sees Beloved as symbolic of black women's collective memory. According to Horvitz, Beloved speaks across generations of Africans and African slaves in the United States, thus creating "the crucial link that connects Africa and America for the enslaved women. She is Sethe's mother; she is Sethe herself; she is her daughter" (Horvitz 1989, 163-64).

5. The bringing together of extreme opposites, the pathos of change and renewal, references the Bakhtinian vision of carnival as a popular impulse that is ultimately "about freedom, the courage needed to establish it, the cunning required to maintain it, and—above all—the horrific ease with which it an be lost" (Holquist 1984, xxi).

Works Cited

Ferguson, Rebecca. 1991. "History, Memory and Language in Toni Morrison's *Beloved.*" In *Feminist Criticism: Theory and Practice*, ed. Susan Sellers. Toronto: University of Toronto Press.

Fields, Karen E. 1989. "To Embrace Dead Strangers: Toni Morrison's *Beloved.*" In *Mother Puzzles: Daughters and Mothers in Contemporary American Literature*, ed. Mickey Pearlman. New York: Greenwood.

Gutman, Herbert G. 1977. *The Black Family in Slavery and Freedom, 1750 - 1925.* New York: Random.

Hirsch, Marianne. 1989. *The Mother/Daughter Plot: Narrative, Psychology, Feminism.* Bloomington: Indiana University Press.

Holquist, Michael. 1984. Prologue to *Rabelais and His World*, by Mikhail Bakhtin. Trans. Helene Iswolsky. Bloomington: Indiana University Press.

Horvitz, Deborah. 1989. "Nameless Ghosts: Possession and Dispossession in *Beloved.*" *Studies in American Fiction* 17.2: 157-67.

McDowell, Deborah E. 1989. "Reading Family Matters." In *Changing Our Own Words: Essays on Criticism, Theory and Writing by Black Women*, ed. Cheryl A. Wall. New Brunswick: Rutgers University Press.

Morrison, Toni. 1987. *Beloved.* New York: New American Library.

Rubenstein, Roberta. 1987. *Boundaries of the Self: Gender, Culture, Fiction.* Urbana: University of Illinois Press.

Stetson, Erlene. 1982. "Studying Slavery: Some Literary and Pedagogical Considerations on the Black Female Slave." In *All the Women Are White, All the Blacks Are Men, But Some of Us Are Brave: Black Women's Studies*, ed. Gloria T. Hull, Patricia Bell Scott, and Barbara Smith. New York: Feminist.

Washington, Mary Helen. 1991. Introduction to *Memory of Kin: Stories About Family By Black Writers.* New York: Anchor/Doubleday.

IV

SEXUALITY

12

We Are Family: Miscegenation, Black Nationalism, Black Masculinity, and the Black Gay Cultural Imagination

Amy Abugo Ongiri

> Desire is always the axis along which different forms of cultural policing take place. And desire across racial and sexual lines was the site for constructing my film *Young Soul Rebel*. The crossing of these lines causes anxiety, undermines binary notions of self/other, black/white, straight/queer.
>
> Isaac Julien

> One of the dangers of being a Black American is being schizophrenic, and I mean "schizophrenic" in the most literal sense. To be a black American is in some ways to be born with a desire to be white. It's a part of the price you pay for being born here, and it affects every black person here.
>
> James Baldwin

Both James Baldwin's assessment of the peculiar predicament of the Black American and Isaac Julien's formulating of the particular transgressive logics of his own work highlight desire as a force and symbol of either radical transformation or radical and traumatic stasis. It would not be difficult to see both of their work as an attempt to come to terms with and "settle" once and for all the problematic of desire as it is figured within an African diasporic tradition, particularly in the discourse of black cultural nationalism to which so much of both their work has been directly and indirectly addressed. In 1989 Marlon Riggs's film *Tongues Untied* revitalized black gay cultural politics by declaring that "black men loving black men is the revolutionary act of our times." This statement finds much of its power in its marking of the complicated intersections of the mythos of miscegenation and representations of black male sexuality present in discourses of gay liberation and post-1950s black nationalism. But the same intersections which charge the statement with its teasingly transgressive and radically unifying revolutionary potentialities also serve to reveal the particular disjointedness of the foundations of its liberatory vision. This paper investigates black nationalism's longing for a masculine, whole subjectivity to compete with the physical and psychic threat of disintegration instantiated by acts of racist violence against the black body. This longing for a unifying wholeness ends up creating a model of desire fraught and overdetermined by the same anxieties around wholeness and purity that cause its creation. Nevertheless, post-1950s black nationalism becomes an essential, yet largely unacknowledged, model for later liberation movements that concern themselves with body politics. Marlon Riggs, Essex Hemphill, Joseph Beam, and other black gay cultural workers structure their critique of the absence of the black body from a discourse of gay rights through a direct reappropriation of black nationalism's discourse on desire and the black body. This restructuring not only highlights the problematic of desire and the body as it has been configured within black nationalism but also calls into question the exclusion of the black body and an acknowledgment of the role of a discourse of black liberation from a discourse of gay rights.

If we are to accept Marlon Riggs's challenge that "black men loving black men is the revolutionary act of our time," it is necessary to examine what might ultimately be at stake in forming or not forming a liberatory vision based in and around the figure of a black masculinity in a crisis of desire. Furthermore, it is necessary to determine why black masculinity most frequently figures within black nationalist discourse as in crisis and why this crisis so frequently centers on and around homosexual desire and a desire for miscegenation. Ultimately, it needs to be determined why it becomes important to police certain desires within the masculinist discourse of black nationalism and who this policing ultimately protects, if anyone. Only this, coupled with an examination of the work of Hemphill, Riggs, and others who challenge the foundational paradigms of liberatory discourses written in the body, will determine if "deviant" desires really pose the challenge that they are supposed to pose to the imagined black nation or to notions of desire scripted by gay rights discourses.

"Black nationalism" marks many various, disparate, and divergent cultural/political expressions, projections, and articulations. However, all of these traditions have been affected and shaped by the double trajectories of the trans-Atlantic slave trade and a racially based political and economic subjugation, which has historically been profoundly physical in its formation. Within that context, desire has been tied to a physicality and various contradictory notions of the body. These notions of the body tended to either celebrate it as the site of a resistant strength and liberatory potentialities or decry the desecration of the black body and reconfigure it as the potential betrayer of these same impulses of strength, resistance, and liberation.

In a 1924 position statement entitled "What We Believe," Marcus Garvey, then president of the United Negro Improvement Association, the most successful Pan-African movement to date, states categorically that "it [the U.N.I.A.] is against miscegenation and race suicide. . . . It is against rich blacks marrying poor whites. It is against rich or poor whites taking advantage of Negro women" (Garvey 1986, 81). The building of the black nation within a diaspora context has always been seen to be contingent on the maintenance of a biologically determined and genetically maintained racial purity, inscribing the individual black body with the investments of a nation. Desire, particularly "wrongfully constructed" desire, then, threatened dissolution of the very bonds of that cultural and racial collective by relocating the personal, subjective body within the realm of the individual, thereby rendering it potentially uncontrollable. Nearly half a century after the formulation of the U.N.I.A. statement, Eldridge Cleaver would, in his polemical condemnation of James Baldwin, construct "Black homosexuality" as the ultimate form, the "extreme embodiment," of a "racial death-wish" negatively conflating homosexual desire with a literal desire for whiteness:

> The white man has deprived him of his masculinity, castrated him in the center of his burning skull, and when he submits to the change and takes the white man for his lover as well as Big Daddy, he focuses on "whiteness" all the love in his pent up soul and turns the razor edge of hatred against "blackness"—upon himself, what he is, and all those who look like him, remind him of himself. He may even hate the darkness of the night. (Cleaver 1968, 103)

In the logic of Cleaver's condemnation of Baldwin, the black body is gendered necessarily male, and it is necessarily caught in the throes of a desire constructed as "wrong" and marked "homosexual." The black body, marked by its maleness and "bad" desire, is then made to enact an entire script of internalized and, though individually enacted, genocidal impulses. For Cleaver, the black male homosexual becomes the locus for anxiety around not only sexuality but also more specifically around a black masculinity in crisis. It is no accident that Cleaver writes *Soul on Ice* from prison; his meditations on heterosexual miscegenation and homosexual desire reveal the profound levels of anxiety around bodily desires that can literally lead not only to imprisonment but to death as well.

In the essay that opens *Soul on Ice*, entitled "On Becoming," Cleaver articulates how the consciousness of his desire for white women, the culmination of that desire in carefully planned and orchestrated acts of rape, and his eventual imprisonment for those acts are formative in the shaping of a self-consciousness driven by an urge to power and a reconstructive vision of masculinity. This vision of masculinity is enabled rather than disabled by the acts of terror that threatened the very existence of black men, precisely as raced and gendered subjects. Rather than simply accept the final symbolic moments of victimized terror in the cultural trope of the lynching scene, Cleaver chooses instead to claim the terroristic power of rapist and outlaw. This is a power that exists as the origin of the lynch scene, but is usually minimized in the symbolic economy of the lynching moment. The entire process of Cleaver's "becoming" begins in an uncomfortable moment of realization that precedes the complete dissolution of self that Cleaver terms "a nervous breakdown":

> an event took place in Mississippi which turned me inside out: Emmett Till, a young Negro down from Chicago on a visit, was murdered allegedly for flirting with a white woman. He had been shot, his head crushed from repeated blows with a blunt instrument, and his badly decomposed body was recovered from the river with a heavy weight on it. I was, of course, angry over the whole bit, but one day I saw in a magazine a picture of the white woman with whom Emmett Till was said to have flirted. While looking at the picture, I felt that little tension in the center of my chest I experience when a woman appeals to me. I was disgusted and angry with myself. Here was a woman who had caused the death of a black, possibly because, when he looked at her, he also felt the same tensions of lusts and desire in his chest—and probably for the same general reasons I felt them. It was all unacceptable to me. I looked at the picture again and again, and in spite of everything and against my will and hate I felt more for the woman and all she represented, she appealed to me. (Cleaver 1968, 10-11)

Cleaver terms the destructive desire of black men for white women a "revolutionary sickness" because of the destructive potential of its force. In Cleaver's words: "I know that the black man's sick attitude toward the white woman is a revolutionary sickness: it keeps him perpetually out of harmony with the system that is oppressing him" (Cleaver 1968, 16). However, a desire for miscegenation and homosexual desire—clearly a nonrevolutionary desire in the logics of *Soul on Ice*—become logically and negatively conflated in Cleaver's account, as both are moments that would seem to challenge easy notions of desire and preset boundaries of the self. As Mary V. Dearborn points out, for the slave owner "[i]ntercourse with a black woman raised troubling but intriguing questions of difference and sameness, of the boundaries of the Self" (Dearborn 1986, 134). Unlike the slave owner's dilemma, however, the dissolution Cleaver works to combat is quite literal. There is much evidence that the decomposing body of Emmett Till played a formative role in the developing consciousness of an entire nation of black people. Mamie Bradley, Emmett Till's mother, insisted, against the explicit instructions of the sheriff's department, that the badly mutilated body of her son not be buried in Mississippi, that it be returned to Chicago, and that she be allowed to conduct an open casket funeral. The figure of Emmett Till's visibly tortured and badly disfigured fourteen-year-old corpse would then be made to stand symbolically for an entire spectrum of abuses borne by the living body of black American history. Juan Williams documents that

> The body would shock and disgust the city of Chicago, and after a picture of it was published in the black weekly magazine, *Jet*, all of black America saw the mutilated corpse.
> It is difficult to measure just how profound an effect the public viewing of Till's body created. But without a question, it moved black America in a way the Supreme Court ruling on desegregation could not match. Contributions to the NAACP's "fight fund," the war chest to help victims of racial attacks, reached record levels. Only weeks before, the NAACP had been begging for support to pay its debts in the aftermath of its Supreme Court triumph.
> The *Cleveland Call and Post*, a black newspaper, polled the nation's major black radio preachers and found five of every six preaching on the Till case. Half of them demanding that "something be done in Mississippi now," according to the paper. (Williams 1987, 44)

For *Soul on Ice*, the dismemberment of Emmett Till's body—which was so badly disfigured it had to be identified by an initialed ring—prefigures the symbolic dismemberment of Eldridge Cleaver's psyche. Cleaver traces both the mutilation and decay of Emmett Till's body in Mississippi and the mutilation and decay of his own psyche both inside and outside of a California prison to a foundational moment of unbounded desire.

In the attempt to resist the threat of dissolution that the Emmett Till narrative provides and to symbolically rebuild a sense of self, it is necessary for Cleaver to isolate and define moments of miscegenation and homosexual desire—which he classifies as manifestations of unbounded, unrestricted desire—as potentially "obvious" disruptions in the maintenance of boundaries of a raced and masculinized self. In Cleaver's account, miscegenation represents a potentially dangerous disruption of the reproductive order, but homosexuality, because it is read as the complete, passive capitulation to white masculinity, represents the potential for the complete dissolution of a resistant black self. For Cleaver, miscegenation and homosexuality also disrupt the narrative of nation since that narrative's primary marker of belonging is inscribed and reinscribed on the bodily collective through processes of heterosexual interaction. If the sanctity of the black nation resides within and is reducible to the essential and individual black body, then it becomes necessary to explain away those bodily impulses that could not easily be said to result in or spring from impulses that positively procreate or sustain that national body and could even be said to threaten the dissolution of the self on an individual level. Besides homosexuality, the ultimate acts of violation against a black nation included in Cleaver's list are "baby rape" and "wanting to be president of General Motors" (Cleaver 1968, 110). In *Soul on Ice*, desire is the marker for actions that are conceived of as highly individual and solely self-profiting enactments of power, acts that threaten the dissolution of the individual black body but also the bonds of the imagined nation. Individuals who are said to exhibit such desires are already not whole and are known, according to Cleaver, to be "sick" (110).

But *Soul on Ice* is obviously not the only cultural nationalist work in which miscegenation and male homosexuality become the locus and focal point for anxiety around the possibilities of cohesion and wholeness in the scripting of the narrative of the black nation directly onto black bodies in an imagined black reality. In the influential *Afrocentricity*, Molefi Asante blames the disintegration of the black nuclear family on "an outburst of homosexuality among black men, fed by the prison breeding system" (Asante 1992, 57). He warns: "We can no longer allow our social lives to be controlled by European decadence" and prescribes instead "guard your minds and you shall save your bodies" (57-58). In the equally influential *Isis Papers*, Dr. Frances Cress Welsing attributes the entire disintegration of the black community to "Black male passivity, effeminization, Bisexuality and Homosexuality" (Cress Welsing 1991, 81). This is achieved, according to Cress Welsing, through repeated literal, ritual, and symbolic castration. A passage from the 1981 manifesto of the First National Plenary Conference on Self-Determination succinctly articulates and limits the boundaries of self, desire, and nation:

> Revolutionary nationalists and genuine communists cannot uphold homosexuality in the leadership of the black Liberation Front nor uphold it as a correct practice. Homosexuality is a genocidal practice. . . . [It] does not produce children. . . . [It] does not birth new warriors for liberation. . . . Homosexuality cannot be upheld as correct or revolutionary practice. . . . The practice of homosexuality is an accelerating threat to our survival as a people and as a nation. (Nelson 1991, 92)

"Self-determination" in black nationalist discourse then becomes the promise of the possibility of individually motivated but communally manifested completion. It is precisely the invocation of a protection against dissolution that is finally a dissolution of the self and nation. It is the body manifesting the local articulation and location of the black nation fixed within a narrowly constructed but nevertheless "self motivated consciousness." In the words of Huey P. Newton, "If you met an African in ancient times and asked him who he was, he would reply, 'I am we.' This is revolutionary suicide: I, we, all of us are the one and the multitude" (Newton 1973, 332).

Though gay liberation could be said to borrow liberally from the discourse and tactics of various black liberation movements including black nationalism,[1] it would also seem, historically, to seek to be free of certain deterministic traps of identity politics, offering instead a diffuse articulation of both place and power. Its articulations of the body have been grounded in ambiguity and the powerful potential of performance, and it is marked by its extreme disavowal of metaphors and tropes of location and place. "Queer Nation"[2] is the continuous, complex elaboration of a joke rather than an attempt to map or mark positively a real geographic or historical landscape. Contrast, for example, Marcus Garvey's classic plea for black liberation (which is still to be heard echoing across certain meeting halls and reggae concerts), "Africa for the Africans, at home and abroad,"[3] with the gay rights slogan, "We are everywhere," or the Lesbian Avengers' playful "answer-back" chant to the statistical attempt to construct solidly and fix a lesbian identity, "Ten percent is not enough, recruit, recruit, recruit!" Rather than create the broad inclusion that this disavowal of place and space gestures toward, it has instead allowed for the appropriation of African-American cultural models, products, and strategies of resistance without a sustained dialogue with the concerns that these models, products, and strategies were created to address. For example, Michael Warner's *Fear of a Queer Planet: Queer Politics and Social Theory* obviously appropriates its title and its radical implications from Cress Welsing's concept that fear of genetic annihilation, or "fear of a black planet," forms the psychological basis for racism and white supremacy. This theory and terminology, which has had and continues to have a widespread currency within black nationalism, first appeared in Cress Welsing's 1970 pamphlet, *The Cress Theory of Color Confrontation and Racism*. The theory gained its most extensive popular articulation through the rap group Public Enemy's 1990 album "Fear of a black Planet," which worked with and through Cress Welsing's ideas to discuss issues of black genocide in a hip hop format. Warner's text, on the other hand, fails to address or even acknowledge the concerns of the theory, its creator, its later permutations, or its radical implications. This is symptomatic of the way in which black liberation movements continue to provide the unacknowledged historical potency to the rhetoric and design of gay liberation.

A cultural politics and expression that is then self-consciously both black and gay exists in an often ambiguous space within either of these arenas, sometimes floating in an equally ambiguous space between the two discourses. black gay discourse often trades openly in black nationalist notions and configurations of nation, family, brotherhood, and the state. However, though black gay cultural politics can seem as dependent on black nationalist discourse as a black nationalist discourse is dependent on its homophobia, the actual fit between a black nationalist discourse and a black gay cultural politics is often imperfect at best. The two discourses often both meet and miss and meet each other in an uneven and unpredictable fashion. For example, in the March '94 issue of *BLK*, cartoonist A. J. Benny sketches two members of the fictional Search Committee for a Chair to head the American black Gay and Lesbian Association. "And guess what?" one of the members whispers to another, "one of the candidates even has a black lover." In Isaac Julien's celebrated 1991 film, *Young Soul Rebel*, the phrase "black and white unite and fuck" floats ambiguously in response to one of the more nationalistically identified characters' exhortation that "it's allright as long as *you* doin' it to *them*!" Marlon Riggs himself was often taken to task in the black gay community for presenting us with the "black men loving black men" slogan and having a white partner. "Why don't you act?" was the question raised. The responses to the contradictions and complexities that face black gay cultural workers and activists attempting to negotiate, construct, and challenge preexisting narratives of nation and black desire are varied enough to suggest that a broad theorizing of a black gay cultural imagination may as yet be an impossibility. It is useful and important, however, to attempt to read certain examples that directly pose questions to the black cultural nationalist assumptions about the black male body, its proper uses and pleasures. Situated as these examples are between a discourse of black and gay liberation discourses, they also serve to take gay discourse to task for the exclusion of the black body in pain from its understanding of a politics of desire.

The film *Young Soul Rebel* was created exactly out of the tenuous cultural and political milieu of black gay culture and could be said to be a complex meditation on the state of the black nation in diaspora and the politics of fucking. It is not so much a critique of black nationalism as it is a critique of the idea of nation. As this paper's opening quotation indicates, the film explores desire as a dynamic and potentially revolutionary force in the undermining of foundational binary notions such as "self/other, black/white, straight/queer" (Julien 1992, 259). Set in the early 1970s in London, the film follows Chris and Caz, two young black male pirate-radio deejays, one of them gay the other straight, in their developing romances, which cut across class and racial lines. In this scenario, processes of desire and sexual interaction become metaphors for processes of creolization, hybridization, and general cross-cultural exchange. Music and audio culture, then, is the medium that translates and transmits various cultural formations into recognizable and consumable commodities for that exchange. Just as George Clinton promises "a chance to dance your way out of your constrictions" in "one nation under the groove," the film and the film's soundtrack offers desire as a thoroughly free-floating, highly individual, and amazingly unconstructed and unconstricted site of resistance to rigid boundaries of the self and the Other. The music, which cuts kinetically across the film's soundtrack, ranges in genre and national origin from Funkadelic's "One Nation under a Groove" (funk, United States), to the X-Ray Spex "Oh Bondage Up Yours" (punk, United Kingdom) and Junior Murvin's "Police and Thieves" (reggae, West Indies). This blend is not inconsequential; as Paul Gilroy points out in the soundtrack's liner notes, "there's a history of this country hidden in its seductive rhythms too." That history is one in which "the blend" would, in fact, become and mean everything. In Gilroy's words: "The special appeal of this alien cultural blend would eventually provide a means to knock back Britain's neo-nazis and their funfree patriotic ideas about how to clean up the country." Desire becomes, in this context, a dynamic and potentially liberating force, and social anxiety is for the film the primary register of the level of cultural interchange occurring. But though *Young Soul Rebel* presents a filmic universe whose moment of political and cultural anarchy represents the limitless, transcendent possibilities for desire, there is also a fairly deep ambivalence toward a total embrace of this moment as either representative of a working solution or as a static paradigm of analysis.

The film is framed by a puzzling subtext that involes the murder by a white man of a young black man in a park, used primarily by closeted gay men for cruising. Caz and Chris both know and have interacted with Ken, the murderer, and T.J. the murder victim. Caz's growing relationship with Billibud, a white punk socialist, is placed without comment up against the violently sexualized scene of murder in the park. In this scene, T.J., a young black "soulboy," is listening to a cassette player and leaning against a tree in the park. Ken, the murderer, approaches, touches T.J., and asks him to turn down the music. When T.J. refuses, Ken forcibly turns off the cassette player, but also accidentally depresses the "record" button, subsequently capturing the entire encounter on audio tape. They proceed to kiss until Ken suddenly strangles T.J., pressing his body hard against the tree. The specter of that murder seeps unevenly throughout the entire film, and in the final "Funk the Jubilee" scene, the punks, soulboys, and hippies, who have gathered in the park for the antijubilee concert and dance, riot with National Front skinheads and police with the audio tape of the murder playing over the microphones in the background. This is clearly meant to be a different sort of audio exchange from the ones taking place in the private rooms, estates, and dance halls that the rest of the film depicts, and it invokes a whole spectrum of other terrorized black bodies captured on tape or in print media, including Emmett Till but also Rodney King and Latasha Harlins.[4] Within the narrative context of the world the film marks and creates, it seems almost not to "fit." However, rather than simply existing as one of the film's narrative contradictions, the murder in the park points toward the limitations and the historical constructedness of desire. No matter how much we might mingle on the dance floor, the specter of the tortured black body will continue to haunt the public sphere.

Just as it has proven impossible to formulate and perform any sort of constructive, communal response to the Queen's Silver Jubilee celebration and the
nationalist impulses that cohere around it, the possibilities for constructive,
creative, cultural interaction seem confined by the film to individual acts of
bodily resistance with desire as the potentially dangerous catalyst. In *Young Soul
Rebel*, the mythos of miscegenation becomes a means for innovatively fixing
and identifying certain histories of oppression around race and sexuality, especially the violent history of lynching that is invoked in the encounter between
T.J. and Ken. However, that same mythology also becomes the vehicle for the
unfixing and challenging of certain rigid and deterministic claims of nationalist
identity politics in all camps. This is most apparent in the positive portrayal of
the mixed-race character, Chris, who has to endure both the harassment at the
hands of the British police and the suspicions of fellow blacks, who are hesitant
to accept his loyalty as genuine. However, this method as a strategy of resistance in the film often appears uneven and uncertain. In the end, Billibud's
"black and white unite and fuck" seems as inadequate a response to questions of
race as the response to homosexual sex given to Caz in an exchange with two
other West Indian men.

> Carlton: Caz, the trouble with you, right—can't always tell what side
> you're on.
> Caz: Now what ya sayin'? What, 'cos Chris is my mate? or 'cos I mix
> with white peop. . . .
> Davis: MAN! White MAN! Nastiness!
> Caz: So dat's wot it's about, yeah? I mix with white man . . . I *fuck* with
> white men!
> Davis: Jesus!
> Carlton: Long as *you* doin' it to *them* . . . innit Caz? (Julien and McCabe,
> 180)

Ultimately, there doesn't seem to be a comfortable way for any of the characters
in *Young Soul Rebel* to settle the question of power, the question of who's doing
it to whom or why. The utopia of the dance floor that the characters share in the
final scene exists as a fleeting moment (which is receding even as we recognize
it), an always already preempted possibility.

Julien's presentation of transgression as power and desire as disruption of
an otherwise static and corrupted order perhaps finds its fullest artistic expression in James Baldwin's *Another Country*, a novel that predated Julien's film by
thirty-one years. In many ways, *Another Country* also predates the mass organization and dispersion of the identity based sociopolitical movements whose
utopian visions are continuously foregrounded and displaced in Julien's work.
While Julien sets up characters who obviously embody and articulate certain
political and cultural stances that converge at particular moments and diverge at

others (Billibud is gay, a punk, a white, and a socialist; Caz is also gay, a soulboy, and black British; Chris is racially mixed heterosexual and also a soulboy),
the utopian vision in *Another Country* is grounded within individual characters
who spring from and float freely within a fairly self-styled humanistic bohemi-
anism. This not only operates differently from Julien's vision of displaced uto-
pias but also stands in stark contrast to the ideas of black nation as articulated by
Cleaver and other black cultural nationalists like him. Through the novel's individual characters, Baldwin attempts to explore the possibilities for a positive
politics of desire that has room for the many rather than the few. However,
much like the charting of the growing relationship between Caz and Billibud
and not unlike Cleaver's creation of a masculine paradigm, the desire in the
utopia that Baldwin creates must be almost entirely scripted in relation to the
dead black body, which is aggressively, explicitly gendered male.

For Cleaver, Baldwin, and Julien, as well as dominant American culture in
general, the black male body represents a cultural overdetermination against
which normative cultural practices must be aggressively mapped out. This is
why the "bye, baby,"[5] of a black male child can be read as such a menacing
sexual threat by men twice his age. The black male body is so overdetermined
that it seems to reach its most convenient symbolic stasis in death. However,
whereas the figure of Emmett Till embodied the complex nobility of a martyr
and the murder of T.J. provides moments for sympathetic identification in a
shared alienation, the death of Rufus Scott in *Another Country* serves only as an
empty catalyst for the interactions of the other figures in the novel. Rufus's
character in *Another Country*, with his chaotic, fractured violence and unrelent-
ing sexuality, could only ultimately be narratively contained in the liminal symbolic space of death. Unlike the bodies of T.J. and Emmett Till, which help, by
their symbolic containment in fixed metaphors of sympathy and martyrdom, to
sustain and contain a discourse on a black masculine sexuality that is constantly
in danger of decomposing, the body of Rufus Scott exists only as an absence
that marks a negative possibility. Terry Rowden is right to describe Rufus's
condition as one that embodies a "dystopia" that makes all the other utopian
possibilities possible (Rowden 1993, 42). Though the relationship between Ida,
Rufus's sister, and Vivaldo, his best friend, is the novel's foregrounded interracial relationship, it is really the relationship between Rufus and Vivaldo that
symbolically "counts." Long after Rufus's suicidal leap off the George Washington Bridge, his memory continues to haunt and charge Vivaldo's every sexual encounter. But this is not simply a case of misplaced sexual longing; it is not
so much Rufus whom Vivaldo desires, but rather what Rufus represents that
Vivaldo longs for. Shortly after Rufus's funeral, Vivaldo—while contemplating
his peculiar dislocation from his childhood home in the Bronx, his current home
in Greenwich Village or Harlem, the place of his sexual coming of age—
remembers that "[t]hey had balled chicks together, once or twice the same

chick." (Baldwin 1962, 116). This memory leads him to an even more symbolically charged memory of an encounter with an almost forgotten black army
buddy:

> There was a girl sitting near them. Who dared whom? Laughing they had
> opened their trousers and shown themselves to the girl. To the girl but also to
> each other. She had understood that their by-play had very little to do with
> her. But neither could it be said that they were trying to attract each other—
> they would never, certainly, have dreamed of doing it that way. Perhaps they
> had merely been trying to set their minds at ease as to which of them was the
> better man. It was out in the open, practically on the goddamn table, it was
> just like his, there was nothing frightening about it,
> He smiled—*I bet mine's bigger than yours is*—but remembered occasional
> nightmares in which this same vanished buddy pursued him through impene-
> trable forests, came at him with a knife on the edge of a precipice, threatened
> to hurl him down steep stairs to the sea. In each of the nightmares he wanted
> revenge. Revenge for what? (Baldwin 1962, 116-17)

It is not Rufus as best friend, brother, musician, or any of the other ways that he
might be characterized within the novel that is ultimately at stake. In the end, it
is simply his narrowly defined "black maleness" that counts. The black male
bodies in *Another Country* become the emptied out vessels through which the
white men, particularly Vivaldo, can negotiate their own positions of sexual
alienation and extreme alienation from community ties and problematic past
histories. In Vivaldo's own words, "[l]ove was a country he knew nothing
about" (Baldwin 1962, 250). In attempting to script that country, Baldwin is,
perhaps, guilty of that of which Cleaver accuses him: sacrificing a certain version of desire scripted in the black male body to create another utopian possibility. Baldwin is, of course, theoretically no more guilty than Cleaver himself. But
rather than free himself in the free-floating detachment of the radical Bohemian-
ism he claims, Baldwin ends up trapping himself in the same metaphors of black
masculinity that confine black men to the status of empty signifiers whose articulations have no place in a utopian possibility. Both the possibilities for a
utopia that could permanently and openly contain or accommodate a black masculinity that doesn't serve the state, the nation, or the race and a black masculinity whose desire is not scriptable in and under traditional terms and conditions
seem, in many ways, just as unthinkable with Baldwin as with Cleaver.

Are the possibilities for a black masculinity that is resistant rather than in
crisis, for the recognition of desires that are neither guided by the oppresive
normativity of the majority nor genocidally bent precluded by the historical circumstances that mark desire in the context of black bodies as "dangerous"? The
work of Essex Hemphill would seem to script other possibilities for "bad" desire
that go beyond either simply marking homosexuality as a sickness and miscege-

nation as a "revolutionary sickness" or, alternatively, seeing in unbounded desire the possibility for utopian fulfillment. Essex Hemphill's "Ceremonies," the short story that frames and titles his first collection of prose and poetry, is a sexual coming-of-age story that finds much of its unambiguous poetic force in the sexual interaction between a middle-aged white shopkeeper and a fourteen-year-old black male customer. In *Soul on Ice*, Eldridge Cleaver accuses James Baldwin of creating in Rufus Scott "a pathetic wretch . . . who let a white bisexual homosexual fuck him in his ass . . . the epitome of a black eunuch who has completely submitted to the white man" (Cleaver 1968, 107). It is, of course, important to note that Rufus Scott never actually engages in any act of anal intercourse either actively or passively within the pages of *Another Country*, but it is this act, in the fantasy of male homosexuality created by black nationalism, that damns black gay sexuality as a marker of weakness, femaleness, and racial submission. Hemphill's profoundly detailed but subtly nuanced accounting of the sexual interaction between the shopkeeper and the boy challenges cultural norms that seem to be unable to figure a sexuality, especially a racialized sexuality, in terms other than those of dominance and submission, "good" sexuality versus "bad" sexuality. The story defies clear-cut pronouncements and easy cultural policing not only because it is the white man who is down on his knees in "submission" but also because Hemphill complicates the notion of desire as something that is or should be ultimately, easily locatable and instantly regimented:

> If we had been caught when we finally began fucking, the law would have charged him with molesting and sodomizing me as a minor because of my age, but the law would not have believed that I wanted him to suck my dick. I wanted him to touch me. I wanted to fuck his ass. I willingly, by volition of my own desires, engaged in acts of sexual passion, somewhat clumsily but nonetheless sure of my decision to do so. (Hamphill 1992, 98)

Neither "the law" nor rigidly defined cultural constructions of sexuality seem capable of figuring or accounting for the narrator's own desires and sexual longings. The actions of his own fourteen-year-old black male body and the desires they seem to signal are as dangerously complicated and open to interpretive possibilities as those of the fourteen-year-old Emmett Till, whose "bye, baby," said to a white woman in a grocery store—a seemingly innocuous bit of defiant bravado resulting from a "dare" from his rural cousins—was read by grown white men as a menacing sexual threat. The narrator knows his desire is something that must be kept dangerously hidden:

> I had to carefully allow my petals to unfold. If I had revealed them too soon they surely would have been snatched away, brutalized, and scattered down alleys. I was already alert enough to know what happened to the flamboyant

boys at school who were called "sissies" and "faggots." I could not have endured then the violence and indignities they often suffered. (97)

In the end, the black male narrator of "Ceremonies" marks his passage into
manhood as a set of definitional memories, moments that define the boundaries
of his masculinity even as he defies them. These moments, marked by a violence as they are, have some of the force of Cleaver's "nervous breakdown,"
Rufus Scott's suicide, and T.J.'s murder in the park; yet they nourish a masculinity that is not only able to protect itself but is also able to recognize its possibilities even in the midst of a daily oppression that is life threatening. It is this
that allows the narrator to see "ceremonies" where others only see sin, to create
an entirely new vision of masculine possibility in the "sexuality and the desires I
could not speak of or name as clearly as I could articulate the dangers"
(Hemphill 1992, 103). The dangers, in the end, will not be this fourteen-year-
old's undoing. In "Ceremonies," even a compromised "love" has a power, and
the negotiations of various positions of power highlight the very fragility of
their enactment.

In an interview with Isaac Julien, bell hooks discussed the ways in which,
within certain strands of black nationalism, desire gets constructed so that
"being with a black person is a kind of an end point"(Julien and McCabe 1991,
130). The intersections of a discourse on miscegenation, homosexuality, and
black masculinity reveal the ways in which simply "being with a black person"
is always, already a mediated experience. When in the final minutes of *Tongues
Untied* Marlon Riggs pronounced, "black men loving black men is the revolutionary act of our time," he is not merely invoking stale black Power rhetoric
(Simmons 1991, 193). He is, rather, complicating our notions of revolutionary
action, black masculinity, and sexual desire and debunking romanticized notions
of love. While we can no longer afford to pretend that "being with a black person is an end" in and of itself, neither can we simply read the act of miscegenation as a transgressive action that necessarily engenders manifold moments of
resistance. The impulses that created nationalism as an impulse of reconstructive
resistance must be renegotiated in order to realize a kind of cultural nationalism
that is not based on fixed points of reference at which you arrive but rather is a
continuous process of location and relocation, a complex series of negotiations
that assert and reassert the foundational importance of freedom, rebuke the poverty of despair, and recognize the intensity of longing as the inevitable components of dreaming a better world.

Notes

1. Examples include the Act-Up "die-in," which is obviously modeled and named

after the Civil Rights tactic of the "sit in" to desegregate public spaces, and the wildly successful 1993 March on Washington for Lesbian, Gay, and Bi Equal Rights and Liberation, which was attended by over a million people. This march had been modeled after the equally successful 1963 March on Washington, which was up until that point the largest demonstration of its kind in United States history. Many moments from the 1963 March on Washington became emblematic of the potential for social change in the United States, including most notably Martin Luther King's "I have a dream" speech as delivered from the steps of the Lincoln Memorial. The 1993 March on Washington for Lesbian, Gay, and Bi Equal Rights and Liberation played off the cultural resonances of the earlier March on Washington to add validity to its claims for civil rights.

2. Queer Nation is a grassroots, direct-action group that uses aggressive and flamboyant humor to combat homophobia and invisibility. The group might stage, for example, a kiss-in at a local shopping mall.

3. Though Marcus Garvey's movement is credited with the widespread popularization of this phrase, Harold Cruse attributes its creation to Martin Delany and a much earlier phase of the Back to Africa movement (Garvey 1986, 4).

4. Both cases, in which an assault on an African American was videotaped, were widely circulated by the American news media. The murder of fifteen-year-old Harlins by a Korean American grocer and the subsequent sentencing of her murderer to less than a year probation and the brutal police assault of Rodney King were made stand-ins for the litany of racist abuse suffered daily by black men and women in contemporary America.

5. The words supposedly mumbled by Emmett Till to Carolyn Bryant on the way out of Bryant's Grocery and Meat Market in Money, Mississippi.

Works Cited

Asante, Molefi Kete. 1992. *Afrocentricity*. Trenton: Africa World.

Baldwin, James. 1962. *Another Country*. New York: Dell.

Beam, Joseph, ed. 1986. *In the Life: A black Gay Anthology*. Boston: Alyson.

Cleaver, Eldridge. 1968. *Soul On Ice*. New York: Dell.

Cress Welsing, Frances. 1991. *The Isis Papers: The Keys to the Colors*. Chicago: Third World.

Dearborn, Mary V. 1986. *Pocahontas's Daughters: Gender and Ethnicity in American Culture*. New York: Oxford University Press.

DeGout, Yasmin, Y. 1992. "Dividing the Mind: Contradictory Portraits of Homoerotic Love in *Giovanni's Room*." *African American Review*. 26.3: 425-35.

Garvey, Amy Jacques. 1986. *The Philosopy and Opinions of Marcus Garvey, or Africa for the Africans*. Dover: Majority.

Hemphill, Essex, ed. 1991a. *Brother to Brother: New Writings by black Gay Men*. Boston: Alyson.

_____. 1991b. "Looking for Langston: An Interview with Isaac Julien." In *Brother to Brother*. Boston: Alyson.

_____. 1992. *Ceremonies*. New York: Plume.

Julien, Isaac. 1992. "'Black Is, Black Ain't': Notes on De-Essentializing Black Identities."In

Black Popular Culture, ed. Gina Dent. Seattle: Bay.

Julien, Isacc, and Colin McCabe. 1991. *Diary of a Young Soul Rebel*. London: British Film Institute.

Mercer, Kobena, and Isaac Julien. 1991. "True Confessions: A Discourse on Images of black Male Sexuality." In *Brother to Brother*, ed. Essex Hemphil. Boston: Alyson.

Nelson, Emmanuel. 1991. "Critical Deviance: Homophobia and the Reception of James Baldwin's Fiction." *Journal of American Culture* 14.3: 91-96.

Newton, Huey P. 1973. *Revolutionary Suicide*. New York: Harcourt.

Rowden, Terry. 1993. "A Play of Abstractions: Race, Sexuality, and Community in James Baldwin's *Another Country*." *The Southern Review* 29.1: 41-50.

Simmons, Ron. 1991. "Tongues Untied: An Interview with Marlon Riggs." In *Brother to Brother*, ed. Essex Hemphil. Boston: Alyson.

Warner, Michael, ed. 1970. *The Cress Theory of Color Confrontation and Racism*. Washington: Cress Welsing.

____. 1993. *Fear of a Queer Planet: Queer Politics and Social Theory*. Minneapolis: University of Minnesota Press.

Williams, Juan. 1987. *Eyes on the Prize: America's Civil Rights Years, 1954-1965*. New York: Penguin.

13

Women on Top, Boys on the Side, but Some of Us Are Brave: Blackness, Lesbianism, and the Visible[1]

Ann Pellegrini

Many of the criticisms lodged by women of color against the exclusions and "blank spots" (Anzaldúa 1990, xx) of white feminist studies in the 1980s (and beyond) are condensed in the title of the 1982 black feminist anthology *All the Women Are White, All the Blacks Are Men, But Some of Us Are Brave: Black Women's Studies*. If the title of that volume declared that such formulas or catchphrases of inclusion as "women and blacks" effectively place some subjects out of bounds, its subtitle—*Black Women's Studies*—called attention to the unmarked whiteness of Women's Studies. To judge from recent criticisms lodged against the intellectual currents and critical practices collected under the name "queer theory," the roster of the brave has increased.

Queer theory has emerged out of (and sometimes broken off from) *both* lesbian and gay studies *and* feminist theory. Although queer theory in its anti-identitarian strain aims to open up, rather than close down, the subjects of sexuality, it too has been assailed from a broad range of intellectual and political positions for its exclusions, evasions, and gaps. To be sure, queer theory's critics do not speak as one. (Nor, it should be mentioned, do its admirers and practitioners.) From a Marxian perspective, for example, Donald Morton accuses queer theory and a particular cadre of influential queer theorists of marching in "veritable lockstep with the mainstream academy at large" (Morton 1993, 130). In thrall to "dominant" academic and intellectual modes of theorizing, which Morton tags "ludic (post)modernism," queer theory is, he argues, of a piece with trends in late-capitalism (Morton 1993, 1995). By "ludic," Morton means "playful," "not serious," and, most damning of all, "apolitical." But it is only by simplifying very different commitments and orientations within queer theory and characterizing all queer theory as a genre of textual studies "concerned with the mechanics of signification, the 'playful relation' of signifier to signified (hence the term *ludic*)" that Morton can reduce its politics to the (in his view) dubious project of promoting "reading practices that 'delay' the connection of the signifier to the signified and disrupt the easy trafficking of meaning in culture" (Morton 1993, 124).

Drawing on terms that usher in the specter of feminine excess trumping masculine order, he calls queer theory "the most recent subversion of the rational" (Morton 1993, 121). It has abandoned radical social change and the theoretical tools that would enable it for so much pomo smoke and mirrors. Interestingly, Morton's list of usual suspects is dominated by women. Thus, if there is any trafficking going on here, it is Morton's traffic—in women. In a new incarnation of *cherchez la femme* (and *cherchez la feministe*), Morton-as-traffic-cop singles out Eve Kosofsky Sedgwick, Teresa de Lauretis, Diana Fuss, and Judith Butler for especial rebuke (139).

If Morton implies that queer theory has been emasculated by an implicitly feminine ludic (post)modernism, for some white lesbian feminists the problem is that queer theory is too much of the masculine. One of the strongest such criticisms has been offered by Sheila Jeffreys, who blasts queer theory for reinstituting a men's club under the banner of a falsely generic "queer." In her apocalyptic assessment of the "queer disappearance of lesbians," Jeffreys accuses some prominent women of collaborating in the lesbian's erasure, outing Judith Butler, Gayle Rubin, and Eve Sedgwick as key coconspirators.

This is a criticism joined, though from a somewhat different angle, by Terry Castle in her "Polemical Introduction" to *The Apparitional Lesbian*. The organizing concern of this lively book is the ways in which the lesbian and the possibilities she names—namely, an erotic commerce between women that exceeds the control of men—have been "ghosted," written and imagined out of existence in Western literature and popular fantasy (Castle 1993, 6). Turning her sights on queer theory, she argues that it, too, participates in this vaporization of the lesbian. Under the sway of continental philosophy, Castle charges, a younger generation of lesbian and gay scholars have deconstructed to oblivion the "very meaningfulness of terms such as *lesbian* or *gay* or *homosexual* or *coming out*" (13). In Castle's view, queer theory's destabilization of what lesbian means has gone so far as to make a nonsense of the lesbian.

In a sly figuration of the "ghost effect," Castle makes Judith Butler stand in for the critical trends she is diagnosing without ever mentioning Butler by name; Butler is identified only as "one such critic (herself lesbian)" (Castle 1993, 14). This parenthetical identification of Butler as "herself lesbian" seems posed as a counterweight to Butler's refusal to specify what lesbian means, indeed to Butler's suggestion that what "lesbian" signifies cannot be specified once and for all (Butler 1991). But does naming Butler a lesbian really serve, as Castle seems to want it to serve, to unmask Butler's arguments as the real nonsense? As if the lesbian truth will out?

It seems to me that asking how and what lesbian means is not the same thing as holding that lesbian means nothing at all or anything you want. It is possible to believe simultaneously that one is, in some real and meaningful sense, lesbian and that "the lesbian" is a cultural construction. This is the tension Butler operates through in "Imitation and Gender Insubordination," when she names herself lesbian. She makes this self-declaration en route to exploring the gap between "being" lesbian and how that lesbian "I" gets "established, instituted, circulated, and confirmed" (Butler 1991, 18). Further, and in an argument that parallels Castle's concerns in *The Apparitional Lesbian*, Butler observes that lesbians, in contrast to gay men, have not been admitted into the realm of the visible, the culturally intelligible, and wonders "how, then, to 'be' a lesbian in a political context in which the lesbian does not exist" (20).

Though I disagree with Castle's representation of queer theory, I do share her concern that in much queer theory, lesbians are not being looked at, but through; 1970s lesbian feminism has come to be the "fall gal" for a new generation of lesbian, gay, and queer theorists. As Biddy Martin has noted, queer theory's moves to differentiate itself from its intellectual and institutional predecessors have too often been achieved at the expense of feminist studies, especially a caricatured version of lesbian feminism, against which queer theory has constructed itself as the vanguard (Butler and Martin 1994, 104). Martin also worries that attempts to complicate "hegemonic assumptions about the continuities between anatomical sex, social gender, gender identity, sexual identity, sexual object choice, and sexual practice" have opened up the field of sexuality by closing down discussions of gender and race, both of which, when and where they do enter the conceptual horizon of queer theory, often end up cast in terms of fixity and constraint (105).

Queer theory's conceptual moves to distinguish between sexuality and gender, such that sexuality is not reduced to an epiphenomenon of gender, have been vital to its development and revitalizing as well for feminist studies, very broadly conceived.[2] However, the move to separate sexuality and gender, even if this is understood as a provisional step to render sexuality and gender distinct for the purposes of sharper historical analysis and critical clarity, may end up disarticulating queer theory from feminist theory. And once queer theory becomes conceived as the academic area "reserved" for the study of sexuality, and once feminist theory gets marked out as the place set aside for the study of gender, it becomes difficult to imagine and enact theories that can investigate the diverse ways in which gender and sexuality articulate each other. Moreover, it is difficult to imagine how either the newly distinguished territories of queer theory or feminist theory could address the problematic of "race," *except* as an afterthought or secondary feature. The segmentation of academic enterprises into distinct territories, each with distinct (read: "proper") objects and identities,[3] does not advance but may actually impede the development of theories and strategies that can conceptualize and address how gender, race, and sexuality are interstructured and interstructuring.[4]

White feminist scholars and white feminist studies have responded in different ways and with varying degrees of success to this challenge to integrate race and racialization into studies of gender. To be sure, this is an unfinished project. But there are important and identifiable traditions in feminist scholarship in which gender is not and has *never* been the privileged object of analysis apart from, say, race or class or sexuality, traditions in which antisexism has been joined from the start to projects of antiracism, anti-homophobia, and economic justice.[5] To assert otherwise would be to misrepresent or overlook the leading roles women of color have played in the development of feminist theory in the academy and out. Moreover, the prominent role played by lesbians of color, such as Audre Lorde, Pat Parker, Gloria Anzaldúa, and Cherríe Moraga, in the imagining and shaping of feminist studies and lesbian studies importantly counters those who would describe, and then on these grounds dismiss, lesbian feminism as "white." As Linda Garber suggests in her important reconsideration of the poetry and identity politics of Judy Grahn and Pat Parker, mischaracterizing the history of lesbian feminism as a movement for and of white women does a gross disservice to the lesbians of color so instrumental to the development, history, theories, and practices of lesbian feminism. This mischaracterization of lesbian feminism has contributed, Garber argues, to the condescension sometimes directed at it by younger feminist and queer theorists writing today.

Let me be clear: I am certainly not asserting that Women's Studies in its institutional forms and feminist theory everywhere and adequately enunciate and work through a conception of gender, race, and sexuality as mutually constituting. (Gender, race, and sexuality do not exhaust the sites in which identity is cast and molded, of course.) Moreover, to claim that gender, race, and sexuality construct and inflect each other does not settle the question of how they have been interarticulated historically, nor does it decide in advance the historical forms these interarticulations will continue to take. If I am here falling into caricatures of my own and portraying the relations between queer theory and feminist theory as more antagonistic and either/or than they actually are, I do so to make a point. Disarticulating queer theory from feminist theory risks, among other things, casting out by forgetting the lessons feminist theory and its various practitioners have learned in their struggles to make race, class, sexuality, and other "Others within" not just additions to, but constitutive features of gender studies.

Failing to remember is one way to repeat with a difference. But there are others. It is, as Evelynn Hammonds observes, one thing to acknowledge that race is not simply a derivative of or addition to sexual difference and quite another to follow up that insight with careful study of "the powerful effect that race has on the construction and representation of gender and sexuality" (Hammonds 1994, 127). This is an undertaking, she says, too few white scholars of sexuality have yet pursued.

Hammonds's essay, written for the second special issue of *differences* on queer theory, represents an attempt to take queer theory at its word. Five years into the institutionalization of something called queer theory—a *very* tenuous institutionalization, granted, and one to some degree launched by *differences*, first special issue on queer theory—Hammonds asks how well queer theory has responded to editor Teresa de Lauretis's 1991 charge to

> problematize some of the discursive constructions and constructed silences in the emergent field of "gay and lesbian studies," and . . . explore questions that have as yet been barely broached, such as the respective and/or common grounding of current discourses and practices of homo-sexualities in relation to gender and to race, with their attendant differences of class or ethnic culture, generational, geographical, and socio-political location. (de Lauretis 1991a, iii-iv)

Later in her introduction, de Lauretis re-marks the kind of critical move she is calling for under the now ascendant term "queer theory." In implied contrast to "gay and lesbian studies," the designation "queer theory" is meant to break through the logjam of "discursive protocols" in which "gay" and "lesbian," and the qualifiers of race and national or local scene that specify just which lesbians and gays are being talked about, fight for pride of place in the titles of organization, publications, and—I would add—academic affiliations (de Lauretis, 1991a, v). Taking the measure of queer theory five years on, Hammonds finds a continuation of, in her words, "the consistently exclusionary practices of lesbian and gay studies in general" (Hammonds 1994, 127). A shift from "lesbian and gay" to "queer" (or from "studies" to "theory"?) accomplishes little, Hammonds implies, if white scholars defer the project of theorizing "differences between and within gays and lesbians in relation to race" or leave it to someone else to do (Hammonds 1994, 130).[6] As if "race"—studying it and having it?—properly belongs to someone else.

Hammonds commends *The Lesbian and Gay Studies Reader* (Abelove 1993, *et al.*), for example, for including essays by many prominent writers of color as well as numerous essays about the sexualities of people of color and how their sexualities are constructed in relation to other fields of power—such as class, gender, and race. But she criticizes the apparent failure of other (and white?) contributors to the volume to integrate questions of race and racialization into the study of sexuality. It is, of course, important to remember that *The Reader* collects and reprints essays written at different times and in different contexts over the past twenty years. Thus, some of the articles Hammonds implicitly rebukes for failing to engage "the work of the writers of color that do appear in the volume" were written *before* the work of these writers was either in general circulation or had even been written (Hammonds 1994, 128). This is in some ways a minor point, since there were other writers of color whose work and challenges were already in circulation when the other essays in *The Reader* were written.

If I am focusing on something I have just characterized as a "minor point," I also think that the broad brushstrokes with which Hammonds sometimes moves in her essay raise some substantive questions about critical genealogies. Earlier I suggested that genealogies of feminisms, including lesbian feminisms, that begin by leaving out the women of color who were writing alongside and in some cases before the white feminists usually given credit (or, as is more the case these days, blame) for "founding" feminisms do not simply misremember history, but they actually construct a narrow history with disturbing implications for the future. It seems to me that the problems with Hammonds's genealogy of lesbian and gay studies and queer theory are of another order, but with related difficulties. Mischarting the chronological relations between and among the essays reprinted in *The Reader* authorizes the attribution of something like "bad faith" to the editors of the volume as well as to individual essayists. It is not, I want to insist, that her concerns about the unexamined whiteness of many of the anthology's critical terms of art—for example, "subjectivity," "sexuality," "lesbian," and "gay"—are misplaced (Hammonds 1994, 128). But the chronology implied in her analysis may collapse the complicated historical and institutional relations between and among feminisms, lesbian and gay studies, and critical races studies. And this too can get in the way of developing alternate critical paradigms for the urgent intellectual and political work that needs to be done now and in the future.

These concerns notwithstanding, Hammonds's overarching criticism of lesbian and gay studies and of queer theory does seem to me on target, namely that the models of inclusion practiced do not go far enough. Women and men of color, inside the academy and out, have been pushing white scholars of sexuality to investigate the ways "race" is sexed and "sex" raced. This intellectual and political project reconceives the "and" linking "women *and* blacks" or "gender, race, *and* sexuality." This other "and" does not secure a neat analogy between otherwise discrete categories. Rather it marks out a different set of relations and demands a different mapping. This is the sort of critical geography called for by Kobena Mercer, when he observes that

> Today we are adept at the all too familiar concatenation of identity politics, as if by merely rehearsing the mantra of "race, class, gender" (and all the intervening variables) we have somehow acknowledged the diversified and pluralized differences at work in contemporary culture, politics, and society. Yet the complexity of what actually happens "between" the contingent spaces where each variable intersects with the others is something only now coming into view theoretically, and this is partly the result of new antagonistic cultural practices by hitherto marginalized artists. Instead of analogies, which tend to flatten out these intermediate spaces, I think we need to explore theories that enable new forms of dialogue. (Mercer 1991, 193)

Mercer cites the work of "hitherto marginalized artists" as a place where the messy contingent spaces "between" identities may be sighted. But I also take him to be arguing that these artists' "antagonistic cultural practices" already represent one such moment of theorizing. In extending to these cultural practices the claim to theory, then, he expands what counts as theory and what counts as cultural intervention.

At this juncture, I want to turn my sights on some recent feature-length films in which lesbianism, and the particular difference it may or may not represent, appears alongside, perhaps even through, blackness as magic sign. The two mainstream films "featured" in the following section exemplify by analogy ways *not* to explore the intersections of identity and difference. I am interested in how and under what conditions "the lesbian" does become visible in these films, and I hope that the analysis brought to bear on them will model one way for queer (and) feminist theorists to "explore theories that enable new forms of dialogue" and ask new kinds of questions about and at the intersections.

"Is This a Black-White Thing?"[7]

In light of the ongoing debates about the place of race in feminist and queer theories, the startling frequency with which recent cinematic portrayals of lesbianism or, better, "lesbianism" (since some of the films in question signify around the bush) have depicted interracial couples consisting of a white woman and a black woman deserves closer scrutiny. So many such feature-length films have come out, and in such a relatively compressed period of time, that this in-

terracial couple has become virtually the cinematic face of lesbianism: *She Must
Be Seeing Things* (1987), *Bar Girls* (1995), *The Incredibly True Adventure of Two
Girls in Love* (1995), *Boys on the Side* (1995), *When Night Is Falling* (1995),
Work (1996), and *Watermelon Woman* (1996).[8]

There are major differences between and among these films, not the least of
which being the different market relations effecting and affecting the distribution and reception of the individual films. Only one was made by a major studio
(Boys on the Side). Three others—*Bar Girls, When Night Is Falling,* and *The
Incredibly True Adventure of Two Girls in Love*—were picked up and released
nationally by major distributors.[9] With one exception—the Canadian film *When
Night Is Falling*—all the films were made in and focused on the United States.
Boys on the Side was directed by a white man, and *Watermelon Woman* is the
first feature-length film by African-American director Cheryl Dunye. The other
five films were directed by white women.

At the risk of eliding differences between and among these films, I want to
offer a schematic of *one* of the ways blackness is working in all of them; this
general claim must be adjusted to fit the scene, and "seen," of each film. In each
of these films, blackness bears the burden of making difference within the same
visible. What Mercer writes of the "tension of sameness" introduced into the
visual field by Robert Mapplethorpe's homoerotic depictions of black male
nudes may also be operating in the films mentioned above. The sameness in
"same-sex" love "transfers the frisson of 'difference' from gendered to racialized polarity" (Mercer 1993, 351). Arguably, this deployment of blackness as
visible difference functions to interrupt or keep off homophobic conceptions of
lesbianism as narcissism by any other name. That is, by articulating lesbian difference through racial difference, the films can avoid, or potentially avoid, homophobic equations of same-sex love with narcissistic love of the same. However, this transfer from sexual difference to racial difference does not disrupt
binaries but displaces them.

The project of putting off the accusation of "too much" self-love can operate hand in hand with a homophobic panic that wants to know, perhaps at first
glance, the difference between homo- and heterosexuality. In *Boys on the Side*,
blackness is joined to both these projects. This female buddy film traces the
adventures of three women, two white (Robin and Holly) and one black (Jane),
as they drive across country, from New York to California. Significantly, their
trip stops short of its target in Tucson, Arizona. But the depiction of Tucson and
the Chicano culture and traditions that are part of that city's fabric as a kind of
utopian *frontera*—where everyone really can get along—turns this detour into
the destination they did not know they were aiming at all along.

This points to the numerous ways in which the film flattens differences
even as it is representing them. The film is more than happy to position itself on
a "lesbian continuum" (to borrow Adrienne Rich's famous formula) and cele-

brate and affirm intimacy between and among women, but it unevenly manages just how far this intimacy may reach. A capsule review in New York's *Village Voice* wryly described *Boys on the Side* as yet another in a series of recent films in which two women meet, fall in love, and do not have sex. The film also seems uneasy about the ripple effects bonds between women may have on heterosexuality once the centrality of women to each other's emotional life displaces men to the position of "boys on the side."

Newspaper advertisements and trailers for the film promoted the distinctively female character of these bonds, referring to the special ties between women and to the envy men felt for the closeness women enjoyed with each other.[10] In the world of the film, this envy becomes a death blow when Holly kills her abusive boyfriend, Nick, in self-defense, and the other two women, who witness the event, conspire to conceal Holly's role in it. In a climactic courtroom scene, when Holly is on trial for murder, the bonds between women seem as much on trial as Holly herself. The film's narrative and its two love stories have been set in motion by two deaths, a man's and a woman's. Nick's death is among the first events depicted in *Boys on the Side*, and the shadow of Robin's imminent death from AIDS is cast over the length of it. It is not clear, then, whether envy's killing sting is directed outward at the ones who incite envy (women-identified-women and/or women-loving-women) or inward at the ones who feel envy (heterosexual men). The self-justifications offered by Holly's new boyfriend (a clean-cut white policeman with the unbelievable name of Abe Lincoln) for turning in the woman he loves give away the film's ideological bottom line, "There's no kind of family without the law." Of heterosexuality? Racial "purity"? Both?

Appearing for the defense at Holly's trial, Robin must offer an accounting that can exonerate the bonds between women of a lesbian connection as well as clear whiteness from the charge of crossing over racial borders. Her speech is worth repeating in full; it is the one moment in the film when men too are explicitly invited to enjoy the same-sex ties that bind: "I don't know what it is, but there's something that goes on between women. You men know that because it's the same for you. I'm not saying that one sex is better that the other. I'm just saying like speaks to like. Love, or whatever, doesn't always keep, but you find what does if you're lucky." The film here labors to conceal the very differences—of race, sexuality, and gender—that it has made its running punch line. Throughout the film, characters have been stating in tones of wonderment, "Jane's gay?" and "She's a black lesbian?" These statements of fact, pitched upward into the form of questions, deny any knowledge of the very thing they pronounce. Lesbianism and blackness are the questions the film cannot stop itself from asking or help itself to answer.

This scene thus reveals that different strategies are necessary to manage and put off the white woman's lesbian possibility. For her, the evasion is brokered on an appeal to a race-neutral conception of sisterly solidarity. As in: "like speaks to like." But this ostensibly race-neutral conception is generated by a racial fix. For how can we (the film's presumptively straight "we") guard against the possibility that this woman-woman identification might cross into or be finally indistinguishable from woman-woman desire? After all, the Radicalesbians' woman-identified-woman was a spokeswoman for just such a convergence cum crossing. What if, in the midst of all this sisterly solidarity and loving but nonsexual touching, a hand, a mouth, a feeling goes astray? Where and how can you tell the difference between female homosociality and female homosexuality? This, I want to suggest, is the work Jane's blackness does. Of the three female friends, Jane is the only lesbian character named as such; she is also the only woman of color. Her blackness visibly marks out the difference between the lesbian and the straight woman she loves and who may even love her in return, just "not in that way." Bearing the representational burden for the threatening difference lodged at the heart of the same (or was it: the threatening sameness lodged at the heart of difference?), her blackness, like her lesbianism, marks the place beyond the pale.

In contrast to *Boys on the Side*, in which blackness marks out differences within the category "woman" by drawing the boundaries between a woman-identification that stops short of desire and a woman-identification that crosses into it, in the 1991 film *Fried Green Tomatoes* blackness demarcates differences within *whiteness*. The film deploys a strategy of "compensatory stereotyping."[11] The whiteness and, so, propriety of a loving relationship between two women is secured by playing it off against stereotypes of put-upon black folk. In this film, lesbianism is raced white and disappears behind the screen of normative and even heroic whiteness.

In *Fried Green Tomatoes*, as in *Boys on the Side*, two women meet, fall in love, do not have sex, and one of them dies. Moreover, in *Fried Green Tomatoes*, as in *Boys on the Side* after it, the character who dies is played by Mary-Louise Parker, who seems to be making a career out of treading the line between woman-woman identification and woman-woman desire. The film represents around the issue of lesbianism, depicting a strong and intense friendship between two white women (the tomboy Idgie Threadgoode and the fem Ruth Jamison), but never committing itself one way or another.[12] Asked whether the film was "really" about two lesbians, director Jon Avnet responded, "You can take it how you want to. I had no interest in going into the bedroom" (qtd. in Parish n.d., 149). The Los Angeles-based Gay and Lesbian Alliance against Defamation (GLAAD) was not so coy; it claimed the film and gave it a Media Award for its positive depictions of lesbians in a film.

I am not particularly interested in settling the question of whether Idgie and Ruth were lovers or just good friends. However, that there can be disagreement on this question indicates some of the weaknesses of "positive images" or a "politics of visibility" as liberatory strategy. Images do not speak once for all. We cannot control for all the different and sometimes even contradictory messages one and the same image or text may open itself to and produce. If GLAAD's recognition of the film commended the identificatory pleasures the film gave some lesbian viewers, the film's representations of its black characters may have foreclosed the pleasures and identifications of some others of its spectators—including some of the lesbian spectators in whose name GLAAD gave *Fried Green Tomatoes* a Media Award.

In *Fried Green Tomatoes'* story within a story, the heroism and goodness of Idgie and Ruth are established by showing their hatred for all forms of prejudice, especially white racism. That Idgie and Ruth are unflagging opponents of racism is indicated in their opposition to the Klan and in their generous concern for the black men and women who live around them and whom they employ. In their turn, these black men and women repay Idgie's and Ruth's kindness with their unflagging loyalty, but we never get a sense of them as independent moral agents.

The film links its criticism of the Ku Klux Klan to its indictment of Ruth's husband, Frank Bennett, whose faults include beating Ruth and being a member of the Ku Klux Klan. Frank's membership in the Ku Klux Klan is one of the ways the film proves what a bad guy he is—as if wife beating would not be sufficient evidence. But, and this is my principal concern with the work blackness does in the film, the white racism represented and criticized in *Fried Green Tomatoes* seems, in the end, to be all about whiteness. It becomes a way of making distinctions within the category of whiteness between "good" white people and "bad" white people; the white racism directed at African Americans, which the film vividly portrays (up to and including a scene where a black male character is whipped by the Klan), is really all about white people. For which lesbians, then, did the film offer "positive" images? As Jackie Goldsby asks, "[W]ho do we mean, after all, by 'our own'" (Goldshy 1990, 10)?

In the end, both *Fried Green Tomatoes* and *Boys on the Side* represent difference to further a universalizing project. Although they invoke a pluralism of differences—depicting differences of erotic choice, gender, race, and class—they persist in wishing these differences away and into some putatively shared transcendent vision in which unlike turns out to be like, and then they can speak to each other.[13] This analogical thinking overlooks the ways in which differences construct, reinforce, contradict, and crosscut each other—and that these fraught crossings do not make them the "same." The failures of the two films discussed above can be instructive as we (an expansive open "we") move to create theories and strategies capable of mapping the intersections of identity.

Conclusions without Foreclosures

One of the most undertheorized aspects of these films is the ways in which differences energize and enlist desire. This possibility produces embarrassment, denial, evasion, uncomfortable silence. In a much-quoted observation concerning the different treatments of race by gay male and lesbian communities, Jackie Goldsby writes, "Dykes politicize it, gay men eroticize it, either perception neutralizing any middle ground on which I can stand and say my piece" (Goldsby 1990, 11). Despite Goldsby's disclaimer, her attempts to theorize about and at the intersections of identity constitute one such "middle ground," however tenuous and revisable it may be. Goldsby's essay—"What It Means to Be Colored Me"—and Goldsby "herself" are both works in progress. She explores the between-spaces, where desires, identifications, histories, imagined futures, self, and other meet, crosscut, and complicate each other in sometimes unpredictable ways. One of her critical insights comes in the form of a question. Discussing her relationship with a white woman, she wonders "where, in the context of lesbian political discourse on race, can we acknowledge that our knowingly crossing boundaries of race and class *is* part of our desire for each other" (11, italics in original). And what would it mean to allow that the eroticization of difference can sometimes be the ground of politics and not its Maginot line?

Rachel Reichman's *Work*, which is centered around an affair between an unhappily married white woman (Jenny) and a younger black woman (June), is one recent film that does thematize the ways in which difference mobilizes desire.[14] With varying degrees of self-consciousness, each woman connects her desire for the other to the transgression of loving across the color line. They do not love "despite" racial difference or as a way to overcome it, but in some sense because of it. June tells a parable in which one woman (a thinly disguised June) desires a second woman (readable as Jenny) because the second woman has been branded a troublemaker. But this branding precedes any act that would qualify the second woman for the category "troublemaker." So, the troublemaker becomes one by virtue of being identified by and coming to identify with the name. The film suggests that transgressive desire occasions—is—this identificatory branding. The reciprocity of one woman's desire for the other both constitutes and confirms that the interpellation has reached its appropriate mark. These two women together make trouble by confounding the lines between desire and identification, other and same.

The film also complicates its treatment of cross-racial desire by attending to the two women's class positions. Jenny and June are both working class, but their ostensibly shared class position means differently because it is inflected by differences of race. The black woman is on her way up and out of the working class; but the white woman seems stuck, when she is not plain losing ground. These reversals of the expected alignment, in which white correlates to more economically privileged and black to less, is not a facile inversion dependent on stereotypes even as they are turned on their head. This flip would not complicate conceptions of race and class because it would allow and encourage audiences to read upside down. In *Work*, however, the rising and falling class fortunes of the black woman and the white woman, respectively, are part of the history of their racial identifications. The ambitions driving June to college and onward to a professional career are as much June's grandmother's as her own. June's aspirations for self-improvement cannot be understood apart from a connection to intimate others, to a particular family history, and to the uplift of "the race."

By contrast, Jenny has no moorings. Jenny's relationship with her husband is noteworthy for its pitch of disconnection. The film follows her from one job interview to another, each for a pink collar job, each unsuccessful. Arguably, her whiteness camouflages her desperation. What does a white working-class woman want? No one asks Jenny, not even Jenny. Her desire for June is marked by a wishful identification with the black woman's class mobility. But without goals or ambitions of her own, these identifications initially cast Jenny even further adrift by opening up another distance between the two women. As the film closes, June is away at college, and Jenny gets a job doing landscaping, an occupation that occasions another crossing over, into traditionally male territory. But her new employ and the way she newly carries her body, as if it is her own, and for the first time, traces the route of Jenny's desire for June as this desire transgresses and is transgressed by identification. Through the intersections of same and different, desire and identification, Jenny comes to identify with another possible future.

Importantly, if this film charts a colonial adventure, it is not the oft-told tale of a white woman rescued by the selfless love of a strong black woman. Rather, *Work* dramatizes ways desire, identification, and difference de- and re-territorialize each other. *Work* thus manages to represent differences of class and race and to draw them through the switchpoints of desire and identification without letting any one difference do all the work or differences stand still. The spare title, *Work*, which is a declaration and a dare, well describes the sometimes tiring, sometimes energizing, but always necessary labor of negotiating the intersections of identity. Work to be done. And different kinds of queer theories to be offered.

Notes

1. Portions of this essay were first written for a talk given at Montclair State University, in April 1996, as part of "Crossing Boundaries: An Interdisciplinary Series with

Lesbian Artists." I am grateful to the organizers of that series for inviting me to participate. Jean Walton pushed me to expand that lecture for a special issue of *College Literature*, and her comments and questions on earlier versions of this essay were immensely
helpful. I have benefited above all from conversations with Liz Wiesen, whose ideas,
queries, and challenges are imprinted across this essay.

2. Key instances of this conceptual move are contained in Rubin's 1984 essay
"Thinking Sex" and Sedgwick's second axiom in *Epistemology of the Closet*, in which
she states, "The study of sexuality is not coextensive with the study of gender; correspondingly, antihomophobic inquiry is not coextensive with feminist inquiry. But we
can't know in advance how they will be different" (Sedgwick 1990, 27). Rubin's essay is
reprinted in Abelove et all., *The Lesbian and Gay Studies Reader*, among other places.

3. For a compelling set of arguments "against proper objects," see Judith Butler's
essay (1994) of the same name.

4. One model of the ways in which lesbian/gay/queer studies, critical race studies,
and a feminist gender studies may complicate and enrich each other without staging a
turf battle over disciplinary domains is offered by *Critical Crossings*, a special issue of
Diacritics edited by Judith Butler and Biddy Martin. In their introduction, Butler and
Martin write that they were initially asked to edit a special issue on gay and lesbian
studies, "and [they] took occasion to broaden the scope of that request to work that interrogates the problem of cross-identification within and across race and post-colonial
studies, gender theory, and theories of sexuality" (Butler and Martin 1994, 3). The title
of this special issue, *Critical Crossings*, not only evokes a conception of identity as inter-
sectionality, but also enacts theoretical movements and critical analyses that intersect,
cross over, and complicate each other. For identity and for theory, this special issue suggests, such "critical crossings" are enabling and necessary conditions. One measure of
the success of this issue in complicating issues of academic "ownership" is that, stripped
of the author-functions of Butler's and Martin's names (especially where the former's
has become synecdochical for "queer theory"), the table of contents is as likely to an-
nounce itself as a special issue on postcolonial theory and critical race studies as on lesbian and gay studies.

5. The arguments presented in this paragraph draw extensively on Butler (1994),
Martin, and Garber (1995).

6. Discussions of the shift from speaking in terms of lesbian and gay studies to
queer theory have usually been focused around the advantages and disadvantages of
"queer." There is need of some substantive discussion of this other redirection: from
"studies" to "theory."

7. Question posed by "Robin" (Mary-Louise Parker) to "Jane" (Whoopi Goldberg)
in the 1995 film *Boys on the Side*.

8. If I were to expand the list to include non-narrative feature films, I would add
Without You I'm Nothing (1990), which poses as a documentary of Sandra Bernhard's
performance piece of the same name. For essays treating this film and its complicated
relations to blackness, see Berlant and Freeman (1993), Walton (1994), and Pellegrini
(1996), in which the relations between blackness and Jewishness are foregrounded. I
have deliberatley left *Go Fish* (1994) off this list. Though the film does feature an interracial lesbian relationship between a Latina and African-American woman, in no way
does it represent the Latina woman as white.

9. Although *She Must Be Seeing Things* received national notice through a review in the *New York Times* (13 April 1988), the film was never released nationally. For a discussion of *She Must Be Seeing Things*, see de Lauretis (1991b, 223-64). See also the audience discussion that followed de Lauretis's presentation of her paper (264-76).

10. I have lifted part of this essay's title from a trailer for the film; its closing line was, "Women on top and boys on the side." (The trailer appeared at the beginning of a video of *The Client*, yet another film featuring Mary-Louise Parker.)

11. See Judith Mayne's discussion of this phenomenon in the films of Dorothy Arzner (Mayne 1991, 125).

12. This strategy of connotation, evasion, and representing around worked commercially. Although *Fried Green Tomatoes* received mixed critical reviews, it was a resounding success at the box office, taking in more than 75 million dollars in its first twenty-two weeks of domestic distribution (figure cited in Parish 1993, 149).

13. For a brilliant treatment of these universalizing strategies in relation to Pauline theology and the difference "Jew/Christian," see Boyarin and Boyarin (1995).

14. In reserving my praise for an independent film, *Work*, I do not thereby imply a neat division and too-neat moral difference between independent films ("good") and mainstream, studio-produced films ("bad"). First, the distinction between independent and studio films is being broken down as major studios purchase independent production companies. In addition, and this is more to my point, failures charged to *Boys on the Side* and *Fried Green Tomatoes* above may also apply to some of the independent films named in the opening catalogue of section two. If I have focused much of my discussion on two studio films, this is because these films reached a wider audience than any of the indies and, consequently, have been more influential in shaping public (read: straight) conceptions of what "the" lesbian "is."

Works Cited

Abelove, Henry, Michèle Aina Barale, and David M. Halperin, eds. 1993. *The Lesbian and Gay Studies Reader*. New York: Routledge.

Anzaldúa, Gloria, ed. 1990. *Making Face, Making Soul/Haciendo Caras: Creative and Critical Perspectives by Feminists of Color*. San Francisco: Aunt Lute.

Bad Object-Choices, ed. 1991. *How Do I Look? Queer Film and Video*. Seattle: Bay Press.

Bar Girls. 1995. Dir. Marita Giovanni. Orion.

Berlant, Lauren and Elizabeth Freeman. 1993. "Queer Nationality." In *Fear of a Queer Planet: Queer Politics and Social Theory*, ed. Michael Warner. Minneapolis: University of Minnesota Press.

Boyarin, Daniel, and Jonathan Boyarin. 1995. "Diaspora: Generation and Ground of Jewish Identity." In *Identities*, ed. Kwame Anthony Appiah and Henry Louis Gates, Jr. Chicago: University of Chicago Press.

Boys on the Side. 1995. Dir. Herbert Ross. Warner Brothers.

Butler, Judith. 1991. "Imitation and Gender Insubordination." In *inside/out: Lesbian Theories, Gay Theories*, ed. Diana Fuss. New York: Routledge.

_____. 1994. "Against Proper Objects." *differences: A Journal of Feminist Cultural*

Studies 6.2-3: 1-26.

Butler, Judith and Biddy Martin, eds. 1994. *Critical Crossings. Diacritics* 24.2-3.

Castle, Terry. 1993. *The Apparitional Lesbian.* New York: Columbia University Press.

de Lauretis, Teresa. 1991a. "Queer Theory: Lesbian and Gay Sexualities: An Introduction." *differences: A Journal of Feminist Cultural Studies* 3.2: iii-xviii.

_____. 1991b. "Film and the Visible." In *How Do I Look? Queer Film and Video,* ed. Bad Object-Choices. Seattle: Bay.

Fried Green Tomatoes. 1991. Dir. Jon Avnet. Universal.

Garber, Linda S. 1995. *Lesbian Identity Poetics: Judy Grahn, Pat Parker, and the Rise of Queer Theory.* Ph.D. diss, Stanford University.

Go Fish. 1994. Dir. Rose Troche. Samuel Goldwyn.

Goldsby, Jackie. 1990. "What It Means To Be Colored Me." *Out/Look* 3: 8-17.

Hammonds, Evelynn. 1994. "Black (W)holes and the Geometry of Black Female Sexuality." *differences: A Journal of Feminist Cultural Studies* 6.2-3: 126-45.

Hull, Gloria, Patricia Bell Scott, and Barbara Smith, eds. 1982. *All the Women Are White, All the Blacks Are Men, But Some of Us Are Brave: Black Women's Studies.* New York: Feminist.

Incredibly True Adventure of Two Girls in Love, The. 1995. Dir. Maria Maggenti. Fine Line Features.

Jeffreys, Sheila. 1994. "The Queer Disappearance of Lesbians: Sexuality in the Academy." *Women's Studies International Forum* 17.5: 459-72.

Mayne, Judith. 1991. "Lesbian Looks: Dorothy Arzner and Female Authorship." In *How Do I Look? Queer Film and Video,* ed. Bad Object-Choices. Seattle: Bay.

Mercer, Kobena. 1991. "Skin Head Sex Thing: Racial Difference and the Homoerotic Imaginary." In *How Do I Look? Queer Film and Video,* ed. Bad Object-Choices. Seattle: Bay.

_____. 1993. "Looking for Trouble." In *The Lesbian and Gay Studies Reader,* ed. Henry Abelove, Michèle Aina Barale, and David M. Halperin. New York: Routledge.

Morton, Donald. 1993. "The Politics of Queer Theory in the (Post)Modern Moment." *Genders* 17: 121-50.

_____. 1995. "Birth of the Cyberqueer." *PMLA* 110.3: 369-81.

Parish, James Robert. n.d. *Gays and Lesbians in Mainstream Cinema.* Jefferson: McFarland.

Pellegrini, Ann. 1996. *Performance Anxieties: Staging Psychoanalysis, Staging Race.* New York: Routledge.

She Must Be Seeing Things. 1987. Dir. Sheila McLaughlin. Sheila McLaughlin.

Radicalesbians. 1972. "The Woman-Identified Woman." *Out of the Closets: Voices of Gay Liberation,* ed. Karla Jay and Allen Young. New York: Pyramid.

Rich, Adrienne. 1993. "Compulsory Heterosexuality and Lesbian Existence." In *The Lesbian and Gay Studies Reader,* ed. Henry Abelove, et al. New York: Routledge.

Rubin, Gayle. 1993. "Thinking Sex: Notes for a Radical Theory of the Politics of Sexuality." In *The Lesbian and Gay Studies Reader,* ed. Henry Abelove, et al. New York: Routledge.

Sedgwick, Eve Kosofsky. 1990. *Epistemology of the Closet.* Berkeley: University of California Press.

Walton, Jean. 1994. "Sandra Bernhard: Lesbian Postmodern or Modern Postlesbian?" In

The Lesbian Postmodern, ed. Laura Doan. New York: Columbia University Press.

Watermelon Woman. 1996. Dir. Cheryl Dunye. First Run Features.

When Night is Falling. 1995. Dir. Patricia Rozema. October Films.

Without You I'm Nothing. 1990. Dir. John Boskovich. M.C.E.G.

Work. 1996. Dir. Rachel Reichman. Not yet released.

Index

Black power, 120

Babha, Homi, 19, 28, 196n4
Back to Africa movement, 245n3
"Badge of inferiority," 5
Baker Jr., Houston, 4
Baker, Josephine, 115n15
Bakhtin, Mikhail, 8, 160, 163, 168,
    170n3, 171n4, 227n5
Baldwin, James, 47, 78, 213, 233, 241-
    243; *Another Country*, 240-242
Baltimore Afro-American, 107, 115n14
Balutansky, Kathleen, 149
Bar Girls, 254
Barbados, 142, 145, 148
Barbarism, 34, 37n10, see also
    Savagery
Barthelme, Donald, 87
Barthes, Roland, 121
Basu, Biman, 7-8
Beam, Joseph, 232
Bell, Bernard W., 210n2
Bell, Derrick, 51
Benin, 33
Benjamin, Walter, 24, 34
Benny, A. J., 238
Bentley, Gladys, 115n15
Berlant, Lauren, 260n8
Bernhard, Sandra, 260n8
Bible, 106
Bill of Rights, 105
Bimbo, 131
Bisexuality, 115n15
Black bodies, 79, 232-236, 239, 241-
    243; male, 238, 243
Black English, 3; speech, 156, 170;
    language, 158
Black female writers, 213
Black genocide, 237
Black masculinity, 213, 242, 244;
    resistant of, 242; sexuality of, 241
Black intellectual, 3n14
Black Muslim, 190-191
Black nationalism, 17, 237-238, 244;
    cultural, 238, 241; of the diaspora,
    238; discourse of, 236; nation and,
    233, 236, 238, 241

Blackboard Jungle, 57
Blackface, 43
Blackmer, Corinne E., 5-6
Blackmun, Justice Harry, 106, 114n10,
    115n13
Blackness, 50, 148, 158, 254
Blake, William, 80, 82
Blockson, Charles, 85; *Black
    Genealogy*, 85
Bloom, Harold, 149
Body politics, 2, 10
Bolekaja critics, 29, 34-35
Boone, Daniel, 177; *Daniel Boone*, 177
Borders, 12, 58; see also Boundaries
Bork, Robert, 78
II.   Boundaries, 3; see also
        Borders
Bowers v. Hardwick, 105-106, 113,
        114n10, 114n12, 115n13
Boyarin, Daniel, 261n13
Boyarin, Jonathan, 261n13
Boys on the Side, 2, 11, 254, 256-257,
        261n14
Bradley, David, 9; *The Chaneysville
        Incident*, 9, 200, 208-210, 211n7
III.   Bradley, Mamie, 235
Brenkman, John, 45
Brennan, Justice William J., 106
Brooks, Neil, 4-5
Brown, Justice Henry, 5, 99
Brown v. Board of Education, 99
Bryant, Carolyn, 245n5
Buchanan, Pat, 45
Burr, Chandler, 114n9
Butler, Judith, 196n8, 248-249, 260n3,
        260n4

Cabral, Amilcar, 28
Caliban, 1-2, 13, 151
Camillo, Guitio, 211n3
Campbell, Horace, 35
Campbell, Maria, 121-122
Canon, 144-147, 152
Cape of Good Hope, 37n5

Padmore, George, 35
Page, Philip, 204
Palmore v. Sidoti, 105
Pan-Africanism, 19-20, 22, 29, 35, 38n19; 7th Congress, 39n22; movement, 233
Papa Legba, 211n5
Paradise Lost, 169
Parker, Mary-Louise, 256, 261n10
Parker, Pat, 250
Parris, Samuel, 144, 151
Parris, Elizabeth, 151
Passing, 2, 5, 84-86, 88-90, 92, 95, 99-103, 110; racial, 100, 102, 107; sexual, 100, 107
Past, 201, 205, 210, 211n7, 220; ancestral, 206, 208; and present, 208, 219; and oral cultures, 210n1
Patterson, Orlando, 18
Pellegrini, Ann, 11, 260n8
People, 79, 81-82
Perreault, Jeanne, 120-121
Petry, Ann, 153n4; *Tituba of Salem Village*, 153n4
Pfeiffer, Michelle, 56
Pfeil, Fred, 48
Philcox, Richard, 153n1
Pisiak, Roxanna, 85-86
Plath, Sylvia, 138n14
Plessy v. Ferguson, 5-6, 98-101, 107, 111-113
Politics, 36; black gay, 232; class, 176; conservative frontier, 186; cultural, 53, 72, 232, 237; of difference, 52; of domination, 65; emancipatory, 36; of fucking, 238; of identity, 55,123, 237, 240; micropolitics, 195; of privilege, 68; racial, 48, 53, 55, 63, 68, 71-72; of representation, 52, 63, 67; of visibility, 256-257; sexual, 79
Positionality, 135
Post-colonialism, 3; contexts of, 144; histories of, 20; theory of, 260n4; writers and, 202

Postmodern, 86, 88, 91; discourses, 89; heroes, 95n4; ludic, 248; novel, 96n6; theory, 92
Post-structuralism, 137n3; theory, 137n3
Povey, John, 29
Project La Churasano, 34-35
Prospero, 12-13
Psychoanalytic theory, 38n20
Public Enemy, 239
Pulp Fiction, 55
Puritan, 147-148
Pyncheon, Thomas, 89; *Crying of Lot*, 88; *Gravity's Rainbow*, 95n4

Queen's Silver Jubilee, 240
Queer Nation, 245n2
Queer Studies, 260n4
Queer theory, 10, 24-252, 260n6

Rabelais, 160-161, 170n3
Race, 90, 95, 103, 114n8, 130-131, 176, 240, 250, 252-253, 255, 257; classifications of, 106; conflict, 59; critical studies, 260n4; cross-racial, 12; culture, 69; definitions, 86; designations, 96; desires, 112; difference, 59; disclosure, 109; discourse, 45; divide of, 60, 100, 178; domination, 66; exoticism and, 103; fictions, 107; hierarchy of, 60, 63; identity and, 65, 69-70, 103, 109-110; index of, 157; justice, 66; loyalty, 102, 111; marker of, 165; masquerade of, 109, 112; and neutral, 256; norms, 133; panic, 102, 107; politics, 71-72; privilege, 68; purity, 71; racial practice and, 43; racialization of, 250, 252; science, 178; studies, 2; suicide, 233; taboo contacts and, 102
Race-ing, 2, 5, 9, 13; de-racing and, 14; raced constructions as, 12; self, 235
Racism, 4, 27, 34-35, 42, 52, 54, 72, 94, 99-101, 119, 127-128, 131,

Contributors

Houston A. Baker, Jr.

Baker is the director of the Center for the Study of Black Literature and Culture, professor of English, and Albert M. Greenfield professor at the University of Pennsylvania. He has published a number of scholarly works including: *Workings of the Spirits: The Poetics of Afro-American Women's Writing* and *Black Studies, Rap and the Academy*.

Biman Basu

Basu is assistant professor of English at the Illinois Institute of Technology in Chicago and the author of articles on Gayl Jones, Toni Morrison, Tsitsi Dangarembga, and Paule Marshall.

Corinne E. Blackmer

Blackmer is assistant professor of English at Southern Connecticut State University. She has published on issues of race and sexuality in the works of Gertrude Stein, Nella Larsen, Carl Van Vechten, Elizabeth Bishop, and Ronald Firbank and has co-edited *En Travesh: Women, Gender Subversion, Opera* (Columbia University Press).

Neil Brooks

Brooks is an assistant professor of English at Huron College, University of Western Ontario, where he teaches American and African-American literature. He is currently working on a book entitled *Passing through Modernism: New Shades of Meaning in the Passing Novels of the Harlem Renaissance*.

Brenda Carr

Carr is an associate professor of English at Carleton University where she teaches Canadian and twentieth-century literatures with an emphasis in women's, post-colonial, and minority literatures. Her current research engages questions of hybrid literary forms and social intervention: twentieth-century poetry, poetics, and politics; trauma literature and testimony theory; and human rights/peace/environmental pedagogies.

Kanishka Chowdhury

Chowdhury is assistant professor of English at the University of Saint Thomas, St. Paul, where he teaches postcolonial literature and cultural studies. He has published articles in *College Literature, Modern Fiction Studies*, and *World Literature Today*.

Robert Crooks

Crooks is an associate professor of English at Bentley College, where he teaches literature, literary theory, and communication theory. He has published essays on issues of races and colonialism in crime fiction, James Joyce, and film reception theory.

Mara L. Dukats

Dukats was visiting assistant professor at Rosary College, where she taught French and Francophone literature and women's writing. She has published articles on feminist literature and Francophone Caribbean writing.

Henry A. Giroux

Giroux is the Waterbury Chair professor of education at Penn State University. His recent books include: *Disturbing Pleasures, Fugitive Cultures: Race, Violence, and Youth*, and *Channel Surfing: Race Talk and the Destruction of Today's Youth*.

Dana Heller

Heller is associate professor of English at Old Dominion University, where she teaches American literature, gender studies, and cultural studies. She is the author of *Family Plots: the De-Oedipalization of Popular Culture* and *The Feminization of Quest-Romance: Radical Departures*.

Helen Lock

Lock is assistant professor of English at Northeast Louisiana University. She is the author of *A Case of Mis-Taken Identity: Detective Undercurrents in Recent African-American Fiction.*

Kostas Myrsiades

Myrsiades is professor of comparative literature at West Chester University and the editor of *College Literature* and *The Journal of the Hellenic Diaspora.* His latest book, coauthored with Linda Myrsiades on Greek Guerrilla Theater is being published by Bucknell University Press.

Linda Myrsiades

Myrsiades is associate professor of English at West Chester University and an associate editor of *College Literature.* She has coauthored and coedited with Kostas Myrsiades four books on modern Greek literature and culture and two books on literary theory.

Amy Abugo Ongiri

Ongiri is a Cornell University graduate student interested in the way in which race, gender, and nation inflect our understanding of African-American literature and culture.

Ann Pellegrini

Pellegrini is assistant professor of English and American literature and language at Harvard University. She is the author of *Performance Anxieties: Staging Psychoanalysis, Staging Race.*